POLITICS IN SOUTHEAST ASIA

DEMOCRACY OR LESS

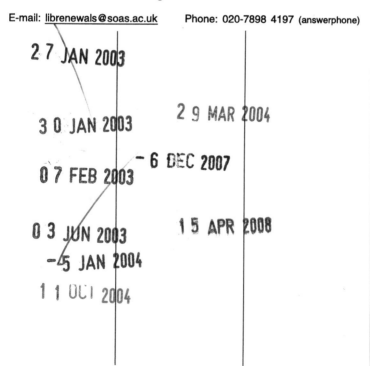

POLITICS IN SOUTHEAST ASIA

DEMOCRACY OR LESS

William Case

CURZON

First Published in 2002
by Curzon Press
Richmond, Surrey
http://www.curzonpress.co.uk

© 2002 William Case

Typeset in Stempel Garamond by LaserScript Ltd, Mitcham, Surrey
Printed and bound in Great Britain by
Biddles Ltd, Guildford and King's Lynn

British Library Cataloguing in Publication Data
A catalogue record of this book is available from the British Library

Library of Congress Cataloguing in Publication Data
A catalogue record for this book has been requested

ISBN 0–7007–1635–1 (Hbk)
ISBN 0–7007–1636–X (Pbk)

For Sakda Prangpatanpon and Prapond Prasertkul who moved
effectively in multiple worlds

Contents

Preface

Few books have appeared that attempt in any theoretical way to make broad sense of the politics of Southeast Asia countries. Put simply, many analysts consider the political regimes of the region's ten countries to be so diverse that meaningful generalizations cannot be made. Indeed, Southeast Asia, at the crossroads of Chinese and Indian influences and buffeted by different colonial legacies and globalizing forces displays a greater spectrum of regime types than perhaps any other part of the world. It thus encompasses sundry forms of democracy, military government, a sultanate, single party dominance, and post-totalitarianism, while historically undergoing some notorious episodes of personal dictatorship.

Hence, most broad brush analyses have done little more than scan the features of individual countries against a checklist of indicators like civil liberties, elections, levels of economic development, and social structures. No systematic explanation for the diversity of regime outcomes has been offered, merely a descriptive stock take, leaving the main organizing principle one of geographic propinquity. At the same time, more sophisticated analyses have scoured for common ground by retreating to specific issue areas, focusing tightly on institutions, legal structures, human rights, the media, economic deregulation, environmental policies, NGOs, and ethnic identities. While useful, these analyses do not cumulate in the kinds of theoretical overviews that are available for the politics of Northeast Asia, Africa, and Latin America.

This book tries to remedy this shortcoming. It begins by narrowing the universe of study to Southeast Asia's five most developed countries, the so-called *"ASEAN 4"* – Indonesia, Malaysia, Thailand, and the Philippines – and Singapore. Of course, the diversity of politics remains wide, featuring pseudo- and semi-democratic regimes, as well as democracies that are fuller, but unstable or "low quality." What is more, the great cultural and linguistic diversity of even this smaller universe has encouraged intense research specialization, with separate scholarly traditions and methodologies growing up in the analysis of each country. In Indonesia, the most influential model has probably been neo-patrimonialism, reflecting the extraordinary centralization of state power in the hands of its long-time leader, Suharto, and the arbitrary ways in which he once wielded it. And even as Indonesia struggles to democratize today, many analysts note the persistence of top-down and personalist orientations amid the continuing weakness of civil society. In Malaysia, much attention has traditionally been given to ethnicity, noting the rivalries between ethnic communities constructed as the Malays and the Chinese which, with the former having gained political ascendancy, has firmed a system of single-party, even executive dominance. In Thailand, the military's historical ascendancy and its dealings with Chinese business people gave rise to an influential bureaucratic polity model. With democratization, however, attention has shifted to a very fluid party system and its interplay with business, especially in the provinces. Investigation of the Philippines, often colored by assumptions of dependency, has focused on a uniquely landed social class, a correspondingly weak state apparatus, a pervasive clientelism that when concentrated produced Marcos's leadership, and a regime change sparked by people power. And in Singapore, analysts have pondered the fusion between the ruling People's Action Party and the bureaucracy, creating an incubus that has spawned good governance and economic rationality within a wholly unaccountable setting.

In order to provide some coherent and systematic explanation for these variable contours, this book takes account of the historical, cultural, and structural conditions that inform mass attitudes and behaviors. But it recognizes too that quite different combinations of these factors can produce similar political outcomes, with the Philippines, Thailand, and Indonesia, for example, converging as the region's new democracies. At the same time, countries that display some important similarities in their structures, like Indonesia and Malaysia, have practiced dissimilar politics, with the military playing a significant role in the first case, but very rarely in the latter one.

In short, amalgams of historical legacies, cultural orientations, and structural constraints may favor political outcomes, but by themselves deliver no determinative impact. Accordingly, this book gives attention to the role of national leaders and elites, measuring the extent to which they are cohesive, thus stabilizing their regime, and the ways in which they energize social constituents, thereby making their regime either more democratic or less. As Barbara Geddes has recently observed with respect to middle-income countries, with "underlying structural causes fairly evenly balanced . . . human choices and serendipitous events – *virtu* and *fortuna* – [can] most easily affect outcomes."[1] Hence, across the *ASEAN 4* and Singapore, this book examines elite configurations that vary in their cohesion and social forces that fluctuate in their levels of participation, finally producing different kinds of regimes. The aim of this investigation has been to provide an empirically rich, yet theoretically informed account of politics in Southeast Asia's most developed countries.

I would like to acknowledge the support of the School of International Business in which I teach. While the imperatives of marketing and management do not always sit easily alongside the concerns of comparative politics, the School has nonetheless been generous in providing research leave and funding. A Griffith University research grant also made possible numerous field trips to Malaysia and Thailand. In addition, I would like to thank the Center for Strategic and International Studies in Jakarta for providing office space and arranging interviews, enabling me to observe a most important democratic transition unfold. I am especially indebted to Hadi Soesastro and Tommy Legowo. The Center of Asian Studies at Chulalongkorn University did the same for me in Bangkok, for which I would like to thank Withaya Sucharithanarugse, the former director. I am grateful also to Peter Alford, *The Australian*'s correspondent in Bangkok, who provided forceful arguments and insights over Blue Eagle. Finally, I thank all those who consented to interviews and discussions, to those who commented on draft chapters, in particular, Bob Elson, Robert Cribb, and Surin Maisrikrod, and to my wife and son, Rebecca and John, who have tolerated the field trips.

Chapter 1

Comparing Politics in Southeast Asia

For about two-and-a-half decades, from the early 1970s until the late-1990s, many countries in Southeast Asia transformed their economies, turning their rice paddies into industrial sites, their rubber plantations into housing estates, and their old tin mining pools into aquatic amusement parks. Indonesia thus bristled with great "mega-projects" – power plants, steel mills, refineries, and naptha crackers – that deepened its manufacturing base. Thailand graduated from rice growing and textiles to agribusiness and automotive parts, then to electronics, wafer fabrication, and pay-per-view TV. Malaysia planned a new national capital from which to dispense electronic government, linking its Cyber City, Vision City, Linear City, Fridge City, and Multimedia Super Corridor. And Singapore offered itself as the Total Business Center, an enclave of bureaucratic probity and scripless trading from which transnationals could conduct their regional dealings.

Accordingly, Southeast Asia gained new international standing. Japanese, Korean, and Taiwanese investors flocked to the region, drawn by the low cost, but increasingly sophisticated production sites that it offered. Europe was attracted by the new markets that resulted, encouraging it to seek new trading relationships. Indeed, even as Europe appeared to be withdrawing into its own economic bloc, its leaders journeyed to Bangkok in 1996 to inaugurate the ASEM (Asia-Europe Meeting), with Helmut Kohl, Jacques Chirac, and John Major meeting Indonesia's President Suharto, the prime minister of Malaysia, Mahathir Mohamad, and Thailand's prime minister, Banharn Silpa-archa, thus flagging Southeast Asia's new rise to prominence. At the same time, the ASEAN (Association of Southeast Asian Nations) gained new stature. Long dismissed as an unfocused "talking shop," able to persist only because it undertook so little, the organization now recruited dialogue partners like the United States and Britain, then served as a key conduit through which to engage China over security concerns in the South China Sea. In addition, Mahathir articulated new forms of regional, indeed hemispheric organization, proposing the EAEC (East Asian Economic

1

Caucus) as a core grouping within APEC (Asia Pacific Economic Cooperation), as well as new programs for South-South cooperation. On the political stage, Singapore's former prime minister, Lee Kuan Yew, challenged the ideological hegemony of Westminster democracy, elaborating the distinctiveness of "Asian values" and the appropriateness of "Asian democracy." Mahathir outlined a program called Vision 2020, marked by "mature" democracy, full economic development, and deep ethnic harmony. And Anwar Ibrahim, then Mahathir's deputy, envisaged in the twenty-first millenium an "Asian renaissance," distinguished by advanced learning, good governance, and social justice.

Southeast Asia's new economic prowess soon impacted on the research agendas of those studying the region. Whereas analysts had once focused on military governments, relations of dependency, clientelism, and low modes of peasant resistance, they began now to investigate the origins and consequences of rapid industrialization. Fruitful comparisons were thus made between Southeast Asia's "tiger cubs" and the NICs of Northeast Asia,[1] helping sharpen debate over the capacity of the state to "pick winners" and the chances of rent-seekers becoming "real capitalists."[2] It also precipitated debate over the effects of growth on social structure, broadly conceptualized in terms of the "new rich," the "new middle class," and the rise of civil society.[3] And because these social changes were associated with political pressures, analysts turned finally to the prospects for democracy.[4] On this score, one notes that the Philippines redemocratized its politics in 1986, followed by Thailand in 1992. The competitiveness of Malaysian elections increased sharply in 1990, with the ruling multiethnic coalition mirrored by another in opposition. Myanmar's military government held elections in 1990, which were won convincingly by the opposition National League for Democracy (NLD). Indonesia underwent a period of liberalization during the early 1990s known as *keterbukaan* ("openness"). And even Brunei consented to the formation of an opposition party in 1995, the Solidarity National Party.

However, though economic growth and social change persisted in Southeast Asia until nearly the end of the decade, democracy's progress was by no means straightforward. Indeed, in Malaysia, the appeal of opposition politics soon faded after 1990 precisely because of a new surge in growth, thus restoring elections to their earlier patterns of limited competitiveness. In Myanmar, the military repudiated the results of its 1990 election outright, while Indonesia, after resolving its rifts in the military, cut short its period of *keterbukaan*. In Brunei, the Solidarity National Party vanished a year after its founding, ending the country's brief experiment with even a truncated party system. And in the Philippines and Thailand, democracy was marred by military coup attempts and corrupt governance. Hence, at least in the short to medium term, one must agree with Jacques Bertrand's conclusion that "there is no clear relationship between growth and

2

democracy in the region."[5] Growth instead produced in Southeast Asia a broad and pulsating spectrum of regime types and changes.

This record was complicated further when, toward the end of 1997, economic growth in Southeast Asia suddenly ceased. Across the region, mega-projects were cancelled, conglomerates fell into insolvency, and new middle classes declined. And while business executives who were well connected subsisted on bail-outs, others were reduced famously to streetside hawking. In these circumstances, many analysts deftly shifted their research agendas once more, seeking explanations for the timing and severity of this economic crisis. In brief, most area specialists attributed the crisis to global forces, focusing on foreign lenders, short-term investors, and currency speculators, their perniciousness exacerbated by the International Monetary Fund. In contrast, neo-classical economists from outside the region tended to blame local borrowers and their patterns of investment, distorted by "cronyist" ties to state officials. And policy analysts, finally, in searching for ways to ease the crisis, drafted plans for recapitalizing banks, restarting production, and coping with the immiseration of dispersed workers.[6]

For many comparativists, though, the economic crisis that so sorely afflicted Southeast Asia seemed to bear new implications for democracy. In brief, just as rapid economic growth and new class formations had not unambiguously favored democracy, neither was democracy everywhere hindered by economic crisis. On the contrary, it seemed that growth, followed by crisis, might best create the circumstances in which existing democracies could be invigorated and authoritarian regimes transformed.[7] Thus, in Thailand, after the crisis hit in 1997, the military refused a plea by the prime minister at that time, Chavalit Yongchaiyudh, that it intervene in politics. Chavalit then lost a no-confidence motion in parliament and was replaced by a reformist government led by the Democrats. Further, in the Philippines, the election in 1998 of Joseph Estrada as president signalled democracy's having passed the "two turnover test" posed by Huntington, helping confirm assessments about stability.[8] But most dramatically, the New Order government of President Suharto collapsed in Indonesia, finally opening the door to new civil liberties and competitive elections.

However, while economic growth, followed by crisis, may in some instances offer democracy's best incubus, transitions are hardly guaranteed. In Singapore, though opposition leaders made new appeals, social forces were instead driven more deeply into the state's corporatist embrace, only trusting the ruling PAP (People's Action Party) to safeguard the country's prosperity. In neighboring Malaysia, though new tensions between Mahathir and Anwar helped enliven the opposition, Mahathir responded with more coercion and controls. Indeed, he declared resolutely that while he had earlier been contemplating retirement after a decade of growth, the crisis made it necessary now that he remain in power indefinitely.[9] Accordingly, he used his country's distorted electoral procedures to renew his tenure toward the end of 1999. Further afield, in Myanmar, even as foreign investors fled, the military government tightened its hold over the NLD. In Brunei, despite astonishing financial scandals, Sultan Hassanal Bolkiah perpetuated his absolute monarchy, firmed by ethnic doctrines, Islamic strictures, and populist entertainments. And Vietnam, far from liberalizing its politics, began now to rescind some of its *Doi Moi* reforms.

In sum, over the past decade, Southeast Asia has displayed a highly diverse record of regime types and change, one that has fluctuated with much independence from economic fortunes. Regimes have also changed independently across national settings in the region, clearly obviating the "snowballing" and demonstration effects that once spread across South America and eastern Europe. Further, in taking a longer view, one observes that social structures, cultural patterns, and colonial experiences, even where broadly comparable, have produced quite different regime outcomes. The Philippines and Indonesia, for example, two large archipelago countries at similar levels of economic development, possessing equally complex multiethnic societies, and sharing long legacies of Western colonial rule, have nevertheless displayed throughout most of the past decade quite different types of regimes. On the other hand, the Philippines and Thailand, so different in terms of their industrial capacity, ethnic and religious structures, and experiences with colonial powers have now converged as two of the region's "new democracies." And finally, in considering the different effects of a single variable, one observes that British colonialism – often cited as the factor most strongly favoring democracy in developing countries[10] – helped to produce semi-democracies in Singapore and Malaysia, a once nominally socialist, though consistently brutal military government in Myanmar, and an absolute monarchy in Brunei.

Hence, while acknowledging the importance of economic trends, international pressures, and social, cultural, and colonial factors this volume demonstrates also their quite variable impact on regime types and change. As noted above, the broad similarities displayed by some Southeast Asian countries have produced very different regimes. At the same time, different sets of factors have cumulated in quite similar political outcomes. Accordingly, this book calls attention to the role of key position holders and decision makers, mediating prominently between contexts and regimes. Indeed, it argues that Southeast Asia, with its gallery of strong leaderships and diverse regime types, offers an especially good format in which to demonstrate the significance of agency, best conceptualized in terms of leaders and elites.

This chapter begins by elaborating regimes as dependent variables, framing possible outcomes in terms of their departures from ideal-type democracy. It next considers some major paradigms through which regimes in Southeast Asia have been analyzed, categorizing them as structuralist, modernizationist, and culturalist. It suggests also that while these approaches provide deep insights, they are by themselves unable fully to explain the fluctuating political records that prevail in Southeast Asia, at least in the short to medium term. They must instead be animated with the tonic of agency. This chapter then offers a short overview of democratic elite theory. It concludes by demonstrating the relevance of analyzing Southeast Asian politics from a democratic perspective.

Regime types

In simple terms, regimes can be understood as the institutions and procedures, both formal and tacit, that order the competitions for, and the exercise of state power.[11] Regimes can also be stable – variously understood in terms of elite cohesion, mass perceptions of legitimacy, and appropriate institutional designs[12] – or they may remain unstable, vulnerable to executive and military coups, ethnic and religious upheavals, and violent class struggles. Moreover, on a second axis, regimes can be classified by the extent to which they feature civil liberties and competitive elections. Of course, a great number of typologies have been developed by comparativists, identifying sundry forms of democracy, authoritarianism, and totalitarianism.[13] But this volume, in focusing on five country cases in Southeast Asia, begins with an ideal-type democracy, then shades across authoritarian categories of semi-democracy and pseudo-democracy. Let us illustrate briefly these three categories in the Southeast Asian setting.

In thinking first about ideal-type democracy, one notes the competing ways in which it has principally been understood: substantive and procedural. Substantive democracy involves equality between classes, ethnic groups, genders, and other forms of identity and affiliation, cumulating in a literature that comes broadly under the headings of social, economic, and industrial democracy. In this view, policies and programs that give rise to social equality must take precedence over institutions and procedures. By contrast, the notion of procedural democracy gives greater attention to civil liberties and regular elections, practices associated with "polyarchy."[14] In evaluating which interpretation is more analytically fruitful, Burton, Gunther, and Higley remind us that social equality may be a precondition for democracy, or it may follow as a policy outcome, but equality and democracy are not the same thing.[15] Indeed, they contend that by conflating these distinct variables, a loss of explanatory power results. As an example, they observe that the former German Democratic Republic, while distributing wealth relatively equitably and remaining ideologically committed to social justice, could hardly be labelled democratic. Accordingly, a consensus has emerged in the study of transitions that democracy is best understood in procedural ways. We will see in our investigation of Thailand, however, that more substantive understandings have reappeared in the study of democracy's consolidation.

In conceptualizing democracy in procedural ways, O'Donnell and Schmitter distinguish between political liberalization (civil liberties) and democratization (competitive elections).[16] This is reminiscent of Robert Dahl's earlier notion of the liberal and inclusionary elements of polyarchy, and is akin to Huntington's more recently differentiating participation from contestation.[17] At base, in ideal-type democracies, civil liberties include free speech, press, and assembly, enabling citizens to participate effectively in politics. And elections must be free, fair, regularly held, and meaningful, enabling governments to be replaced. More specifically, elections are free in that the voting franchise is inclusive. They are fair in that incumbent governments eschew any partisan use of state agencies, facilities, and funding. They are regularly held within fixed time frames, probably recorded in a constitution. And they are meaningful in that elected chief executives and legislators control the state apparatus, not cabals of generals, bureaucrats, and business elites nestling in "reserve domains."[18]

Of course, no democracies in the real world conform fully to this ideal type. But when they depart egregiously from these ideals, even if stopping short of leaving the democratic category altogether, concerns arise over quality. On this count, Juan Linz scrutinizes the quality of professional politicians, their willingness to engage in corruption, flirt with semi-loyal or anti-system oppositions, or tolerate illegal violence against "enemies of the state and democracy."[19] And indeed, in two of Southeast Asia's democracies today, the Philippines and Thailand, rural *caciques* and provincial "god-fathers" have respectively held influence over law-makers, enabling them to benefit extensively from corrupt practices. We shall see too that in the Philippines in 1998, President's Ramos's commitments to democracy seemed briefly to waver. And in Thailand, though Chavalit's entreaties to the military were rebuffed and he was replaced as prime minister, business elites gained entry to the senate, then resisted economic reforms. Thus, while the Philippines and Thailand can today be categorized as formally democratic, satisfying the procedural requirements of civil liberties and elections, doubts persist over quality. Concerns grow even deeper in the case of Indonesia's new democracy.

In specifying democracy's twin dimensions, O'Donnell and Schmitter have also supplied the tools by which to capture something less, in particular, regimes that are not only tainted by low quality, but tinged with authoritarian residues. In what can be categorized as a semi-democracy, then, governments regularly hold elections, thus offering a snapshot of propriety on voting day. But they have limited civil liberties beforehand, thereby hindering opposition parties in contesting effectively. More specifically, opposition parties are permitted to organize, operate head-quarters, solicit contributions, select their own leaders and candidates, then recruit cadres and core constituencies. On the other hand, they are prevented from reaching wider audiences by the government's owning most media outlets, they are restricted in circulating their own party publications, and they are barred from organizing mass rallies, even during campaign periods. And opposition leaders who persist, one notes, are targeted with lawsuits or detention. Further, on the electoral dimension, outcomes may be skewed through delineation exercises that involve malapportionment and multi-member districts. And government candidates may make heavy use of state resources in campaigning, practices winked at by election commissions. In these circumstances, opposition parties are able to articulate the grievances of core constituencies, though only in muted ways. And they are able to win enough legislative seats that they can hold the government at least mildly accountable, though never so many they can replace the government, at least at the national level.

In Southeast Asia today, the best examples of semi-democratic regimes are Malaysia and Singapore. In both settings, opposition parties encounter all of the restrictions on civil liberties enumerated above. They confront separate challenges, however, on the electoral dimension. In Malaysia, the dominant party in the ruling coalition, the UMNO (United Malays National Organization), favors its ethnic Malay constituents over urban Chinese by weighting rural districts heavily. But then, in trying to keep these same districts from falling to the party with which it competes for Malay votes, the more Islamicist PAS (Pan-Malaysia Islamic Party), its candidates sprinkle their campaign appearances with "development grants," warning darkly that development will cease if they lose. By contrast, Singapore's ruling party, the PAP, has fashioned some multi-member districts that require inter-ethnic team candidacies. It is thus difficult for small opposition parties to contest in these districts, especially when their coffers are repeatedly drained by defamation suits and fines. In these ways, Malaysia's ruling coalition usually wins around 60 per cent of the popular vote, which, when filtered though single member districts and a first-past-the-post system, enables it to claim a far larger share of the seats in parliament. Singapore's PAP usually takes 95 per cent of the country's parliamentary seats – and displays great anxiety and imposes new controls when it gets something less.

With elections in semi-democracies so clearly contrived, what can governments hope to gain from them? As is well known – though never well-measured – they win a shred of legitimating cover. Put simply, by remaining able to claim that they have consulted electorates, governments can more plausibly justify their statuses before local and international audiences. Thus, however disingenuously, Mahathir has been able to advise his critics, "If you don't like me, defeat me in my district."[20] Second, elections enable leaders peacefully to ratify their statuses before one another – in the manner that Schumpeter envisioned.[21] A good example involves the tensions between Singapore's prime minister, Lee Kuan Yew, and his successor, Goh Chok Tong during the early 1990s. As we will see in

Chapter Three on Singapore, after Lee taunted Goh, "lecturing" him publicly about the need to appeal to Chinese-educated constituents, Goh responded by resigning his seat, staging a by-election, and, in a "resounding win," capturing nearly three-quarters of the vote. Lee Kuan Yew then shifted his criticisms to Western democracies and even neighboring Malaysia. Third, elections in semi-democracies provide opportunities for governments to re-energize constituencies, organizing campaigns and staging much pageantry. At the same time, for those who insist still to vote against the government, elections may serve as "safety valves," venting and abating their dissident impulses. Moreover, when districts vote in this way, they are revealed to the government, providing it with valuable "feedback mechanisms"[22] – and thus, increased scope for investigative or retaliatory actions.

Beyond semi-democracies, one finds pseudo-democracies, a category in which elections are also held regularly. However, these elections are rigged, while civil liberties are nearly extinguished, with rights of expression, information, and assembly all rigidly controlled. But the most striking qualitative difference between semi- and pseudo-democracies appears in the respective approaches taken toward opposition parties. Put simply, in pseudo-democracies, opposition parties are permitted no autonomy, with governments interfering deeply in their formation, organizational structure, selection of officers and candidates, fund-raising, and campaigning. Thus, while opposition parties may win legislative seats, they are barred from performing even limited accountability functions. In addition, the elections through which they gain entry to the legislature are not only rendered less competitive than in semi-democracies, they are also less meaningful. Most notably, these legislatures seldom possess any serious role in policy making. Policy is instead the prerogative of unelected chief executives, then to be shared with top bureaucrats, generals, and favored business elites.

The Southeast Asian record offers several good examples of pseudo-democracies. In the Philippines, President Marcos always took care to hold elections – even organizing five plebiscites during the martial law period. However, he rigged these contests grossly in order to favor his KBL (New Society Movement), deploying a rough formula of "guns, goons, and gold." He also bypassed opposition members who managed still to enter the congress, opening *barangay* (local assemblies) as direct conduits between his cabinet and constituencies. Further, during 1974–78, General Ne Win operated the Burma Socialist Program Party (BSPP), reliably winning elections and stacking the parliamentary *Hluttaw*. However, while Ne Win was chair of this party, he remained outside the parliament, basing his state leadership more securely in the military. Finally, though Cambodia has agreed to hold elections that have been organized externally by the United Nations, candidates and voters have participated in these contests at great peril. And warring between party leaders afterwards has resulted in the *de facto* repudiation of electoral outcomes.

8

However, it was Indonesia during the presidency of Suharto – a period labeled the New Order – that best institutionalized a pseudo-democracy. The press was tamed through quite arbitrary licensing requirements, while opposition parties, NGOs, and trade unions were tightly constrained. Hence, though the government permitted two opposition parties to operate, it recast them as vacuous "OPPs" (*organisasi peserta pilihan*, election participant organizations), then intervened deeply in their organizational affairs. As one example, the government pushed for a new leader of the non-government PDI (Indonesia Democracy Party) in 1986, replaced him in 1993 after he dared to delay in nominating Suharto for the presidency, then pushed him anew to replace his replacement, namely, Sukarno's daughter, Megawati. Irrespective, though, of who led the PDI, opposition parties were forbidden to organize branches in Indonesia's rural areas, precisely where most votes were to be found. No such prohibitions were placed on the government vehicle, however, *Golkar* (*Golongan Karya*, or "functional groups"), sent down by Suharto to contest elections every five years, then promptly garaged afterward. In addition, Suharto thickened the insulation round his presidency by refusing to sit in the legislature or submit to direct election. His tenure was instead renewed reliably through an electoral college, the members of which he had appointed himself or screened beforehand.

At this point, the analytical worth of distinguishing between semi- and pseudo-democracies must be underscored. One clear difference lies in the amounts of legitimacy that respective governments are able to claim.[23] Unlike Mahathir, Suharto could never justify his holding state power by inviting opposition parties to unseat him. And unlike Malaysia, Indonesia was never mistaken by even its most sympathetic foreign observers as democratic. Thus, while Suharto gained some of the benefits from elections enumerated above, his rule was legitimated less by electoral activities than raw economic performance. And when growth finally ceased, his pseudo-democracy collapsed – even as semi-democracies persisted in Malaysia and Singapore. Thus, semi-democratic regimes, characterized at least by a limited competitiveness, may stabilize more readily than pseudo-democracies, their presence indicating that a national leader has forged stronger ties to elites and social constituents. Pseudo-democracies, in contrast, characterized by greater coercion, may mask a fragility of inter-elite and elite-mass relations, though only so long as growth continues.

Finally, in supplying a referent with which to delimit our typology of full, semi-, and pseudo-democracies, a regime of "hard" authoritarianism can be specified, one which offers no trace of civil liberties or elections. And in Southeast Asia, one finds that this category of hard authoritarianism still abounds. The military government of Myanmar, having been "stunned" by its election in 1990, has since refused to conduct any more. In addition, it ruled that the *Hluttaw* that had been elected was in a fact a constituent assembly, not a parliament, and that its true purpose was thus to draft a constitution, not form a government. Even so, the military did not convene the *Hluttaw* for two-and-a-half years. In addition, Brunei has closed its regime once again, even before a first election could be held. And Vietnam and Laos, though ceasing their totalitarian mobilizations, have similarly refused to protect civil liberties or hold national elections. However, these cases – involving three low-income countries and one that is high-income, but unindustrialized – lie outside the scope of this volume. Where poverty enervates society, or where petroleum extraction principally enriches the state, the autonomy of elites is easily shown, a configuration reflected in the hard authoritarianism that prevails. Accordingly, this book investigates Southeast Asia's lower middle- and middle-income countries, those inhabiting a "political transition zone"[24] in which elites must not only engage one another, but interact with social forces, thereby producing in complex settings a variety of full, semi-, and pseudo-democracies.

Theories of political change

In attempting to explain regime types and change in Southeast Asia, a great range of approaches has been used. We can capture many of them, however, under structuralist, modernizationist, and culturalist headings. These approaches are similar in that they attach little importance to agency. They hold different expectations, though, about the prospects for democracy in Southeast Asia.

Structuralist accounts assume the presence of epic constraints that combine in determining regime outcomes. These structures may take different forms, including levels of economic development, class relations, ethnic identities, historical legacies, international contexts, and sundry other phenomena. They may also be static or dynamic, evolving at different rates. However, though taking different forms, unfolding at different speeds, and combining in various ways, structures are never freely chosen. Indeed, approaches that attach much significance to agency are dismissed by structuralists as "strategies of analytic simplification."[25] Thus, a structuralist methodology, frequently conducted in terms of historical comparisons, involves identifying forces and the ways in which they evolve and combine, driving the collectivities of actors who inhabit them to organize their politics, economies, and societies in predestined ways. As examples, Harold Crouch has used domestic political structures to gauge the limited prospects for regional cooperation in Southeast Asia.[26] Jomo K.S. has focused on class relations in Malaysia to explain patterns of uneven economic development.[27] Rabushka and Shepsle have demonstrated the implications of multi-ethnic social structures for democratic breakdown, using Malaysian experiences as a central case study.[28] And David Brown has combined state and ethnic structures to develop an explanation for varying amounts of political stability and unity in the region.[29]

But it has probably been Richard Robison, Kevin Hewison, and Garry Rodan who have been most committed to using structuralist models as a way of explaining political regimes in Southeast Asia. They have prefaced their analysis by arguing strongly against the voluntarism that prevails in the transitions literature, its contingency appearing, in their view, to erode scope for theorizing.[30] They have focused instead on the implications of steady capitalist development. Briefly, they contend that in the late-industrializing context of Southeast Asia, a capitalist class has been nurtured within the state apparatus through protection and subsidies. And because of the exclusionary nature of these exchanges, they have necessarily been carried out under authoritarian cover. However, as capitalist development continues, a point is reached where bourgeois "accumulation is facilitated more by competition in a market than by state patronage."[31] And hence, with markets allocating resources more efficiently than the state, maturing capitalist classes seek finally to break free. These classes then press the state to be more transparent in its allocative processes. They call upon it also to mediate impartially between different elements of competing capital. But apart from anomalous Singapore, Robison *et al* observe that governments operating authoritarian regimes have found it difficult to meet these new structuralist requirements. In these circumstances, capitalist classes push separately for democracy – so long as they do not feel threatened by lesser classes.

The analytical attraction of structural forces, of course, lies in their promise of enhanced opportunities for generalizing about political change. But the "bloodless social science"[32] that results ignores the fact that the progress of structures is sometimes modified, even negated by the deliberate and near-term calculations of elites. As we will see, business classes in the Philippines and Thailand, the most developed in the region, were sooner motivated to seek democracy by their desire to gain rents than any functional need for greater transparency. They opposed Marcos because he had shunted many of them aside, diverting state favors to new sets of cronies. And after Marcos was removed and politics were democratized, these elites rushed in to claim the newly vacated monopolies. In Thailand, new provincial business elites pushed for more political openness in 1988 in order to gain access to parliament, then control the tendering of state contracts. Moreover, after the military coup of 1991, business elites based in Bangkok revealed their great ambivalence over democratic procedures, sitting as comfortably in the cabinet of General Suchinda as they had that of his democratic predecessor, Chatichai Choonhavan.[33] In short, these were not once nurtured, now mature capitalist class with a structural need for democracy. They were motivated instead by instrumentalist calculations about access to state benefits, prompting them to support democracy in some cases and resist it in others.

Second, capitalist development within discrete national arenas may not only be slow, but its progress may be reversed. And in such instances, having hitched one's predictive hopes to a *telos* of capital's structural requirements may generate even less certainty than tracking voluntarist behaviors. The unforeseen nature of Asia's economic crisis is revealed by the IMF managing director, Michel Camdessus, having characterized the East Asian economies in March 1997 as "the very essence of globalization – open, dynamic, economies that continue to amaze the world with their rapid growth and economic development.[34] A year later, analyses were produced presaging the "end of Asian capitalism."[35] Clearly, then, structures can themselves evolve or decline in quite rapid and unpredictable ways. Further, in weakening the region's capitalist classes, the economic crisis had implications for democracy that again tested structuralist expectations. For example, the crisis more severely affected the industrializing bourgeoisie in Indonesia than in Malaysia. But it may be precisely because so much of Indonesia's capitalist class was weakened that the country was able to move forward, however haltingly, in democratizing its politics. In Malaysia, by contrast, where the capitalist class was wounded, but remained coherent, it was able to pressure the government for financial bail-outs. And because these bail-outs were unpopular with society more generally, they were accompanied by tighter authoritarian controls.

In sum, structuralist accounts identify a range of economic, social, historical, and external factors that must be brought into any full explanation of regime types and change. But structures do not by themselves determine regime outcomes. Rather, they are better understood as generating pressures that leaders and elites then mediate. And this mediating activity, involving near-term calculations and behaviors, amounts to a voluntarism that can seriously distort the impact of structures, thus compounding the incertitude with which structures are already afflicted.

A second kind of paradigm guiding the study of Southeast Asian politics can be labeled modernizationist. At base, modernization theories, first introduced during the 1950s–60s, hinged less on the structural requirements of the capitalist class than the attitudinal changes of the middle class, arguing that economic growth, urbanization, greater literacy rates, and organizational know-how help to stimulate middle-class participation in politics. And in crude terms, the need to accommodate this broad-based participation led ineluctably to democratic openness.[36] Of course, this thesis lost favor among comparativists toward the end of the 1960s, with the economies of developing countries stagnating or, where they grew, leading sooner to political "disorder."[37] In these circumstances, many comparativists were drawn to the activism of dependency theory, or they adopted the bland stability bias of systems theory and structural functionalism.

However, the rapid industrialization of South Korea and Taiwan during the 1970s–80s, in defying dependency's logic, opened yet another gap between theoretical expectations and real-world experience. Accordingly, analysts turned now to state capacity, in particular, the strategies by which the state could beat free markets and accelerate growth.[38] But then, as growth transformed the social structures of Korea and Taiwan, analysts began to peer once more through the lenses of modernization theory in order to scrutinize new middle classes.[39] And gradually, middle classes came slowly into focus in Southeast Asia too. Indeed, throughout the region, a great bloom of housing estates, designer goods, automobile showrooms, and golf courses provided the bearings for new middle-class living.

But if the middle class in East Asia, in displaying new careerist ambitions and consumerist longings, began to take on the appearance of its counterpart in the West, would there also be convergence over attitudes toward democracy? Samuel Huntington outlined some reasons for thinking so. While once he had warned that modernization did not amount to institutionalization, and that economic growth in developing countries sooner led to authoritarian controls than democratic procedures, he has seemed more recently to offer a new perspective. Specifically, in his study of democracy's "third wave," he observed,

> [I]ndustrialization led to a new, much more diverse, complex, and interrelated economy, which becomes increasingly difficult for authoritarian regimes to control. Economic development created new sources of wealth and power outside the state and a functional need to devolve decision making. More directly, economic development appears to have promoted changes in social structure and values that, in turn, encouraged democratization.[40]

Accordingly, in his account of democratization in the Philippines during the mid-1980s, Huntington notes the "crucial role" of the "business community." But he emphasizes also the activities of middle-class professionals, especially "non-politician doctors and lawyers" who volunteered their services to citizenship watchdog groups and opposition candidates.[41] In short, it was the middle class that gathered in the streets in opposition to Marcos, giving rise finally to the "miracle of EDSA." And it appeared to be the middle class too that helped resist the military during "Black May" in Bangkok, parking their BMWs out of harm's way and coordinating their activities over their hand phones and pagers.

Much analytical attention was thus given to the new middle class in various Southeast Asian settings.[42] But as investigation deepened, the gloss went off Huntington's new optimism, with middle-class ardor for democracy emerging as quite contingent. For example, in Malaysia, Singapore, and Indonesia much of the middle class remained employed by the bureaucracy, greatly tempering its political activism. And Brunei too, through its many entitlement programs, showed the capacity of the state to uplift a middle class, than smother it politically in sultanism. Further, the middle classes in these countries were ethnically segmented, with mutually

13

suspicious indigenous communities and Overseas Chinese finding it difficult to organize collectively. And middle classes were also divided by the different occupational categories they contained, with professionals and managers sitting uneasily alongside clerical and sales personnel. And finally, even where the middle class might coalesce, then press for its own inclusion in public policy making, it remained wary of the mass politics and majoritarian principles that would open the door more widely to organized workers and farmers. Accordingly, the middle class remained unlikely to enter any broad coalition led principally by the working class – identified by Rueschemeyer *et al* as historically democracy's most reliable agent.[43] Indeed, even in the Philippines, after the middle class had helped to democratize politics, it scaled back its activism, acquiescing finally in what some analysts have labelled "oligarchic" democracy.

Hence, in nuancing the argument about economic growth and the middle class, the central lesson emerging from James Morley's important volume, *Driven by Growth*, is that rapid annualized economic growth rates account less for democratization than the level of development that is finally attained.[44] Put simply, the most highly developed countries in Northeast Asia – Japan, South Korea, and Taiwan – all democratized their politics. Countries in Southeast Asia would surely do likewise, once their growth rates had accumulated over time in higher development. But as Andrew MacIntyre reflected in a work published in 1994, even if one could assume continuous growth rates of 7 per cent – an assumption quite invalidated by the region's economic crisis toward the end of the decade – it would have taken Malaysia 17 years, Thailand 27 years, the Philippines 41 years, and Indonesia 46 years to reach the per capita income level enjoyed by South Korea in 1990.[45] Thus, modernization theories focusing on middle-class attitudes – like structuralist accounts fixed on capitalist development – must make bold assumptions about lineal progress in order to gain explanatory power. In the meantime, though, Southeast Asia's new middle class has remained quite ambivalent toward democracy. While elements of the middle class helped to democratize regimes in the Philippines, Thailand, and perhaps Indonesia, their commitments have been much weaker in Malaysia and Singapore. Hence, it seems most accurate to suggest that the middle class desires better governance, but probably not mass politics, generally prompting it to seek no more than reformed authoritarianism.[46]

Nonetheless, if the middle class has been unable to coalesce so far in any broad, modernized push for democracy, perhaps the finer actions of civil society can succeed in gaining some "political space." Hence, civil society – an atomized entity of NGOs, neighborhood groups, religious and cultural associations, philanthropic organizations, trade unions, and social movements – emerges in many ways as the next phase in the modernization paradigm, even standing on the threshold of fragmented post-modernity. On this count, in surveying the rise of civil society in Europe, John Hall

14

demonstrates that literacy and a mass print culture helped to forge a necessary political awareness.[47] Other analysts identify similar processes of modernization at work throughout the developing world today. Lester Salamon has thus heralded an "associational revolution," one that "may prove to be as significant to the latter twentieth century as the rise of the nation-state was to the latter nineteenth."[48]

Indeed, one does find in Southeast Asia today the early stirrings of civil society. Moreover, if these new civil society organizations are traceable to modernizing processes, they draw much of their impetus from the "negative consequences" of rapid industrialization. Thus, new middle-class issues of consumer rights, environmental degradation, and gender inequalities combine with working-class resentments over labor exploitation and social marginalization to galvanize civil society. And in some cases, governments have responded positively to these concerns by cooperating with NGOs in important ways.[49] In the Philippines, Fidel Ramos consulted with a coalition called People's 2000 over developmental programs associated with his Philippines 2000 agenda. In Thailand, the government invited coordinating committees of rural NGOs to participate in forming the Sixth and Seventh National Development Plans (1986–90 and 1991–95). In Malaysia, the Federation of Malaysian Consumers' Association (FOMCA) and the National Council of Women's Organizations were invited by the government to participate in the National Economic Consultative Council held in 1990, helping devise a program to succeed the New Economic Policy. And in New Order Indonesia, the minister of population and environment, Emil Salim, met regularly during the 1980s with the Indonesian Environment Network (*Wahana Lingkungan Hidup* Indonesia, WALHI).[50]

But like the middle class in Southeast Asia, it remains too soon to argue that civil society has made significant headway in balancing state power and gaining political space. Nicos Mouzelis notes that a key aspect of the modernity upon which civil society relies is a rule of law that guards against state arbitrariness.[51] Hence, in Southeast Asia, where legal structures mostly remain poorly developed, the question to be asked is less one about how much space civil society is able to claim than how much the state is willing to cede. And if governments have sometimes consulted with NGOs, they have more often dismissed them. Tadashi Yamamoto thus concludes,

[T]he public sector rarely appreciates the advocacy agendas associated with many NGOs. While experience varies around [East Asia], many governments at the central and local levels regard NGOs as special interest organizations that do not keep the broader public interest at heart, as threats to social unity, or simply as private organizations placing additional burdens on government bureaucrats.[52]

15

The impatience often felt by government leaders toward NGOs is amply illustrated by Prime Minister Mahathir's once dismissing them publicly as "thorns in the flesh."

Hence, while state apparatuses in Southeast Asia have displayed great porousness before high-level cronies and first families, they have insulated themselves more stoutly against civil society. Deploying a variety of strategies, then, the state has coopted civil society leaders, supported organizational rivals, and imposed steep coercion. Hence, in Malaysia, for example, NGOs are registered under the Societies Act, then segmented into "friendly" and "political" societies.[53] And if the government has then worked closely with organizations like FOMCA on social welfare issues, it has sharply confronted those like *Aliran* and the Consumers Association of Penang that have sought greater public accountability. Indeed, dozens of NGO leaders were arrested in a security sweep in 1987, known as *Operasi Lalang*. Malaysia and New Order Indonesia also imposed controls on press freedoms, usually through licensing requirements and ownership patterns. Further, they countered resurgent Islamic movements by organizing respectively the co-optive IKIM (Malaysian Institute of Islamic Understanding) and the ICMI (Association of Indonesian Islamic Intellectuals), then suppressed autonomous sects as "deviationist." In Singapore, the government has tightly incorporated labor on behalf of foreign investors through a state sponsored front, the National Trades Union Congress. In the Philippines, Marcos targeted labor leaders for "salvagings" by death squads. And in Thailand too, labor leaders continued to "disappear" until the early 1990s.

Finally, quite apart from state actions, civil society has itself been divided over democracy's worth. As Garry Rodan reminds us, many NGOs and social movements have been geared more closely to ethnic identities, religious revivalism, and, in the past, communist insurgency than to any democratization of politics.[54] As brief examples, some Muslim groups in Malaysia have demanded an Islamic state, one in which policy is made by a *shura* of appointed religious scholars rather than by elected representatives. A high official in Thailand's Buddhist *sangha*, Kittiwutto, once intoned during the 1970s that it was an act of faith to kill Communists. And indeed, to confirm the patriarch's fears, Southeast Asia once bristled with Communist labor fronts, radical student movements, and guerrilla groups. In consequence, though the region's civil society was vital in the past and may be gaining density today, its commitments to democracy are unclear. Civil society remains a variable whose origins and outlooks must themselves be explained, rather than used reflexively as a tool by which to predict democratic outcomes.

In sum, many of Southeast Asia's most important countries remain lower middle- and middle-income ones, attaining a level of modernization with ambiguous implications for democracy. Of course, in the wake of economic crisis, once timorous middle classes may now be more easily activated. And as recovery imposes new demands on ethnic minorities, women workers, and the environment, civil society too may gain greater coherence. But much will depend also on the kinds of strategies that leaders and elites now deploy, engaging one another and re-energizing social constituents – thus suggesting the very cautious use one must make of modernizing assumptions. As Karen Remmer has observed, "The modernization approach, along with the major theoretical alternatives that crystallized during the 1970s, simply leaves analysts standing too far away from the world of political actors and agency to offer insights into these varied longitudinal and cross-sectional patterns of interaction between economics and politics."[55]

A final paradigm used to assess politics in Southeast Asia can be labelled culturalist. And it is here, perhaps, that analysts have travelled furthest across boundaries of area specialization and discipline. One thinks in particular of Clifford Geertz's notions of "thick description" and an "interpretative theory of culture,"[56] Benedict Anderson's study of traditional Javanese "imaginings" and their modern-day cultural impacts,[57] and James C. Scott's uncovering the "everyday forms of resistance" mounted by peasants when cultural norms have been breached.[58]

More recently, though, analysts guided by culturalist assumptions have turned to gauging the prospects for democracy in Southeast Asia. And while the structuralists and modernizationsts have impatiently awaited democracy's imminent arrival, the culturalists have warned of its great delay. In brief, the culturalists argue that timeless or reinvented patterns of cultural values amount to finely calibrated status systems that enforce the divisions between leaders and tame followings. In consequence, social relations – whether in politics, business, or ordinary encounters – have remained personalist and informal, yet rigid and steeply unequal. Furthermore, many analysts have suggested that despite the constructed nature of ethnic identities, these sentiments are still deeply etched across the face of Southeast Asia, reinforcing the top-down affiliations and mass-level tensions that negate possibilities for collective class action. Indeed, in this view, the ease with which state leaders have been able to divide social constituencies ethnically, then mobilize them culturally helps not only to explain democracy's delay, but the rapidity with which economic growth once took place. As a rough guide to the region's division of labor, Overseas Chinese, while broadly excluded from political life, have been recruited as investors, contractors, technicians, and retailers. And indigenous followings, though politically enfranchised, have mostly been conscripted into factory places, agriculture, and petty trade.

Michael Vatikiotis, in *Political Change in Southeast Asia*, has perhaps made this culturalist argument most forcefully. He begins by identifying

17

"top-down control" and "acquiescence to power" as traditional, yet still compelling orientations within the region's political culture. He then sets out to discover the roots of these orientations, peeling away the relatively recent accretions of wayfaring Islam, European colonialism, and Cold War ideologies, finally exposing "indigenous models of kingship."[59] Clark Neher and Ross Marlay observe similarly that while patron-clientelism may be waning, "Asian cultures still stress hierarchy, status, gratitude, reciprocity, and personalism." They then trace these values squarely to the "Buddhist views [and] Hindu beliefs that permeated mainland Southeast Asia in the centuries immediately preceding the Christian era. . . . Kings found attractive those Indian forms and rituals that reinforced their power [and permitted them to pose as] reincarnations of Shiva, Vishnu, or Indra."[60] Finally, David Martin Jones reveals in much detail the cultural bases for the unaccountable politics and unreliable business contracts that he characterizes as endemic in the region. In Thailand, for example, he charts the links between immutable Buddhist *kharma*, unchangeable gradients in status, and the "joys" of social dependence. In Indonesia, he detects in "Javanese political psychology . . . its underlying pessimism and its susceptibility to messianic appeal." And in Malaysia, he asserts that Islam has helped reinforce the "traditional sacral and magical attributes of rule."[61] In sum, area specialists taking culturalist approaches contend that irrespective of fluctuating economic records and processes of class formation, attitudes continue to militate strongly in Southeast Asia against democracy.[62]

However, one must caution against attributing to cultural patterns such ironclad determinacy. To be sure, because cultures link individuals, collectivize identities, and regularize expectations in cross-group encounters,[63] they help to color the contexts in which politics take place. But as is often observed, culture fails to solidify as an independent causal variable. Instead, it can be reinvented consciously by elites who seek to firm constituent loyalties. And it can be woven by elites into their fabric of legitimating "mentalities."[64] On the other side, culture can be contested by constituents, who, in then sometimes abandoning their leaders, defy cultural norms and contribute even to regime changes. One recognizes, then, that culture, far from posing a constant and immutable force, is heavily negotiated, thus revealing its partly voluntarist character.

On this score, Jones himself detects shortcomings in unleavened culturalist accounts. He perceives that lore about ancient Javanese kingships and Confucian bureaucrats does not filter unaided into contemporary outlooks on politics. Instead, "traditional ideas" must be "reinvented" or "revitalized" by what he at various junctures labels "indigenous," "ruling," "traditional scholar," and "technocratic" elites. He elaborates a "problematic elite nationalism" in colonial Asia and describes democratization in Taiwan as "elite-driven."[65] Accordingly, Jones now fortifies his argument with a large measure of agency, reinterpreting culture as a strategy by which elites re-energize constituent support. More specifically, he observes that throughout East Asia, elites have industrialized their economies and transformed their societies. But then to perpetuate their statuses and authoritarian regime forms, they resort to a menu of culturalist cues and appeals.

To illustrate Jones's thesis, it is perhaps worth recalling an observation made by Malaysia's national leader, Mahathir. After warding off a challenge to his leadership of the UMNO at its general assembly in 1996, Mahathir reminded his audience that "according to Malay tradition . . . it is impolite for someone who sits in the same committee or cabinet to challenge another who also happens to be his boss."[66] The UMNO's permanent chair had earlier made the same point, advising that while leadership challenges were formally permitted in the party's constitution, actually to mount one flouted cultural understandings: "According to Malay tradition, it is treachery."[67] In sum, this need for cultural reminders shows clearly that culture cannot by itself stratify societies, perpetuate loyalties, and determine regime types. Instead, as Jones comes to demonstrate, culture is curated, then exploited by elites, helping greatly to firm his account of authoritarianism's persistence in Malaysia, Singapore, and New Order Indonesia.

On the other hand, though Jones does not consider it explicitly, the possibility of elites failing to reinvent culture – or doing so inappropriately – might help equally to explain the authoritarian breakdowns and transitions to democracy that have occurred in the Philippines, Thailand, and most recently in Indonesia. As Hewison *et al* note, by itself, "the most serious flaw in the culturalist approach is the incapacity to explain tensions in authoritarian regimes."[68] Indeed, notions of slow-moving patrimonialism and habitual mass deference fail utterly to square with recent manifestations of popular upsurge, that is, the "people power" and *reformasi* movements that have in some instances been steeled by mob violence. What is more, these contemporary activities have taken place against an historical backdrop of Communist insurrections, regionalist upheavals, and Islamic militancy. Hence, by introducing elites who fail to craft cultural appeals, or who do so with great clumsiness, we begin to observe divergences from mass expectations. In this way, culture can be given the dynamism necessary for moving beyond authoritarian persistence in order to explain democratic change. As one example, there are reasons for thinking that Suharto's increasingly stilted ideas about Javanese kingship and his reinvention of the *priyayi* ethos finally struck social forces as absurd, especially in the Outer Islands, thereby intensifying the resentments against him.[69]

In sum, paradigms that rely on determinist structures, modernizing processes, or fixed patterns of culture – their assumptions grounded respectively in capitalism's requirements, middle-class attitudes, the cumulation of civil society, and timeless patterns of clientelism – are unable to account fully for political regimes in Southeast Asia. Even where business classes do seek democracy, their motivations are mixed, seeking as much to reconstitute cronyist ties as to institute free markets. Middle classes too adopt uncertain postures, remaining either dependent on the state and sceptical of mass politics, or actively, though ineffectively, participating in civil society. And culture, finally, only helps to perpetuate authoritarianism where it is skillfully reinvented. Hence, the principle variables contained in these paradigms unfold in ambiguous ways. To see which way, one must look to agency, best conceptualized in terms of national leaders and elites.

Elites, social forces, and regime outcomes

References to leadership and elites, though usually *ad hoc*, are commonplace in analyses of Southeast Asian politics. Indeed, it is difficult to overlook the roles in regime types and change that have been performed by Sukarno, Suharto, Marcos, Mahathir, Sarit, Ne Win, Lee Kuan Yew, and Ho Chi Minh – as formidable a roster of national leaders as one will find in the developing world. But leadership, in its contingency, appears difficult to theorize. Accordingly, few accounts attempt to do more than document the origins of leaders, then trace weak links to their policy preferences. The broader collectivities of elite persons and factions are given even scantier treatment, introduced only to fill gaps in heavily determinist accounts or to animate chronological narratives.

However, Harold Crouch and James Morley, in nuancing their modernization approach to change in East Asia, begin to uncover the importance of inter-elite relations. Most notably, they find that Singapore has been able to avoid democracy in part because elites in the PAP have remained "extraordinarily unified since the party's formation in the 1950s . . . The lack of factional conflict within the ruling party has given little opportunity for the emergence of a strong opposition." Elites in New Order Indonesia also displayed much unity, enabling them similarly to avoid democracy for more than three decades. Crouch and Morley thus conclude that "a long-established cohesive elite can often obstruct political change even when other factors are pushing in the direction of change."[70] By contrast, "the less cohesive an elite, the less it is able to resist pressures toward liberalization and democratization." Unfortunately, these analysts give no particular weighting to elites within their long directory of modernizing forces. But importantly, they acknowledge the implications of inter-elite relations for the persistence of regimes.

Moreover, in two seminal analyses of Southeast Asian politics, Donald Crone usefully broadens the focus from inter-elite to elite-mass relations.[71] He begins by forcefully arguing that the main organizational base for elite statuses in the region remains the state.[72] He then shows that where state elites use "collaborative mechanisms" to deepen their social support, they increase their autonomy and capacity, enabling them better to purse their industrializing aims. Specifically, state elites in Singapore created a "paternalistic, corporatist structure" through which to gain the support of labor. Elites in Malaysia forged "a multicommunal political 'directorate'" in order to retain the loyalties of different ethnic groups.[73] Further, in doing this, elites in Singapore and Malaysia were able to generate surpluses with which to fund social welfare, thereby reinforcing their prior social support. By contrast, elites in New Order Indonesia, Thailand, and the Philippines created few collaborative mechanisms, provided little welfare, and hence, gained comparatively little capacity. Indeed, elites under Marcos followed the market "toward disaster," greatly alienating social forces. In sum, though Crone never explicitly addresses the conditions in which democratization might take place, he nonetheless highlights the analytical significance of elite-mass relations in the Southeast Asian setting.

At this juncture, we can begin to forge a rough template by which to order our analysis of regime types and change. In brief, one investigates the inter-elite relations noted by Crouch and Morley to learn whether a regime is stable or unstable. One investigates the elite-mass relations studied by Crone to account for a regime's being authoritarian or democratic. Hence, in Southeast Asia – its context marked historically by pervasive colonialism and extensive bureaucracies, state-led or state sanctioned processes of industrialization, low to medium levels of development (with the exception of highly developed Singapore), socially "constructable" ethnicities, politically "re-inventable" cultures, and quite contradictory international pressures – one finds that elites have generally been cohesive and societies quiescent, enabling many authoritarian regimes to persist. Thus, where democratization has taken place, it has involved elites who have lost their cohesiveness, and hence, their managerial capacity, leaving them vulnerable to social forces grown at least momentarily participatory. These surges in participation, in turn, are rooted in contextual changes (e.g., economic growth, followed by decline), perhaps magnified by great leadership incompetence (e.g., inappropriate cultural appeals, "excessive" predatory behaviors, and conspicuously stolen elections). However, any democracy that results can only reach equilibrium if elites regain their cohesion. This involves elites acknowledging one another as rightful contenders, social forces as legitimate participants, and elections as the most efficient way in which to structure their competitions.

Democratic elite theory

Elite theory, while duly enumerated in most texts on comparative politics that survey analytical frameworks, has never gained the prominence that at various stages structuralism, modernization theory, political culture, systems theory, and class analysis have enjoyed. Elite theory has instead been too often associated with *elitism*, a belief not only in the inevitability of

21

elites – even in the course of social revolutions[74] – but the normative rightfulness of their statuses and privileges. Put simply, elite theorists have been thought guilty of much worse than the stability bias seen generally to tarnish the field of comparative politics. They have accepted, even celebrated elites who have resisted socioeconomic mobility and reform, permitting at most some circulation within their own cabals in order to freshen their memberships and sharpen their cunning. Indeed, among the classical elite theorists, Mosca appears to have been contemptuous of democracy, at least in his early writings. Pareto was associated with the rise of Italy's fascist politics during the 1920s, while Michels too was branded "an apologist for Fascism."[75]

During the 1970s, however, elites were reviewed in a more positive light. Their collusion was recast as cooperation, while their narrow processes of circulation became rule-bound competitions. Thus, in developing typologies of variable behaviors, Putnam identified a category of elite "solidarity," Di Palma elaborated a notion of "restrained partisanship," and Field and Higley described relations of "consensual unity."[76] Elites who organized their relations in these ways competed openly, but not violently. Instead, they moderated their competitions with formal rules and tacit under-standings which, while in many ways culturally unique to their milieus, seemed universally to involve two broad kinds of restraint. First, elites avoided systematically undercutting the statuses and resources of other elites, purging their rivals from high positions, dismantling their organiza-tions, and forcing them into prison or bankruptcy. The penalties for political defeats, in short, were softened. Second, when elites moved outside their configurations to mobilize support, they avoided inflaming social grievances. Of course, elites made ethnic, class-based, and regionalist appeals – as they must in order to re-energize their followings and perpetuate their standings. But they did this skillfully, stopping well short of provoking mass uprisings that would threaten the elite collectivity.

In a stronger version of this thesis, elites were seen even to be useful in managing societies that were scarred by sectarian or ideological rivalries. Where elites had earlier been viewed as artfully manipulating social tensions in order to underpin their own standings, they were seen now to cooperate in easing these tensions – under-mobilizing supporters, holding countries together, and in some cases conforming to democratic procedures. Nordlinger thus charted the "regulatory behavior" of elites in "divided societies." Lijphart examined strategies of "elite coalescence" in "plural societies." Lijphart also credited elites with the capacity to forge grand coalitions atop their constituent "pillars," practices that sometimes unfolded in what he labeled "consociational democracy."[77]

During the 1980s–early 1990s, elites were given an even more surprising role, able not only to manage societies and maintain democracies, but even to commence democratizing processes. In their path-breaking analysis of democratic transitions in southern Europe and Latin America, O'Donnell and Schmitter focused closely on elites, especially those based in the state apparatus. They framed elite factions in terms of "soft-liners" and "hard-liners," then famously asserted that "there is no transition whose beginning is not the consequence – direct or indirect – of important divisions within the authoritarian regime itself."[78] Of course, if democratization must begin with elites, a question arose over what might motivate them to open the regimes upon which their statuses depended. O'Donnell and Schmitter responded simply that soft-lining elites were driven by a new awareness of the benefits of "electoral legitimation," bracing their hold on state power with societal consent.[79] Lest one conclude from this, though, that elites have no choice but one day to legitimate their rule by democratizing, O'Donnell and Schmitter reminded us too that "no transition can be forced purely by opponents against a regime which maintains the cohesion, capacity, and disposition to apply repression."[80]

Questions about the pressures and calculations that converted elites into democrats helped to invigorate the field of democratic elite theory.[81] Indeed, from the mid-1980s through the early 1990s, scholarly attention shifted dramatically from structural determinants to elite-level contingency, thus producing a vast new literature. In a summary guide to its methodological steps, one began by addressing the sundry crises, legitimacy gaps, and drops in performance that strained elite relations and enlivened social forces. One turned next to the ways in which soft-lining elites based in the state began to negotiate with those in opposition, reaching agreements that were variously conceptualized as "pacting," "crafting," "accordism," "garantismo," and "settlements."[82] In this way, soft-liners could regulate the pace of democracy's progress, made manifest in state-led or heavily brokered processes of "transformation" and "trans-placement." However, where state elites remained divided, then failed equally to make deals with the opposition, they risked their regime's unmodulated "replacement."[83] As we will see, if the first mode of transition better describes the experiences of Latin American and southern Europe, the second captures the sparser democratic record of Southeast Asia, hence illustrating the great contextual differences between these regions.

During the mid-1990s, however, democratic transitions everywhere grew scarcer, thus inaugurating among those studying regime change a period of what Kuhn might have designated as "normal science."[84] In brief, analysts lowered their sights in order to focus more closely on their existing inventory of democracies, addressing the puzzles of stabilization and quality that together denote consolidation.[85] Further, in appearing to have exhausted the possibilities for theorizing elite contingency, they reviewed the legacies of prior regime forms, various types of institutional designs, and the opportunities for mass-level participation. Indeed, a key theme in Linz and Stepan's empirically rich volume is that the kind of authoritarianism that exists beforehand helps to mould democracy's transitional pathways – and hence, the nature too of later "consolidating tasks." Because Spain's authoritarianism under Franco, for example, had featured a "usable" bureaucracy, a legal culture, and robust civil society, its transition to democracy and consolidation were more easily achieved than in the once totalitarian countries of eastern Europe.[86]

However, while the study of democratization continues to unfold, we are guided by two insights as we make our way into Southeast Asia. First, to gauge whether a regime is stable or unstable, one investigates the distinct, logically prior relations between elites, especially within the state. Second, in gauging the prospects for authoritarianism or democracy, one assesses mass attitudes, in particular, the extent to which contextual factors render them quiescent or participatory. These dimensions yield a simple four-cell table of possible outcomes, though one makes the usual allowances for continuums.

	Elite cohesion	Elite disunity
Quiescent constituents	**Stable authoritarianism**	**Unstable authoritarianism**
Participatory society	**Stable democracy**	**Unstable democracy**

Where elites are cohesive, they can perpetuate authoritarianism, readily paying the costs in terms of economic inefficiencies, social unrest, and international sanctions. Myanmar's political record shows this vividly. But where elites lose cohesion, their authoritarianism grows unstable. In this situation, whether one authoritarian regime will merely be replaced by another or will instead give way to democracy depends on mass attitudes and the contexts in which they form. In crude terms, where societies remain quiescent, mired in low levels of industrial development, fractured by sectarian identities, and frozen in cultural traditions, elites can mobilize, yet contain social forces through simple appeals and mentalities. Accordingly, instability in these circumstances will produce no more than high-level executive and military coups – a revolving-door authoritarianism. The political record of Thailand best illustrates this outcome, punctuated by nearly a score of coups between its revolution of 1932 and its re-democratization sixty years later.

Conversely, where industrialization articulates new classes, sectarian identities soften in pluralist forbearance, or cultural traditions dim amid occupational mobility, social forces may find that the primary appeals made by elites lose resonance. These forces may instead grow active when after a long period of growth, widely inspiring a new sense of personal efficacy and organizational know-how, severe crisis sets in. It is at this point that quiescent constituents may become participatory civil societies, then press for democracy. Of course, if elites retain enough cohesion, they can resist these pressures – an outcome demonstrated by Malaysia during the late 1990s, notwithstanding the deep rift between Mahathir and Anwar. But if in these conditions elites lose their cohesion, their regime may give way to democratic pressures. The Philippines in 1986, Thailand in 1973 and in 1992, and Indonesia during 1998–99 each democratized their politics in this way. One observes too that national leaders in these cases, unaccustomed to making concessions to oppositions and activated social forces, did little to prepare for the transitions that took place. Hence, as noted above, democratization in Southeast Asia has involved opposition-led replacement, rather than state-modulated transformation or negotiated trans-placement. Nonetheless, for democracy thereafter to persist, elites must regain their cohesion – lest it fall prey to "conspiracies involving few actors."[87] This progress appears only to have been completed in the Philippines. However, even here, the terms under which Philippine elites have gained cohesion suggest their democracy remains low quality.

In sum, the aim of this book is to account for the extent to which political regimes in Southeast Asia are stable or unstable, as well as authoritarian or democratic. It may be, of course, that over the long haul, the lineal projections and democratic expectations of the structuralists and modernizationists will finally be borne out. Notwithstanding anomalies like Singapore and Brunei, the correlations between wealth and democracy at the global level are compelling. On the other hand, it may be that in the hands of innovative elites and their ideologues, cultural features will pose perennial hindrances. However, these paradigms cannot by themselves explain the jagged short-to-medium term surges and reversals that make up Southeast Asia's fluctuating record, producing a greater diversity of regimes than is found in any other region. Attention must thus be given to agency, conceptualized as leaders and elites who mediate between societies in context and regimes as outcomes. Taking this nimbler approach offers quicker analytical payoff than gazing upon structured, modernized, and fully democratized horizons, or alternatively, culturally enforced authoritarian settings.

Southeast Asia: a democratic perspective

This volume, though including a short chapter on Singapore, focuses most closely on those countries in Southeast Asia that are lower middle- or middle-income, operate largely capitalist economies, and have at least some experience with democracy. The rich country of Brunei is thus excluded, as is the very poor country of Myanmar, having mostly missed out on the boom of the early to mid-1990s. The poor and post-totalitarian countries of Vietnam, Cambodia, and Laos are also left out. In this way, the dissimilarities in contextual factors between our sample countries are reduced, placing in sharper relief the role of elites in producing different types of regimes. At the same time, we can focus at some junctures on the contextual dissimilarities that remain, again spotlighting the role of elites in cases where they produce similar regime outcomes.

Hence, what are sometimes labelled the *"ASEAN 4"* are explored in this volume – Indonesia, Malaysia, Thailand, and the Philippines[88] – along with the highly developed city-state of Singapore. While for analytical reasons, political economists frequently locate Singapore in the one-time "tiger" community of Northeast Asian NICs, enabling them to trace the contours of its developmental state, one notes that Singapore is deeply embedded in Southeast Asia, historically deriving much of its trading wealth and investment returns from exchanges with its neighbors, while also sharing much of their cultural ambience.

Country chapters are ordered beginning with Indonesia's pseudo-democracy and its recent transition, followed by Southeast Asian countries that in varying measure have shown enduring records of something more. Hence, this volume investigates next the stable semi-democracy of Singapore, the newly contested semi-democracy of Malaysia, the unconsolidated democracy of Thailand, then concludes with the stable, but low quality democracy of the Philippines. Of course, such sequencing and nomenclature evoke a normative preference for democratic regimes. But after examining Southeast Asia closely, questions over who benefits most must nuance our judgements about democracy's worth. Too often in Southeast Asia if democracy limits state power, it then benefits those social forces that possess most resources, namely, metropole business conglomerates, landed families, provincial godfathers, and rural *caciques*.[89] In extending analysis from democratic transitions to consolidation, sceptics are thus not without basis for dismissing democracy in the Philippines as "oligarchic" and Thai democracy as "bourgeois," observing that despite the formal change in political regimes, no better distribution takes place. At the same time, if authoritarianism appears to offer great gains, with developmental states once quickening industry and socialist ones sometimes promoting equality, its risks are now widely recognized too. For every Lee Kuan Yew or even Mahathir, one encounters the avariciousness of a Marcos, the brutality of Myanmar's generals, and the murderousness of Cambodia's Pol Pot. Hence, this book contains an implicit endorsement of democratic procedures. But it seeks more to deploy the concept as a neutral organizing principle and object of study.

On this score, it is easily shown that Southeast Asia's political record can usefully be entered into debates over democratization.[90] In particular, though the region has been characterized from a democratic perspective as the "world's most recalcitrant,"[91] we have seen that its experiences fluctuate considerably, even within the subset of the five country cases analyzed in this volume. Colonial experience, both British and American, helped to democratize politics during the 1940s–50s in Singapore, Malaysia, and the

Philippines. And amid democracy's "second wave" after World War II, Indonesia democratized its politics too. Of course, Thailand, was never formally colonized by the West. Instead, it opened its doors to fascist Japan during the war, incurring legacies that perhaps hindered democracy's progress. Nonetheless, as noted above, factional divisions between military elites enabled restive students and workers to push through democracy during the mid-1970s – the first democratization in the region to have sprung from internal forces.

Despite this democratic momentum, however, Southeast Asia soon suffered a "reverse wave." Democracy was thus eroded in Indonesia by the radical populism of Sukarno and rebellions in the Outer Islands, in Singapore by the strong-willed industrializing of Lee Kuan Yew, in Malaysia by Malay "ultras" seeking ethnic redress, in Thailand by generals who gradually muted their factional differences, and in the Philippines by economic stagnancy and Marcos's opportunism. Thereafter, though, national leaders and elites gained uneven amounts of cohesion. Social forces emerged too which, in a context of structural changes, modernization, and fading tradition, sometimes mounted challenges that were cast in explicitly democratic terms. In these circumstances, as noted above, the Philippines, Thailand, and most recently Indonesia all redemocratized their politics. What is more, in cases where national leaders and elites succeeded in resisting these pressures, they did so in part by invoking democracy's idiom. Singapore and Malaysia thus innovated the notion of Asian democracy – a regionalized variant of semi-democracy – grounded in reinvented cultural themes of top-down Confucianism and the Melaka Sultanate. Thus, in varying measure, Carl Trocki concludes that "democratic forms, including elected legislative bodies and executives, regular elections, political parties, written constitutions, and formal guarantees of political and individual human liberties have become part of the legitimizing apparatus of most Southeast Asian nations."[92]

In consequence, while many political economists studying Southeast Asia have turned to economic crisis and uneven recovery, and sociologists have focused on changing social formations, safety nets, and coping strategies, comparativists should keep an eye on democracy. Indeed, this book tries to show that democracy's progress in different Southeast Asian countries can be compared in more than trivial ways. And it attempts to demonstrate also that in making comparisons, attention must be given to agency, conceptualized in terms of leaders and elites.

In doing this, each country chapter opens by locating its analysis in the broader context of Southeast Asia, enumerating some important similarities and differences. It then addresses leaders and elites, specifying their institutional or social grounding and the quality of their relations. In Southeast Asia, the state is still the most potent base for elite statuses, with the executive positions and bureaucratic apparatuses introduced through

27

European colonialism still retaining their centrality. But we will also see that the business conglomerates with which the state in some cases now closely interacts have come also to buoy up elites. The quality of relations between elites, then, unfolding mainly in the state, but also across business, determines the regime's stable or unstable character. Next, analysis turns to elite-mass relations, identifying in each country setting the forces that most strongly shape mass attitudes. Ethnicity, religion, and class solidarities are thus considered. Local and regionalist sentiments are addressed where appropriate, though not in any systematic way, owing to restrictions on the book's length, as well as its theoretical focus. Finally, these forces cumulate in mass outlooks which, amid variable elite capacity to mediate and manage, can broadly be categorized as quiescent or participatory, thus helping to account for the regime's authoritarian or democratic character. A description of the regime form then follows, cast in terms of civil liberties and elections.

In concluding these studies, the country chapters explore a key issue that in each setting provides additional insights into national politics. In Indonesia, the transition from pseudo-democracy to a fuller democracy is examined, followed by assessments of the Habibie presidency and Abdurrahman Wahid's first year in office. In Singapore, questions are briefly addressed about the worth of elections as a way of ratifying power relations between elites. In Malaysia, attention focuses on the general election in 1999, waged amid severe elite-level rivalries between Mahathir and Anwar. In Thailand, an analysis of the general election of early 2001 is presented, arguing that recent increases in democratic quality may jeopardize stability. In contrast, an analysis of the most recent election in the Philippines, held in 1998, argues that while the country's democracy is stable, it remains low quality – an evaluation seemingly verified by the subsequent policy performance of President Joseph Estrada and the manner of his removal. Much the same assessment might be made of Indonesia's new democracy, given the performance and impeachment of Abdurrahman Wahid as president.

Chapter 2

Indonesia

—▪◆▪—

Perpetuating and Changing a Pseudo-democracy

With Indonesia's territorial reach, immense population, and legacy of anti-colonial struggle, it has in geo-strategic and historical terms been viewed as the heavyweight of Southeast Asia. Further, its ethnic tensions between "indigenous" communities and Overseas Chinese, as well as its Islamic resurgence, have seemed emblematic of social structures and pressures in the region. And its economic record has illustrated, indeed magnified regional trends, involving first a dependence on commodities exports, a transition to foreign investment and labor intensive manufacturing, a cronyism taken to new heights, and a crash to new lows.

However, from the perspective of this book, it is Indonesia's political record that most deserves attention, illustrating many of the regime types formed elsewhere in the region. As configurations of national leaders, elites, and social forces evolved over time, they produced an unconsolidated democracy during the 1950s, an unstable form of semi-authoritarianism during the early 1960s, a long period of pseudo-democracy that persisted until the late 1990s, then a fuller democracy today. But within this record, it is Indonesia's pseudo-democracy – the much studied New Order – that most stands out. For three decades, it generated political stability, however unjust, and rapid economic growth, however uneven. Thus, the speed with which this pseudo-democracy finally broke down astonished Southeast Asianists, in something of the same way that the collapse of the Soviet Union did the rest of the world. Accordingly, this chapter focuses mostly on the origins, operation, and change of the pseudo-democratic New Order.

In first stabilizing his regime, the national leader, Suharto, artfully managed elites. In particular, rather than unifying elites, Suharto divided them into rival factions, then balanced them, skillfully administering patronage and sanctions. Further, in perpetuating the pseudo-democratic character of his regime, he contained social forces, deploying a variety of incentives and controls. Elites thus skirmished continuously, but were unable seriously to challenge Suharto. Social forces sometimes rioted, but were more often quiescent, indeed, a disembodied "floating mass."

Of course, Suharto's balancing and containment strategies required large amounts of resources. At the start of his tenure, he gained these resources through new inflows of foreign investment and aid. Then, during the petroleum boom of the 1970s, he vastly increased his revenues, enabling him to promote local business conglomerates. Finally, with the decline of petroleum prices during the 1980s, he returned deftly to foreign investment, this time generating export manufactures. However, throughout these policy swings, Suharto accumulated enough resources that he was able to placate most elites and at least some social forces, while the economic growth that took place helped legitimate his rule more broadly. In these circumstances, his regime remained stable, even if graced by the barest of democratic procedures.

But after three decades in power, Suharto was confronted by severe economic crisis. International currency traders got wind of the indebtedness of local banks and conglomerates, then speculated in ways that eroded the local *rupiah*. As loans then turned bad and foreign investors fled, local businesses failed in large numbers. Suharto now stood bereft of the resources with which to manage elites, causing the divisions he had long husbanded to widen. And as elites in the state bureaucracy, security forces, and business conglomerates drew increasingly apart, some began openly to challenge Suharto's leadership. Further, with middle-class hopes now blighted, students grew participatory, helping inadvertently to prompt mob violence. In this context, still more elites turned against Suharto, evaluating him as endangering, rather than promoting their statuses. And in May 1998, they forced Suharto out, finally setting in train a transition to fuller democracy.

As elsewhere in the region, with such unyielding national leadership, the democratization that took place involved an opposition-led replacement. But as we will see, though this implies a far-reaching transition, social forces soon lost momentum while elites regained some cohesion, thereby limiting the pace and extent of change. In brief, under Suharto's successor, B.J. Habibie, civil liberties and competitive elections were introduced. But this was undertaken in ways that restrained the opposition, enabling only "cautious" reformers to emerge. Thus, while Habibie's party, *Golkar*, was dealt a great setback when finally parliamentary elections were held, and Habibie was himself forced out of the presidential contest some months later, the broader collectivity of elites and patterns of distribution largely persisted. And though this limited progress raised questions about the quality of Indonesia's new democracy, it appeared to have improved prospects for stability.

This chapter begins with a note on analyzing New Order Indonesia. It then provides some background, charting the regime types that preceded the New Order, the route by which Suharto came to power, and the ways in which he managed elites and social forces. Next, it outlines the pseudo-democracy that he operated, marked by tight constraints on civil liberties and rigged, though regular elections. This chapter turns then to economic crisis, new elite and mass tensions, and the transition to fuller democracy that followed. It concludes with assessments of Suharto's successors as president, B.J. Habibie and Abdurrahman Wahid.

Analyzing New Order Indonesia

In New Order Indonesia, inter-elite and elite-mass relations have often been likened to a pyramid[1] – capped by a paramount national leader, staffed with an elite collectivity, and resting on a broad social base that while mostly flat, was nonetheless distinguished by a new middle class and the first stirrings of civil society. While this metaphor describes roughly, of course, the political life of many Southeast Asian countries, Indonesia was distinguished by the extent to which its leader, President Suharto, elevated himself gradually over other elites in the military, bureaucracy, and business. With unusual astuteness, he dispensed patronage in ways that placated elites, yet sorted them into countervailing groups, an approach that can best be conceptualized as patrimonialist.[2] He also deployed similar, though necessarily more distant strategies toward society, variably rewarding diverse forces. Most notably, new urban and landowning middle classes were heavily subsidized, while more traditional and formally demarcated categories of workers, peasants, and fishers were only lightly benefited. Other social forces, meanwhile – student activists, critical journalists, and labor organizers – were often harshly suppressed. Hence, at this level, Suharto's approach can be understood as corporatist.[3] Finally, Suharto tried to obscure his arbitrary behaviors with highly formalized institutions, a fussy legalism, and regular, though uncompetitive elections. Taken together, the patrimonialism that ensnared elites, the corporatism that disciplined society, and the elections that offered a shred of legitimating cover provided the armature for Suharto's pseudo-democracy.

For more than three decades, Suharto operated in these ways, limiting the interpretative angles from which to scrutinize his rule. Hence, neither the structuralists or modernization theorists, scouring for democratizing pressures in economic growth and social differentiation seem able to account for the New Order's persistent authoritarianism. Nor can culturalist approaches, in tracing long contours of social passivity, explain the suddenness of collapse when finally it came. In short, the quest for structures and processes favoring political change – an autonomous bourgeoisie, a democratizing middle class, feisty NGOs, a new labor militancy, and small-holder resistance – seems fruitless during most of the New Order. One can track the emergence of these forces, but seldom their effective participation, suggesting the scant utility of frameworks centering on class identities and civil society formations. Instead, causality flowed more heavily from the top, washing over society, blanketing it in quiescence, and confining it to private goals. Suharto thus promoted an industrializing bourgeoisie, yet divided it ethnically in order to diminish it politically. He fostered a new middle class, yet one that remained dependent on the government, often for employment, but more generally for protection from the lesser classes surrounding it. And he bundled industrial and agricultural workers into docile fronts, offered a few programmatic benefits, then suppressed their residual grievances with military coercion.

Further, in trying to explain this authoritarian persistence, area specialists who weave some cultural factors into their analyses take note of the collectivist, yet hierarchical norms that color Indonesian outlooks. In brief, political change appears to have been frustrated by a mass-level culturally induced passivity, conceptualized variously as fatalism or resilience, and reaching its apogee in "*bapak*-ism" (paternalism). In recounting these arguments, Harold Crouch observes that "to the extent that the Javanese 'Idea of Power' continues to predominate in Indonesia, the prospects of democratization must be seen as slight."[4] Of course, he acknowledges that Javanese "ideas" have been challenged in Indonesia by Outer Island cultures and an expansion of education, creating some scope for more participatory sentiments. But he nonetheless contends that "there is little to suggest that the democratic culture has acquired deep roots in society. Traditional attitudes are still an obstacle." However, as we shall see, though these norms have surely flourished, they were asserted more strongly by Suharto's ideologues than they were cherished by society. In addition, Suharto always gave much attention to developmental performance and populist programs – suggesting that any cultural deference holding society in check had materially to be reinforced. Hence, when development ceased during the late 1990s, Suharto's cultural reinventions were quickly discarded. In sum, economic growth and social differentiation failed to democratize Indonesia's politics in any straightforward way. On the other hand, once democratization began, social forces were unchecked by any culturally-induced sense of fatalism.

Hence, structures, modernizing processes, and cultural patterns, while doubtless important factors, by themselves forge no more than a context. To explain more fully the regime types and changes that emerge, one must recognize the pivotal role of agency. In focusing closely on Indonesian experience, R. William Liddle provides some methodological advice:

> I have, of course, no crystal ball, only an approach that says: pay attention to politicians and other public individuals acting in context. Assess the environment, both domestic and international, from which they draw resources. Observe closely how they accumulate, mobilize, and deploy those resources, and how others react to them.[5]

Thus, in analyzing the New Order, we can ask the following questions. How did Suharto accumulate so many resources? How did he distribute patronage in ways that maintained elite loyalties, rather than fueling elite ambitions and encouraging challenges? On what basis did he organize social forces? And how did he couple his populist programs with reinvented culture and legitimating mentalities, ensuring that once given, they were not converted autonomously into resources that could be turned back against him? In short, how was it that Suharto could perpetuate his rule over a vast, rapidly industrializing, and deeply pluralist country for more than thirty years? And how was it that in the end, he plummeted so swiftly, giving way to a period of reform?

Suharto's rise to paramountcy

Indonesia's regime during the 1950s can be formally classified as democratic, featuring civil liberties, a parliamentary election, and a constituent assembly designed to enshrine these procedures. However, this democracy gained little stability. First, though the Dutch had colonized Indonesia for three centuries, they provided local elites with comparatively little tutelage in democratic procedures, deploying a restricted assembly they labeled the *Volksraad*, as well as some local and regional fora. Further, the war-time occupation by Japan that followed exposed these elites to militant strategies of mass mobilization, inspiring them when preparing for independence to write a deeply unitary, even "fascist" charter, the Constitution of 1945.[6] Finally, because the Dutch attempted after the war to retake Indonesia, these elites grew even more embittered. And thus, after winning their anti-colonial struggle, they dismantled Dutch federalist arrangements for governing the archipelago, then reintroduced their unitary rule.

Notwithstanding these impediments, Indonesia's elites set aside the 1945 constitution in order to create a parliamentary democracy in 1950. They did this in part to demonstrate their political moderation before the West, thus quickening the process of Dutch withdrawal, while gaining a broader international recognition.[7] But if this democracy was animated by social forces, then applauded overseas, it never gained stability through elite cohesion. Accordingly, governments during the 1950s were short-lived, bogging down in policy immobilism and economic lassitude. Deep tensions existed also between the president, Sukarno, and his military commander, Nasution, periodically generating fears of a coup. And conflicts roiled within the military itself, pitting those at the center against regional commanders in the Outer Islands. Thus, when elections were held in 1955 – the only competitive parliamentary elections the country would hold for nearly another four-and-a-half decades – they did more to crystallize then to resolve elite rivalries. In a field of several dozen competing parties, organizations, "voters associations," and local notables, votes were mostly apportioned across four major parties, each separately pursuing a

33

bureaucratic, Muslim traditionalist, Outer Island Islamic, and communist agenda.[8]

President Sukarno, who resented being eclipsed by his prime ministers during this period, exploited the social and regionalist tensions that elections had deepened. In 1957, he cooperated with the military in imposing martial law, then two years later revived the Constitution of 1945. He conceptualized the regime he formed as a "guided democracy," one in which he operated as "president-for-life."[9] In this configuration, though some civil liberties were still tolerated, electoral processes were formally terminated, producing a rare regime type that can be categorized as semi-authoritarianism – an intrinsically unstable form of politics that permits social activism, but no electoral outlets.

In this situation, Sukarno relied upon the military to contain fissiparous forces, especially in the Outer Islands. At the same time, in energizing social constituencies with which to balance the military, he turned to the Indonesian Communist Party (PKI). In these ways, the PKI and the military began strongly to compete, the first organizing peasants and plantation workers into labor unions, the latter seeking to wrest these constituencies away, affiliating them through a "joint secretariat" called *Golkar* (ie., *Golongan Karya*, "functional groups"). Moreover, as their rivalries intensified, they were militarized, with the PKI seeking to break the military's monopoly on weaponry in order to carry out land seizures, then organize the peasantry into an armed "Fifth Force." One notes too that these competitions unfolded in a context of hyper-inflation, food and clothing shortages, radicalized foreign policies, and much diplomatic pressure from the United States.

By keeping the PKI and the military at loggerheads, Sukarno perpetuated his own paramountcy. The PKI was unable to overtake Sukarno, needing him for protection against the core of the military that remained loyal to Nasution. And the military, though often suspicious of Sukarno, was hampered in removing him by the many units and services that still respected his nationalist standing and ideologies. In 1965, however, Sukarno fell ill, leaving him unable to modulate these elite-level tensions. In these circumstances, some generals appear to have begun plotting against Sukarno, scheduling a coup for Armed Forces Day (October 5), an event that would have brought large numbers of troops loyal to them into Jakarta.[10] However, other officers still favoring Sukarno, especially in the presidential guard, appear to have collaborated with PKI leaders in striking first, killing six of the generals in an action that came to be labeled *Gestapu*.[11]

At this juncture, one of the top surviving officers, Suharto, commander of the strategic reserve, appeared on the scene. And after gaining the support of some troops and dispersing the rest, he moved against rebellious officers and PKI leaders, executing them summarily or interning them in prison camps. Throughout 1965 and well into the next year, this campaign was extended to the rural areas of Java, Bali, and parts of Sumatra, often using Muslim organizations antagonized by land seizures to slaughter PKI supporters, finally instigating the deaths of perhaps a half-million.[12] At the same time, Suharto looked beyond the military and Muslims to recruit students and the nascent middle class, thus forging a "New Order coalition." And in broadening his support, he began gradually to push past Sukarno. In 1966, through a document known as "*Super-semar*" (executive order of 11 March) that the president was pressured to sign, Suharto assumed much executive authority. In 1967, he became acting president, then president in his own right a year later. And in 1970, Sukarno died while under house arrest.

In the early stages of his leadership, Suharto was no more than first among equals within the elite collectivity. However, he recognized much better than Sukarno the need for economic recovery – enabling him to gain the resources with which to manage elites and contain social forces. Thus, with few other options at this stage, he took the advice of some free market technocrats. And foreign investors and aid donors, in surveying Indonesia's rich commodities base and new market openness, were duly attracted. Hence by the early 1970s, Indonesia achieved annual growth rates of 6–7 per cent, a record that it would perpetuate until the late 1990s.

However, in bowing to the strictures of free markets, Suharto was unable to centralize patronage. Instead, elites in the military and bureaucracy began tapping independently into the new surpluses that were created, colluding with foreign investors and skimming overseas aid. Further, this enabled foreign investors to win control over key economic sectors – most visibly made manifest in Japanese companies that forged partnerships with local Chinese, then wrested the textiles industry from indigenous owners. In these circumstances, the student groups that had been recruited into the New Order coalition grew alienated over corruption, foreign investment, and the role of the Chinese minority in business. Devout Muslim groups were also disturbed by the generals' high living in Jakarta.

As Suharto's New Order coalition began to unravel, some elites began to challenge him by appealing to social resentments – a key indicator of deepening elite disunity. In particular, General Sumitro, the head of a key security agency called *Kopkamtib* (Operational Command for the Restoration of Security and Order) mobilized university students, attending their discussion groups and seminars. He also took up the grievances of Muslim leaders. Meanwhile, General Ali Murtopo, heading a rival organization called *Opsus* (*Operasi Khusus*, Special Operations), sought ways to counter Sumitro. An opportunity arose in 1974 when Japan's prime minister visited Jakarta, attracting large numbers of student demonstrators. Sumitro appeared in order to address the students, then concluded by urging them to disperse. However, they soon gathered anew, destroying Toyota showrooms and burning some market places. Soldiers arrived, and a number of students were shot. Suspicions focused quickly on Ali Murtopo's role in instigating these actions, evidently in order to discredit Sumitro by linking him to the violence.[13]

This rioting came to be known as *Malari* (an Indonesian acronym for "disaster of 15 January"), and it emerged as the benchmark against which to measure the violence of subsequent mass actions in Jakarta. Suharto, however, soon turned it to political advantage. Specifically, he gained new ascendancy over elites in the military, expelling Sumitro from the army and closing down Ali Murtopo's *Opsus*. At the same time, though imposing new limits on students, he took up their grievances, now barring foreign investors from some economic sectors. J.A.C. Mackie thus concludes,

> One of the most important results of the *Malari* episode was that it brought home to all New Order leaders just how dangerous it could be for the stability of the regime if mass protests of that type were to be exploited by any of them to serve their own interests in the internal power plays constantly going on within the leadership circle. Sumitro's abrupt dismissal served as a clear warning to other members of the circle that they would not in future be permitted to make any bids whatever for popular support outside it . . . in the wider ranks of society.[14]

However, because part of Suharto's response involved his limiting foreign investment, questions arose over how economic growth – and the patronage resources it afforded – could now be sustained. A solution appeared when during this juncture the OPEC induced a quadrupling of world petroleum prices, dramatically increasing Indonesia's revenues. To be sure, the state petroleum company, Pertamina, so rapidly squandered these revenues that it slipped into insolvency in the middle of a global petroleum boom, a scandal that sparked new criticisms of Suharto.[15] Indeed, doubts emerged over whether the military would even support his bid for re-election as president in 1978. But Suharto succeeded in resuscitating Pertamina, restoring it as a fount of patronage in time for a new surge in petroleum prices in 1979. And it was at this point, then, after disciplining elites through *Malari*, then coopting them with resources from Pertamina, that most analysts consider Suharto to have established his paramountcy.

The national leader and elites

Suharto concentrated an astonishing amount of state power in his presidency, enabling him to manage elites.[16] From his office on the edge of Jakarta's Medan Merdeka, he issued presidential "decisions," "instructions," and "decrees," then firmed them with patronage and sanctions. In brief, as commander-in-chief, he presided over the armed forces, enabling him to promote, transfer, and retire commanders. As chief executive, he freely appointed his ministers, though rarely convened them, while maintaining control over the bureaucratic rank-and-file through sundry organizations and programs. Further, as head of the Guidance Council (*Dewan Pembina*), he drafted his government's list of candidates, ranking loyalists high, while dropping those who had been less reliable. And in presiding over the economy, he helped to set objectives through the National Economic Planning Board (*Bappenas*) and the Investment Coordinating Board (BKPM), then oversaw the distribution of commodities through the State Logistics Board (BULOG).

But Suharto went even further then this, intervening deeply in the world of business. During the 1980s, he transferred control over all state contracts for construction and supply to a unit within the presidency's State Secretariat, the influential "Team 10."[17] At the same time, he was able to amass patronage resources through a range of tax-free and non-audited "charities" and foundations, the now notorious *yayasan*. Here, Suharto accumulated "contributions" from grateful business elites, levies from state banks, and taxes on everyday transactions, then recycled them through the enterprises of his family and friends, or dispersed them – with much fanfare – at the mass level to build clinics, orphanages, and mosques. Indeed, in investigations conducted after his ouster, Suharto's *Yayasan Supersemar* was revealed to have been funded through a 2.5 per cent levy on the profits of eight state banks, including the central bank, Bank Indonesia.[18] And though dedicated officially to education, 80 per cent of its funding was given over instead to land purchases, stock acquisitions, and loans for business cronies. This pattern was replicated by other *yayasan* controlled by Suharto, irrespective of their charitable or religious missions.

After distinguishing his presidency in these ways, Suharto identified three kinds of elites as necessary for his government's structure and functioning. The task asigned to military elites involved internal security-checking ethnic tensions, Islamic revivalism, secessionist movements, and labor indiscipline. Bureaucratic elites provided administrative order, implemented government programs, and provided middle-class employment. And elites operating large business conglomerates, mostly ethnic Chinese, carried out developmental agendas, secured foreign capital, and provided much funding for New Order institutions and Suharto family businesses. One notes also that these elites were not confined to their respective roles, thus enabling them to range across different arenas. Military officers, for example, often held positions in the bureaucracy and state enterprises through the practice of *karyaan* (i.e., secondment). They were also involved deeply in business, linking up frequently with Chinese partners in order to operate diverse services and extractive industries. Top bureaucrats too went into business, setting up their own family conglomerates, gaining state contracts, and appointing their children (*anak pejabat*) to executive positions. These children could then move back into politics, taking top posts in *Golkar*'s party apparatus.

Suharto thus drew freely upon his powers as president to promote elites. But then, to prevent their one day growing able to challenge him, he cultivated their factional rivalries. For example, in recruiting top military commanders, he turned often to Christians and Sumatrans, then later to devout Muslims, knowing that their ethnicity or religiosity weakened rapport within the mainly Javanese officer corps. As added insurance, he rotated his commanders regularly, then capped their careers at a fairly young age of retirement. Cabinet ministers, further, were divided by their factional memberships, whether free market technocrats, nationalist "technologues," ethnic redistributionists, or ordinary rent seekers. They were also normally dropped from the cabinet after completing a single term, two at most. In business, ethnic Chinese were heavily favored, Suharto knowing that in undertaking their developmental tasks, they could never challenge him politically because of the ethnic resentments they faced. Indeed, while their drawing close to Suharto and accumulating wealth may have gained them some protection from state bureaucrats, they grew proportionately more vulnerable to social forces. By contrast, opportunities for indigenous people were proportionately truncated, especially during the 1990s when they were mainly confined to Suharto's relatives, top "bureaucratic families," and a handful of favored entrepreneurs. Most other indigenous business people, while not cut off from state contracts completely, were offered only enough to keep a lid on their grievances. Let us investigate relations between Suharto and these different kinds of elites more fully. They tell us much about the conditions in which national leaders can emerge, then perpetuate their paramountcy.

Suharto and the generals

During the "revolution" that was waged against the Dutch, the civilian government under Sukarno "allowed" itself to be captured. However, the regular and irregular units that made up the armed forces, while consisting largely of groups sponsored first by the Japanese or mobilized later by crime bosses, continued the struggle, albeit ineffectively.[19] And though it was as much international pressure as local guerrilla activity that encouraged the Dutch finally to withdraw, the armed forces were able afterward to make special claims to state power. Specifically, they asserted that they had sprung from society in ways that made them a true "people's army," and they had afterward made far greater sacrifices for independence than civilian leaders had. In these circumstances, the doctrine of the "middle way," later *dwi-fungsi* (dual function) was devised, denominating the military's security and sociopolitical roles. On this basis, military officers would later take posts in the cabinet, the bureaucracy, and state enterprises, especially lucrative ones like Pertamina and BULOG. The military also erected its own territorial command structure, one that closely paralleled the state bureaucracy and extended down to the village level. Further, it formed *Golkar* in 1964, incorporating mass organizations as functional groups in order to counter the PKI. And it operated many of its own businesses too, especially in logging, transport, and financial services, overstating the extent to which it had funded its own field operations during the revolution in order to gain a precedent.

For historical reasons, then, the military gained a large role in Indonesia's political life and economy. Indeed, as we have seen, Suharto himself emerged from its ranks, first marginalizing Sukarno, then strengthening his own presidency. However, in doing this, Suharto gradually became distinct from, and more powerful than the military. Accordingly, he perpetuated its standing in order to enforce social quiescence. At the same time, he developed new strategies by which effectively to manage the armed forces. In brief, he rewarded loyal officers with promotions, business licenses, housing subsidies, loans, medical programs, educational opportunities, and gifts. But he also cultivated their factional rivalries, ones that involved officers from Java and those from the Outer Islands, "financial" officers and more professional ones, different generations with different training experiences, varying attitudes toward nationalism and Islam, and conflicting estimations of democracy's worth. In this way, Suharto promoted, yet divided military elites, denying them cohesion, but preventing their rivalries from boiling over.

Of course, military elites sometimes grew alienated by these manipulations. At such junctures, they worked stealthily to undermine Suharto, usually by turning a blind eye to student demonstrations and press exposes. In other instances, they even confronted him directly, as retired officers did in the Petition of 50 episode during the early 1980s, the warning by the armed forced commander, Benny Murdani, over the first family's business dealings in 1988, the imposition of Try Sutrisno as vice-president in 1993, and the encouragement given Sukarno's daughter, Megawati, in ascending to the presidency of an opposition party toward the end of that year. Nonetheless, it appears that after *Malari*, Suharto dealt effectively with the military's subsequent feints, responding with transfers, demotions, diminished benefits, Islamicization campaigns, or outright purges. In this way, he transformed the armed forces into his own *pemadam api* (fire extinguisher). One illustration of the military's performing this role involves ethnic conflicts in Central Java during the mid-1980s, flaring first in Solo, then spreading to Semarang, Pekalongan, Kudus, and Magelang. In response, the military loaded up a C-130 transport plane with troops and equipment, duly tracking the rioting across the province and stamping it out.[20]

Suharto and the bureaucrats

Suharto relied upon Indonesia's vast bureaucracy to carry out his developmental programs and broadly to offer at least nominal middle-class employment. But then to retain his grip, Suharto responded with familiar balancing strategies. Thus, throughout his tenure, Suharto shifted favor between two major factions in cabinet, the economically nationalist technologues (best represented by B.J. Habibie as minister of research and technology) and the liberalizing technocrats (found mostly in the finance ministry, the central bank, and *Bappenas*).[21] In good economic times, Suharto favored the technologues, seeking to "leap frog" Indonesia's technological development into such areas as aviation and shipbuilding. But in lean times, he turned to the technocrats, deftly regaining the confidence of the IMF and World Bank, foreign investors, and local export manufacturers. Of course, during these periods of technocratic ascendancy, many Chinese business people grew more prosperous still. Hence, to offset the indigenous grievances that resulted, Suharto could turn to a third, though lesser faction, Islamicist, collectivist, and thus deeply suspicious of ethnic Chinese and free markets, and best represented in the Ministry of Agriculture and Cooperatives. Finally, throughout this fluctuating record, there were persons and factions geared simply to patronage, capturing rents through positions known locally as *basah* ("wet"). Such positions could be found in all bureaucratic agencies but were especially plentiful in Pertamina, BULOG, the department of industry and trade, the department of mining and energy, and various state developmental banks.

While balancing elite factions at the cabinet level, Suharto extended his controls deep into the bureaucratic apparatus. Much of Indonesia's bureaucracy was located in the interior ministry. Its members were given a distinct corporate identity through their compulsory membership in the KORPRI (Indonesian Civil Service Corps), indeed, the only social organization they were permitted to join. Further, the KORPRI was obliged through the doctrine of "monoloyalty" to ally at least informally with *Golkar*. Moreover, these controls extended even into private lives of bureaucrats, with their needing permission from their supervisors for marriage and divorce. Wives were then inducted into an organization called *Dharma Wanita*, with their rankings paralleling those of their husbands in the KORPRI. What is more, during times when Suharto was not obliged to Islamicize his demeanor, he delineated bureaucratic identities in Javanese ways, reinventing aristocratic ideals of *priyayi* detachment. Finally, in a great display of *bapak*-ism, he provided annual bonuses to bureaucrats, the checks all bearing his name. Of course, even with bonuses, bureaucratic salaries were not sufficient, impelling most civil servants to moonlight or extract *pungli* (*pungutan liar*, illegal levies) in return for their services. But Suharto, while evidently tolerant of these activities at the elite level, disdained such mass-level entrepreneurism, prompting him regularly to complain of corruption.

Suharto and the conglomerates

Suharto's business activities, mostly involving Chinese partners, close personal relatives, and bureaucratic families, have inspired a great number of scholarly analyses and media exposes.[22] At base, Suharto is seen to have dealt with business elites in ways that met two distinct, but related aims: accelerating economic growth, yet perpetuating his paramountcy. To do this, Suharto relied upon Chinese business elites to help carry out his government's infrastructural projects, as well as to guide his own family members in their dealings. In addition, a limited number of indigenous business elites were allowed to emerge. Because they were frequently the offspring of bureaucratic elites, they offered conduits through which to exchange patronage for support. And because they were nurtured on state contracts in construction, they did little to deepen industrialization, but may have helped to temper criticisms that Suharto favored the Chinese.

However, while these elites collectively built up much infrastructure, developed vast conglomerates, and fueled high growth rates, they gained little entrepreneurial dynamism or export competitiveness. They depended instead on state protection, subsidies, and favorable privatizations through which to dominate local markets, especially in areas like commodities distribution, food processing, power generation, upstream intermediates, toll roads, telecommunications, and property. Further, when petroleum revenues were high during the 1970s, Suharto arranged cheap financing for these activities through a range of state development banks. And when petroleum prices declined during the 1980s, and hence the capacity of Suharto to provide funding, local and overseas lenders eagerly took up the slack. Indeed, these lenders were much encouraged by Indonesia's economic vitality – even if generated less by business elites than the newly deregulated, small- and medium-sized exporters of labor-intensive manufactures.

It is worth exploring in slightly more detail the nature of relations between Suharto and the conglomerates. Apart from the great intrinsic interest these relations created, they help us to understand the economy's mounting vulnerability to crisis which, in the absence of deep elite cohesion, finally divided elites, brought down Suharto, and destabilized the regime. We have seen that early in his tenure, Suharto relied on free market reforms. But after *Malari* and the rise in petroleum prices, he turned to state-led strategies for rapid industrialization. However, his circumstances differed in two important ways from those of Sukarno's economic nationalism a decade or so earlier.[23] First, because of high petroleum prices, Suharto had far more resources to work with than Sukarno ever had, enabling him to industrialize much more rapidly. Secondly, while Suharto took a state-led approach, he remained less ideologically sceptical of private capital. Indeed, because business elites during this period were almost always Chinese, their enrichment posed no direct challenge to Suharto's paramountcy.

In addition, Suharto valued the effectiveness of many ethnic Chinese in business, a feature he had observed while a divisional commander in Central Java during the 1950s. There, far from Jakarta, he had joined Chinese entrepreneurs like Mohamad "Bob" Hasan to arrange supplies, smuggle commodities, and finance new ventures – activities for which Suharto was removed for a time from his command.[24] But after becoming president a decade or so later, Suharto reactivated these relations. In this way, Hasan emerged as Indonesia's "timber king," establishing a cartel over plywood, pulp, and paper. Liem Sioe Liong, head of Salim Corporation, was able similarly to gain control over cement factories, flour milling, and instant noodles production. Over time, a core collectivity of perhaps 50 Chinese business elites emerged, known colloquially as *cukong*, including Eka Tjipta Widjaya in plantations and cooking oil, Hendra Rahardja and Ciputra in property development, Prajogo Pangestu in logging, and Sjamsul Nursalim in finance. Accordingly, while the Chinese constituted only a tiny minority in Indonesian society, they are commonly estimated to have controlled roughly 70 per cent of the country's non-landed wealth.[25] But even as they diversified and formed great conglomerates, they dutifully reciprocated, assisting Suharto in his industrializing agenda, while filtering a portion of their rents back into his *yayasan*.

During the early 1980s, oil prices fell. Nonetheless, Suharto responded at first with a new burst of patrimonialist behavior. In particular, he extended state favors to indigenous business people, mostly his own family members, though usually in alliance with established Chinese. Thus, his half-brother, Probosutedjo, joined Liem Sioe Liong in controlling the marketing of cloves – the essence of popular *kretek* cigarettes – while his cousin, Sudwikatmono, joined Liem in running cement production. Import licenses, sole distributorships, and equity holdings were later transferred to Suharto's children, with middle son Bambang controlling the importation of plastics and Kalimantan's citrus production, while youngest son, Hutomo Mandala Putra ("Tommy"), was given allocations of crude oil to export and petrochemicals to distribute. Later, Tommy also inherited – though badly mismanaged – the clove market.[26]

It was also during this time that under the auspices of Team 10 state contracts were issued to the heads of bureaucratic families lodged at the peak of the state apparatus. Indeed, the state secretary himself, Sudharmono, began building his family conglomerate during this period. But Team 10 began also to promote a few indigenous business elites outside the bureaucracy, like Aburizal Bakrie, Fadel Muhammad, Fahmi Idris, and Arifin Panigoro. However, because this last category of elites could potentially energize social constituencies in a way that the Chinese could not,

Suharto remained wary. He thus limited their numbers and hampered their activities, opposing Bakrie's election as head of the head of the Chamber of Commerce and Industry (KADIN), for example, and apparently delaying the resort developments of Bakrie Brothers on Bali.

Petroleum prices fell a second time during the mid-1980s, so sharply reducing state revenues that Suharto now recognized that the state could no longer serve as the motor force behind industrialization. Hence, in order to attract foreign investors and motivate local exporters, Suharto returned once more to market reforms. Banking was liberalized in order to increase credit, requirements were eased on foreign ownership, and the import licenses affecting the intermediate goods necessary for exports were pared back. Accordingly, large amounts of foreign lending and investment began to enter Indonesia. It was during this period too that small- and medium-sized, mainly Chinese-owned companies sprang suddenly to life, geared to low-tech, labor-intensive manufacturing. In this way, Indonesia rapidly became an important exporter of garments, footwear, plastic goods, household articles, and low-grade electronics, helping perpetuate the country's high growth rates, despite the decline in petroleum prices.

However, while exports by small- and medium-sized producers surged, few business elites gained any international competitiveness. Indeed, while licenses affecting the imported components and materials necessary for export manufacturing were rescinded, controls over upstream goods destined for local markets remained, especially in petrochemicals and foodstuffs. In addition, Suharto began now to hand over state assets and service contracts to business elites directly, using the reformist idiom of privatization to legitimate these transfers. Richard Robison summarizes the ways in which privatization was carried out: "Where state companies were being sold they went to well connected conglomerates and politico-business families at low prices and without open and transparent divestiture procedures, reinforcing the system of concentration and monopoly."[27] Thus, *Satelindo*, a profitable, state-owned satellite communications system was privatized to Bambang's conglomerate, *Bimantara*. And Suharto's eldest daughter, Siti Hardijanti Rukmana ("Tutut"), operating *Citra Lamtoro Gung*, won control over key toll roads and television broadcasting. Privatization, then, while transferring some state assets into putatively private hands, hardly amounted to market reforms.

In sum, Suharto skillfully managed business elites, balancing them in ways that extended industrialization, but also his own paramountcy. Hence, if the growth that resulted was at one level based on export manufactures, it also involved dealings between Suharto and business elites that came popularly to be delineated as cronyism, thus infesting the economy with distortions and inefficiencies. By using state power, Suharto created the protected circumstances in which Chinese business elites undertook development projects, confident that no matter how rich they might get, their ethnicity would prevent them from confronting him politically. Similarly, while later promoting some indigenous business elites, he relied on their family ties, bureaucratic statuses, and limited numbers to perpetuate their loyalties. And even below the elite level, Suharto dispensed some functional minimum of patronage to small-time indigenous contractors in order to ease their discontents. We see, then, that in Indonesia's economy, if some sectors grew competitive, many others did not – a configuration that could only be maintained overall by steady inflows of foreign capital.

To conclude this section, we have seen that Suharto as national leader was able artfully to manage the elite collectivity. He cultivated rivalries between different elites, thus dividing military generals, top bureaucrats, and business tycoons along functional, religious, and ethnic lines. However, he then dispensed patronage and sanctions in ways that dampened leadership challenges and inter-elite struggles. In this way, Suharto poised the elite collectivity on the knife's edge, imbuing it with neither the cohesion into which he might have been absorbed as simply another member, nor tilting it toward the outright disunity that in destabilizing his regime would even sooner have threatened his paramountcy.

Elite-mass relations

While the New Order record shows how elite relations can be managed in ways that stabilize a regime, it shows also how social quiescence can be encouraged, thus perpetuating authoritarianism. More specifically, the national leader, Suharto, retained many of the corporatist mechanisms that Sukarno had introduced, organizing functional groups based on occupation, religion, gender, and sundry other identities. Indeed, Suharto took this strategy to new lengths, generating a panoply of group acronyms, uniforms, and colorful assemblies. In addition, where Sukarno had mobilized functional groups through inspiriting appeals, Suharto depoliticized them, deadening them with top-down controls. And finally, while Sukarno had then halted elections, allowing social pressures to build, Suharto held elections regularly, thus venting through brief apertures the participatory impulses that accumulated.

But if corporatist organizations bring benefits to leaders and elites, they may sometimes be spurned by the social forces they contain. The All-Indonesia Workers' Union (SPSI), for example, the New Order's official labor front, failed conspicuously to enforce even the government's own minimum wage. The *Dharma Wanita*, ostensibly a women's organization, was derided as no more than a wives' organization. Hence, to perpetuate social quiescence, Suharto reaffirmed corporatism through an elaborate, though shallow construction of legitimating mentalities, some populist redistributions, and failing all else, steep coercion. In this way, society came

44

officially to be conceptualized in the New Order as the "floating mass," disconnected utterly from political life, its brute energy dedicated to rapid industrialization.

In terms of legitimating mentalities – validations that fall short of well-articulated ideologies – one encounters the first notes of corporatist justification in the Constitution of 1945, a document revived by Sukarno in 1959 and awarded near sacral status under Suharto.[28] The constitution's principal author, Dr. Soepomo, had been much influenced during the inter-war years by European fascism. He thus borrowed heavily from the doctrines of organicism and integralism, estimating that they correlated with Indonesia's social diversity, but also with cultural virtues of hierarchy and consensus. Further, while society might be sorted into functional groups, competitions between them could be muted through the mantra of *Pancasila*, a collection of short injunctions unveiled by Sukarno in 1945 in order to defuse Islamic pressures and secularize the regime. And under Suharto, *Pancasila* was transformed into a more rigid mentality of corporatist control, then rigorously disseminated through an educational campaign known as "P-4," geared mostly to indoctrinating civil servants, but also business people and students. Indeed, new notions were elaborated of "*Pancasila* democracy," "*Pancasila* economy," and even "*Pancasila* labor relations." Moreover, after functional groups had been suitably informed by *Pancasila*, they could safely be embraced in the "big *Golkar* family," then as delegate "fractions" in a consultative parliament. Similarly, while perpetu-ating a national motto of "unity in diversity," Suharto attempted during the 1980s to imbue the Outer Islands with a reinvented Javanese ethos of *priyayi* ideals. Indeed, by the middle years of his tenure, Suharto's leadership style came increasingly to be characterized as aloof and enigmatic, in the imagined manner of a Javanese king, thereby complementing the floating mass, its gaze quite hollow, though respectfully cast upward.

Legitimating mentalities must be firmed by performance if they are to remain effective. Thus, under the New Order, the benefits accruing to social forces who conformed to corporatist guidelines were cast as security (*keamanan*), order (*ketertiban*), and development (*pembangunan*). Indeed, the value of stability and order could be highlighted by recalling through state-controlled media outlets the mayhem of Sukarno's leadership, with the class-based tensions he cultivated erupting finally in mass conflagration. And development, portrayed in terms of growth and equity, could be similarly emphasized, with the New Order's self-sufficiency in rice production, public health care, family planning, education programs, and career opportunities contrasting starkly with the scarcities and hyperinfla-tion under Sukarno. Accordingly, Liddle states plainly the ways in which performance colored popular perceptions of the New Order: "The regime [was] in fact legitimate in the minds of probably a majority of members of the politically aware public because of its developmental record."[29] Suharto thus crowned himself with an epithet that was both traditionalist and modernizing, *Bapak Pembangunan*, the father of development.

Of course, development benefited some groups more than others, creating scope for social resentments. Accordingly, in adhering to the collectivist strictures of the 1945 constitution, Suharto appeared to soften market forces, redistributing benefits to sample audiences of indigenous poor. Most notably, his government set up an extensive, if inefficient range of cooperatives, ostensibly giving a boost to small, indigenous business people and farmworkers. Cooperatives were also supplemented by *ad hoc* decrees, Suharto introducing the *Desa Tertinggal* ("Backward Village") program, for example, through which to make modest amounts of credit available to villagers. Suharto also made regular use of *Banpres* (Presidential Assistance) and *Inpres* (Presidential Instruction), providing funding for schools, health care, and roads. And he delivered some important subsidies too, easing the cost of electricity, petroleum products, cooking oil, and food staples. Moreover, in giving this populism a personal touch, Suharto repaired often to countryside to conduct "dialogue sessions," smiling broadly as he dispensed advice about the importance of hard work. Farmworkers then grinned, looked down, and contemplated this advice, forming asymmetrical exchanges that were duly broadcast on state-run TV.

Finally, for social forces unassuaged by corporatist organizations, legitimating mentalities, substantive performance, and populist redistributions, the government turned to coercion. Richard Tanter records the ways in which the New Order's vast security apparatus engaged in "militarization, comprehensive domestic political surveillance, and intermittent but persistent state terror."[30] Accordingly, organizations like *Kopkamtib*, with "virtually no effective internal limits on the rights and powers of the . . . commander,"[31] its successor *Bakorstanas*, the Armed Forces Strategic Intelligence Agency (*Bais ABRI*), and the State Intelligence Coordinating Agency (BAKIN) addressed a succession of social challenges. During the mid-1960s, these agencies focused on apparent Communist sympathizers, variously executing, imprisoning, exiling, and blacklisting. Later, during the 1970s–80s, as the government began to shed unneeded elements within its New Order coalition, it targeted student activists, then militant Islamic groups. And if, after 1990, these security agencies eased their attacks on Muslims, they focused more intently on labor. Finally, throughout the New Order, security agencies and military units operated against critical social organizations and NGOs, independent journalists, Outer Island secessionists, and troublesome gangsters. In sum, quite in contrast to Sukarno, the New Order under Suharto did much to enforce social quiescence.

A stable pseudo-democracy

In managing elites, Suharto propped up his own paramountcy and stabilized his regime. And in dispersing social forces, he was able also to perpetuate authoritarianism. Nonetheless, Suharto also found functional advantages in embroidering his regime lightly with democratic procedures, thereby producing the New Order's pseudo-democracy. In this situation, civil liberties were tightly constrained, while elections, though regularly held, were rigged – in important respects a reversal of the semi-authoritarian patterns followed by Sukarno and hence, possessing greater intrinsic stability. On this score, we recall that while causality flows more strongly from inter-elite and elite-mass relations to regimes, the institutions that result filter back, thus reaffirming elite behaviors.

Civil liberties and elections

In the New Order's pseudo-democracy, the limits that were posed on civil liberties were at base quite standard authoritarian fare, even if articulated through extensive legalism, much of its traceable to the colonial period. Communication was thus dampened by laws against subversion, with punishments meted out even for "insulting" the president. The press was hindered by the information's ministry's licensing requirements, the patterns of family ownership, and a "telephone culture" in which generals and bureaucrats regularly placed admonitory calls to editors.[32] Topics barred from media reporting included presidential succession, the Suharto family's business dealings, and tensions attributable to ethnicity, religion, "race," and class (contained in the acronym SARA, *suku, agama, ras, antargolongan*). Further, free assembly was hampered by the corporatist controls described above, tightly demarcating political parties, labor unions, and NGOs.[33] Parties were thus subjected to the *fusi* (fusion) law of 1973, requiring that the nine opposition parties existing at that time be collapsed into two, the United Development Party (PPP), linking four Muslim groups, and the Indonesian Democracy Party (PDI), which convened nationalist and Christian entities. In these circumstances, Andrew MacIntyre observes that "the fusion created artificial new political organizations which were fraught with internal tensions," eroding their capacity to contest elections.[34] Further, the government intervened in these parties' internal processes of leadership and candidate selection, then prohibited their forming party branches at the sub-district and village level where most votes in Indonesia were to be found. Indeed, the PPP and PDI were not even permitted to conceptualize themselves as an opposition, but rather as OPPs (*organisasi peserta pemilu*, electoral participant organizations), enabling them sometimes to consult with the government, but never to hold it accountable, much less replace it. Finally, with respect to social organizations, ranging from political parties to hiking clubs, the *asas tunggal* (sole principle) legislation of 1983 required their steadfast commitment to *Pancasila*. And the *ormas* (mass organization) law passed two years later specified more closely the terms under which they could legally be registered.

In these circumstances, elections in New Order Indonesia featured little competitiveness, even if regularly held. Two kind of elections were organized, the first involving popular voting for members of the People's Representative Assembly (DPR) and provincial and local assemblies, the second involving members of the People's Consultative Council (MPR) who selected the president. Suharto agreed to begin holding DPR elections in 1971, seeking to display a greater legitimacy than Sukarno had possessed. But then to reduce competitiveness, his government refurbished the military's old *Golkar*, plied it with state funding, then staffed it with loyal bureaucrats and military figures. Indeed, Indonesia's six million bureaucrats, pledged to *Golkar* through the doctrine of monoloyalty, were in many elections awarded two voting cards.[35] Moreover, in deepening its constituencies, *Golkar* avoided the limits on grass-roots organizing that were imposed on the PPP and the PDI.

But even after manipulating the party system, the government persisted, seeking now to shape campaigning, balloting, and vote counting. Hence, if during the five-week campaign period restrictions on parties were eased, only *pesta demokrasi* ("festival of democracy") took place, studded with pageantry, rock concerts, and celebrity appearances. Further, on election day, "thugs" were sometimes deployed from organizations like the *Pemuda Pancasila* (Pancasila Youth), menacing the polling places or provoking disturbances with which to discredit the opposition.[36] And finally, in the 1997 DPR election, after the polls were closed and the ballots collected, the General Election Institute, lodged in the interior ministry, undertook the last and "least transparent" stage of the vote counting, with only five officials able to access the electoral results database, among them Suharto.[37] In these ways, *Golkar* was able routinely to capture around 65–70 per cent of the popular vote, then utterly dominate the DPR.

But what, then, did legislators do in the New Order's pseudo-democracy? During most of Suharto's tenure, the DPR contained 500 seats, including 100 (later reduced to 75) that were reserved for the military. And though this assembly was formatted with regular sessions, delegate "fractions," and specialized policy commissions, it remained deeply subordinate to the president, never rejecting any of Suharto's legislation, never proposing any of its own. Members who openly protested were simply removed, inspiring the neologism, "*di-recall*." This encouraged others to observe closely the refrain of the "4 D's": *daftar, duduk, duit, diam* (register, sit down, take your pay, stay quiet). Indeed, the value of a seat in the DPR lay mainly in the patronage that it brought, earning its members secure, semi-detached housing in the special compound at Kalibata, as well as numerous other perquisites and business opportunities.

During the year after the DPR election, the MPR election for the president and vice-president was held. Here, all 500 members of the DPR sat with 500 additional members recruited from regional and functional groups. The MPR was officially the country's highest political body, not only operating as an electoral college, but also producing a document of broad social and economic planning (*Garis-garis Besar Haluan Negara*) However, because Suharto had selected or vetted virtually all the members of the DPR, and because he chose or approved the delegates from regional and functional groups, Indonesians were long treated to the spectacle of Suharto appointing the electors who in turned appointed him as president, while ratifying too his choice of vice-president. There can be no better exemplar of pseudo-democratic procedures.

Contextual changes in the late New Order

During the New Order's last decade-and-a-half, profound contextual changes took place, finally altering class formations, cultural patterns, and hence, mass attitudes. In particular, because of the new emphasis on labor-intensive manufacturing, large numbers of people were uprooted from their villages and shifted to urban centers, finding employment in factory places and informal sectors. And though these workers mostly benefited in absolute terms, relative inequalities worsened and social ties were disrupted, thus fueling new grievances. In these circumstances, the New Order's corporatism, mentalities, performance, and populism – strategies geared mostly to rural populations – lost much of their effectiveness in maintaining social quiescence. Indeed, while Suharto continued to run dialogue sessions with farmers, he never dared similarly to engage audiences of factory workers.

The grievances that resulted seemed often to gain expression through Islam. Indigenous members of Indonesia's middle class, for example, sometimes finding it difficult to adjust from rural collectivism to steep urban careerism, now graduated from their "statistical" Islam to more demanding modernist codes. Students began increasingly to articulate grievances at campus mosques, recognizing that after the severe crackdowns of the 1970s, Islam offered the only reasonably safe outlet for their activism. And workers, finally, severed from their rural support groups after migrating to urban production sites, used more intense forms of Islam as a sounding board for their class and ethnic resentments. On this score, Bresnan recounts the Tanjong Priok "incident" of 1984, pitting dockworkers galvanized by Islamic preachers against the military, culminating in scores of deaths.[38] Islamic militancy gained an anti-Chinese tenor too, with bombing attacks carried out against Liem Sioe Liong's Bank Central Asia and even the ancient Buddhist monument of Borobudur.[39]

Suharto responded by reconfiguring his image, undertaking a pilgrimage to Mecca, then appending the given name "Haji Mohammed" to his existing sobriquet, *Bapak Pembangunan*. He sought also to gain approval from Muslim intellectuals, forming the ICMI (Indonesian Islamic Intellectuals Association) in 1990, then recruiting a number of well-known Islamicists such as Amien Rais, Adi Sasono, Sri Bintang Pamungkas, and Nurcholish Majid. He gave it prominence by persuading his minister of technology, Habibie, to serve as its chair. The organization then appealed to social constituents through its think tank, CIDES (Center for International and Development Studies), its newspaper, *Republika*, and through a symbolic share issue by its own *yayasan* that was broadly pitched to Muslim families.[40]

However, this Islamic resurgence continued to test Suharto. In brief, while some Muslim members of the ICMI seemed placated by this organization, "activists" conspired to use it for their own ends, working steadily to Islamicize the state more deeply than Suharto had intended. Meanwhile, other Islamic leaders remained apart from such state agencies in order more freely to make criticisms. Abdurrahman Wahid, for example, leader of the traditionalist *Nahdlatul Ulama* (Awakening of the Traditional Religious Teachers), condemned the ICMI for risking sectarian strife, and he set up his own organization, the *Forum Demokrasi* (Democracy Forum), with which to counter it. At the mass level too, many charismatic *kiai* (Islamic religious teachers) skirted Suharto's corporatist structures and programs, then jeered his new Muslim commitments. And finally, these activities gave rise to new interpretations of Islam, diversifying from the simple *santri-abangan* dichotomy observed by Geertz into traditionalist, modernist, and neo-modernist strands, giving rise to a spectrum over which Suharto was unable to impose any state-sanctioned version.

But if Suharto's record in coping with Islamic resurgence seemed uneven, he appeared even less able to deal effectively with more straightforward expressions of student and working-class discontents. In Indonesia's vast industrial estates, workers had for some time been restive, striking throughout the 1980s over working conditions. But these outbreaks were usually spontaneous and leaderless, and hence, were quelled swiftly by the military. In 1994, however, a strike took place in the north Sumatran city of Medan, closing down manufacturing activities for a number of days. And though the strike finally turned violent, acquiring an undisciplined ethnic tone, its scope suggested that its origins had been planned and coordinated. Accordingly, the government publicly identified the Indonesian Prosperous Labor Union (SBSI) as responsible, an unregistered federation that now competed head-on with the government's own corporatist front, the SPSI.

Discontents over urban poverty continued to mount, gradually finding expression through the PDI, now led by Sukarno's daughter, Megawati.

Indeed, with popular nostalgia over Suharto's charisma and political radicalism spreading, Megawati was hailed as the politician best able to resolve inequalities. And grasping the nettle, she stated publicly in early 1996 that she would allow her name to be put forward as a presidential nominee – increasing greatly the support her party could expect in the next year's DPR election. Suharto responded clumsily, ordering an extraordinary meeting of the PDI through which to depose Megawati as leader. Further, when her supporters refused to surrender party headquarters in Jakarta to her successor, security units and hired thugs attacked them, triggering a riot that came to be known as *Sabtu Kelabu* (Gray Saturday). This attack on PDI headquarters marked the capital's most serious upheaval since *Malari*.[41] In addition, Suharto handled it far less effectively than the earlier confrontation – with few accepting his government's explanation that the violence was really the fault of the People's Democracy Party (PRD), a small group of students and workers. Accordingly, in hindsight, some analysts have characterized the attack on PDI headquarters as having so increased public sympathy for Megawati that it marked the beginning of the end for Suharto.

Nevertheless, having appeared to clear the stage, the government readied itself to contest the 1997 DPR election. Indeed, Harmoko, the head of *Golkar*, while serving also as information minister, sought to raise his party's popular vote from the 67 per cent it had won in the 1992 to a more resounding 70 per cent. He thus stumped the country, inaugurating a "yellow-ization" (*kuningisasi*) campaign in which building fronts, walls, curbs, and trees were all painted in *Golkar* yellow. Bureaucrats attended *Golkar* rallies in large numbers, and their ranks were supplemented by paid audiences.[42] And the media grew effusive in its support of the government. However, throughout the campaign, social grievances continued to surge, thus souring the festival quality. Indeed, new forms of religious and class-based violence, sometimes tinged with ethnic resentments, now flared across the archipelago, thus testing the capacity of the military to keep order. Indeed, the most serious incidents took place where they were least expected. In Kalimantan, for example, ethnic Dayaks clashed with migrant Madurese in the west, while Islamic elements burned shopping centers identified with the Chinese in the south, killing 123 persons in a single incident.[43]

Against this backdrop of spiraling violence, students and workers began to organize in support of Megawati, even though she had been ousted as PDI leader. In these circumstances, the only credible opposition party, the PPP, showed new vigor too, intensifying its Islamic appeals and criticisms of Suharto. Indeed, as the campaign wore on, wherever the supporters of Megawati and the PPP crossed paths with *Golkar* cadres, they clashed, despite the restrictions that had been placed on their operating simultaneously in disputed districts. Further, though the motorcycle processions that had become a feature of campaigning in Indonesia were this year officially banned, they still appeared in great numbers, their riders often dressed in Palestinian-style *khafiyah*. Youth gangs appeared on the streets too, confronting police boldly, then fleeing down side alleys. Older generations of onlookers expressed astonishment over this youthful militancy that had not been seen since the mid-1970s.

But if the character of electoral campaigning was different in 1997 than it had been in years past, its outcomes were much the same. Indeed, the only surprise lay in *Golkar* exceeding its target, winning 74.5 per cent of the vote. But analysts assessed this as over-kill, upsetting Suharto's elaborate pseudo-democratic framework. With the discredited PDI winning only 11 seats, it could not even place members in all twelve of the DPR's policy commissions, thus diminishing displays of consensus. Hence, a recount was hastily organized in North Sumatra, yielding an additional 64,000 PDI votes and the necessary legislator.[44] However, this boost remained a small one, meaning that the PDI still lagged far behind the PPP, which had won 89 seats. In consequence, some observers suggested that opposition politics in Indonesia would soon take on an even greater Islamic stridency. Suharto, then, seemingly inconvenienced by Harmoko's having done his work too well, shunted the *Golkar* leader from the information ministry to a vacuous cabinet post without portfolio, then into the speaker's slot in the MPR/DPR.

In sum, as labor-intensive manufacturing accelerated during the final decade or so of the New Order, it changed contextual factors in ways that made it more difficult for the government to enforce social quiescence. New middle- and working-class grievances appeared, finding expression through Islamic resurgence, student activism, labor militancy, and opposition politics, activities that often acquired ethnic overtones. Of course, Suharto responded by borrowing habitually from his kit of control strategies. He made new concessions to Islam, allowing it greater resources and autonomy. On the other hand, he harassed students and workers, while removing Megawati from the PDI. Nonetheless, Suharto faced social forces that had been greatly activated by his own industrializing choices. And hence, at precisely the juncture in which he needed to operate most skillfully, he demonstrated a diminished capacity to do so. It remained only for him to lose capacity also for managing elites for regime change to take place. In these circumstances, the 1997 DPR election, though appearing to produce for Suharto a great victory, turned out to be the last that he would wage.

Transition from pseudo-democracy

Toward the end of 1997, amid East Asia's economic crisis, Indonesia's economy began swiftly to contract. Suharto was thus suddenly stripped of the resources he needed to manage elites and contain social forces. Of course, he struggled to regain support, transmuting his developmentalist appeals into nationalist resentments, then rallying the country against the conditionalities imposed by the International Monetary Fund (IMF) and the capital flight carried out by the local Chinese. Nonetheless, the rivalries between elites, once so artfully husbanded by Suharto, broadened now into disunity, affecting bureaucratic agencies, the business community, and finally the military. Up through these fissures surged mass-level grievances, articulated first by middle-class students, then delivered with deadly force by riotous urban mobs. At this point, another wave of elites in the cabinet, the DPR, and *Golkar* abandoned Suharto, while members of a military faction that still supported him misplayed their hand badly. And it was in this context that Suharto fell finally from office and his pseudo-democracy was changed.

Economic crisis

After the DPR elections in mid-1997, political activity subsided. Though the PPP delayed in endorsing the electoral results and even contested some vote counts in the courts, it finally returned to the fold. But several months later, East Asia's economic crisis began to set in. At first, it appeared that among the countries that were affected, Indonesia would be best able to cope, drawing upon the expertise of its top technocrats, honed so sharply by past experiences with economic shocks. Specifically, Bank Indonesia officials had resisted pegging the *rupiah* firmly to the U.S. dollar, preferring instead a more flexible band. In this way, they avoided squandering the country's foreign exchange reserves in the kind of futile monetarist defense that had been mounted in Thailand. However, currency traders and international fund managers began to scrutinize the indebtedness of Indonesia's banks and conglomerates more closely, then quickened their disinvestment and the *rupiah*'s decline, eventually causing the currency to lose more than 80 per cent of its value against the U.S. dollar. And with businesses unable at such low exchange rates to repay their dollar-denominated loans or to import necessary capital goods and components, industrial production soon slowed. Inflation surged proportionately, even as workers were shed in large numbers.

With indices rapidly worsening, Indonesia turned to the IMF for help, quickly signing an initial agreement in October 1997, then a more formal one in January next year. Thus, through a fifty-point program, the IMF provided some $40 billion in loans. However, the IMF also imposed its trademark conditions, demanding that the Indonesian government cut public spending in order to generate a small budgetary surplus. Fuel subsidies, in particular, were to be removed. In addition, the IMF demanded much market deregulation. The aviation industry promoted by Habibie would thus lose its subsidies, the plywood cartel operated by Bob Hasan would be dismantled, and many of BULOG's commodity licenses would be withdrawn. Suharto's son, Tommy, was also targeted, with his monopoly on clove marketing and his new tariff preferences on auto imports both scheduled to be abolished.

The IMF package was met in Indonesia with great ambivalence. Many elites and members of the middle class were offended by their country's evident loss of sovereignty, indeed, the haughtiness with which conditions seemed to be imposed. The image of the bespectacled Suharto hunching over to sign the agreement while the IMF chief, Michel Camdessus, looked on with folded arms pricked even the sensitivities of the president's strongest critics. At the same time, though, many cheered the imminent disbanding of the Suharto family's conglomerates. Equally, local economists reacted with ambivalence to the IMF agreement, expressing doubts about its imposing contractionary measures upon an economy that was already rapidly contracting. What was really needed, they suggested, was the rescheduling of business' short-term loan obligations in order that it could restart production. These economists suggested too that while monopolies and rent seeking had long posed inefficiencies, this could not explain the timing or the rapidity with which the economy was now collapsing. Rather, they argued, the causes lay in panic among foreign investors, those who possessed little specific country knowledge and were driven by "herd effects." But it was precisely because of this panic, most agreed, that the IMF's program, even if flawed in its prescription, had faithfully to be implemented.

Thus, in first accepting the IMF's conditions in October, Suharto appeared to be acting as pragmatically as he had in earlier crises, suspending his patrimonialist behaviors, then restoring the economic levers to technocratic control. The finance minister, Ma'rie Muhammad, was thus able to close a number of banks that had been identified as violating regulations, including those associated with Suharto's family members, Bambang and Probosutedjo. In addition, Widjojo Nitisastro, Radius Prawiro, and other technocrats from early in the New Order were trundled out once again. And finally, after announcing a national budget that met with disapproval from the IMF because of its basing projections on unrealistic valuations of the *rupiah*, the finance ministry dutifully responded by drafting a new one.

In time, though, Suharto began to deviate from his course. Evidently frustrated by the *rupiah*'s failing to recover quickly, he supported a proposal for a currency board system, one in which monetary policy would be removed from the much distrusted central bank in order that the *rupiah* could be pegged rigidly to the U.S. dollar. But if the IMF had endorsed currency boards in other settings, it demonstrated convincingly that it was inappropriate in Indonesia because of the country's diminished foreign exchange reserves and poorly supervised banking system. Suspicions emerged also that the new monetary peg was designed mostly to restore value to

Suharto family assets, strengthening the *rupiah* just long enough that the president's children could convert the rest of their assets into dollars.

Debate over the currency board system bogged down in stalemate with the IMF, preventing any constructive policy making for some months. During this time, Suharto stopped short of finally instituting the board, thus avoiding breaking with the IMF outright. But he refused also to abandon the proposal. In this way, Suharto was able at least for a short time to benefit from the uncertainty he perpetuated, preventing the *rupiah* from falling as much as it might have. Specifically, with currency traders fearful of being caught long on dollars during the brief upturn in the *rupiah* that any currency board would mean, they ceased to sell the *rupiah* down. Suharto, in short, while squeezed into a very tight space, was trying to conduct at a global level the kind of balancing he had long practiced at home. It also came to light that while the BULOG's monopoly on rice imports was removed, it was nonetheless issued foreign exchange with which to make purchases, a measure that though defended publicly as necessary to ease food shortages, seemed aimed instead at discouraging competitors. Meanwhile, the beneficiaries of clove and plywood cartels manoeuvred to keep their arrangements intact.[45] And Bambang was permitted to reorganize his bank, then reopen it under a new name, while Probosutedjo reopened his after gaining a court order.

In grappling with the IMF, however, Suharto soon displayed a new recklessness, leaving him for the first time in his tenure to appear quite disoriented.[46] In the past, as we have seen, he was able to juggle his patrimonialism with the technocratic requirements for economic growth. Even as he had deregulated the economy during the 1980s, key partners, relatives, and bureaucratic families had been able still to benefit, swapping their crude import monopolies and sole distributorships for new access to bank credit and upstream industrial projects. But in 1998, the conditions imposed by the IMF on Suharto, whether appropriate or not, forced him to choose between patrimonialist and technocratic domains. And he seemed finally to be plumping for his family. Meanwhile, food shortages, unemployment and inflation brought more hardship across Indonesia, circumstances made worse by a severe drought and falling petroleum and timber prices overseas. Per capita income thus plummeted during this period from US$1100 to around US$300. Consumers were unable to obtain imported pharmaceuticals. Spare parts for vehicles became increasingly scarce. Indeed, the *Far Eastern Economic Review* observed, "Since World War II, no large country's economy has fallen faster (Indonesia's economy contracted about 14 per cent in calendar 1998), or further (its economy grew at an annual rate of 7 per cent from 1990 to 1997)."[47] And it was in this extraordinary context that Suharto lost the resources with which to manage elites.

Elite disunity

In the oft-quoted refrain of O'Donnell and Schmitter, democratic transitions take place in the fissures between elites who operate the authoritarian regime itself.[48] Haggard and Kaufman later deepened this insight, showing that among middle-income countries, divisions between elites have most often been precipitated, or at least exacerbated, by economic crises: "Economic downturns affect the loyalty of the military-political elite directly by reducing the ability of the government to deliver material benefits."[49] Of course, where military elites possess "corporate insulation," bureaucrats retain technocratic capacity, and business elites transcend their rent seeking to step up productivity, they may revive the economy, regain their unity, and perpetuate their regime. On this score, Haggard and Kaufman cite the experiences during the early 1980s of South Korea under Chun Do Hwan and Chile under Pinochet. However, where elites fail to revive the economy, their disunity may deepen, thus destabilizing the regime and ushering in democracy. Here, among other cases, Haggard and Kaufman present the Philippines in 1986.

Under Suharto's leadership in Indonesia, we have seen the military possessed little insulation. Rather, the military was exposed to, and colluded deeply with, elites in the bureaucracy, business, and *Golkar* apparatus. Further, technocrats in the cabinet were regularly overruled by factions of technologues, ethnic redistributionists, and ordinary rent seekers. And business elites, finally, in building their conglomerates in a highly politicized setting, failed to attain much export competitiveness. Thus, during 1997–98, with elites unable to halt economic decline, they started to split. And then, while holding a variety of motivations, some began openly to confront Suharto.

One begins this roster with Amien Rais, a university lecturer who had worked through a number of modernist Muslim organizations to vent grievances over the ethnic Chinese dominating business.[50] In 1990, however, Amien was persuaded that Suharto was showing Islam greater favor, prompting him to join the ICMI, then even to emerge as a protégé of Habibie. Further, Amien was elevated to the head of the ICMI's Council of Experts, thus providing him with large research budget. He was also given a column in *Republika*, enabling him regularly to condemn the *Kristenisasi* (Christianization) of Indonesia's elite. And finally, he became the head of *Muhammadiyah*, an important social organization of some 25 million modernist urban Muslims. However, after gaining elite standing in these ways, Amien changed his assessment of Suharto once more, claiming that he "could no longer stomach being used by Suharto, particularly since Suharto was on his way to ruining the country."[51] Thus, after openly criticizing Suharto's dealings with a U.S.-based mining company in Irian Jaya, he resigned from the ICMI in 1997. And then, later in the year, he declared that he would challenge Suharto for the presidency at the MPR election scheduled for March 1998. His candidacy was quickly endorsed at an important Islamic gathering in December, "a clear sign that Suharto [was] losing his grip on the constituency of 'modernist' urban Muslims who served as an important new source of support for him in the early 1990s."[52]

Grievances were then expressed also by some managers of state enterprises, with Djiteng Marsudi, the head of the national electricity company, PLN, testifying at a hearing held in December by a DPR committee. He began by welcoming the government's having partly privatized energy markets, but then complained bitterly of his company being forced to buy expensive, even unnecessary electricity from the new independent producers. The PLN was in consequence saddled with large deficits, a condition he attributed to "outsiders" – though leaving little doubt that he meant consortia involving Suharto family members and foreign companies. Djiteng then added, "I realize the risks from speaking up about this now. But I have to say this openly for the sake of our country."[53] Indeed, he went further, advising that "economic deregulation should be coupled with a 'political' deregulation to prevent political power from controlling the economic sector." Analysts observed that never before had a top-level bureaucrat openly vented such grievances. Even *Golkar* legislators were encouraged, calling for more disclosures from Djiteng. As one DPR member noted shrewdly to the press, "The time is right for PLN to ask for changes since the government currently is looking for changes as it has shown by liquidating banks owned by 'those people.' I hope we all understand what I mean by 'those people.'"[54]

In January 1998, Adi Sasono, the secretary-general of ICMI and director of CIDES, called for a "national dialogue" in order to address the economic crisis.[55] He appealed specifically to Amien Rais, Megawati, and Abdurrahman Wahid. It was unclear what this body's precise agenda should be. It was also unclear whether ethnic Chinese would be allowed any role, given Adi's past criticisms of their business activities. Still, he was proposing nothing less than a new mediary institution, one quite outside Suharto's corporatist framework. And it seemed geared to forging new elite-level understandings, perhaps even mobilizing new social constituencies. What was more, Syarwan Hamid, former chief of the army's office of political and social affairs and now deputy speaker of the MPR/DPR, seconded the proposal, stating, "Yes, we need a dialogue, especially one that relates to pressing matters relating to the future of the people."[56]

As strains between elites in the state apparatus appeared, one detected a new surge in opposition. Amien Rais now crossed forthrightly to the opposition forces, helping to galvanize student demands for Suharto's removal. In addition, he gained support from some indigenous business elites – a critical development in that while student groups can be potent,

Huntington notes that "by themselves, [they] do not bring down regimes."[57] As O'Donnell and Schmitter suggest, "One class condition which does seem unavoidable for the viability of the transition is that the bourgeoisie . . . regard the authoritarian regime as 'dispensable.'"[58] Accordingly, the opposition was much strengthened when Arifin Panigoro, head of the important *Medco Energi* conglomerate, began to join Amien Rais at political meetings. Arifin's conglomerate had once benefited greatly from oil drilling contracts issued by Team 10. But he had grown deeply alienated by Suharto's continuing to skim oil revenues in the context of crisis.[59]

Hence, in February 1998, a month before the MPR election was scheduled to be held, Arifin and Amien attended a discussion group organized by the Center for the Study of Strategy and Policy in order to ponder political and economic reform.[60] The meeting focused explicitly on ways of redefining the functions of the MPR/DPR in order to make elections more competitive. On this score, Arifin argued that because Amien had so recently energized students, it was possible now to galvanize "people power" against Suharto. He recommended too that Amien's international standing be strengthened by making contact with the foreign media. And he proposed finally that large demonstrations be organized at the MPR/DPR building in order to halt its proceedings. Clearly, Arifin's alienation ran deep. Though he was himself a delegate to the MPR, he called for its presidential election to be made competitive. And while he had once benefited from Suharto's patronage, he now demanded economic reforms. However, Arifin's statements were evidently conveyed to Habibie, then to Suharto, causing him abruptly to be removed from the MPR and placed under "city arrest." For Suharto, Arifin's actions would surely have confirmed the folly of his promoting indigenous business elites.

Criticisms over the government's approach to the economic crisis were also expressed by a prominent Chinese business elite, Sofjan Wanandi. As chief executive of the Gemala Corporation, Sofjan headed one of Indonesia's largest business conglomerates, assembling vehicles and manufacturing batteries. He was also head of the Jimbaran Group, a loose organization that had been set up at Suharto's request in order to collect 2 per cent of the profits of major conglomerates, then distribute the proceeds to small- and medium-sized indigenous businesses. But while indulging Suharto in these ways, Sofjan had also emerged over time as an advocate for Chinese business and market reforms. And now, in early 1998, he began even to criticize the government openly, dismissing as "meaningless" a new "love the *rupiah*" (*cintai rupiah*) campaign that had been proclaimed by Suharto's daughter, Tutut, in order to bolster the local coin. Accordingly, the military detained Sofjan, interrogating him in several lengthy sessions about his suspected involvement in a bombing incident traced to the PRD[61] – a dramatic indicator of the extent to which elite relations were now strained. Indeed, while the military had long benefited from its exchanges with Chinese business, its commanders now asserted that the Chinese were responsible for the economic crisis. In a much publicized action, they broadened their attack, with officers making "threatening phone calls" to Chinese business elites, while Suharto exhorted the community to repatriate what he claimed was its $80 billion in offshore holdings.[62] Moreover, there were suspicions that throughout Indonesia, regional military commanders were instigating anti-Chinese violence, not only to gain indigenous social support, but even to accelerate social upheavals, perhaps prompting the IMF to ease its conditions.[63]

As tensions deepened, Suharto showed little of his earlier capacity to manage elites. To the contrary, his actions seemed to alienate them more deeply. Hence, as the MPR election drew near, Suharto announced that his choice for vice-president should be someone knowledgeable about information technologies, strongly hinting at Habibie. Accordingly, Bambang Triantoro, a former military chief of social and political affairs, proposed publicly that the incumbent vice-president, Try Sutrisno, be given a second term. At this point, Emil Salim, once a key technocrat in the government and later an environment minister, nominated himself for the vice-presidency. These unofficial nominations, made by persons who had recently been top position holders in the state, constituted significant violations of Suharto's prerogatives. And their impact, of course, was heightened by Amien's having earlier declared his own candidacy for the presidency.

To be sure, despite these elite-level tensions, Suharto still controlled institutional procedures. Hence, as he prepared for the MPR election, he placed a two-week ban on public demonstrations. And then, to enforce it, he brought 25,000 army troops into Jakarta. In this way, the MPR/DPR building was ringed deeply by defenders, preventing any disruption of the proceedings inside. The MPR session, then, broadcast on state television, ran according to form, with cameras panning the delegates chuckling or yawning during interminable speechmaking. Unofficial candidates were never acknowledged. No mention was made social unrest. Suharto and Habibie thus stood unopposed, relieving the 1000 MPR delegates of even having to vote in unanimously registering their preferences.

In the cabinet reshuffle that followed, Suharto performed similarly, freely exercising his formal prerogatives, while refusing to engage alienated elites. Indeed, he simply dropped prominent ministers whose allegiances he doubted, like the technocratic finance minister, Mar'ie Muhammed, the environment minister, Sarwono Kusumaatmadja, and the minister for transmigration, Siswono Yudosuhodo. And then, in a display of great hubris, he appointed in their place his long-time business partner, Bob Hasan, as minister of trade and industry, and his daughter, Tutut, as social services minister. He also appointed Fuad Bawazier as finance minister, a former director-general of tax collection, but now the treasurer of *Yayasan Sejahtera Mandiri*, a Suharto family "charity." It was widely noted too that Fuad chaired the Jakarta Stock Exchange board of commissioners, of which Suharto's second daughter, Siti Hediati Prabowo was a member.[64] Faisal Basrie, a noted economist at the University of Indonesia, assessed the new line-up: "Most of them are Suharto loyalists and would do anything to serve the president's interests. This once again demonstrates that the president has not paid heed to widespread criticism of nepotism, collusion, and corruption."[65]

Participatory society

The 1998 MPR election not only deepened the alienation of many elites, but also intensified student grievances. Hence, even as Suharto imposed his ban on demonstrations, student protests broke out in Jakarta, Bandung, Surabaya, and Ujung Pandang. At Atmajaya University in Jakarta, a huge banner, clearly visible from the MPR/DPR building, was unfurled demanding that the delegates not "rape" their consciences. Students thus amplified the call made by Amien Rais for Suharto to step down, then took up broader issues of business reform and price rises. Further, they began to develop cross-campus networks, establishing leadership contacts through which to coordinate their activities. They conducted "long marches" from their campuses, then converged in city-based "student forums." And they disseminated their messages through student newspapers, hand phones, pagers, and practiced use of the internet.[66]

As the students intensified their activities, the military met them with unexpected restraint, with some military elites appearing even to make soft-lining overtures. In particular, General Wiranto, recently appointed armed forces commander, declared that the military also favored political reforms. He thus permitted student demonstrations to take place so long as they were confined to campuses. He also invited student leaders to a dialogue session. In taking the cue, General Susilo Bambang Yudhoyono, the new chief of sociopolitical affairs, then stated that military was "working on a plan to hold dialog with students and other government critics. . . . Regional and lower military commands should not wait for further instruction from [armed forces] headquarters. They can hold discussions without waiting for our permission."[67]

On this score, as O'Donnell and Schmitter observe, "once the government signals that it is lowering the costs for engaging in collective action. . . . [f]ormer political identities reemerge and others appear *ex novo* to expand, beyond anyone's expectations, the public spaces the rulers decided to tolerate at the beginning of the transition."[68] Accordingly, while the government under Suharto had long suppressed "self-organized and autonomously defined political spaces," what O'Donnell and Schmitter once labeled a "resurrection of civil society" appeared now to be occurring.[69] Specifically, artists, journalists, professionals, and consumer groups now grew more participatory. For example, during the MPR session, Ratna Sarumpaet, a prominent playwrite and leader of a pro-democracy group, *Siaga*, organized a "people's summit" in north Jakarta at which Amien Rais and Megawati were scheduled to speak.[70] She and other organizers were arrested, but immediately gained much media attention, as well as public expressions of support from Goenawan Mohamad, former editor of a major news weekly, *Tempo*. A leading academic, astronomer Karlina Leksono, joined with members of *Suara Ibu Peduli* (Voice of Concerned Mothers) outside the Hotel Indonesia on Jalan Thamrin, Jakarta's main thoroughfare, then mounted a demonstration over fast rising milk prices.[71] Former cabinet ministers, top university officials, and members of alumni associations began also to take up student demands. And consumers organized small gatherings outside shopping centers and markets where they protested against inflation. The *Jakarta Post*, in order to reveal the depth of new middle-class alienation, summarized the results of a poll that had been commissioned in early 1998 by the Voice of Concerned Professionals in Jakarta: Among "middle class professionals . . . a staggering 98.25 percent of those polled agreed with the need for economic and sociopolitical reform to deal with the crisis."[72]

In addition, urban workers began to forge links with students, their grievances surging in tandem with transport and electricity costs. Thus, during the MPR session, while student protesters remained confined to campuses, workers tried to demonstrate on the highway in front of the MPR/DPR building, an action evidently coordinated by the SBSI leader, Muchtar Pakpahan, from his hospital bed. Then, in early May, the representatives of 30 Jakarta-based workers' groups gathered with University of Indonesia students for a series of meetings, cooperating in ways that were replicated in Surabaya and Bandung.[73] Increasingly, then, the names of labor activists were included on the lists of speakers at student rallies. Finally, there is evidence that student demands began also to resonate with farmworkers, hemmed in by new industrial states, dispossessed by golf courses, and subjected to price distortions by first-family manipulations. Exclaimed one farmer in an interview with the *Far Eastern Economic Review*, "After 30 years, nothing is changing, and we are sick and tired of it."[74]

At such junctures, O'Donnell and Schmitter observe that the resurrection of civil society, peaking finally in "popular upsurge," may "frighten" even those soft-liners who had sponsored it, expecting fully to control its progress.[75] In particular, soft-liners may find that the social forces they had appealed to attempt now to sweep past them, quickening the pace and extent of regime change. Indeed, General Wiranto's offers of dialogue were ignored by student leaders from the most important universities. Protests at campuses round the country then intensified, peaking in clashes with security forces in Central Java. Moreover, students began planning in early May a massive rally in Jakarta for Indonesia's Day of National Resistance, commemorating an anti-colonial action against the Dutch.

Wiranto thus stepped back from his soft-lining role, now warning students that stronger action would be taken against them. And if Wiranto retreated to a more hard-line posture, a rival military faction that had been pitted against him by Suharto took a harder line still. In brief, while Wiranto had earlier been trying to engage student leaders, the commander of the Strategic Reserve, General Prabowo Subianto, had for some months been operating in more complex ways, mobilizing Islamic student elements on the one hand and "disappearing" political activists on the other. And now that Wiranto was trying to contain students, Prabowo was widely suspected of advancing the cycle by inciting mob violence.[76] In this scenario, Prabowo calculated that violence would discredit the students, thus providing a pretext for stopping reforms. It would also spotlight Wiranto's inability to keep order, thereby opening the door to Prabowo's own rise within the military command.

Hence, media reports speculated that while Suharto was out of the country attending an Islamic conference in May, troops loyal to Prabowo shot four students during demonstrations at Jakarta's Trisakti University.[77] The mob violence that erupted in neighboring districts was then stoked by well-organized bands, systematically prising open the security doors of shopping malls, encouraging looters to enter, then setting the buildings alight. However, the violence grew so intense – targeting business premises associated with the Suharto family, gutting much of Jakarta's Chinatown, and leaving well over a thousand people dead – that Suharto's return from overseas inspired little confidence that he could restore order.[78]

In this situation, another cohort of elites abandoned Suharto, recognizing that far from perpetuating their statuses and managing their relations as he had in the past, his leadership – overtaken by events and diminished by old age – was exposing them to mass fury. The MPR/DPR speaker, Harmoko, having overseen *Golkar*'s electoral victory the year before, now demanded publicly that the president step down. And when Suharto responded by promising elections, then attempted to convene a "reform council," the persons he selected – fourteen economic ministers from his previous cabinet – all refused. In a widely quoted riposte, one nominee asked, "Are you crazy? The people will burn down my house."[79] And the military, meanwhile, simply stood aside as many thousands of students occupied the MPR/DPR building and its grounds. Analysts agree that it was at this point that Suharto recognized his position as untenable – even if Wiranto never confronted him directly.[80] He thus stepped down on May 21, apologizing in a remarkable resignation speech for any "mistakes and shortcomings," then transferring power to his vice-president, B.J. Habibie.

To conclude this section, we have seen that economic crisis reduced Suharto's capacity to manage elites, turning modulated rivalries into open disunity. Crisis also diminished Suharto's capacity to contain social forces, closing off career paths, factory employment, and subsidy programs. Thus, as Haggard and Kaufman observe, crisis "increases the likelihood of political protest 'from below,' and reduces the capacity of ruling elites to manage the resulting distributive conflicts."[81] This insight can be nuanced slightly by suggesting that it is rapid economic growth beforehand – articulating new classes and transferring new skills – that erodes the setting in which social quiescence prevails. And it is economic crisis afterward that encourages participation, with social forces now rising through the fissures between elites. Indeed, with soft-lining elites appearing, however briefly, social forces were readily activated. And when hard-lining elites miscalculated, social forces erupted in violence.

Transition to fuller democracy

Suharto's ouster and the transition that followed have been characterized by most analysts as a process of bottom-up "replacement,"[82] one in which social forces have grown highly participatory. This suggests that in contrast to transitions closely modulated by elites, the pace is rapid and its extent far-reaching. Accordingly, Huntington suggests that replacement is the mode of transition least likely to consolidate.[83] With elites having failed to strike bargains with the opposition, their statuses and interests are threatened, encouraging them finally to mount an authoritarian backlash.

The account offered here, however, demonstrates that just as regimes can be too strongly credited with intrinsic properties, so too can transitional pathways. In particular, while the notion of replacement highlights correctly the ascendancy that social forces can gain, it prolongs this ascendancy beyond what can always be perpetuated. It also underestimates the capacity of elites to regenerate cohesion and hence, the strategies by which they can respond to social forces, except through crude authoritarian backlash. Accordingly, this section will show how elites were able to limit the pace and extent of the democratic transition, then conduct founding elections in ways that left most elite statuses intact. Further, it argues that because many elites were able to safeguard their statuses Indonesia's new democracy possesses unexpectedly good prospects for stabilizing.

Habibie's presidency

As the concept of replacement would suggest, the new national leader, Habibie, began swiftly to liberalize politics, dismantling state controls over media reporting, labor organizing, and the formation and internal workings of opposition parties. And he began to democratize politics too. Although

Indonesia's constitution seemed to permit Habibie to finish out Suharto's term until 2003, he agreed to schedule a fresh election for the DPR within a year, soon to be followed by a presidential election in the MPR. Furthermore, while Suharto had always taken care to screen the MPR's regional and functional delegates, Habibie now gave greater autonomy over selection to the provincial assemblies and a new election commission. He agreed also to make governorships and many local positions elected ones, then promised a referendum on East Timorese autonomy, a *de facto* offer of independence.

However, Habibie acted also to moderate the transition. Of course, as the former overlord of high-tech innovation, he lacked grassroots support, thus encouraging him to pose now as a reformist in order to retain office. He at the same time, though, bracketed his reforms with moves to strengthen his hand for the day when elections had finally to be held. For example, when some retired generals within his own ruling *Golkar* challenged his leadership of the party during mid-1998, he called upon Wiranto to silence them. Moreover, when a special session of the MPR was held toward the end of the year, one that diluted or delayed some proposals for reform, Habibie ordered Wiranto to use Muslim vigilantes to suppress the student protests that followed, an action resulting in a dozen more deaths.[84] Further, a tape recording of a conversation between Habibie and his attorney-general was leaked in early 1999, revealing his selectivity in prosecuting business elites for corrupt practices. Specifically, Habibie ordered only those associated with opposition parties to be targeted, among them, Arifin Panigoro. Toward the end of the year, an audit by an international accountancy firm revealed that top strategists for his election bid had extracted some US$80 million in illegal commissions from the newly recapitalized Bank Bali. It was widely suspected that this money would be used for influencing MPR members – thus putting IMF assistance at risk. In addition, though Habibie permitted opposition parties to organize, he attempted still to intervene in the affairs of the one that could best challenge him. Specifically, his government refused to acknowledge Megawati's regaining leadership of the PDI at the party's fifth congress in October 1998, instead supporting a rival congress that had been held two months earlier.[85] Finally, though Habibie also eased formal controls over trade unions, activists on the ground still faced a "security approach." In attempting to reach workers, they were regularly confronted by low-level bureaucratic obstacles and intimidation by thugs. In sum, evaluations of Habibie's commitments to democracy remained equivocal. While ratifying the transition, indeed trumpeting his contributions to *reformasi*, his counter-moves led him popularly to be identified as "status quo."

At the same time, with Suharto removed, social forces grew less participatory. Student groups lost organizational coherence, while urban mobs dispersed in more common forms of criminality. Elites, meanwhile, regained some of their cohesion. During the New Order, Habibie had been deeply distrusted by the military because of his resorting to Islamicist tactics and his meddling in procurements. But now, in consenting to an election, yet lacking mass constituents, Habibie plainly needed the military's help. Wiranto, in turn, amid alarming new disclosures about the military's brutality in East Timor, Aceh, Irian Jaya, and elsewhere, sought the legitimating cover of civilian leadership. And both figures, of course, found themselves tarred by their long-time patronage from Suharto. Hence, at this conjuncture of great mutual need, Wiranto was authorized by Habibie to remove Prabowo from the military, thus consolidating his command. And Habibie was supported by Wiranto in the ways enumerated above.

More broadly, in then perpetuating the statuses of elites, Habibie retained most of the cabinet ministers and top bureaucrats that he had inherited from Suharto. Indeed, there are indications that his government turned a blind eye to their accelerating corruption during the run-up to the election that could mean their removal – a kind of golden handshake executed under the table. Further, to the extent that he could, Habibie appeared to shield indigenous business elites from IMF bank closures and painful restructuring, then permitted them even to regain some wealth through high deposit rates and new credit flows.[86] And finally, Habibie arranged that the fall of Suharto, however precipitous, be suitably cushioned. In particular, Suharto's Jakarta residence was resolutely protected from waves of student protesters, while his business affairs remained insulated from serious investigation. His children, meanwhile, though made to resign their board positions and sometimes even to face charges, retained most of their properties, equities, and overseas holdings.

Thus, even as Indonesia remained in economic crisis, Habibie was able to regenerate some elite cohesion. At the same time, social forces lost participatory vigor. Hence, in borrowing an institutionalist idiom, though tempering its dichotomous assumptions, a configuration of "weak state, weaker society" emerged in Indonesia, one in which the transition proceeded less rapidly and extensively than the concept of replacement demands. In these circumstances, elites permitted founding elections to take place without their resorting to authoritarian backlash.

"Founding elections"[87]

Despite democratization by opposition-led replacement, the procedures and outcomes of Indonesia's parliamentary and presidential elections cannot be characterized as far-reaching. To see this first in the case of the DPR election in 1999, we can specify on two dimensions what far-reaching electoral activities would look like in the case of Indonesia, then assess the empirical short-fall. These dimensions involve the nature of institutional rules created to govern the elections and the policy aims put forth by the competing parties. To be sure, this is not to argue that significant shifts on these dimensions would necessarily "suit" the peculiarities of the Indonesian setting, thereby enhancing the prospects for democratic consolidation. On the contrary, such shifts would correlate instead with the general concept of replacement, with some of them inviting authoritarian backlash.

In terms of institutional rules, a far-reaching transition would change Indonesia's presidential system to a parliamentary one, thus avoiding the twin pitfalls of "delegative democracy," with executive dominance on one side and deadlock between the executive and legislature on the other.[88] Indeed, it is now well established in the literature on democratization that a parliamentary system poses fewer risks in terms of executive abuses and destabilizing clashes.[89] Second, all the seats in the DPR would be made elected ones, thus removing the military's appointed members. Third, single member districts (SMDs) would be replaced by provincial-based proportional representation. Of course, while SMDs promise closer links between representatives and their constituencies than proportional representation does, a trade-off exists in that they tend to promote pork barreling and to exclude third parties. In Indonesia, however, SMDs were often promoted by reformists, breaking with New Order legacies of unitary administration and intense party bossism. Fourth, a transition that was far-reaching would introduce a neutral election commission to replace the General Election Institute. Further, state bureaucrats – from ministers to local officials – would be barred from mobilizing voters in partisan ways. Sixth, the official three-party system, enforced by the New Order's *fusi* legislation, would be dismantled, permitting parties freely to organize and compete. And finally, strict controls would be imposed on campaign financing, helping stem the rise of dreaded "money politics." Let us consider the changes in Indonesia's institutional rules by these benchmark measures of a far-reaching transition.

In mid-1998, the interior ministry commissioned a group known popularly as the "team of seven" to draft new election laws for the MPR/DPR, the electoral system, and political parties. The team determined first that it had no mandate to change the Constitution of 1945, thus leaving intact a powerful presidency. The MPR was also preserved, meaning that the election of the president would remain indirect. Second, while the team of seven sought initially to remove the military delegates from the DPR, it soon "experienced 'the reality' of [military] pressure."[90] Thus, upon reflection by the incumbent DPR, elected, we recall, in 1997, the military was left with a sizeable bloc of 38 seats. Third, though the team proposed an election law introducing single member districts, the DPR rejected it. With none of the party leaders wishing to see their control over party affairs diminished, they together conspired to make only limited concessions to district-based sentiments. In this way, a hybrid *sistem semidistrik* emerged, one in which proportional representation remained at the provincial level, though representatives would finally be chosen based on their district-level performance. However, it was difficult to gauge the reformist impact of this arrangement. In the view of one foreign assessment team, the system – "without exact precedent or parallel anywhere else in the world" – risked "anomalous results" and "confusion and dissatisfaction."[91] Thus, while Adam Przeworski has famously adjudged "uncertainty" as a necessary condition for electoral fairness, Indonesia's new laws introduced a kind that appeared unhelpful.[92]

In terms of the other three issues, though, the team of seven made greater headway. A new election commission (KPU) was formed that chose as its leader Rudini, a much respected former home minister. A further reform was introduced when the DPR agreed that bureaucrats could not make use of their official posts to promote political parties. Of course, *Golkar* resisted this bitterly, given its long-time reliance on local officials to cajole village voters. But Habibie finally accepted it. Further, a new party law was adopted that permitted fairly easy registration, relieving parties of their obligations to *Pancasila*. And though another "team" was subsequently formed to decide which of the 150+ parties that had registered should be permitted finally to contest the election, the culling appeared to be carried out pragmatically, leaving a field of 48.[93]

In sum, by the terms of the new institutional rules adopted for Indonesia's founding elections, the transition cannot be regarded as far-reaching. To be sure, a new election commission, the non-partisanship of bureaucrats, and revisions to the party law all indicated that a transition was underway. But the retention of a powerful and indirectly elected president, the reserving of seats in the DPR for the military, the ambiguities lurking in the election laws themselves, and the refusal to regulate campaign finance all suggested real limits.

Turning now to the policy aims pursued by competing parties, let us consider again what a far-reaching transition would have looked like in the Indonesian setting. In the context of replacement, one would expect many of Indonesia's opposition parties to have strongly denounced the New Order and its many elite hold-overs, thus testing the statuses of elites in the military, bureaucracy, and business. Most notably, these parties would demand that the military be confined to a security role, dislodging it not only from the legislature, but also from its "reserve domains" in the bureaucracy and economy. Second, these parties would call for federalist power-sharing, abolishing the unitary controls, reinforced by the military's territorial command, that have so alienated the Outer Islands. Third, amid severe economic hardship, these parties would make strongly populist appeals, promising redistributive programs, support schemes, cheap credit, and subsidies. In addition, this populism would likely be edged with sectarian cues, namely, an intensification of revivalist Islam with anti-Chinese overtones. One would also expect this populism to be coupled with feisty economic nationalism, venting social resentments against the multilateral agencies and globalized financial patterns seen by many to have worsened the country's economic crisis. And finally, of course, demands that the Suharto family be punished would be expressed, given the extent to which their webs of corruption were widely blamed for triggering the crisis to begin with.

Let us check again our theoretical expectations against Indonesia's empirical record. Despite the pledges made by all parties to reform, Habibie's ruling *Golkar*, of course, avoided criticizing the military's practice of *dwi-fungsi*. In seeming contrast, the leaders of the most important opposition parties – Megawati, now heading the Indonesia Democracy Party of Struggle (PDI-P) and Abdurrahman Wahid of the National Awakening Party (PKB) – joined Amien Rais and the Sultan of Yogyakarta in demanding the military give up its seats in the DPR. But this "Ciganjur declaration," as it was labeled, was issued only after renewed pressure from students, and it only called for the military's departure to take place in another six years. In this same vein, though the DPR now passed new laws on decentralization, and the military ceased its seconding officers to the bureaucracy, these reforms fell short of federalist guarantees or any serious limits on the military's own deeply penetrative command structure. And finally, in rehearsing her party's nationalism, Megawati denounced Habibie's independence offer to East Timor, thereby taking a stand more to the military's liking.

Similarly, on class and ethnic issues, while Megawati was acclaimed by mass audiences as favoring the poor, she released few programmatic details, intimating instead a non-binding message of feminine "caring."[94] Leaders of other major opposition parties, meanwhile, remained even more muted on class inequalities. Nor did any of them test the transition's reach, however dysfunctionally, by seizing opportunities to mobilize sectarian jealousies. In particular, the PDI-P remained avowedly secular, the PKB maintained the "traditionalist" Muslim tolerance of its leader, Abudurrahman Wahid, and even *Golkar* drew back from the revivalist Islam it had begun to express. Moreover, these parties blamed neither globalized forces nor Suharto family dealings for Indonesia's great hardship. Only the PDI-P's Kwik Kian Gie, tipped to be the key economics minister in the event of his party's coming to power, canvassed a nationalist policy response of fixed exchange rates, though in close consultation with the IMF.

Some smaller opposition parties, however, though stopping short of radical positions, gained more the kind of stridency one would expect in a context of transition by replacement. Amien Rais, now leading the National Mandate Party (PAN), called forcefully for the DPR to be fully elected, the state bureaucracy to be decentralized, foreign investment to be regulated, and Suharto to be placed on trial – thereby challenging the standings of many elites. At the same time, Adi Sasono's People's Sovereignty Party (PDR), a breakaway group from *Golkar*, intensified demands for a "people's economy," marked by new funding for cooperatives and cross-ethnic redistribution. Further, in steeling his campaign with great personal charisma, Islamic militancy, and heavily subsidized state lending, one would have deduced that amid replacement, Adi was building a powerful platform. And finally, a raft of other Islamicist parties appeared, seeking the right social gradient for their sectarian appeals.

In these circumstances, with the major political parties adopting moderate postures, one would have expected that in the DPR elections, held June 7, the smaller, more strident parties would have forged ahead. But when official results were finally announced some two months later, the PAN won only 7.5 per cent of the vote, the PDR only 3 per cent, and the strongly Islamicist parties collectively but 15 per cent. Thus, a plurality of the vote, nearly 34 per cent, went to the PDI-P, greatly overshadowing *Golkar*'s 23 per cent and strengthening Megawati's claims to the presidency. Moreover, with Megawati having emerged as a cautious reformer, the military soon signaled it could live with her by acknowledging publicly that a woman could become president. One also notes here that at least some business elites had grown comfortable enough with Megawati that they had made contributions to her party. In these circumstances, there was no need for *Golkar* to be "'helped' to do well" by distorting the vote count – the advice once given by O'Donnell and Schmitter on behalf of rightist parties in order to preempt authoritarian backlash.[95] In particular, Indonesia's founding elections, while appearing to unseat *Golkar*, advanced cautious reformers over more strident oppositionists, while featuring no anti-system radicals at all. Elite statuses and interests were thus unthreatened.

Of course, the DPR election was only the first phase in a two-step process leading finally to the MPR election for the presidency. This progress was protracted, however, involving a hiatus of more than four months. And it was made complicated by the need to select 200 more electors from regional and functional groups, thus quickening the horse trading between parties that had already been made brisk by the fact that none of them had won a DPR majority. Nonetheless, the center stage was held by the two largest vote-getters, the PDI-P and *Golkar*. Megawati then raised her party's front-runner status by gaining intimations of support, however, coy, from Abdurrahman Wahid, leader of the PKB. Habibie, however, was fast gathering funding, eyeing the MPR's floating voters who were widely reported in the press to be available for $1 million each.

But despite this new competitiveness, with the MPR election to be decided within this narrow spectrum, the outcome would, from the perspective of many elites, appear not to have mattered. To be sure, a victory by Megawati, by installing a woman president, might have antagonized many revivalist Muslims. And a victory by Habibie might have roused students and urban mobs from their deep *desencanto*. But given the moderate postures of both these figures, as well as the rough balance in risk attending their candidacies, elites in the military and business appeared willing to accommodate either of them.

Over time, however, Megawati's support from the PKB weakened, with Abdurrahman Wahid stayed by the Islamicist sentiments of his followings. It appeared too that while the serenity of Megawati's campaigning style had entranced mass-level voters, it was ill-suited to the instrumentalist dealings of the MPR members. Accordingly, in early October, Amien Rais, now hardening his opposition to Megawati, gained selection as the MPR's head. And soon afterward, the Golkar secretary-general, Akbar Tanjung, won the speakership of the DPR. On the other side, though, Habibie was dragged down by the Bank Bali scandal, his fund-raising methods embarrassing MPR delegates before middle-class audiences and the IMF. Further, his attempt to resolve the East Timor issue in ways that would add lustre to his aura as a reformer exploded with nationalist resentments. Hence, in contrast to Suharto's putative nation building, Habibie came now to be disparaged as *Bapak Disintegrasi* (Father of Disintegration). In these circumstances, he could expect no better from his erstwhile collaborators in the military than electoral neutrality.

In addition, during the interim between elections, Amien Rais unveiled a new "central axis" (*poros tengah*), giving a coherence and weight to the Islamicist parties that previously they had lacked. And in planting this axis squarely between Megawati and Habibie, Amien began rallying Muslim forces behind Abdurrahman Wahid. At the same time, Megawati refused still to press her candidacy vigorously, causing her support in the MPR to soften further. And Habibie, finally, in delivering to the MPR his accountability speech – no more than a staid ritual under Suharto, but now an arena for critical feedback – met with rejection, forcing him finally to withdraw from the race. Thus, when the MPR election was held on October 20, *Golkar* members were split, with many of them going over to Abdurrahman. And in gaining some support too from the military, Abdurrahman suddenly ascended to the presidency, winning 373 votes to Megawati's 313.

Abdurrahman Wahid, at once a secular democrat and Sufi mystic, moved quickly after his victory to reassure elites. In brief, he helped next day to bring about Megawati's election as his vice-president, thus calming her elite-level supporters, as well as her disillusioned social constituencies. Moreover, Habibie was allowed a soft landing, repairing to his new think tank in downtown Jakarta, the Center for Democracy and Human Rights. In addition, though Abdurrahman had pledged to combat corruption, he remained quite ambivalent over prosecuting Suharto. Similarly, though seeking to mollify the IMF in ways that would restore lending, he heartened local business elites by declining to appoint any tough-minded technocrats to his new cabinet.

But most importantly, Abdurrahman dealt gingerly with the military. Of course, by this time, the military's infamy had deepened, attributable first to its brutality in East Timor, then to its loss of the province. And this enabled Abdurrahman to pare back the military's role in politics, now appointing a civilian as defense minister and a naval officer as armed forces commander. Nonetheless, he took care to set aside for General Wiranto the Ministry of Political and Security Affairs. He also reserved for the military some new domains, namely, the ministries of mining and transport,[96] historically regarded as *basah* portfolios, wet with ambrosial patronage. And finally, he made no mention of the military's sinewy command structure that continued to truss up the archipelago.

In sum, Indonesia's MPR contest for the presidency, like the earlier one for the DPR, underscored the moderate character of its founding elections. It thus helped also to cap the country's less than far-reaching transition. However, it was in part because these outcomes were measured that authoritarian backlash was in the early months avoided, hence brightening the prospects for democracy's stabilizing. One must be cautious, then, in attributing to regimes and transitional pathways any strongly determinative qualities. Elites may autonomously regain some cohesion, while social forces, notwithstanding the inspiriting contexts in which they dwell, may lose some participatory zeal.

Democratic quality and stability

As analysis turns from democratic transitions to consolidation, new issues of quality and stability grow important. These issues are addressed in some detail later in this volume when we focus on Thailand and the Philippines, countries that democratized their politics more than a decade ago and illustrate well the dilemmas of consolidation. today. In Indonesia, though, even at this very early stage of democratic experience, we can identify attempts by the government to pursue reforms, as well as the impact they have had on regime equilibrium.

During 2000, President Abdurrahman Wahid's first year in office, attempts were made to raise democracy's quality on a number of dimensions. But one quickly discovers that increases in quality that were rapid and concerted run counter to stability, threatening the interests of the many military and business elites who had survived the New Order's collapse. We will see too that disputes over prerogatives erupted between the president and new members of the MPR/DPR. In consequence, the government's pursuit of democratic reforms in Indonesia, while probably not risking any overt authoritarian backlash, nonetheless provoked sundry resistances and destabilizing actions. Abdurrahman thus responded by slowing the pace of reform, emphasizing stability over quality.

Let us begin by specifying in the Indonesian case some areas in which democracy's quality might have appropriately been extended. First, the civilian government required clear supremacy over the military,[97] scaling back the reserve domains that have long been enshrined by the doctrine of *dwi-fungsi*. Second, as state power was wrested from the military, it should then have been shared by the presidency and legislature in ways that increased executive accountability, yet ensured policy making coherence. The country otherwise remained at risk of delegative democracy, especially in view of its presidentialist legacies, or conversely, crippling deadlocks and policy immobilism. Third, the government had also to devolve power to local government, thus relaxing Jakarta's unitary grip. Larry Diamond and Svetlana Tsalik have recently demonstrated in theoretical terms how strong local governments help to deepen democracy, practicing the virtues of smallness, close-up accountability, and checking the center.[98] In the case of Indonesia, greater fiscal autonomy also appeared necessary for placating the resource-rich provinces of the Outer Islands, though it had to be carried out in ways that did not unduly antagonize poor ones.

Fourth, in shifting discussion from politics to the economy, Indonesia needed to quicken the pace of its recovery. To be sure, the correspondence between democracy and levels of socioeconomic development remains unclear. But it is difficult to imagine Indonesia's democracy gaining quality without achieving growth rates that would restore business enterprises to solvency and workers to gainful employment. Further, to the extent that recovery depended on attracting foreign investors and rationalizing local business operations, the judiciary had to be strengthened, safeguarding contracts and property rights. More broadly, the courts and police had to be reformed in ways that strengthened the rule of law, helping also to tame Indonesia's spiraling criminal activities and streetside vigilantism.

Fifth, at a social level, party appeals and policy outputs had to be made in ways that would mitigate ethnic and religious tensions. More specifically, parties should pitch their appeals to multi-ethnic constituencies, rather than amplifying Indonesia's manifest social hatreds. Indeed, where sectarianism persists, elections help to rigidify social inequalities, thus jeopardizing the democracy of which electoral contestation is meant to be a key constitutive element. Finally, on an international dimension, Indonesia's democracy required international support, taking the form of discrete guidance and generous funding assistance. On this score, one must recognize the tensions between Western trade unions, human rights groups, and democratizing institutes on one side and foreign investors on the other, the latter easily spooked by competitive elections and labor organizing. In each of these areas, then, let us turn now to evaluating briefly the progress made during Abdurrahman's first year as president, highlighting the tradeoffs between democratic quality and stability.

On the critical issue of establishing the supremacy of civilian leadership, Abdurrahman appeared at first to make headway. In a much publicized episode, he removed General Wiranto from his cabinet, albeit through circuitous methods. He then secured Wiranto's acquiescence by offering some guarantees, namely, providing the general with "nonactive" status in order to minimize loss of face, while promising an amnesty for any human rights violations that might one day be investigated. Similarly, Abdurrahman succeeded in easing many serving officers from the bureaucracy, while retired ones assumed a lower profile in *Golkar*. But beyond this, attempts to raise democracy's quality on this score were limited. In particular, a constitutional amendment passed in August 2000 safeguarded the military's 38 seats in the DPR until 2004 and in the MPR until 2009. A second amendment appeared also to prevent military personnel from being tried under any new laws for past human rights abuses. Hence, even where changes were made to the Constitution of 1945 – a document readily harnessed to authoritarian aims – they did more to insulate the military from accountability than to register democratic progress. What is more, Abdurrahman remained silent about the military's pervasive territorial command structure. Left undisturbed, this parallel apparatus enabled the military to continue, indeed to intensify, its pressuring regional administrators, while collaborating with, or extorting from, local business people.

To be sure, retreating from quality in these ways might have been necessary if Indonesia's new democracy was to persist. Put simply, with historical rivalries in the military evolving now into tensions between reformists and more numerous recalcitrants, there was need to avoid antagonizing the hard-liners. Hence, when a new reformist commander of the Strategic Reserve, General Agus Wirahadikusumah, revealed to the press the large-scale embezzling of his predecessor, he met with such opposition that Abdurrahman, rather than risking confrontation with hard-liners, finally accepted Agus's removal.[99] Abdurrahman rightly assessed that after easing top generals from the cabinet and bureaucracy, he had to tread carefully in moving more deeply to reform the military's internal dealings. Though the military was now so widely despised that it would probably have shrunk from any direct coup against civilian leaders, it remained able to make considerable "trouble" when challenged on its own corporate turf.

Moreover, there was evidence that quite apart from the factional loyalties that top generals might hold, their orders were increasingly ignored in the field. Indeed, as Indonesia's military gained a character that Linz and Stepan have labeled "nonhierarchical,"[100] it seemed to fuel, rather than quell, mass-level violence. More specifically, as regional commanders sought to exploit local dynamics, they appeared to exacerbate religious conflict in Ambon, with the army supporting Muslims and the local police siding with Christians.[101] In these circumstances, Abdurrahman's dispatching his vice-president, Megawati, to Maluku in order to calm the violence merely revealed more fully his government's ineffectiveness. Alternatively, the suspicion that he sought deliberately to spotlight Megawati's incompetence by thrusting her into an irresolvable conflict augured no better for able governance. In addition, even as Abdurrahman tried to dampen separatist tensions in the province of Aceh, negotiating avidly with local leaders and promising a referendum over the introduction of Islamic law, elements in the military continued to commit atrocities, quickly eroding local confidence in Jakarta's good faith. In East Timor, while Abdurrahman attended a United Nations summit in September in New York, mobs galvanized by local militias massacred three UN workers while security forces looked on, exposing the president to severe public criticisms from other national leaders. In Kalimantan, while Abdurrahman tried to reassure foreign investors, regional commanders were widely suspected of protecting land seizures, illegal mining activities, and unlicensed timber felling. And finally, destabilizing actions occurred even in Jakarta, with bombing attacks taking place on the attorney-general's chambers, the stock exchange, and the residence of the Philippine ambassador.

Marzuki Darusman, the attorney-general, attributed the bombings in Jakarta directly to military hard-liners. Indeed, he observed in the press that whenever police investigations drew close to the military, they soon afterward ceased.[102] However, Abdurrahman's second defense minister, Mohammad Mahfud M.D., seemed better to articulate the president's new thinking, advising publicly that the military should not be wrongly accused: "If the military goes on strike for one hour, the country will be shattered."[103] Accordingly, in terms of civil-military relations, gauged early in Abdurrahman's presidency to be his greatest area of reform, the pace of democratization soon slowed. Abdurrahman came to recognize that his moving too swiftly to raise quality, while not provoking the military to open confrontation, seemed still to trigger destabilizing actions.

A second area of democratic reform involved the sharing of state power between the presidency and legislature, thereby alleviating the imbalances created by Suharto. On this count, institutional progress appeared to take place as the DPR acquired a competitive party system and new powers to pass laws. Further, the MPR, made up largely of the DPR, decided to meet annually in order to "review" the president's performance, thereby enhancing executive accountability. However, the good will between Abdurrahman and the MPR/DPR was soon tested, with the president at one stage dismissing the legislature as a "kindergarten," while denying that it possessed the constitutional power to scrutinize his policy decisions.[104]

As relations grew strained, Abdurrahman began to pare back the cabinet of "national unity" that he had formed after his election, expelling several ministers from parties other than his own. In doing this, he offered the barest of pretexts, usually alleging corruption, then proceeded to make what were often assessed as dubious appointments. Abdurrahman was thus criticized by DPR members and the MPR leader, Amien Rais, for his hasty dismissals and appointments, his off-the-cuff commentary to the press, his frequent travels abroad, and even some instances of apparent corruption. In particular, Abdurrahman was revealed to have taken funds from BULOG, while casually accepting assistance from the Sultan of Brunei, promptly generating scandals that were labeled "*Buloggate*" and "*Bruneigate.*" It may be that Abdurrahman operated with good intentions, namely, to gain the funding with which to ease discontents in Aceh. But his informal and unaccountable methods appeared reminiscent of Suharto's "off budget" activities.

Many observers anticipated that after the annual session of the MPR had been held in August 2000, democratic reforms and economic recovery would resume. Abdurrahman would either give a reasonable account of his presidency, conceding his failings and outlining new strategies in order to restore confidence in his leadership, or he would be impeached, paving the way for a new president. But neither outcome occurred. Instead, Abdurrahman offered a lackluster speech, yet managed to mollify the MPR with a pledge to turn over day-to-day administration to Megawati. However, he appeared afterward to renege, ceding little new authority to his vice-president. Indeed, he reshuffled his cabinet, sacking more ministers from Megawati's PDI-P and *Golkar*, then replacing them with loyalists from his own PKB. Accordingly, Abdurrahman survived his first year as president, though can hardly be said to have respected the notion of executive accountability. On this dimension, it was perhaps Abdurrahman himself who posed the greatest obstacle to raising democratic quality.

On the third issue of regional autonomy, we recall that new laws had been passed under Habibie to devolve administrative power and fiscal policy. Indeed, decentralization was to range beyond Indonesia's twenty-six provinces to its 300 districts.[105] Meanwhile, provincial governments would be permitted to retain 15 per cent of the export earnings on petroleum from their provinces, 30 per cent on natural gas, and 80 per cent on mining and timber products. Abdurrahman, upon gaining the presidency, appeared committed to implementing these reforms. Indeed, early in his tenure, he spoke even of holding an independence referendum for Aceh, just as the one that had been organized in East Timor. At the same time, Amien Rais recommended a thorough-going federalist system. And a much respected official from the interior ministry, Ryaas Rasyid, was appointed to oversee decentralizing programs, signifying the seriousness of the government's proposals.

Questions soon arose, however, over the capacity of district-level officials to undertake the administrative tasks with which they were now to be entrusted.[106] Further, the retention of greater export earnings by the resource-rich rich provinces meant less could be distributed among poorer ones, exacerbating the rural imbalances and immiseration that even before the economic crisis were quite serious in Indonesia. At the same time, no amount of autonomy and revenue-sharing seemed likely to appease militant secessionists, particularly in Aceh, but also in Irian Jaya. And interior ministry officials in Jakarta, fearing for their livelihoods in the capital, began to dig in their heels against decentralizing reforms. Hence, during 2000, an uncertain process took place through which Jakarta began to negotiate terms with individual districts. Implementation was scheduled to begin at the start of 2001, though if anything, a crazy quilt of uneven administration seemed likely to result.[107]

In terms of economic recovery during Abdurrahman's presidency, only the slightest gains were made. To be sure, Indonesia's GDP was projected to grow by nearly 4 per cent in 2000. But analysts warned that at this rate, it would take another seven years before the economy would regain its size prior to crisis. Further, there were doubts that even this 4 per cent rate could be sustained. High petroleum prices during 2000, again the engine of Indonesia's economic growth, were sure to fall. At the same time, foreign investors remained wary, shunning Indonesia's manufacturing and property sectors for more favorable markets elsewhere, especially in China. In these circumstances, the *rupiah* remained fragile, subject still to sharp devaluations, while nearly half the country's GDP was committed to servicing foreign loans.

Of course, the IMF now offered more appropriate guidelines than it had upon its first arriving in 1997. And with the key to restarting Indonesia's economy held to be recapitalizing the banks and restructuring the conglomerates, a new agency, the Indonesian Bank Restructuring Agency (IBRA) was introduced. Similar to such agencies in other countries affected by the crisis, the IBRA's task was to acquire assets from companies made insolvent by the crisis, sell them to new interests, often foreign ones, and repay creditors, thereby easing the banks' bad loans. But after more than a year of operation, while technically conforming to IMF strictures, the IBRA managed to sell few of the assets that it had acquired.[108] What is more, managerial control of these assets was usually left in the hands of the conglomerate bosses from whom they had been seized.

Accordingly, little corporate restructuring was deemed to take place. Indeed, there were fears that as Abdurrahman's tenure in office lengthened, patterns of government-business relations were coming again to resemble those of the New Order, even if less centralized and lucrative. In particular, as business elites grew bolder, they drew closer to Abdurrahman in seeking his favor.[109] And as Abdurrahman realized the need to accumulate resources with which to re-energize support, especially in the *Nahdlatul Ulama* that he had once led, he began to respond in patrimonialist ways. Many government officials defended Abdurrahman's behaviors as necessary for retaining local business expertise, the basis for any economic recovery. However, Kwik Kian Kie, Abdurrahman's first coordinating minister of the economy, retorted bluntly that most of the country's conglomerate bosses belonged in jail.[110] In these circumstances, Indonesia's economy grew no more attractive to foreign investors. And local business elites gained no new access to export markets.

Abdurrahman thus faced a sharp dilemma. On the one hand, he needed to restructure Indonesia's business dealings in ways that would quicken economic recovery and alleviate poverty. On the other hand, he had to avoid alienating business elites: despite their corporate insolvency, they still held enough wealth that they could collaborate with military hard-liners in fomenting disorder. In addition, democracy's new competitiveness seemed to require that Abdurrahman not only tolerate some cronyist behaviors, but that he participate in them directly. Put simply, Abdurrahman, as surely as his predecessor, Habibie, had to amass patronage resources, then deliver them to critical constituencies. Hence, on this count too, the tradeoffs between democratic quality and stability became clear.

Similarly, attempts to reform Indonesia's judiciary in ways that would rationalize business dealings grew weaker over time. Early in his tenure, Abdurrahman succeeded in replacing nearly half of the supreme court judges. In addition, military officers were no longer recruited to the bench. However, Marcus Mietzner has shown how the president later intervened quite arbitrarily in the judiciary, thus preventing it from gaining new institutional autonomy.[111] For example, Abdurrahman ordered that ongoing investigations of the Texmaco group, a conglomerate headed by his associate, Marimutu Sinivasan, be halted. He also offered pre-emptive clemency to Suharto – as he had to Wiranto – in the event of the former president one day going to trial. At the same time, Abdurrahman personally ordered the arrest of Suharto's son, Tommy, over the bombing of the Jakarta Stock Exchange. And when the police refused because of a clear lack of evidence, Abdurrahman responded by sacking the chief of police. He also demanded that the former head of the central bank, Syahril Sabirin, be investigated over the Bank Bali scandal, though less because of any evidence than because Syahril had earlier been involved in closing two banks operated by the *Nahdlatul Ulama*.[112] Mietzner thus concludes, "With the president using his executive powers to influence the legal apparatus, and openly violating guidelines set to ensure public accountability, the government has lost some of its credibility in implementing legal reform." Accordingly, political maneuverings and commercial dealings remained undisciplined by the rule of law in Indonesia. And high-level transgressions were paralleled in the streets by a great surge in criminal activities and vigilante reprisals.

Shifting to the social level, we have seen how ethnic and religious tensions have persisted Indonesia. Hence, in order for elections to be held in ways that would avoid inflaming these tensions, political parties had to broaden their constituent appeals across sectarian lines. And indeed, after Abdurrahman succeeded Habibie as president, his tolerant demeanor set the tone, with party elites now ceasing to express even tacit criticisms of the local Chinese. However, if ethnic relations between the indigenous and Chinese communities improved, religious tensions between Muslims and Christians grew worse, most notably in Maluku. Further, while local rivalries exacerbated by military elements appear mostly to have been responsible, some political parties also joined in the fray. Most notably, Amien Rais, leader of the PAN and head of the MPR, now sullied his middle-class program of political reform with calls for holy war against the Christians in Maluku.

Indonesia's religious violence spilled over into debates about direct presidential elections. On one side, Abdurrahman remained committed to direct election, viewing it as necessary for extending democratic reforms. However, some analysts feared that with Indonesia's social terrain growing increasingly polarized, direct election would encourage political parties to galvanize mass support through religious appeals. And victory, then, by either the Islamic constituencies of the *poros tengah* or the secular and nationalist followings loyal to Megawati would so antagonize the loser that Maluku's experiences might then be replicated across large parts of the archipelago.[113] Accordingly, these analysts counseled that presidential elections remain confined to the MPR: with members of the electoral college sheltered from the scrutiny of their impassioned constituencies, they seemed better able to reach peaceful compromises. Hence, at this level too, it appeared that stabilizing Indonesia's new democracy demanded limits on its quality.

Finally, on an international plane, extending democracy required much skillfully calibrated assistance. Indeed, ever since democracy's transition in Spain was hastened during the 1970s by the prospect of inclusion in the European Union and agricultural support schemes, analysts have acknowledged at least the subsidiary impact of external factors. In Indonesia, then, various democratic advocacy groups provided much funding and advice during 1998–99 for institutional designs. Large teams of international observers monitored the electoral processes in the DPR and MPR, generally attesting to democracy's advance. In these circumstances, Indonesia gained much supportive publicity through the international media, while receiving the encouragement of many governments in the West.

More recently, however, Indonesia appears to have fallen from international favor. The United States criticized Abdurrahman for his attending a meeting of non-aligned countries in Cuba, while the U.S. ambassador publicly expressed his deep frustrations over mounting corruption in Indonesia.[114] In addition, with Indonesia's military seeming to regain some influence in politics, alongside its refusal to disarm the militia in East Timor, the U.S. Congress again imposed an embargo on arms shipments. Likewise, the IMF and World Bank threatened repeatedly to withhold their tranches of new loans. And finally, these increasingly stern international postures were unmitigated by any foreign trade or investment incentives that reward democracy's progress. On the contrary, with globalizing strategies driven exclusively by markets, patterns of foreign investment have responded not to democratic reforms, but to corporate returns, hence shunning Indonesia almost entirely.

In sum, upon Abdurrahman Wahid's surging past his rivals to gain the presidency in 1999, he was gauged by sober minded analysts as the "best of the worst," thus inspiring a pale optimism. And during the next months, he attempted to extend democratic reforms on a number of dimensions. However, where the interests of still powerful elites were put at risk, raising democracy's quality impinged on stability. Military hard-liners, indebted business elites, centralizing bureaucrats, and even an arbitrary Abdurrahman himself thus mounted resistances to democracy's progress, although stopping short of any fully blown backlash. Afterward, however, tacit understandings appeared gradually to be reached, thereby slowing democracy's pace. Hence, amid the investigations, sackings, bombings, religious tensions, and low currency valuations that scarred Abdurrahman's first year in office, it also became possible to detect some elite-level forbearance. Observers are thus right to say that Indonesia's democracy is low quality. But they probably understate its stability.

Nonetheless, as tensions deepened between Abdurrahman and DPR members, he was finally removed by a special session of the MPR, convened in July 2001. Abdurrahman mounted a spirited resistance, first attempting to declare emergency rule, later calling his Muslim supporters into the streets. And the MPR countered in ways that raised doubts over constitutionality. Accordingly, the behaviours of both sides support our assessments about Indonesia's low quality democracy. However Abdurrahman finally withdrew and was peacefully succeeded by his vice-president, Megawati. She then formed a cabinet, which, if surprising many analysts by its inclusion of technocrats, also contained an attorney-general who was expected to approach human rights questions with great wariness. Megawati doubtless recognised that such caution was the price of democratic stability.

Conclusions

The political record of New Order Indonesia provides an exemplar of pseudo-democracy, characterized by few civil liberties and regular, though rigged elections. This record also shows one way in which this regime type could be stabilized, namely, by a collectivity of elites that was neither fully cohesive or disunified, but instead managed artfully by a paramount leader. At the same time, society remained quiescent, contained by corporatist institutions, legitimating mentalities, developmental performance, and coercion. However, the leader's industrializing strategies, finally tilting toward labor intensive manufacturing, altered the context in which social quiescence prevailed. Corporatism, mentalities, and coercion thus all lost effectiveness, while performance became most conspicuous for its inequalities. In this way, quiescent constituents grew poised for participation.

Indonesia thus also shows a way in which a pseudo-democracy can be changed. In particular, as economic crisis denied Suharto the capacity to dispense patronage and sanctions any longer, elites who had never gained full unity began now to divide in uncontrolled ways. Further, because Suharto then clung to power, and because elite divisions were more strongly made manifest in spiraling competitions between military hard-liners than any sustained appearance of soft-lining negotiators, the transition that took place involved a bottom-up replacement. Specifically, as divisions between elites grew wider, social forces were suddenly uncorked, producing student demonstrations, middle-class activism, and the violence of the urban poor. In this situation, with elites evaluating Suharto as endangering, rather than perpetuating their statuses, they abandoned him, forcing Suharto to step down and the transition to begin.

However, the concept of replacement implies a rapid and far-reaching transition which, in deeply threatening the interests of elites, grows vulnerable to authoritarian backlash, probably taking the form of an executive or military coup. Accordingly, it has been understood as the transitional pathway least likely to stabilize. But Habibie's presidency demonstrates the capacity of elites to regain some cohesion. They were then able to influence, if not closely to regulate, the pace and extent of the transition, thus obviating the need for any heavy-handed backlash. At the same time, social forces lost much of their participatory vigor, dissipating in petty factions, rival movements, and atomized attempts to cope with economic hardship. Thus, even while instituting civil liberties and scheduling elections, Habibie was able to perpetuate elite statuses. And though his ruling *Golkar* and, indeed, his own candidacy, were finally thwarted by founding elections, new oppositionists came to the fore who must be characterized as cautious reformers. In these circumstances, elite statuses persisted – giving Indonesia's new democracy unexpectedly good prospects for stabilizing.

However, during the first year in office of Habibie's successor, Abdurrahman Wahid, attempts were made to extend reforms, especially in terms of civil-military relations, administrative decentralization, and the relations between business and government. And in threatening elite interests, these reforms incurred destabilizing actions, making clear the tradeoffs between democratic quality and stability. Abdurrahman thus retreated, leaving the military to retain control over most of its internal dealings. Decentralization became a matter of widely dispersed negotiations, thereby appearing to meet the concerns of some regional elites, but also safeguarding the livelihoods of many Jakarta-based bureaucrats. And finally, through the IBRA, some gains were made in terms rationalizing the business scene, but not so many that the statuses of business elites were seriously diminished. In these circumstances, Indonesia's new democracy remained marred by low quality, but seemed likely to persist. Indeed, it was precisely because reforms were limited or rolled back that prospects for stability were improved. Few observers expect that Abdurrahman's successor, Megawati, will alter these patterns substantially.

Chapter 3

Singapore

—◆—

A Stable Semi-democracy

Singapore has attracted scholarly attention on a variety of counts, but two stand out. First, it has rapidly industrialized, then acquired a highly sophisticated service sector, thus earning its place as Southeast Asia's most developed country. Indeed, notwithstanding its limited technology gains and exposure to weak regional markets – its links to Indonesia's banking industry, in particular – Singapore has weathered the recent economic crisis while avoiding many painful adjustments. Second, despite the emergence of a large middle class and suggestions that society is generally growing more participatory, social forces have failed to cumulate in any strong pressures for democracy. Indeed, it may be precisely because the state is regarded as having so ably developed the economy, then safeguarded its gains, that social forces have been deterred from seeking any regime opening – thereby again confounding the modernizationists.

Accordingly, Singapore's size, level of development, social structure and a host of other factors render it quite unlike any other countries investigated in this volume. And given its anomalies, questions can rightfully be asked about how applicable Singapore's lessons might be to the rest of the region. We will see, however, that it is these contextual differences on one side, and some similarities in regime outcomes on the other that enable us to focus comparatively on the intervening role of elites. Singapore thus takes its place in this volume, although its analysis is comparatively brief.

Singapore in the region

Even amid Southeast Asia's much celebrated diversity, Singapore appears unique, thus seeming to limit the generalizations that can be made about its politics. Most obviously, Singapore is a small country – a mere city-state – its main island barely 30 miles across and containing a population of less than four million. Malaysia stands to the north, with a population nearly six times greater. Indonesia looms to the south, with a population more than 50 times greater. In addition, Singapore's ethnic composition is conceptualized

81

as three-quarters Chinese, making it the only country in the region with an ethnic Chinese majority.

These territorial and demographic factors have helped to shape Singapore's socioeconomic development. For example, unlike the rest of Southeast Asia, Singapore possesses few natural resources or even agricultural hinterland, thus denying it the farmer populations, rice culture, plantation sectors, and agribusiness that remain so vital elsewhere. Accordingly, Singapore has industrialized with greater urgency, commencing this process during the mid-1960s. Moreover, in doing this, the country's small domestic markets obviated any common strategy of import substitution, as well as the political contours and class structures that this model entails. Singapore had instead to export its manufactures right from the start, prompting it to gain competitiveness through efficient state enterprises and foreign investment.

In consequence, Singapore has been distinguished too by its "strong" state capacity, the large measure of foreign investment relative to GDP that it has attracted, and the high per capita income levels that have resulted, reaching US$33,000 in 1997.[1] Indeed, for many comparativists, Singapore's state strength has given it greater affinity with the NICs of Northeast Asia than with its neighbors in Southeast Asia.[2] Further, in exploiting it geographic location, Singapore has functioned since colonial times as the region's transshipment node, then forged ahead into financial services, casting itself as the "total business center" in order to host the regional headquarters of transnational companies. And yet, even while globalizing its economy, Singapore has remained politically insular, its small size and ethnic Chinese character engendering a deep sense of national vulnerability.

But if Singapore is distinctive in terms of its social and economic development, this helps nonetheless to underscore this book's methodological theme. In particular, despite the great socioeconomic differences between Singapore and the rest of the region, the country's politics display some important parallels with Malaysia, Thailand during the 1980s, and even New Order Indonesia.[3] More specifically, Singapore's government has regularly held elections, but limited civil liberties beforehand, thus ensuring its iterated return to power. Indeed, these procedures, amounting to a semi-democracy, were once ennobled as "Asian democracy" by Singapore's leader, Lee Kuan Yew, a notion that was readily embraced by some other leaders in the region, in particular, Mahathir Mohamad. Furthermore, Singapore's elites have blurred the lines between their ruling party, the state bureaucracy, and the commanding heights of the financial sector.[4] They have then developed their statuses within the close nexus between the ruling People's Action Party (PAP), key ministries, and the country's "big four" banks. Finally, Singapore's elites have managed social forces through top-down policies favoring the middle class, while imposing corporatist controls on ethnic communities and labor. They have alloyed these strategies also with strong developmentalist performance, legitimating mentalities, and coercion.

Thus, in analyzing Singapore, one is struck by the efficiency of its state interventions in the economy, the level of development that has resulted, its small population size, and its middle-class character. The regime's semi-democratic outcome, however, is more commonplace. Put simply, despite the great socioeconomic gulf that lies between Singapore and its neighbors, great similarities persist across their political regimes. Structures, culture, and modernizing processes are thus indeterminate, encouraging one to ascribe similarities in regime outcomes either to utter coincidence or deliberate elite choice. And in examining the leadership of Lee Kuan Yew and to some extent his successor, Goh Chok Tong, one can perhaps argue more forcefully here than in any other Southeast Asian setting for the preeminence of choice.

Inter-elite and elite-mass relations

During the colonial period, Singapore served as the commercial center for Britain's possessions on the Malayan peninsula. It was thus the staging ground for British capital investment that flowed up-country and the outlet for rubber and tin that flowed to markets overseas. Singapore and Malaya were thus characterized by different, if complementary economies, as well as inversely articulated social structures. However, as the British prepared to decolonize during the 1950s, they in some measured democratized the politics of both settings.

In introducing democratic procedures to Singapore during the 1950s, a competitive party system and vital trade union movement took root. Thus, through elections in 1959, Lee Kuan Yew led the PAP to power, a party joining English-educated, middle-class professionals and the representatives of Chinese-educated students and workers. However, the PAP was confronted by a stagnant economy, generating high rates of unemployment and ethnic tensions between the Chinese community and local Malays. It thus searched for a new industrializing strategy, settling finally on the import substitution that constituted the orthodoxy at that time for late-industrializing countries.

To increase the size and viability of its local market, Singapore's government proposed a "merger" with Malaya. The prime minister of Malaya, Tunku Abdul Rahman, responded favorably, calculating that he could balance the influx of Singapore's ethnic Chinese by at the same time including the indigenous populations of British possessions in northern Borneo. Thus, with British approval, the merger took place in 1963, with Malaya, Singapore, Sabah, and Sarawak forming the new Federation of Malaysia. This merger was an unhappy one, though, unable to resolve ethnic suspicions, especially at the elite level. Some Malay politicians campaigned in Singapore's legislative elections in 1963, stirring Malay grievances that helped later to trigger serious rioting. And during Malaysia's general election in 1964, Chinese politicians from Singapore, including Lee Kuan Yew, campaigned in Kuala Lumpur. Though they made little headway, Tunku Abdul Rahman was piqued. He then expelled Singapore from the federation in 1965.

Its import substitution thwarted, the PAP government searched for new strategies. It seized swiftly, then, upon export-oriented manufacturing. To do this, the government began by building up state capacity, creating a pilot agency, the Economic Development Board (EDB), through which to devise industrial policies. A range of statutory boards and state enterprises, known locally as government-linked companies, was then set up through which the state could undertake business activities. What stands out about these entities is their efficiency, indeed, their frequent profitability. But even more important for industrialization than this state investment was the foreign direct investment that Singapore attracted. Indeed, within the EDB lay the Special Projects Division, targeting new industries, forging linkages between them, then recruiting transnational firms.

Unable now to gain unhindered entry to the Malaysian market, the government had to provide an unusual set of incentives in order to attract foreign investors. First, state decision making was "insulated" from social forces, thus not only increasing efficiency, but avoiding official corruption.[5] More specifically, by regulating closely the volume of state contracts and by refusing to impose tariffs, bureaucrats were left with few favors to sell. Moreover, in disciplining the PAP's electoral activities, party officials solicited no "campaign contributions" from transnational firms. On the contrary, the government dramatically reduced corporate tax rates. And yet, it provided much infrastructural support – the power grids, telecommunications networks, transport hubs, and harbor facilities necessary for industrialization.

At the same time, the government refrained from promoting local business elites, largely confining Singapore's business activities to finance, property development, simple processing, and trading. This spared transnational firms even nominal competition in local manufacturing. In addition, the government closely modulated the work force. Specifically, it tamed the trade unions in order to make cheap labor available, at least during the early phases of industrialization. It later set up educational facilities, producing the managers, engineers, and professionals required by transnational corporations. In this way, though foreign investors have been permitted to repatriate their profits freely, they have left a residue of corporate taxes which, along with local executive salaries and wages, have enabled Singapore to prosper. Indeed, in November 1998, more than a year after the economic crisis first struck, foreign currency reserves stood at nearly US$75 billion, two-and-a-half times that of the Southeast Asian country with the next largest reserves, Thailand.[6]

In sum, in Singapore, the patterns of state power and social relations upon which foreign investment has depended involve first, a disciplined PAP and a highly structured, yet entrepreneurial bureaucracy. The party and bureaucracy thus form the twin organizational bases for elite statuses in Singapore, a configuration that better reflects the legacies of Singapore's socialist beginnings than the strict requirements of a Korean-style "hard" or developmental state. Further, these organizations sustain elites in the cabinet and upper echelons of the civil service, then swiftly converge beneath these platforms. What historically has been distinctive about this elite collectivity, however, has been the near absence of local conglomerates able to sustain business elites. Indeed, a common observation has been that Singapore's most entrepreneurial elements have been found in the bureaucracy, closely engaging foreign investors. Finally, Singapore's industrialization has required a well-trained, though politically passive middle class, much of which is likewise lodged in the bureaucracy, as well as a modestly waged, though motivated work force, available for employment by transnational firms. Thus, a steeply articulated socioeconomic structure has emerged in Singapore, yet one that as we shall see, while justifying inequalities with norms of consensus, has held out prospects for merit-based mobility.

Cohesive elites

After gaining internal self-government, Singapore featured a democratic regime. However, it was operated by elites who were disunified over game rules and policy visions, thus making it unstable. As we have seen, in forming the PAP, a faction of English-educated, middle-class professionals led by Lee Kuan Yew had coalesced with a another representing Chinese-educated students and workers. Together, they sought first to gain home rule from Britain, then to contest founding elections. However, after achieving these aims, the PAP's factions quickly turned against each other, then formally split in 1961. Thus, the middle-class professionals remained in power under Lee, retaining the PAP label. The local business and working-class faction formed the *Barisan Sosialis* (BS, Socialist Front), while going into opposition.

The PAP then strengthened its grip on state power, harassing the BS and the trade unions. Most dramatically, prior to elections in 1963, the PAP used the police special branch to mount a sweep called Operation Cold Store, "obliterat[ing] the BS's top level leadership."[7] And while it then won the elections, the PAP continued to jail opposition leaders and deregister trade unions until again holding elections five years later, a contest regarded as establishing Lee's paramountcy as national leader. In this way, with the

PAP's middle-class professionals and bureaucrats gaining ascendancy over the BS's Chinese-educated trade union leaders, Singapore's elite collectivity was made compact and cohesive. And in this way too, though the regime's democratic procedures were truncated, it reached equilibrium.

Within the PAP, elites have structured their interactions in deeply opaque ways. They have selected from among the party's base membership a small number of cadres who in turn vote for the party's central executive committee (CEC). The national leader, first Lee Kuan Yew, later Goh Chok Tong, then operated through this committee to make key bureaucratic appointments and select party candidates. Ooi Can Seng thus contends that "in a circular manner, the CEC is elected by selected members which the CEC must have approved before," inevitably giving rise to some cronyist exchanges.[8] Similarly, James Cotton characterizes the PAP as a "convenient electoral machine for maintaining in office an elite which is ultimately self-selected, self-promoted, and self-defined." During his tenure, Lee Kuan Yew stood "at the center of the network of patronage which the party exists to legitimize."[9] Nonetheless, the top appointees in Singapore's bureaucracy have generally been regarded as "talented." And the recruitment of candidates for parliament has been characterized by a concern for high educational and professional achievements. Without any broader account-ability to party members, the merit of these selection processes can only be attributed to uncommon leadership preferences, externalized norms, and processes of elite socialization.[10]

At the same time, we have seen that since the end of merger and the loss of ready access to Malaysian markets, elites in the PAP and the bureaucracy have favored transnational firms over local business. From the start, they doubted the political loyalties of local business which, after severing its ties to British capital during the 1960s turned frequently to the *Barisan Sosialis*. Though socialist, the BS appeared at least to be nationalist. In addition, Singapore's elites remained unimpressed by local management styles and technologies. Hence, they sought to encourage large-scale manufacturing and exports to the West, rather than the small-time banking and property development in which local business tended to cluster. During the mid-1980s, though, Singapore's Western markets began to slump amid global recession, causing the economy to contract. And in these circumstances, elites took a new look at local business, recognizing its potential to tap existing networks of Overseas Chinese, then boost Singapore's trade and investment within the region, producing the country's "second wing."[11] The PAP thus formed new committees through which to convene local chambers of commerce and employers' associations, seeking their inputs into plans for greater regional integration. The PAP began also to admit local business people directly into its own organization, even recruiting some directors of Singaporean companies as candidates for parliament. However, this progress may have been slowed by the recent economic crisis, with Singapore's traditional Western markets having fared better than its new regional ones. The country's elite collectivity must thus be regarded as still made up principally of top position holders in the PAP and the bureaucracy. And since the late 1960s, their interactions have never been less than tightly cohesive.

Quiescent, but sophisticated social forces

Singapore's elites, in confronting social forces, resorted first to controlling labor through corporatist controls. During the 1960s, then, independent unions were closed, and their workers absorbed into the state-sponsored National Trades Union Congress (NTUC) or dispersed across in-house unions. But the coercion associated with corporatist organizing has also been tempered with populist benefits – a strategy that has been facilitated by, but has also contributed to, the rapid industrialization that Singapore has undergone. Thus, while prohibiting central bargaining and strike action, the National Wages Council has granted steady pay increases and year-end lump sums to the workers in NTUC affiliates. In addition to easing worker grievances, this strategy has helped to phase out labor-intensive industries, thus attracting transnational firms geared to higher technologies and value-added production. Further, through the Housing and Development Board, the PAP has offered working-class families public accommodation (while threatening to cut funds and take back units for development projects)."[12] It has also offered working-class children subsidized education (while heavily shaping their curriculum and steering them away from universities into polytechnic and vocational training). And finally, the PAP has grudgingly subsidized basic medical care (while quashing any notion of broader social welfare schemes). In sum, Singapore has imposed corporatist controls upon its workers. Yet, through the redistribution of some of the surpluses earned through its rapid industrialization, workers have also been placated.[13]

David Brown observes that in many respects the government has extended these corporatist techniques into the realm of ethnic identities.[14] During merger with Malaysia, Singapore's elites stressed "multiracial" tolerance, but carried out affirmative action programs by which to uplift the Malays. However, in a harsher setting after merger had ended, elites emphasized the need for merit-based competition. Thus, while avoiding discrimination against ethnic communities, they ceased their pro-Malay policies. And hence, amid the worsening disparities that followed, Singapore's elites confronted new social tensions. In this situation, though allocating public housing in ways that avoided ethnic ghettos, and setting up electoral constituencies that avoided marginalization, elites discovered limits to the effectiveness of their integrative approach. New policy orientations thus reinforced ethnic identities, involving a corporatism that was reflected even in the state-sanctioned formation of "community self-help organizations."[15] In particular, the state engaged the Chinese community through the Chinese Development Assistance Council. It reissued some benefits to the Malays through the *Mendaki* program. And it approached the Indian community through the Singapore Indian Development Agency.

Singapore's elites have also reinforced their corporatist organizing with legitimating mentalities. As a new country made up predominantly of migrant populations, local traditions available for reinvention have been scarce. And until recently, elites avoided tapping the deeper cultural heritage of the Chinese mainland for fear that this would spotlight the oddity of their own English-language backgrounds and hence, the inappropriateness of their leading Chinese-educated constituencies. Accordingly, elites have emphasized themes able to unify different linguistic groups and classes, namely, the threats posed by outsiders to Singapore's well-being. This produced a "state of siege" outlook after Singapore was expelled from Malaysia, followed by the more regularized "garrison mentality" of a small Chinese island in a "sea of Malays."[16] During the 1980s, though, threats to Singapore came less from Malay neighbors and mainland traditions than invidious Western cultures, seen subtly to be eroding the country's work ethic and international competitiveness. More specifically, Singapore faced the twin evils of Western liberalism and welfarism, with elites attempting to counter them now by placing new value on traditional Chinese norms of consensus and family responsibility. As elites elaborated these notions into a mentality, they urged local Chinese to augment their dialects with Mandarin and rediscover the virtues of Confucianism. Indeed, an Institute of East Asian Philosophies was set up to disseminate these cues and give them scholarly standing.

These early efforts to counter Western culture, however, failed to resonate with social forces, often mystifying the Chinese, while arousing ethnic Malay and Indian suspicions. Hence, Singapore's elites commissioned their ideologues more simply, yet widely to energize constituencies, relaxing their insistence on Mandarin, then finding in Islam some collectivist virtues matching those of Confucianism. Indeed, Singapore soon set the pace in elaborating "Asian values" – a code by which steeply paternalistic hierarchies were made acceptable through broad-based consensus. A more finely articulated notion of "shared" or "core values" was then heralded as a "national ideology," exalting country above community, society above self, and family as the most basic social unit.[17] In doing this, Singapore mapped out the route by which to compete with the West, thus perpetuating economic expansion and prosperity. Moreover, this mentality had a political guise, Asian democracy, with civil liberties made redundant by consensus and elections merely registering the popularity of indispensible incumbent governments.[18] Hence, in providing some political legitimacy without risk, some feedback in the form of fluctuating margins of electoral victory, and the means by which ideologically to defy the West, this notion of Asian democracy was readily taken up, indeed, further embroidered, by the national leaders of neighboring countries.

But more important than corporatist organizing and legitimating mentalities has doubtless been Singapore's record of development. We have seen the ways in which economic growth has made possible a variety of populist programs which, in their shrewd execution, have extended growth. But economic expansion has also opened broad avenues by which social forces have been able to fulfill many of their careerist and consumerist longings. And however fleeting, it is the intense and replicable joy of such pursuits that helps to dissuade middle-class Singaporeans from challenging the government – even as they learn to lobby mildly through conservationist groups, women's organizations, and the arts community.[19] Many observers have noted in the Singapore setting a syndrome of middle-class "*kiasu*-ism," an acceptance of ruthless personal advancement and rapacious acquisition so long as one outwardly remains anonymous and conformist.[20] As made manifest in consumerism, one finds an anxiousness, a compulsion to shop with greater sophistication than one's peers, a desire made keen by close living in housing estates, and irrepressible by the absence of safe outlets for political activism. Indeed, to see how effective elites have been in plugging political outlets with consumer goods, one need only to visit the malls along Singapore's boulevards, especially during Christmas in Confucian, indeed, episodically anti-Christian Singapore. Shopping has also been a main motivation for the government's envisioning an "intelligent island," wiring the country's 750,000 households to the internet in order to boost e-commerce.[21]

Finally, of course, for social forces impervious to corporatist controls, legitimating mentalities, and developmental opportunities there remains in Singapore – as surely as in New Order Indonesia or Malaysia – a fair measure of coercion. Indeed, political activism in Singapore risks black-listing, shunning, lawsuits, tax investigations, lost business opportunities, and detention without trial. We will explore this dimension more fully in the following discussion on regime type.

Semi-democratic regime outcome

Since the late 1960s, elites in the PAP and bureaucracy have maintained their deep cohesion. Hence, in eschewing purges and competitive social mobilizations, they have avoided the coups and uprisings that are the hallmarks of political instability. Indeed, among the countries examined in this volume, Singapore's elites doubtless operate the regime that has been most stable.

Let us focus in this section, then, on the regime's semi-democratic character. Singapore's elites, in unveiling the notion of Asian democracy, have tapped the nearly universal legitimacy that democracy seems now to command, as well as some regional sanction for authoritarian controls. In doing this, the government has remained vigilant toward the dangers of liberalism and majoritarianism. In its view, liberalism risks puncturing the consensus upon which social hierarchies must rest. Majoritarian principles threaten merit, offering a route by which less meritorious populations can band together in demanding welfare. Indeed, in a worst-case situation, majorities could even turn out the government, delivering state power into less competent hands. Hence, to retain its grip on the state and perpetuate development, Singapore's elites have limited civil liberties and truncated electoral procedures, tapering their democracy of the 1960s into semi-democracy.

Civil liberties

With respect to civil liberties, the government has tightly controlled information flows, reinforcing its legal restrictions with distinctive patterns of media ownership. In brief, the Newspaper and Printing Press Act of 1974, passed initially to ward off foreign influences, imposes a basic legal framework, requiring the local print media to enhance "the unity of Singaporeans." News coverage and advertisements thus emphasize the virtues of patriotism, courteousness, speaking Mandarin, and rearing families. To ensure this mission's success, a publicly listed company called Singapore Press Holdings owns all of Singapore's daily newspapers. And though its equity is prized by foreign mutual funds, it features also a category of management shares with special voting rights that can only be held by nominees of the Ministry of Information and Arts.[22] In addition, while registered opposition parties are permitted to circulate their own papers – the Workers' Party publishing *The Hammer* and the Singapore Democratic Party *The New Democrat*, for example – they attract few advertisers, and their formats pale alongside the "sleekly produced" *Petir* (Thunderbolt) of the PAP.[23] Furthermore, though foreign publications are available in Singapore, those that report on local affairs are regularly obliged to carry government rebuttals lest they face limits on advertising and circulation or even outright bans. Finally, with respect to electronic communications, the government requires that persons and organizations operating websites on the internet that carry political, ethnic, or religious content register with the Singapore Broadcasting Authority. Political videotapes, further, are prohibited. And though Singapore is a major manufacturer of satellite dishes for export, Singaporeans are barred from owning them.[24]

While limiting communication, the government has also imposed controls on assembly. As mentioned above, the government began with organized labor shortly after Singapore's expulsion from Malaysia, incorporating highly politicized unions into the state-sponsored National

Trades Union Congress. The NTUC leader, a member of the PAP, has been brought into the fold as a cabinet minister. Likewise, other top NTUC officials have been given positions in key government agencies like the EDB and the Housing and Development Board (HDB).[25] The country's workers, meanwhile, though generally awarded adequate pay scales by the National Wages Council and housing by the HDB are prevented from bargaining collectively over conditions or wages. Indeed, one of the hallmarks of Singapore's industrializing strategies has involved its labor controls, readying the country's work force for transnational firms.[26]

In addition, the government introduced the Societies Act in 1967, registering all voluntarist groups, then discriminating sharply between those geared to political and nonpolitical activities. For example, when the Law Society attempted to comment on amendments to the Newspaper and Printing Presses Act that were introduced in 1986, the government warned expressly against professional organizations participating in politics. It then set up a rival Academy of Law – amply illustrating that a "denser" civil society, far from spawning new liberalism, may open new conduits of state control.[27] Further, the government has focused particularly closely on political cooperation across class lines – especially when alloyed with ideology or religion. In 1975, after student activists called attention to the plight of workers who had been retrenched, the government brought the National University of Singapore's Student Union under the watchful eye of the education ministry – paralleling the new assertiveness of education ministries in Malaysia and Indonesia during this time. In 1987, the government arrested 22 members of Catholic Church organizations who had promoted middle-class awareness of the conditions endured by foreign workers, charging them with plotting a Marxist revolt. The government carried out these detentions through the Internal Security Act (ISA), its bluntest weapon against autonomous participation. Anxious to gain a finer legal grounding, however, the government then passed the Maintenance of Religious Harmony Act in 1990, reinforcing the "separation of religious faith and social activism."[28] Legal bans have also been imposed on performance art and forum theater, "non-scripted art forms" that are prone to spontaneous political messages.

It is important to note, however, that while the government has dampened free assembly through legal codes and coercion, it has attempted also to display responsiveness. Ministerial "walkabouts" were introduced in 1982, while PAP parliamentarians hold weekly "meet-the-people" sessions. Ooi Can Seng also catalogues a range of officially sanctioned "grass roots organizations" including Residents' Committees, the People's Association, and Citizens' Consultative Committees. Within these arenas, PAP parliamentarians seek to explain government policies, local residents make some responses, and "recreational, welfare, and social needs" are met.[29] Further, Community Development Councils were introduced in 1996, strengthening these grass roots organizations and facilitating new services such as upgrading housing estates and providing child-care centers.

The government has also innovated some mechanisms that have more closely targeted the middle class, dissuading it from participating in more autonomous ways.[30] The Feedback Unit was set up in 1985 under the auspices of the Ministry of Community Development, inviting middle-class views. Government Parliamentary Committees were introduced in 1987, opening up still more consultative arenas. And the Institute of Policy Studies was created in 1988, organizing seminars and lectures. However, while Singapore is surely distinguished in the region by these many innovative arenas for assembly, there are doubts about how much the government values the inputs and feedback that it obtains. As Prime Minister Goh Chok Tong once lamented, "People think you just open up the space . . . and Singapore will be well run because the best ideas will emerge . . . How many people have the time to read through the papers . . . do you think they have the time to reflect?"[31]

Electoral contestation

Singapore's government has not been content to restrict civil liberties. It has steadily narrowed the regime's electoral dimension too. To be sure, formal elections have been regularly held since the 1950s. Further, their procedures have been exhaustively recorded in the Parliamentary Elections Act, thereby posing a nonpartisanship that would seem to level many of the advantages enjoyed by the PAP. As we have seen, campaign contributions are sharply restricted. Vote-buying and even party funding for transporting voters – so prevalent in the region's "fuller" democracies in the Philippines and Thailand – appear never to take place. Campaign rallies are vigorous and serious events, while voting is compulsory. Election day, then, presents the snapshot of propriety that is characteristic of a stable semi-democracy.

But what renders a semi-democracy something less than full democracy is that in addition to the limits imposed on civil liberties, opposition parties are systematically impaired before election day arrives. Garry Rodan notes that in Singapore, qualified persons are strongly discouraged from joining the opposition: "In a city-state where the government is not only a substantial employer, but also the major dispenser of commercial contracts, there is a perception that careers and business interests can easily be jeopardized by association, however indirect, with opposition parties."[32] The government also regularly files lawsuits against opposition party leaders for libel or, more deviously, supports these leaders in suing one another, as it did during the struggle between the Singapore Democratic Party and the Singapore People's Party during the mid-1990s.[33] On this count, Ooi records an illuminating response made by Goh Chok Tong when asked why he did not react promptly to allegations made against the PAP by an opposition candidate, Tan Liang Hong, during campaigning for the 1997 general elections: "I did not want to answer all these because I was hoping that he would go further by our silence and then libel the Minister for National Development or myself or whoever he wants to libel."[34]

What is more, the government has practiced much gerrymandering, dispersing pockets of opposition support. At the same time, it has fashioned most wards into "group representation constituencies," that is, multi-member districts contestable only by slates of up to six candidates with at least one drawn from an ethnic minority group, thus imposing a nettlesome requirement that tests further the opposition's scant resources. The government has also called elections with great suddenness, typically a year or two before the end of its term, then permitted no more than the nine days required by law for campaigning. Further, the government controlled media gives far more attention to PAP candidates than it does to opposition parties. Finally, questions have been raised also about the secrecy of balloting. The number of counting centers has been steadily increased, enabling the preferences of particular residential areas easily to be identified. The ballots also each contain a numbered counterfoil, allowing an even finer trace.[35]

Notwithstanding these electoral controls, opposition parties made steady gains against the PAP during the past two decades. Appealing to middle-class irritation over meddlesome public policies that have ranged from eugenics to gum sales, as well as to more recent working-class grievances over cost-of-living increases, opposition parties have won nearly 40 per cent of the popular vote. The government thus lost a by-election in 1981, bringing the first opposition MP – Joshua Jayaretnam of the Workers' Party – into parliament since the 1960s. A second opposition member entered parliament in the election of 1984, and a total of four appeared in 1991.

Of course, this vote should not be interpreted as any groundswell in support of government turnover. In surveying the region, Singaporeans recognize that they have made too many gains to put them at risk. They seek at most a stronger opposition through which to vent discontents and check PAP policies. Still, the government frets over a "freak result" and its loss of power. It thus admonishes voters over their responsibilities, and then, in a twist, establishes mechanisms by which to hold *voters* accountable. For example, beginning in 1986, the government has been placing parliamentarians on Town Councils that are responsible for urban services, then warning voters that opposition MPs will be unable to deliver. Nonetheless, in the 1991 election the opposition countered with its most effective campaign strategy ever, winning four seats by contesting in less than a majority of districts, thereby assuring beforehand the government's victory. In short, the government sought to blunt the opposition's electoral appeal by sharing some real power. The opposition made some electoral gains by refusing to take it.

In these circumstances, the government has introduced still more electoral innovations. In particular, just as the government deactivated civil society by setting up corporatist groups, so has it sought to weaken political society by fabricating an artificial opposition. Thus, in 1984, it introduced a category of "non-constituency MPs," carefully summoning up to three defeated opposition candidates to appear in parliament. In 1990, it created an even more rootless category of "nominated" parliamentarians, recruiting up to six eminent, though nonpartisan persons from the professions or business. Together, these MPs have been permitted to engage in parliamentary debates and thus to "sharpen up" government MPs, but they have been prevented from voting against the government on money and constitutional bills or from mobilizing mass followings through opposition appeals.[36]

Finally, when the opposition attempted to repeat its 1991 strategy in the 1997 general election – again contesting less than half the parliamentary seats – Goh Chok Tong responded forcefully. After having promised a more caring leadership than that which had been exercised by his predecessor, Lee Kuan Yew, he now threatened bureaucratic retribution. Specifically, he vowed to suspend housing "upgrade programs" in wards that failed to return the PAP. "They'll become slums. That's my message," he intoned.[37] What is more, just weeks before election day, the number of candidates required for many of the group representation constituencies was increased from four to fuller complements of five or six, sharply raising the bar for the opposition.[38] Indeed, this combination of bureaucratic partisanship and procedural manipulation brought the PAP great electoral success, enabling it to reverse the decline in popular vote totals that it had been suffering since 1980. It thus won 82 of the 83 seats in the parliament. One notes also that when presidential elections were held in 1999, the screening measures attached to candidates were so stringent – requiring candidates to have served as top-level bureaucrats or business executives – that the Council of Presidential Advisors approved the candidacy of only one figure, closely identified with the PAP.

In concluding this section, one might ask what really is achieved by Singapore's holding general elections? Since the end of the colonial period, the government has steadily limited civil liberties and curbed electoral procedures – to the extent that it must create a surrogate opposition to stand in for the one that it has nearly extinguished. Elections do little, then, to hold the government accountable. Nor do they even provide accurate feedback to the government about social discontents. When Goh Chok Tong threatened to turn the wards voting against him into slums, he could hardly expect the electorate to register any sentiment but fear. However, if elections in Singapore do not permit opposition parties and social forces to challenge the government squarely, they do enable elites in the PAP to contest peacefully against one another. In short, elections contain the rare strain points that test the party's central executive committee. A vignette from the early 1990s helps to illustrate this.

In 1990, Lee Kuan Yew retired as prime minister. He was succeeded by Goh Chok Tong, then a top bureaucrat, while Lee's son, Lee Hsien Loong, became deputy prime minister. In 1991, Goh called snap elections, seeking power in his own right and some "breathing space from [his deputy] whose rise to the top spot appear[ed] inevitable."[39] However, the PAP slipped from the 63 per cent of the popular vote that it had garnered in 1988 to 61 percent this time round, thus adding to the assessment often made of Goh that he was merely a "seat-warmer."[40] The election showed also that the PAP was losing more support in working-class districts than in middle-class ones, prompting Lee Kuan Yew publicly to "lecture" Goh about speaking more Mandarin and reading Chinese newspapers.[41] Hence, in a quest for "self-renewal," Goh resigned from his seat in 1992 and staged a by-election in his multi-member district of Marine Parade. In a "resounding win,"[42] Goh took 72.9 per cent of the vote. For governments that refuse to hold elections, there can be no resounding wins, thus suggesting negatively the value of elections even in semi-democracies. In this instance, they enabled Goh Chok Tong to secure his tenure for at least another decade, while his reprover, Lee Kuan Yew, shifted his criticisms to neighboring countries.

Conclusions

Although Singapore possesses many contextual factors that are quite unlike those of other countries in the region, its regime shares many similarities with the pseudo- and semi-democracies of New Order Indonesia, Malaysia since the early 1970s, and Thailand during the 1980s. As such, Singapore offers an opportunity to focus comparatively on the intervening role of elites, mediating contextual diversity into similar politics. In Singapore, elites have been assessed by most analysts as tightly cohesive, thereby stabilizing their regime. And because they have perpetuated the quiescence of social forces, even as modernization has taken place, they have been able to scale back their regime to a semi-democracy. Indeed, it is only because the government merely contains opposition parties, rather than intervening more deeply in their internal affairs, that we are prevented from classifying the regime as pseudo-democratic. Accordingly, Singapore has avoided the practice of New Order Indonesia whereby opposition parties, funded mostly by the state, were expected to reciprocate by joining in the nominating of Suharto for president. Instead, Singapore's opposition parties have often boldly confronted the PAP – though at great personal cost and with little political effect.

However, some observers suggest also that as Singapore's economy and social structure continue to evolve, elites in the PAP and the bureaucracy, even if remaining cohesive, will be forced to democratize their regime more fully. Let us very briefly consider what forms these challenges might take and what the commensurate prospects for fuller democracy might be.

Structuralists and modernization theorists generally invoke the changing requirements of maturing capital and the restlessness of the middle class as finally loosening the grip of authoritarian governments. Most close observers of the Singapore scene, however, doubt the applicability of this thesis. The country has rapidly industrialized and boosted its financial sector by skillfully engaging foreign investors, not by nurturing local business. They have argued also that with much of the middle class grounded in salaried bureaucratic positions, rather than flourishing in individualized professional life or business entrepreneurship, it possesses little incentive to democratize.[43] Indeed, the participatory impulse of civil society reverberates only weakly in Singapore through conservationist groups and women's organizations.

If not the bourgeoisie or the middle class, what then of Singapore's working class, its contributions to compulsory superannuation schemes helping subsidize the infrastructural demands of foreign investors? Cho-oon Khong warns explicitly that "as the state's corporatist organization of society comes under increasing strain, the state finds it difficult to keep its co-opted organizations under control. Coordination of policy becomes more difficult too, as does winning compliance."[44] In these circumstances, while workers still respond to government threats to withdraw populist benefits, they grow steadily more resentful, perhaps one day tilting toward the opposition. But in a sense, the government has already faced its greatest test posed by labor. For three decades, workers have been employed in large assembly plants, ones that have usually been owned by foreigners, potentially deepening their grievances. But despite the comparative ease with which workers could in these conditions have been mobilized, they have remained incorporated and placated. And if now their resentments are mounting, this takes place at precisely the moment in which they are being dispersed across smaller production sites, geared increasingly to information technologies and services. Hong Kong's experience demonstrates well the ease with which labour is weakened when industrial processes are decentralized.

Finally, W.G. Huff has noted Singapore's declining measures of total factor productivity (TFP), attributable to its failure to gain technology transfers from the foreign investors it attracts. Thus, to prolong its economic growth, Singapore must inspire greater "economic creativity." One way to achieve this, notes Huff, would be for Singapore's government "to give way to political liberalization."[45] And indeed, the country's small local businesses, especially in high-tech sectors, clamor regularly for the loosening of state controls, hoping to bolster their statuses and competitiveness. But Huff notes also that Singapore may choose a different route by which to raise TFP. Rather than easing its political controls, it may redouble its promotion of selected individuals. He quotes Lee Kuan Yew: "There are relatively few people who are above average. It can only be the task of the government to find those few and then to say: Go!"[46] In a similar vein, Rodan recounts the ways in which Singapore is busily transforming itself into an "information hub." While business is given free access to satellite television, ordinary viewers are confined to "more content-controllable" cable TV.[47] And while households are wired to the internet, many transmissions are effectively monitored, filtered, and blocked. Finally, for those who still doubt the capacity of Singapore's elites to finesse the contradictions between globalized processes and local controls, consider their management of the recent economic crisis. Though extending a "second wing" deep into Malaysia and troubled Indonesia, countries whose economies contracted sharply in 1998, Singapore escaped with the briefest of downticks. This comparative performance appears to have done much to revitalize public recognition of the capacities of elites in the PAP and the bureaucracy, thus easing pressures for their greater accountability. But the next general election, due to be called before early January 2002, will, like previous elections, only partly reveal mass sentiments.

Chapter 4

Malaysia

——◆◆——

Semi-democracy with Strain Points

Politics in Malaysia can be conceptualized in terms of a steep pyramid, similar in some respects to the one we have explored in New Order Indonesia. At its apex looms a national leader, Mahathir Mohamad, tightly concentrating state power in his prime ministerial office, then dispensing benefits to elites in patrimonialist ways. Further, he has incorporated social forces into ruling party apparatuses, crafted mentalities based on ethnicity, Islam, and "Asian values," generated a record of developmental performance, yet also resorted at many junctures to coercion. And finally, while he has regularly held elections – within his own party, as well as for parliament – he has conducted them in ways that must be regarded as semi-democratic.

But if these features bear parallels to those of New Order Indonesia, Mahathir has also been more constrained in his behaviors by elites, social forces, and the regime form itself that these categories have produced. In brief, he has not been so able to manage elites as Suharto once did, poising them on the knife's edge between unity and disunity. Instead, elites have perpetuated a legacy of cohesiveness that in many respects antedates Mahathir. And in then waging their factional competitions, even if bounded, they have sometimes tested Mahathir's paramountcy. Indeed, until his ouster, Suharto never confronted the kind of elite-level challenges that Mahathir has, posed first by his trade and industry minister, later by his deputy and finance minister.

Furthermore, Mahathir was central in implementing a complex set of socioeconomic policies which, in its partial fulfillment, has fed back to ring him tightly with new social pressuress. In particular, more than simply quickening industrialization, Mahathir has sought to promote indigenous Malays in business. We recall that in Indonesia, Suharto admitted only a few members of the indigenous community to the economy's commanding heights, namely, his relatives, the bureaucratic families, and some well-connected contractors. Instead, through a primitive, but effective approach, he mostly recruited Chinese to carry out industrialization, knowing that no

99

matter how rich they might get, they could never challenge him politically because of their ethnicity. In Malaysia, however, Mahathir systematically invoked programs of reverse discrimination, their directives and quotas known collectively as the New Economic Policy (NEP). And the aim of this policy was to stay the Chinese, while "breeding" Malay capitalists.

In doing this, however, Mahathir changed the context in which social attitudes are formed, thus inviting new challenges to his regime. During the 1970s–80s, while the NEP advanced the Malays and surely re-energized their support, Chinese grievances swelled inversely. And during the 1980s–90s, more fundamental challenges emerged from within the Malay community, finally confronting Mahathir with the test that Suharto had feared most. Specifically, while the NEP had at first placated the Malays, it imbued them with heightened expectations, organizational know-how, and corporate self-confidence. But during periods of economic downturn – when patronage and business opportunities grew scarce, and burdens were unevenly shared – many of them shed their quiescence in order to demand Mahathir's ouster and even a change of regime. Further, as these challenges matured, they evoked new social forces, specifically, the new middle class, civil society, youth cultures, and several kinds of Islamic revivalists.

In responding to these elite- and mass-level challenges, Mahathir has also been constrained by some electoral processes associated with his regime. We are reminded that regimes are best understood as outcomes, their institutions the product of inter-elite and elite-mass relations. But over time, they may gain an integrity that filters back at least modestly to inform elite behaviors. On this score, one notes that Mahathir has doubtless debased many of his country's key institutions, most notably the parliament, judiciary, the press, the police, and the monarchy. And yet, in defending his leadership before elites, he has had still to wage electoral contests within the United Malays National Organization (UMNO), the dominant party within the ruling *Barisan Nasional* (National Front). And in defending his prime ministership before social forces, he has had regularly to lead the *Barisan* in general elections. To be sure, these elections have been preceded by many controls that have greatly advantaged Mahathir. This is, after all, the hallmark of semi-democracy. But Mahathir has had no military delegates, regional representatives, or functional groups to tap at the UMNO general assembly, as Suharto once did in the MPR. And in preparing for general elections, if Mahathir has used the police special branch to gauge voter sentiments, it is difficult to imagine his calling upon the army commander to campaign for the *Barisan* in the way Suharto's General Hartono once did for the *Golkar* in 1997, donning the party's yellow jacket, sitting on the dais alongside Tutut, and declaring all soldiers to be *Golkar* cadres.[1]

Hence, in Malaysia, UMNO assembly elections and general elections have been contested respectively by powerful factions and feisty oppositions. And in these circumstances, not all top posts in the UMNO's party apparatus have been won by Mahathir's favorites. Nor in general elections have all parliamentary seats and state assemblies been won by the *Barisan*. Of course, this has failed to cumulate in any leadership change, much less any change of regime type. But electoral processes have served nonetheless to register the grievances of elites and social forces, thereby constraining Mahathir, at least moderately, in his political maneuverings and policy choices. By contrast, in navigating Indonesian elections, Suharto long enjoyed plain sailing, securing MPR unanimity and bureaucratic monoloyalty, while disembodying the floating mass.

This chapter begins by providing some background, first describing British colonial policies and the contextual factors that resulted. It does this in some detail, because continuities with the colonial period are perhaps more pronounced in Malaysia than in any other Southeast Asian country. Put simply, this chapter argues that while the British helped unify local elites, they divided ethnic communities, thus dooming their last-minute efforts to institute democratic procedures. Indeed, while elites were able to perpetuate democracy for more than a decade after independence, they were abandoned finally by their respective ethnic constituencies during the 1969 elections. And amid the mass-level violence that followed, elites closed the regime, reorganized their relations, and re-energized Malay loyalties through the NEP. Only then were they were able to restore the regime to at least a semi-democratic posture, one that has persisted for more than a quarter-century.

Next, this chapter investigates the two most important arenas in which Malaysia's semi-democratic politics are conducted, the UMNO assembly elections and general elections – the rough counterparts, perhaps, to the MPR and DPR elections in New Order Indonesia. In UMNO elections, the party's leader and elites compete for top posts in the party apparatus. In then waging general elections, they lead the *Barisan* in competing for mass support across a wider, multi-ethnic electorate. This chapter also considers the impact of the recent economic crisis on Malaysian politics, showing that despite the tensions between Mahathir and his deputy, elite cohesion has broadly persisted – much in contrast to elites in Indonesia who, while once artfully managed, so rapidly unraveled. Finally, to demonstrate the persistence of Malaysia's semi-democracy, indeed, its "high quality," this chapter provides an analysis of the 1999 general elections.

Malaysia in the region: colonial distinctions

The British formally colonized the territory of Malaya for less than a century, but left behind important residues in the economy, society, and politics. To begin, they geared the economy to commodities production, mostly rubber and tin, then opened it to outside forces, especially foreign investment, labor migration, and export markets. Throughout much of its colonial record, then, Malaya featured one of the most open economies in the world. However, the British also created a pattern of state interventions, enabling them to reserve the best agricultural land and most promising tin fields for British-owned plantation and mining companies. Further, in order to avoid overproduction, they shifted indigenous Malay cultivators from rubber to *padi*.[2] And they imposed various restriction schemes whenever the price of rubber needed additional support. Similarly, the British passed legislation to protect colonial tin smelting interests from foreign, principally American competition.[3] They also invoked a broader imperial preference during the 1930s, barring the importation of textiles from Japan in order to tilt the market toward British manufacturers. Jomo K.S. thus concludes that "Britain's commitment to free trade was only in so far as it served its own interests. . . .[W]hen capitalists of other nationalities began to pose a serious challenge to British interests in this free-trade situation, the colonial government did not hesitate to violate its espoused commitment to this 'cherished principle.'"[4]

While developing Malaya's economy in these ways, the British also created a "divided" or "plural" society – rendering ethnicity a more pressing factor, perhaps, than in any other Southeast Asian setting.[5] First, the British recruited a small number of indigenous and hence, "sovereign" Malays nominally to operate the state apparatus. Nine traditional sultans thus served as the heads of state, while lesser aristocrats were sprinkled throughout the bureaucracy's lower echelons. Mass-level Malays, for their part, were confined to peasant agriculture and fishing. Next, to work the tin mines that Malay small holders and fishers rarely entered, the British encouraged the mass migration of Chinese. In this way, some Chinese rose to gain ownership over the mines, then used debt bondage and secret societies to enforce labor discipline among their countrymen. However, as the British introduced more capital intensive methods, they wrested away ownership, now prodding the Chinese into revenue farming, commercial trading, and urban artisanry. Finally, because the British had owned most rubber estates from the start – thus dampening the acquisitive hopes of the Chinese and discouraging their seeking work in this sector – they relied upon ethnic Indians as tappers. Thus, long after independence, most Indians remained on these estates, even if some in their community gravitated to new factory places, scaled the trade union hierarchies, or rose in the professions.

A shrill polemic persists over whether the British adopted a cynical strategy of divide and rule or a more functional one of ethnic and occupational harmonization.[6] On a more theoretical plane, questions have also arisen over whether ethnic identities are reflexively primordial or filtered rationally through class fractions.[7] Either way, colonial policies and the identities they created helped to shape Malaysian society profoundly, thus limiting the possibilities for democracy. As Rabushka and Shepsle have observed in their study of developing countries with divided societies, elections become censuses that crystallize political inequalities, worsening ethnic tensions, sparking social violence, and finally breaking down democratic regimes.[8]

Nonetheless, in preparing to decolonize Malaya during the 1950s, the British abandoned their pre-War authoritarian controls in order now to institute a democracy. Doubtless they were motivated in part by a desire to shield their investments from unchecked local governments. They wished also to contrast their new electoral principles with the violence of the Communist insurgency that raged at the time ("fictionalized as the 'Emergency' primarily for the purposes of insurance claims"[9]). Hence, the British exposed local elites to consociational methods through a series of Communities Liaison Committee meetings.[10] They at the same time consented to the formation of political parties. And then, in careful increments, the British organized local elections in Penang in 1951, in Kuala Lumpur in 1952, and finally an election for the federal council in 1955, the forerunner of a national parliament. Independence was granted in 1957.

But the party system that emerged remained tethered to the underlying socioeconomic structures. In brief, Malay civil servants and peasants gathered in the UMNO, expressly to protect their "special rights" against Chinese interlopers. Big Chinese traders formed the Malayan (later Malaysian) Chinese Association (MCA) in order to defend their business interests. And Indian leaders formed the Malayan (ie, Malaysian) Indian Congress (MIC), hoping to gain a toehold in both politics and the economy. Indeed, so firmly intertwined were these parties and ethnic identities that the efforts by some local elites to uncouple them, even when encouraged by the occasionally contrite British, were spurned by other elites and mass-level constituents. Most notably, when the UMNO founder and president, Dato' Onn, tried to open his party to Chinese members in 1950, he met with such protest that he resigned. And his subsequent attempts to build a multi-ethnic Independence of Malaya Party (IMP) failed utterly to attract electoral support.[11]

In these circumstances, elites continued to galvanize constituent loyalties through ethnic appeals and parties. However, they learned also to cooperate autonomously across ethnic lines, finally solidifying their relations through a party coalition. Specifically, in an arrangement known informally as the "the bargain" and recorded obliquely in the constitution, elites shared out the resources that had been apportioned to them by the British. Malay elites in the UMNO, now led by Tunku Abdul Rahman, held most state power, filling the prime ministership and staffing the bureaucracy. And Chinese elites in the MCA operated those economic sectors not controlled by foreign, mainly British investors. Moreover, in then exchanging resources, top UMNO officials gained some personal wealth through special share issues and directorships in Chinese-owned companies. They also set up several state programs like the Rural and Industrial Development Authority through which to promote a limited number of mass-level Malays in small business. In turn, top MCA officials became ministers of finance and commerce, while limited numbers of Chinese were employed in the bureaucracy's technical departments. And a small number of Indian elites in the MIC, finally, were embraced by these arrangements, gaining a cabinet seat, judicial positions, and places in business and the professions.

The terms of the bargain were sealed through a party coalition known as the Alliance, enabling the UMNO, the MCA, and the MIC effectively to contest elections. Specifically, the Alliance's component parties generated enough ethnic appeals that they were able easily to defeat any non-communal parties like the IMP. At the same time, because their respective ethnic constituencies were still separated by great spatial and sociocultural distances, the Alliance could mute these appeals, yet still defeat more sectarian parties. One thinks especially here of the Pan-Malay(si)an Islamic Party (PMIP, later PAS), a group that broke from the UMNO in 1951, as well as the Democratic Action Party (DAP), successor to the PAP after the expulsion of Singapore from Malaysia in 1965. Accordingly, elites in the Alliance were able to operate a stable democratic regime for more than a decade after independence. This regime was stable because elites remained unified, sharing out resources in accord with the bargain. And it was democratic because the British had made it so – rather than because of the participatory outlooks of social forces.

The May 13th incident

During the 1960s, however, as moderate economic growth took place in Malaysia, it brought some of the developmental gains anticipated by modernization theorists, but delivered finally the sting feared by Hunting-ton.[12] In particular, rapid urbanization brought the Malays and Chinese into closer proximity, raising awareness and sharpening their resentments over the inequalities that came squarely into view. Further, improved literacy rates enabled these resentments to be communicated more widely. Thus, "segmental isolation" – so necessary, according to Lijphart, for providing elites with the discrete pillars of constituent support atop which they can cooperate – began now to erode.

It was in this context that the Alliance prepared in 1969 to contest its third general election since independence. As in previous elections, the coalition staked out the centrist position implicit in the bargain, acknowl-edging ethnic identities, but emphasizing forbearance. Campaigning over Radio Malaysia the day before the election, the Tunku affirmed,

The Malays have gained for themselves political power. The Chinese and Indians have won for themselves economic power. The blending of the two with complete goodwill and understanding has brought about peace and harmony, coupled with prosperity to the country.[13]

However, the PAS on one side and to some extent the DAP on the other attacked the Alliance's bland posture. Many Malay constituents duly abandoned the UMNO, questioning the value of the party holding state power while their stake in the economy dwindled in relative terms. Equally, many Chinese constituents turned from the MCA, alienated by the mismatch between their economic statuses and their political and cultural rights. Thus, while the election returned the Alliance to power at the federal level, the coalition was gravely weakened, losing its two-thirds majority in parliament, as well as its control over several state assemblies.

In celebrating these gains, the Chinese in Kuala Lumpur mounted "victory" processions, entering Malay neighborhoods and crying "*balik kampung*" ("go back to your village"). Malay street gangs then mounted counter-demonstrations. Thus, three days after the elections, in an incident known locally as "May 13th," the capital erupted in extraordinary violence.[14] And though the military restored order, Malaysia's democracy was suspended, the parliament closed for nearly two years while PAS and DAP leaders languished in detention. Malaysia was then governed by the National Operations Council, comprising top Alliance figures and military commanders.

After the rioting, elites in the UMNO began reorganizing their relations and re-energizing their Malay constituents. To do this, they ousted the accommodationist national leader, Tunku Abdul Rahman, in what has been characterized as a "palace coup."[15] Indeed, Mahathir Mohamad, a first-term MP who had just lost his seat, gave weight to this action, penning an open letter in which he admonished the Tunku that "the Malays whether they are UMNO or [PAS] supporters really hate you, especially those who had lost homes, children and relatives [during May 13th] because of your 'give and take' policy. . . . [I]t is high time you resign as our prime minister and UMNO leader." He further chided the Tunku because, "although the country was in a state of emergency you were engrossed playing poker with your Chinese friends," and he demanded that the MCA be excluded from the next cabinet line-up. Mahathir then signed off by declaring his willingness to be jailed for "conveying . . . the feelings of the Malays."[16]

Tunku Abdul Rahman responded by persuading the UMNO Supreme Council to oust Mahathir from the party. But he was himself so weakened that during 1970, he finally stepped down as prime minister, then later as UMNO president. In this way, his deputy, Tun Abdul Razak, emerged as Malaysia's national leader, a figure more attuned to mass-level Malay sentiments. Tun Razak then restored Mahathir to the UMNO in 1972, appointed him to the senate, then readied him to head various ministries. He also began recruiting a wider coterie of well-educated Malay *"ultras,"* consulting them over ways in which now to tilt the bargain more steeply toward their constituencies. Together, Tun Razak and his advisors proceeded to tighten the UMNO's grip on state power, then strike deeply into the economy. Let us briefly examine their strategies.

While the parliament remained closed, Tun Razak reduced the electoral competitiveness that in 1969 had so weakened the Alliance. Most importantly, he absorbed many opposition parties into his ruling coalition, thereby expanding the Alliance into the *Barisan Nasional*.[17] Far from diluting the UMNO's centrality, however, the coalition's swelling membership enhanced it, pitting many of the non-Malay parties against one another. Most notably, the MCA was forced now to compete with the *Gerakan* and other non-Malay parties for candidate selection and cabinet positions. Furthermore, Tun Razak drew the PAS into his ruling coalition, promising positions in a rapidly expanding bureaucracy. But the PAS, rather than sharing state power with the UMNO was vastly overshadowed, and it returned to opposition several years later. Finally, the DAP refused to join the *Barisan*, and its leader remained in detention for allegedly having helped to spark the May 13th rioting, thus leaving the party quite adrift.[18]

Having weakened the opposition, Tun Razak turned next to the parliament, imposing limits on its agenda as a condition for its reopening. Specifically, he introduced new sedition laws that barred all debate over Malay special rights, then ordered that parliament add them as constitutional amendments. In this way, the statuses of the sultans (signifying Malay sovereignty) and the official standing of Malay language (scheduled to become the main medium of education) could be firmly "entrenched." But even more importantly than the sultans and language, these amendments would safeguard the deep inroads into the economy that the UMNO proposed now to make, a progress of reverse discrimination that favored the Malays and was labeled the NEP.

The New Economic Policy

In explaining May 13th and their loss of voter support, UMNO officials devised a strongly materialist account. In particular, they focused on the disparities in equity ownership between ethnic communities. Collectively, the Malays held about 1.5 per cent of the country's equity, the Chinese around 23 per cent, and foreign investors the rest.[19] Of course, they said little about the gaping inequalities *within* ethnic communities, a major factor, claims David Brown, for so many Malays having fled their "racial patrons" in the UMNO for the more equitable "developmental patronage" of the PAS.[20] Hence, while these officials duly introduced two policy "prongs" through the NEP – one targeting poverty irrespective of "race" and a second seeking to sever the nexus between ethnicity and occupation – they gave most attention to latter aim. Enough benefits would be shared across Malay constituencies, then, that ethnic support could be energized. But benefits would also be concentrated in order to thrust up new managers, big business owners, and shareholders.

Tun Razak formally released the NEP in 1972 through the Mid-term Review of the Second Malaysia Plan. The policy was then articulated with quotas through the Industrial Coordination Act of 1975. In this way, the advancement of Malay constituencies, ennobled by the revived use of the shibboleth *"bumiputera"* (a Sanskrit term denoting "sons of the soil"), could be quantitatively gauged. Henceforth, 75 per cent of all local university places would be reserved for *bumiputra*,[21] imbuing them with new training. Next, state enterprises were set up to employ new Malay graduates, thus providing them with managerial skills. Private businesses, meanwhile, both Chinese-owned and foreign, were required to set aside 30 per cent of their positions at all levels for Malay executives and workers, or risk losing their operating licenses. Finally, state contracts for construction and supply were awarded almost exclusively to Malays who had set up their own contracting firms, helping transform managers and executives into entrepreneurs.

But the measure of Malay advancement given greatest priority involved ownership of corporate equity. On this score, a broad target of 30 per cent was again introduced. However, just as many Malays marked time in state enterprises while en route to more entrepreneurial activities, so too did much of their equity have to be held "in trust" while they learned how effectively to manage it. Indeed, in early allocations of share issues, many Malay recipients simply sold off their windfall to local Chinese buyers. Similarly, many of those who received business licenses and state contracts merely "fronted" for Chinese-owned companies, relationships that were disparaged as "Ali-Baba" schemes. Hence, the government now formed great holding companies to acquire assets. The main institutions were *Pernas* (National Trading Company) and *Permodolan Nasional Berhad* (PNB, National Equity Company), the latter eventually becoming one of Malaysia's biggest companies. Further, the government set up a *bumiputra* unit trust through which to dispense high dividends, the *Amanah Saham Nasional*. In this way, the Malays could be prevented from selling the assets that were held in their name, but nonetheless benefit from corporate earnings. And then to celebrate their new statuses, they were offered *bumiputra* discounts of 10–15 per cent on home purchases in new middle-class estates.

As mentioned above, one consequence of the NEP was that small- and medium-sized Chinese business people and workers grew steadily more alienated, especially during the 1970s-early 1980s when the policy was most ardently imposed. At the elite level, however, Chinese were able to maintain or even increase their business stakes. This was attributable to two factors.

First, despite the market distortions caused by the NEP, Malaysia's economy continued to grow until the mid-1980s, largely because of the discovery and export of petroleum and natural gas. It was during this time too that even as Malaysia uprooted foreign investors from commodities production, it attracted new ones in manufacturing, especially in electronics. Secondly, while the MCA's hold over financial ministries was loosened by the UMNO, Chinese business elites learned directly to interact with top UMNO officials, thereby retaining at least covert access to state contracts, loans, licenses, and share issues. The continued expansion during this period of Robert Kuok's business empire, Quek Leng Chan's Hong Leong Group, and Khoo Kay Peng's Malayan United Industries offer clear examples of this.[22] Hence, James V. Jesudason concludes that despite the NEP, "Chinese businesses do not appear to have lost out markedly, certainly not as much as they initially feared."[23] Of course, in relying now on connections with the UMNO, many Chinese business elites grew less attuned to export markets than local politics. They thus avoided manufacturing in order to concentrate in easier product areas that offered quicker returns, most notably property development and finance. At a time, then, when the Malays were learning new business skills, the quality of Chinese business practices appeared to slip. Nevertheless, one observes that as their activities converged, important avenues for elite cooperation persisted across ethnic lines.

In sum, the new national leader, Tun Razak, reorganized, but did not disunify elite relations, establishing a pattern that Zakaria has characterized as "hegemonic" with accommodationist elements.[24] Specifically, Tun Razak greatly elevated the UMNO over the MCA, but did not remove Chinese elites from business. And military elites safeguarded these adjustments, entering into, then departing the National Operations Council on terms specified by the prime minister. Thus, despite the social upheaval of May 13th, the regime remained stable. In addition, Tun Razak re-energized the UMNO's Malay constituencies, providing them access to business through the NEP. Of course, this came partly at the expense of mass-level Chinese, intensifying their grievances. But because at least one ethnic community was now placated, the socioeconomic divisions that had been erected by the British, then inflamed by processes of modernization, were made more manageable. Henceforth, the UMNO could more easily win Malay votes than during the 1969 election. And to the extent that the MCA was *less* able to win Chinese votes, the community could be neatly contained through state repression. Indeed, a rash of discriminatory measures was introduced during this period, even scrutinizing the claims of many Chinese to Malaysian citizenship.

In these circumstances, Tun Razak adjudged in 1972 that it was safe to restore at least some of the regime's democratic dimension, producing what can be recognized as a semi-democracy. As the prime minister confided, "So long as the form is preserved, the substance can be changed to suit conditions of a particular country."[25] Of course, during the decades after his death in 1976, these terms would fluctuate, with controls sometimes tightened over the Malays or eased among the Chinese, often in correspondence with Malaysia's changing economic fortunes and Islamic resurgence. But despite these recalibrations, the semi-democracy fashioned by Tun Razak endured.

Semi-democratic regime outcome

From the perspective of elites, democracy presents both costs and benefits, the relative weights of which shift across contexts. Costs, of course, include constituent interventions in elite position holding and policy making, as well as the risk of spontaneous mass violence during electoral contests. Democracy's benefits may include its electoral mechanisms for resolving elite disputes, monitoring and mobilizing constituent support, discharging social grievances, and generating perceptions of legitimacy. Where elites are cohesive and social forces quiescent, elites normally look askance upon democracy's costs and avoid it. But where elites confront participatory social forces, they may agree to democratize, grasping its compromise benefits. Specifically, elites recognize that democratic procedures make their statuses less certain, but still offer them reasonable prospects. On the other hand, continuous broad-based repression of social forces that have grown participatory, while oftentimes viable, poses great inefficiencies. Elites thus apply it as only a last resort.

The Malaysian record illustrates, though, the ways in which historical factors can prompt some departures from this logic. In particular, Malaysian politics were democratized at independence, producing general elections, as well as elections within the parties of the ruling coalition. This was carried out, however, less because of participatory social forces and obliging elites than colonial preferences. Moreover, it was precisely because elites were untested by social participation that they perpetuated the democratic procedures they had inherited. Put simply, because ethnic divisions and relatively low levels of development left society quiescent, democracy posed few of the costs enumerated above while reliably renewing elite statuses.

We have seen that afterward, though, in a context in which rapid urbanization sharpened ethnic tensions, social forces grew more participatory. This erupted finally in the violence of May 13th that sorely tested elite statuses. In this situation, elites reassessed democracy's costs as outweighing its benefits, then scaled it back in semi-democratic ways. Most notably, new restrictions were imposed on civil liberties, while procedures governing general elections were tightened. It is at this point, then, Malaysia's political record breaks somewhat from its distinctive colonial experience, then converges with a more modal trajectory.

Indeed, this semi-democracy correlated closely with new patterns of elite-mass relations. Specifically, with elites introducing the NEP's reverse discrimination, mass-level Chinese were alienated, thus requiring regime closure. But because the policy also placated the Malays, scope was created for reopening the regime. It thus became possible during the 1970s even to absorb the PAS into the new *Barisan*, then a more avowedly ethnic party than it is today. What is more, elites found ways of stabilizing their semi-democracy through the discretionary application of the NEP. While this policy's directives and quotas weakened the positions of MCA politicians, it spared most top Chinese business people. In these circumstances, the conduits between the UMNO and Chinese business grew more direct, conveying symbiotic exchanges. In sum, with social forces divided, then unevenly rewarded in ways that restored Malay quiescence, the regime was calibrated in semi-democratic ways. And by perpetuating elite-level cohesion, especially in the UMNO, but also across ethnic lines, this semi-democracy could reach equilibrium.

However, we will also see that under the NEP, the Malays were gradually readied for participation once again. Through a stream of university places, positions in state enterprises, state contracts, licenses, and share offers they gained new organizational know-how and self-confidence. And hence, to bolster their new businesses and portfolios, they began to participate more vigorously in the UMNO, contesting its divisional and branch-level posts. Further, during periods when the UMNO had more – or less – patronage to dispense than was usually the case, they quickened their participation, thus helping to pump up elite competitions. In the circumstances, Mahathir responded by tightening electoral procedures within the UMNO too, imposing a "bonus votes" scheme through which to flush out challengers, then abolishing it when it threatened to work against him. After cowing the party's Supreme Council, he also quite arbitrarily changed the number of nominations necessary for making candidacies official, slapped a one-off ban on "campaigning" for posts, then finally pushed through general assembly resolutions and Supreme Council recommendations that the party's top leadership posts go uncontested. In this way, the semi-democratic controls over civil liberties and general elections were extended to the UMNO assembly elections.

This section traces the contours of Malaysia's semi-democratic regime, delineating its key arenas, namely, the assembly elections in the UMNO and the general elections held for parliament and the state assemblies. These two electoral sites distinguish semi-democracy as it is practiced in Malaysia. It is through UMNO assembly elections that the national leader asserts his paramountcy over other elites; it is through general elections that the leader re-energizes his social constituencies. Further, as Diamond has recently argued, some correspondence exists between the competitiveness of general elections and the internal workings of political organizations, thereby reinforcing any broader "culture of democracy."[26] It can be demonstrated, then, that despite new restrictions imposed on the UMNO assembly elections, more competitiveness remains than in the PAP's central executive committee, imbuing Malaysia's semi-democracy with greater vibrancy than Singapore's.

In addition, this section examines the patterns of inter-elite and elite-mass relations that causally precede, yet are guided by, the semi-democratic regime that has emerged. In analyzing UMNO assembly elections, we will see that these patterns have been punctuated by sharp factional struggles. Yet the strain points that resulted have afterward subsided, signaling the persistence of elite cohesion. Further, in analyzing general elections, we will see that that the government has surely done much to tighten civil liberties and electoral procedures. But it has also perpetuated social quiescence through legitimating mentalities and a record of performance.

Elite relations and UMNO general assembly elections

In Malaysia, the most important organizational bases for elite statuses have been the UMNO party apparatus, the state bureaucracy, and the business conglomerates. And indeed, there has much overlap between them, with the UMNO historically subsuming top civil servants (giving rise to "adminostrocrats"[27]) and later promoting top business people, primarily Malay, but also Chinese (thus fueling "money politics"). Accordingly, in Malaysia's semi-democracy, the most important elite-level competitions have been waged through the UMNO.

UMNO general assembly elections have often been conceptualized as Malaysia's "real" elections.[28] It is by winning party posts in the UMNO's apparatus that one gains access to state positions. And with the NEP having paved the way for state participation in the economy, it is through posts in the UMNO that one gains business opportunities too. Thus, with the UMNO so strongly determining the relative fortunes of elites, competitions in elections have sometimes been fierce, especially during periods when the party gained new benefits to dispense (i.e., after the NEP was first set up during the mid-1970s, as well as amid privatization during the mid-1990s) and when it had fewer (i.e., amid economic recessions during the mid-1980s and late 1990s). These competitions have also been sharpened by different commitments on such issues as Malay culture, Islam, and the merits of globalization. At the same time, however, party procedures have ensured that while elites compete rigorously, they do not do so at all costs – thus helping to reinforce their prior cohesion. Accordingly, given the centrality of the UMNO assembly election for elite competitions, it is necessary to examine its workings in some detail.

Today, there are nearly 2.8 million ethnic Malays (and some indigenous people in the eastern state of Sabah), who are members of the UMNO.[29]

At base, they are arrayed in some 18,000 branch organizations, a webwork that knits together Malaysia's urban areas and many rural *kampung*. Local branches vary in size, though can contain as many as 150 members. They hold general meetings annually, each time electing some of their members to represent them at the UMNO's divisional level. Currently, the party has 165 divisions, corresponding in Peninsular Malaysia and parts of Sabah with the country's parliamentary districts. These divisions then hold their own elections every second year, choosing a "head" and ten committee members – the status with which one at last gains importance.[30]

Hence, the competitions between members to gain divisional posts in the UMNO have grown vigorous. In years when the party holds it triennial elections, divisions have each nominated persons for posts at the party's national level, then sent their divisional head and committee members to attend as delegates, or further, to stand simultaneously as candidates. As delegates, divisional officials have typically been able to barter their votes, either settling quickly for airfare to the capital, luxury hotel rooms, packets of cash, and perhaps an overseas holiday, or they have "floated" as long as possible, seeking more lasting assistance in politics or business. Candidates, in turn, in mobilizing delegate support, have contested one of 25 elected positions in the UMNO Supreme Council, the presidency and deputy presidency of the party's Youth (*Pemuda*) and Women's (*Wanita*) wings, one of three elected vice-presidencies, and, at the pinnacle, the party's presidency or deputy presidency.[31]

The desirability of these positions has been enhanced by their paralleling so closely the hierarchies of Malaysian government and business. In years when general elections are held, divisional heads are normally chosen also as UMNO candidates for state assemblies or parliament (with usually two state assembly districts lying inside parliamentary ones). As assemblymen, they may be appointed to their state government's executive council or to committees possessing important regulatory powers. Committees with authority over land usage have been especially prized. In particular, members of these committees can win land grants for the construction companies they often own, either rezoning the land quickly or selling it at great profit, or subcontracting out work on office blocks and housing projects – frequently to "Chinese . . . developers who might otherwise have faced difficulty in getting access to land."[32] In addition, assemblymen may gather up posts on key municipal councils, football clubs, and charities, nodes that lengthen opportunities for transacting patronage.

Further, at the national level, backbenchers in parliament may gain operating licenses or contracts, state bank loans, some privatized state assets, and discounted equity in restructured Chinese- or foreign-owned firms (preferably allocated just before their public listing and price rise). They may also be appointed to the boards of state enterprises, thereby fattening their parliamentary salaries with directors' fees. Finally, at the fountainhead, parliamentary frontbenchers may capture the real "plums," gaining elite statuses as cabinet ministers, deputy ministers, and parliamentary secretaries. Here, with the approval of the prime minister, they are able to arrange licenses, tenders, restructuring, and privatizing on a much grander scale, channeling state resources to valued constituents.

The UMNO, moreover, while serving as the bridgehead to state resources, has been able to amass many of its own. Through the NEP, the UMNO has set up portfolios of "two-dollar" firms, then nurtured them with state construction projects and operating monopolies. Many of these firms were gathered together under holding companies like Fleet, *Hatibudi*, and Renong, then placed in the care of assorted "trustees" and "proxies." Later, as part of the UMNO's reconstitution as the UMNO *Baru* (New UMNO) – an episode we will explore in the next section – its assets were technically divested and perhaps more professionally managed. Either way, whether dispensing state resources or those more nominally its own, the UMNO has emerged as the principal avenue along which ambitious Malays have advanced their standings in politics and business. Indeed, these twin enterprises in Malaysia have nearly become seamless.[33]

Stakes have thus been high in UMNO elections, with candidates freely able to contest vice-presidential posts, Supreme Council seats, and the leadership positions the Youth and *Wanita*. Above this level, however, members have been discouraged from contesting the party presidency and deputy presidency, for these offices normally correlate respectively with Malaysia's all-powerful prime ministership and the deputy prime ministership. Aspirants have instead been advised that sedate processes of seniority, retirement, and planned succession should take their course. Still, despite UMNO lore about inviolate leadership, the party constitution has historically permitted challenges to top position holders so long as they are supported by two divisional nominations. Hence, in scanning the UMNO record, one notes that the deputy president has been challenged in five of the party's six elections held between 1978 and 1993 (with 1978 marking the first such election after Tun Razak's death), while the president has been challenged twice during this period, in 1979 and 1987.[34]

In evaluating these elections and the candidates who have contested them, some analysts have sensed slight ideological differences, the extent, for example, to which candidates might favor global capital, deeper Islamicization, and limits on Chinese cultural displays. But these outlooks seem flexible, inclining most observers to see little more than personalist appeals and patrimonialist spoils.[35] Ideology, then, has turned historically on simple calls for Malay protection and unity, more recently on Malay assertiveness and entrepreneurship. And candidacies have routinely been funded through unprincipled "money politics." Nonetheless, while one might disparage the scant ideologies of those contesting UMNO elections, there can be no gainsaying the competitive framework in which they have done so, their grassroots aspirations filtering persistently upwards even as leadership prerogatives weigh heavily down. Thus to the extent that these exchanges have been transacted in electoral ways, the UMNO can historically be conceptualized as internally democratic.[36]

Elite-level 'strain points'

This section briefly records some of the elite-level competitions that have been waged through UMNO general assembly elections. As we will see, these competitions have sometimes grown intense, to the point where one can question whether elites were any longer cohesive. Further, these competitions sometimes spilled out of the general assembly, then raged through parliament, the judiciary, and the media, raising additional questions about the extent to which UMNO elections helped to guide elite behaviors. But in focusing closely on strain points, this section seeks purposively to pose a hard test for claims about elite cohesion and regime stability. It will show that despite episodes in which elite relations were tested, elites drew back from prolonged periods of social mobilization – a key indicator of disunity. There were, then, no coups or mass uprisings – key indicators of regime instability. Indeed, after Singapore, Malaysia has probably possessed the most stable regime in the region.

During the mid-1970s, as the government began to intervene deeply in the economy through the NEP, elites in the UMNO began struggling over the greater benefits that the party now had to dispense. Accordingly, new factions emerged that could roughly be distinguished by their leadership styles, administrative capacities, and generational memberships. As we have seen, Tun Razak began recruiting some Malay advisers that he gauged would be helpful in implementing the NEP. This group included his cousin, Hussein Onn, the newly rehabilitated Mahathir, Tengku Razaleigh, and Musa Hitam. Displaying high educational levels and strong ethnic commitments, this faction was labeled – though without reference to Indonesia – the "new order."

Sharp resentments over the sudden rise of this new order were felt by a looser grouping that can collectively be called the "old guard." It was nominally led by Tunku Abdul Rahham, appearing to plot his return to power. But this faction's main driving force was Harun Idris, the chief minister of Selangor, a pivotal state that encompasses Kuala Lumpur. And though Harun was equally dedicated to the NEP, his charismatic rhetoric and old-time populism were dismissed by Tun Razak as inappropriate for the policy's new planning and restructuring tasks.[37]

As factional tensions deepened, Tun Razak sought to confirm the new order's standing at the 1975 UMNO general assembly election, advancing his proteges as the party's vice-presidents. However, in brusquely declaring, rather than skillfully placing his proteges, he offended many delegates, thus inviting an electoral challenge from Harun Idris. Hence, to sideline Harun, Tun Razak offered him a diplomatic posting overseas, a soft form of traditional sanction in UMNO politics. Harun rejected the offer, however, causing Razak to respond with firmer sanctions, namely, by filing corruption charges.

Shortly afterward, however, in January 1976, Tun Razak died. He was succeeded by his deputy, Hussein Onn. And when Hussein passed over several senior party officials to select Mahathir as his deputy, he now triggered resentments within even the new order. In addition, Hussein began clashing anew with Harun Idris, removing Harun as Selangor's chief minister, then expelling him from the UMNO, measures that were quite unprecedented. Indeed, the party's Supreme Council quickly overruled Hussein, thus readmitting Harun to the party. Factional tensions then surged once more, with Harun mobilizing Malay constituents in the streets, and Hussein Onn calling in security forces. The home minister, Ghazali Shafie, played an ambiguous role, jailing protagonists from both factions and forcing bizarre, televised confessions about social beliefs. Indeed, the conflict only subsided in 1978 when Harun finally was sentenced to six years in prison, and the Tunku was mollified with an invitation to address the UMNO general assembly.

One concludes from this episode that because the UMNO had so tightened its grip on state power and extended its reach into the economy, competitiveness increased within the party for its many new benefits. Moreover, the factions that emerged reflected the changing backgrounds of elites, with a youthful new order now elbowing aside the old guard notables. Most importantly, Mahathir gained the deputy prime ministership, while Tengku Razaleigh became director of a variety of new state enterprises associated with the NEP. However, while elite relations were strained, they remained cohesive, signaled finally by Harun Idris's gaining a pardon. Indeed, he later resumed his political career, while directing various UMNO-owned enterprises. Thus, despite tensions at the top and increased pressures from below, Malaysia's regime remained stable.

In 1981, Hussein Onn stepped down, and Mahathir succeeded him as prime minister. But Mahathir, having earlier helped to set up state enterprises through which to promote Malay business people while deepening industrialization, seemed now to display some ambivalence over the merits of these interventions. Indeed, early in his tenure as prime minister, he declared his government's new commitments to privatization. Further, during an economic recession in the mid-1980s, his finance minister, Daim Zainuddin, began sharply to cut back on state expenditures. It was in this context that Mahathir announced that the NEP would be held in "abeyance."

It soon appeared, though, that this new austerity was not being uniformly imposed. In particular, a cluster of business proteges associated with Daim retained his favor, while many small- and medium-sized Malay-owned companies were left to drift. Resentments set in, crystallizing finally in the formation of new UMNO "teams" as the party approached its assembly election in 1987. This occurred in the wake of the NEP's having transformed the general assembly's delegations, replacing many of the bureaucrats and school teachers that it had initially attracted with business people. In these circumstances, Mahathir's "Team A" appeared to retain the loyalties of top corporate Malays (*korporat Melayu*). "Team B," led by Tengku Razaleigh, now trade and industry minister, appealed to deeply alienated smaller business people. Razaleigh thus challenged Mahathir for the UMNO presidency, even gaining the support of Mahathir's former deputy, Musa Hitam.

The UMNO's assembly election that took place in 1987 was the most competitive that had ever been waged. And, by many accounts, it was also the most unfair.[38] Only after much bargaining and vote buying, capped by some dubious ballot counting, a mysterious black-out, and a notorious break for prayers (during which much last-minute lobbying took place), was Mahathir able to ward off Razaleigh's challenge. However, Razaleigh persisted, seeking through the parliament, the courts, the media, and public rallies to secure a new assembly election. Mahathir as quickly responded, ordering a dramatic sweep in late 1987 known as *Operasi Lalang*, arresting sundry opposition parliamentarians and social critics.[39]

However, after some brief respite, it appeared that Razaleigh might nevertheless be successful in getting the high court to order a new assembly election. Mahathir's lawyers responded now with a "kamikaze defense," prompting the judge to order the UMNO's deregistration.[40] In this situation, Mahathir formed the UMNO *Baru*, then barred Team B members from joining it. In turn, Razaleigh organized his faction into what gradually solidified as an alternative Malay party, the *Semangat '46* (ie., the Spirit of '46, the year in which the original UMNO had been founded). However, at this stage, Razaleigh remained committed to reviving the original UMNO. He thus began a new legal challenge that made its way finally to the supreme court. But as Razaleigh appeared to draw close to a favorable outcome, Mahathir arranged for the removal of the lord president and several key judges.[41] Razaleigh's suit was then duly struck down by the acting lord president. It was during this period, then, that Mahathir's reputation evolved from an ethnic *ultra* and promoter of "mega projects" to a wrecker of institutions.

With the re-registration of the UMNO thus blocked, Razaleigh prepared to contest the 1990 general elections, using *Semangat '46* as his vehicle. However, as economic recovery became more evident during 1989–90, the UMNO *Baru* replenished its patronage resources, quickly dampening the new interest of many Malay business people in opposition politics. Hence, these constituencies returned swiftly to the UMNO. Further, though the *Semangat '46* lingered in opposition, it suffered a steady stream of defections. Razaleigh finally wound up his party, then rejoined the UMNO during its 1996 assembly election. And during the run-up to the 1999 general election, he was even touted briefly as Mahathir's likely successor.

In assessing the significance of this strain point during the late 1980s, one notes a context of economic growth, followed by recession, greatly alienating many of the business people that the party had promoted. Party patronage had now grown scarce, yet austerity was unevenly imposed, with Malay business elites favored over small- and medium-sized business people. The resentments this caused enabled Razaleigh to gain new constituencies with which to challenge Mahathir for national leadership, beginning with the UMNO assembly election, but then ranging across a variety of institutional arenas. And Mahathir then reacted in ways that clearly abused these institutions, tightening press controls, purging the lord president, and doubtless squeezing the registrar of societies. However, though Mahathir thus truncated the UMNO into the UMNO *Baru*, the next assembly election, held in 1993, was also quite competitive, indicating the ways in which Mahathir could still be constrained by procedures. One could also argue that the readmission of Razaleigh into the UMNO three years later, followed three years after that by widespread speculation over his succeeding to the party presidency indicated clearly the persistence of elite cohesion.

A third strain point in the UMNO record took place during a period of rapid economic growth in the mid-1990s. This was the period too during which the government began more seriously to privatize important state assets, elevating it now as the main form of patronage and delivering it usually through untendered state contracts and other opaque forms of transfer.[42] Competitions stiffened commensurately within the UMNO as factions vied to control privatizing processes.

Hence, as the party's 1993 election approached, questions arose over whether Mahathir's deputy at that time, Ghafar Baba, would be challenged by the new minister of finance, Anwar Ibrahim. Ghafar was an old-style politico who, while having little knowledge of complex economic and international issues, remained skilled in mobilizing village-level followings. Mahathir had thus recruited him in 1986 after the surprise resignation of his first deputy prime minister, Musa Hitam, then helped him to win the UMNO deputy presidency in 1987. In contrast, Anwar had first gained attention during the early 1970s when, as a radical student leader and founder of an influential Muslim organization called ABIM (Islamic Youth Movement of Malaysia), he had been detained for nearly two years under the ISA. But in 1982, with his charisma and organizational abilities having caught Mahathir's eye, he was co-opted into the UMNO. Anwar's fortunes then rose swiftly throughout the next decade. And as he gathered up party positions and ministerial portfolios, finally becoming finance minister in 1991, his interests diversified from social justice and Islam into sustainable economic growth, Malay competitiveness, and indeed, an Asian "renaissance."

During these boom times Mahathir's policy aims mostly coincided with Anwar's, leading most observers to believe that Anwar was his chosen successor. But Mahathir's personal ambitions may have encouraged him also to fear the rapidity with which Anwar was now coming up. Specifically, though Anwar had pledged that he would never contest the UMNO deputy presidency while held by someone else, his supporters intensively canvassed the party's divisions and branches. Further, through a management buy-out, they gained control over the New Straits Times Press, the firm controlling the country's leading English-language daily. Thus, as Anwar's "juggernaut" gained steam, he agreed to contest the deputy presidency after all, making his announcement while flanked by nine of the country's 13 chief ministers, nine of fourteen cabinet ministers, and 16 UMNO deputy ministers. This show of strength left its mark on the party's grass roots, its divisions soon giving 145 nominations to Anwar and seven to Ghafar. And despite Mahathir's then invoking UMNO traditions and patterns of deference, implying the sanctity of incumbency, Ghafar recognized the futility of his defending his post. Hence, even before the assembly convened, a humiliated Ghafar staged a staggered series of resignations from all his party and government posts, then repaired to Jakarta.

Anwar was thus free at the UMNO general assembly to advance his candidates into the party's three elected vice-presidencies and Youth leadership position. Dubbed the "*wawasan* team" (vision team), these candidates articulated images of the "new Malay" (*Melayu baru*), the "scientific Malay," indeed, the "global Malay," confident in dealing with Chinese business people at home and mastering new technologies and languages abroad. The UMNO Youth then elaborated these sentiments through a resolution that called for "a revolution of the 'Malay minds' . . . to make Malaysia a knowledge-based society."[43] The *wawasan* team duly gained the endorsement of the assembly delegates, sweeping all the positions that it contested.

The significance of this last strain point lies in the ways in which economic recovery and new forms of patronage rekindled elite competitions in the UMNO. Anwar's faction thus pushed past the incumbent, Ghafar Baba, seemingly violating UMNO traditions and unnerving Mahathir. But the election showed also the greater sophistication with which elite competitions had now to be waged. In particular, the *wawasan* team graduated smartly from the short-term, reactive style characteristic of earlier factional battles, giving much attention now to public relations and bold images, then quietly tapping privatized assets and influencing delegates. And though the faction would disperse over the next several years, many of its innovations endured. Indeed, one candidate associated with Ghafar observed that the *wawasan* team victory "should be viewed as success for the country as it reflected a national transition – from an era of agriculture to that of industry, commerce, and the corporate sector."[44]

However, if one can also read in this statement the recovery of enough elite cohesion that the regime remained stable, one notes that Mahathir was more muted in his congratulatory messages. Indeed, he used his adjournment speech to recommend that those accused of money politics be barred from contesting UMNO posts, then proposed an extraordinary UMNO assembly through which to pass necessary amendments. Later, in preparing for the 1996 assembly election, he would further discourage challengers by tampering with the nominations process, forbidding campaigning, and finally forcing a resolution that suspended elections for the presidency and deputy presidency, thus securing his own position, while freezing Anwar in his. And in 1998, amid economic recession, Mahathir's relationship with Anwar would be more tested still, forming a strain point at that year's UMNO general assembly that will be evaluated in a later section.

Elite-mass relations and general elections

After elites have waged their competitions at UMNO assembly elections, they engage social forces through general elections. In Malaysia's semi-democracy, the conduct of general elections can be distinguished from the ways in which they are held in a pseudo-democracy. Although civil liberties are in many ways similarly curtailed, opposition parties retain greater autonomy over their internal workings and canvassing of constituent support. Further, while many electoral procedures are distorted, balloting, vote-counting, and reporting are carried out fairly, thus rendering elections less "rigged." In these circumstances, while the UMNO-led *Barisan* has been returned reliably to power, the opposition can win some local contests, gain a foothold in parliament, and impose accountability in limited amounts.

More specifically, in terms of civil liberties, Malaysia's home ministry has usually allowed opposition parties, trade unions, professional associations, and other kinds of cause-oriented and cultural groups to operate at modest levels. And on occasion the government has even responded positively to the grievances they have raised, promoting rural development, for example, easing the barriers to tertiary education, and even rolling back unpopular levies on new toll roads.

However, the government has also acted systematically to cap such participation. It has blocked opposition parties from circulating their party newspapers outside their memberships. It has registered and circumscribed NGOs through the Societies Act, then branded them explicitly as "political." It has prohibited trade union leaders from holding posts in political parties, while barring students through the Universities and University Colleges Act from any formal political activities at all. In addition, free communication has been hindered by the government's ownership of much of the electronic media, while the *Barisan*'s main component parties monopolize major dailies through the companies to which they are allied. Independent publications, meanwhile, are regulated by the licensing requirements of the Printing Presses and Publications Act, and their investigations are hampered by the Official Secrets Act. Finally, public assembly is curbed by the Police Act, requiring permits for gatherings of more than five persons. And any organizers who persevere can be jailed indefinitely without trial under the Internal Security Act (ISA), a remnant of "preventive detention" practised by the British during the Emergency a half-century ago. In sum, while opposition parties and NGOs in Malaysia possess some organizational autonomy, they are hindered in freely mobilizing constituencies or communicating their views, thus posing grave impediments to their effectively contesting elections.

In terms of electoral procedures, the government has regularly held general elections since independence, dissolving parliaments within the five-year time frames specified by the constitution. Further, with the seeming exception of postal votes, secret balloting and vote counting have been carried out fairly, and the results have been promptly reported. The prime minister, put up by the party that wins these elections, has always held sway over the state bureaucracy and military, thus signaling the meaningfulness of his office. And opposition parties, though seriously hobbled, have fought elections vigorously, even defeating *Barisan* candidates in some districts.[45] In consequence, the government has taken elections seriously enough that it has responded to constituent demands. We have seen the ways in which the UMNO re-energized Malay loyalties through the NEP. But it has also offered them rural development schemes, Islamicizing programs, and preferential cultural policies.[46] At the same time, under the banner of the *Barisan*, the UMNO has grudgingly respected the core concerns of its Chinese and Indian constituents, leaving them some space in which to operate their businesses, preserve their dialects and religious rites, and educate their children in non-Malay vernaculars, at least at the primary level. Thus, writes Crouch, "the government [has been] careful to respond to the expectations of a large part of the society . . . because competitive elections [have] continued to be held."[47]

However, though opposition parties can gain entry to Malaysia's parliament, they are prevented from winning the majorities necessary to control it. Election day, then, while presenting the necessary snapshot of propriety, obscures the underlying limits on civil liberties. It also obscures many abuses in the electoral procedures themselves, including the twin ills of gerrymandering and malapportionment that in a single member district system exaggerate the weight of rural Malay districts, the areas in which the UMNO has historically reaped most its votes. Indeed, Edmund Terence Gomez reports that when districts are averaged across Malaysia, one rural vote is worth two urban votes.[48] Furthermore, elections are called abruptly, leaving poorly funded opposition parties little time to prepare for them. And the candidacies that these parties then declare are sometimes rejected by the election commission, usually because of petty mistakes made in nomination papers. Finally, because opposition campaigners seem better able to galvanize their audiences than government speakers can, campaign periods are kept brief, usually about a week, and open-air rallies are banned, ostensibly for fear of violence. Of course, ministers in the *Barisan* remain able to hold mass rallies, disguising them as official addresses.[49] And throughout their campaigning, they make unabashed use of government workers and state-owned facilities and equipment. They can also tip wavering voters with on-the-spot development grants and occasional vote buying, practices that have been more sanctioned than checked by the election commission. In these circumstances, notes Crouch, "the Malaysian electoral system [has been] so heavily loaded in favor of the government that it is hard to imagine that the ruling coalition, as long as it remained united, could be defeated in an election."[50] And the *Barisan*, then, in closing its grip on parliament, has freely passed legislation, amended the constitution, manipulated standing orders and question time, and appointed its loyalists to the largely ceremonial upper house.

Opposition parties have fared better at the state level, at different times forming state governments in Kelantan, Terengganu, Penang, Sarawak and Sabah. However, even here the government has worked to reverse these outcomes, sometimes fomenting disorder and imposing emergency rule. James Chin records that this pattern was established early on by Tunku Abdul Rahman.[51] In 1966, shortly after the inclusion of the East Malaysian states into the new Federation of Malaysia, the chief minister of Sarawak refused to yield to Malay (and Melanau) demands that land-owning rights be extended to non-indigenous populations. The Tunku then pressed for the chief minister's resignation, declared a state of emergency, imposed a new government, and altered the Sarawak constitution in ways that blocked the former chief minister's return. In Kelantan, we have seen that Tun Razak persuaded the PAS to enter the *Barisan* during the early 1970s. But after the PAS then won a majority in the state assembly of Kelantan, Tun Razak insisted on exercising his prerogative of appointing the PAS leader of his choice as the state's new chief minister. After the PAS resisted, the UMNO organized rallies that finally provoked riots in Kelantan's capital of Kota Baru, thus establishing a pretext for emergency rule.[52] The government then organized snap elections and defeated the PAS, thereby helping to drive the party back out of the *Barisan*. Finally, in Sabah, after the ruling Sabah United Party (PBS) defected from the *Barisan* during the 1990 election campaign, the UMNO responded by setting up its own party branches in the state, withholding federal development assistance, and forging a rival coalition to contest against the PBS in the state election in 1994. And while the PBS won, the UMNO applied relentless pressure afterward, finally putting the PBS leader on trial for corruption, then luring party defectors with financial incentives. The PBS government quickly collapsed, and it was replaced by a local *Barisan* coalition that agreed to rotate the chief ministership among its components.

In sum, skewed electoral procedures, prefaced by limits on civil liberties, form the parameters of Malaysia's semi-democracy. Sundry laws and stratagems enable the UMNO reliably to retain power at the parliamentary level; emergency powers sometimes encourage it to retake power at the state level. In consequence, uncertainty during general elections has usually involved little more than the fluctuating margins of support earned by the UMNO's non-Malay partners, the extent to which the *Barisan* will keep its two-thirds parliamentary majority, and the outcomes of the by-elections the government occasionally contests.

Still, one concludes by underscoring that general elections in Malaysia have not been so vacuous as the ones held in New Order Indonesia. Civil liberties, though limited, have remained vital enough that opposition parties can choose their own leaders, organize branches throughout the country, and openly criticize the government. Electoral procedures, though distorted, have enabled these parties to enter the parliament and even to form state governments. And though the opposition can never really contemplate forming a new federal government, it has nonetheless been able to keep the *Barisan* mildly accountable, embarrassing it with disclosures about banking scandals, business abuses, and sundry personal peccadilloes.

Perpetuating social quiescence

While inter-elite relations determine whether a regime is stable, elite-mass relations determine the extent to which it is democratic. Put simply, elites can control quiescent societies – either trolling lightly for constituents or leaving social forces at rest – enabling them to operate an authoritarian regime. But where elites are confronted by societies that have grown participatory, they may compromise by agreeing in some measure to democratize their politics.

We have seen that Malaysia's political record was most democratic during the decade after independence, despite the country's comparatively low level of socioeconomic development. To explain this early democratization, Jomo tries to identify some participatory attitudes, rooted in the "little traditions . . . of the peasant masses" which, when steeled through anti-colonial struggles and labor organizing, gave rise to a "democratic impulse." He thus concludes that the "popular traditions in Malay and other indigenous Asian cultures" cumulated in a "democratic tendency."[53] However, Gordon Means counters that "because aristocratic Malay elites were well-represented in the colonial administration, Malays from the Malay States were slow to develop voluntary social and political institutions."[54] He describes the UMNO's founding in 1946 as an "artificially high state of mobilization," meant less to demand independence than to refuse it, at least until the British had reaffirmed the Malays' indigenous standing over the Chinese. Hence, in taking a longer view, one detects more social quiescence than participation, meaning that political democracy, like national independence, was mostly introduced from on high by the British. Of course, local elites then perpetuated this democracy, though only so long as their statuses were unchallenged by it. On this count, Means describes the elite-mass relations that underpinned democracy during the 1950s–60s:

> [O]nce elections are over, the Malays tend to withdraw to their daily activities and are not motivated for participation in voluntary associations seeking to influence public policy on a continuing basis. Rather, the Malay masses seem content to leave politics to political leaders who are expected to act as trustees for the interests of their Malay constituencies. . . . Leaders [in turn] have patronizing and manipulative attitudes toward their constituents.[55]

Of course, we have also seen that the resentments of the Malays – and the Chinese – began to mount during the 1960s as urbanization drew these communities in closer view of one another. And these resentments caused them to grow more participatory in the 1969 elections, spurning elites in the ruling Alliance, then erupting in spontaneous violence. In consequence, far from invigorating democracy, greater mass participation helped to break it down, with Malaysia placed under emergency rule for nearly the next two years.

During this hiatus, elites in the UMNO devised the NEP. And in then alienating the Chinese, but placating the Malays, they formed the patterns of mass attitudes upon which a semi-democracy could be operated. Of course, many Malays began soon afterward to participate more robustly inside the UMNO. Further, the factionalism that resulted sometimes spilled over from the UMNO into general elections, especially after periods of economic recession. In this way, Malaysian politics gained new levels of competitiveness as they approached elections in 1990 and 1999. However, the government also responded with new levels of coercion, again narrowing civil liberties and electoral procedures in order to extend its tenure.

But elites in the UMNO have also used more than coercion in dampening participatory mass attitudes. In particular, they have developed legitimating mentalities, often embroidered with light sloganeering. Hari Singh records the ways in which elites have reinvented traditions of Malay loyalty and treachery, invoking the Melaka sultanate as their behavioral referent.[56] They have thus alluded regularly to classical Malay texts like the *Sejarah Melayu* and *Hikayat Hang Tuah*, then celebrated social hierarchies through "feudal honorific titles" such as *datuk* and *tan sri*. Of course, they have been less able during Mahathir's tenure to make use of Malaysia's king and traditional Malay rulers, with Mahathir viewing these potentates as a drag on his executive prerogatives. But elites in the UMNO have nonetheless invested heavily in renovating Malay ceremonies and pageantry in order to encourage mass deference. Historically, they have also deepened Malay loyalties to the UMNO by stoking fears of the Chinese, calling regularly for the "Malay unity" that underpins "Malay dominance." In addition, during the 1970s, anti-communist appeals could be used, coinciding with the fall of Vietnam, but directed more poignantly against the local Chinese, recollecting the role of parts of the community in the Emergency. And finally, when factional tensions within the UMNO have erupted in discrete strain points, gaps in available mentalities could be plugged with greater innovations. For example, as Mahathir dueled with Razaleigh during the late 1980s, he initiated a "loyalty with the people campaign" (*semarak*), accompanied by the bouncy, distinctly un-martial Loyalty Song (*Lagu Setia*).

However, after raising Malay loyalties in these ways, UMNO elites have calmed ethnic passions, thus preventing new outbreaks of major ethnic violence. Indeed, after stirring ethnic fears, they have typically collaborated with their *Barisan* partners in warning that only they have the capacity to guard against recurrences of May 13th rioting. Hence, shortly after May 13th, even as the government developed the NEP, it composed a softer score of *Rukunegara* ("pillars of the nation"), calling for civility and social tolerance that were in some ways reminiscent of *Pancasila*. In addition, the government has moved tactically beyond Malay dominance to highlight the "*Barisan* way," a style of consultation in cabinet that has occasionally yielded policy adjustments favoring the Chinese. And during the mid-1990s, Mahathir went further even than this, unveiling his Vision 2020 of full development, one strand of which was a new integrated Malaysian identity of "*bangsa Malaysia*" that partially eclipsed the dyadic and vexatious idiom of "Malay/non-Malay." Indeed, while once labeled a Malay *ultra*, Mahathir came now to take on the mantle of the Tunku, wisely mediating relations between ethnic communities – though this time with the difference that underlying sources of social grievance had been put right. In addition, while asserting that *bahasa Malaysia* should remain the national language, Mahathir called for the reintroduction of English into educational curricula, essential for remaking his country into a "knowledge-based" society. And his deputy, Anwar, extolled even the benefits of Malay students studying Mandarin and learning something of Confucianism.

But more critical for social quiescence than legitimating mentalities and manipulated ethnic sentiments were widespread perceptions that the UMNO-led *Barisan* had delivered the goods. Indeed, throughout most of the 1990s, Malaysia's economy attained nearly double-digit growth rates, producing new business elites and a broad middle class whose membership clearly spanned ethnic communities. Mahathir attributed these economic gains in Malaysia – and indeed, throughout East Asia – to Asian values of obeisance, consensus, and thrift. And in paralleling new initiatives in Singapore, his ideologues helped to develop notions too of Asian democracy. Further, even when crisis struck and Malaysia's economy began to contract, Mahathir responded not by reviewing Asian values, with consensus appearing to have mutated into cronyism, but instead by launching crude nationalist attacks on outsiders, the speculators and neo-colonialists who operated from countries that supposedly had been enfeebled by their liberal belief systems and excessive democracy. In sum, elites in Malaysia did much to perpetuate social quiescence, incorporating social forces into ethnically based parties, then imposing controls on civil liberties and elections. But they also justified the semi-democracy that resulted with reinventions of cultural deference, modulations of ethnic sentiments, and regular reference to their industrializing performance.

In these circumstances, though Malaysia has long featured some vigorous opposition parties, and has even acquired the faint outlines of civil society, social forces have been unable to extract from elites any fuller democracy. With respect to opposition parties, we observe that they usually perform well after periods of economic recession. But it is on this count, perhaps, that modernization theory is stumped, with recession, rather than steady growth, fueling new middle-class interest in a more competitive party system. Further, with economic recovery, this interest in accountability dissipates rapidly, revealing it to have progressed little beyond a longing for boom times. Indeed, a pioneering study of mass attitudes in Malaysia that was conducted during the high-growth years of the mid-1990s found little support for democracy, or even much understanding of what democratic procedures involve.[57] In these circumstances, politicians who had left the UMNO for the *Semangat '46* returned, calculating that even the scraps of patronage they might now be allotted would be more than they would receive in opposition. And the new middle class returned also to the *Barisan*, providing the government in 1995 with one of its greatest electoral victories ever.

The weakness of mass attitudes necessary for making opposition parties competitive is reflected also in the performances of NGOs and trade unions. To be sure, Jesudason observes that after the general election in 1969, as the UMNO absorbed many opposition parties into its *Barisan* coalition, NGOs sprouted as new outlets for dissent.[58] In particular, new consumer and environmental groups emerged, the best known of which were the Consumer Association of Penang and the Environmental Protection Society of Malaysia. Political reform groups arose too, like *Aliran*, the Catholic Resources Center, the Selangor Graduates Society, and more recently, *Suaram*, *Gerak*, *Gagasan*, and the Coalition for People's Democracy.[59] During the late 1980s, the Malaysian Bar Council resisted the government strongly over the removal of the lord president and supreme court judges, then again during the late 1990s over the trial proceedings involving Anwar Ibrahim. Women's groups also appeared during the 1980s–90s, like *Tenaganita*, Sisters in Islam, and the National Council of Women's Organizations.

But despite this growing roster, Jesudason notes too that if NGOs began to proliferate after 1969, their participation has been weakened by several factors.[60] Many NGOs have relied upon the efforts of a few "passionate men," rather than any deeper social activism. Further, these leaders have been drawn from a narrow middle-class segment, mainly lawyers, rather than business people and other professionals. Memberships too, have been ethnically skewed. While NGOs committed to Islam have attracted Malays, those addressing broader issues of public interest have recruited heavily from among the Chinese and Indians. And finally, the vitality of NGOs has been sapped by the threat of state coercion, especially after *Operasi Lalang* in 1987, leading them to suspend their links with political parties. In sum, Malaysia may have acquired a "denser" civil society since 1969, but one that remains substantially co-opted, ethnically fragmented, and repressed by the state.

Finally, despite the spread of factory employment in Malaysia, organized labor has generally been regarded as ineffective. More than one-third of the country's work force has been organized by unions affiliated with the Malaysian Trades Union Congress (MTUC), a federation that unlike the SPSI in New Order Indonesia and the NTUC in Singapore has maintained its independence from the state. And yet, with many workers also members of the UMNO's grass roots structure, attempts by the MTUC to form a new labor party in opposition have been hampered by fears of dividing worker loyalties.[61] What is more, when MTUC leaders have nevertheless joined existing opposition parties or launched major strikes, the government has often responded by arresting them under the ISA or setting up rival unions. Indeed, the government has been strongly encouraged in this by its alliances with international capital. For example, though the Ministry of Manpower once consented to electronics workers in Malaysia's free trade zones organizing along industrial lines, it soon pared back its authorization to in-house unions, having been threatened by transnational firms with swift disinvestment to other sites in Asia.[62] Hence, given its internal weaknesses, external pressures, and inability to forge any cross-class coalitions, organized labor has been unable to participate in ways that have more fully democratized Malaysian politics.

In sum, while social forces have stirred periodically in Malaysia, they cannot yet be characterized as participatory. Middle-class indifference to accountability during periods of rapid economic growth has weakened the opposition parties. Ethnic divisions have weakened the NGOs and trade unions that make up civil society. In these conditions, the government's deployment of legitimating mentalities and coercion have completed the task, confining social forces to a posture whereby elites need concede no more than a semi-democracy.

At the same time, one observes that if elites in the UMNO have modulated ethnic and class sentiments in ways that have encouraged social quiescence, their efforts to use Islam have as often handed over the tools of resistance. Historically, Islam has been felt most strongly in the rural Malay states of the peninsula's north, a region in which the rhythms of peasant life long conformed to the requirements of commercial agriculture and subsistence. And in this setting, education was offered in limited amounts, oftentimes through rustic *pondok* schools. During the 1970s, however, the NEP's scholarship schemes drew many of these students to universities in Kuala Lumpur and the West. Once in the capital, they grew keenly aware of social inequalities and rural-urban disparities. And when studying overseas, they were equally confronted by Western hedonism and their own profound sense of dislocation. Accordingly, even as the PAS was absorbed into the UMNO, Islamic students formed ABIM, then chose Anwar Ibrahim as their leader. And under Anwar's charismatic tutelage, students made increasingly strident criticisms of the UMNO, protesting fervently on behalf of impoverished *padi* farmers and urban squatters. Thus, amid an Islamic resurgence that swept across Asia and a student militancy that spanned the globe, the 1970s witnessed a great wave of Muslim student activism in Malaysia.

It was in this same NEP incubus that a broader category of middle-class Malays began also to form. And in having been so brusquely transported from the *kampung* to dense urban living, then saddled with new managerial tasks and parental fears, many middle-class Malays grew acutely concerned about the erosion of primary relationships and the rise of "social ills." Many of them appear also to have been troubled by the corrupt dealings they encountered, festering in the tight nexus between their bureaucratic roles and business dealings. In these circumstances, more rigorous approaches to Islam began to resonate among middle-class Malays – contributing to the pressures for a response from the UMNO.

The government responded to this Islamic revivalism with its trademark combinations of coercion and patronage. On the one hand, Anwar was detained for nearly two years under the ISA. Moreover, Mahathir, then serving as minister of education, tabled the highly restrictive Universities and University Colleges Act. And in 1981, the government added stringent amendments to the Societies Act, mainly it seems to contain the ABIM. On the other hand, we have seen that the PAS was absorbed into the *Barisan*

127

throughout most of the 1970s, then given control over a full ministry. A division for Islamic affairs was created in the Prime Minister's Department. And the year after Mahathir ascended to the prime ministership, he cunningly recruited Anwar into the UMNO, then rapidly escorted him up through the party's apparatus and cabinet hierarchy. He also provided meaningful concessions in the form of an Islamic university, an Islamic bank, and an Islamic insurance scheme, then rationalized the administration of Muslim law and enhanced the jurisdiction of *syariah* courts.

But if Anwar and many of his colleagues in ABIM entered the UMNO, the PAS departed the *Barisan*, then asserted in opposition a more strongly revivalist, indeed militant demeanor. Of course, this posture intimidated many middle-class Malays, leaving the PAS to perform poorly in the 1986 general election. But it appeared gradually to deepen the party's roots in the rural Malay states. Thus, in dispensing its developmental largesse, the UMNO discriminated systematically against villagers associated with the PAS, often fracturing village-level relations. In these conditions, local partisans avoided one another at traditional functions, worshiped in separate mosques, and forbade their children to enter into cross-party marriages. There is evidence too that the UMNO deployed goons while preparing for by-elections in the region, finally killing a PAS supporter in Lubok Merbau.[63] And in the "Memali incident" in 1985, an Islamic commune led by Ibrahim "Libya," a charismatic figure associated with the PAS, was attacked by security forces, resulting in the deaths of fourteen villagers and four police officers. In analyzing the impact of this confrontation, Jomo and Shabery Cheek record that

> the Memali incident shocked PAS militants into recognising the repressive character . . . of the state. . . . Despite much PAS rhetoric about martyrdom (a fate exalted in Islam) . . . of the victims . . . of Memali, the PAS leadership probably recognized that PAS was hardly prepared mentally, let alone physically and organizationally, for violent struggle.[64]

In these conditions, the PAS began to elaborate its revivalism with themes of neo-modernist tolerance, accountability, and good governance. And in coalition with the *Semangat '46*, it gained control over the Kelantan state assembly in 1990, then defended its strong majority in 1995. However, once securely in office, the PAS *menteri besar*, Nik Aziz Nik Mat, pledged to Islamicize all state institutions, the economy, and culture, while introducing too the *hudud* code of punishments. Of course, the UMNO responded by warning of the inappropriateness of such rigid Islamicization in a plural society. Beyond this, it reminded the PAS that forging an Islamic state would require constitutional changes, an outcome that the *Barisan* was empowered to block. And for good measure, the UMNO slowed federal development spending in Kelantan to a trickle. However, despite the economic stagnancy that resulted in Kelantan, we shall see in this chapter's final section that the PAS was able to win much more in the general election of 1999, gaining control over a second state assembly, while making deep inroads in parliament.

Another Islamic organization that gained prominence during this time posed further challenges to the UMNO. Known as *Al Arqam*,[65] this organization at one level operated a network of Muslim communes, clinics, and schools on soundly orthodox lines. In pursuing a modernist agenda, however, it welcomed new technologies, erecting computer rooms, engineering workshops, and sound studios. But most importantly, *Al Arqam* grew adept at business, operating small firms engaged mostly in the production of *halal* (religiously acceptable) food products. In this way, it gradually built up assets valued at US$120 million. Hence, in retaining an orthodox religiosity, yet fusing it with new entrepreneurial zeal, *Al Arqam* began to compete for the loyalties of the Malay middle class – a category that the UMNO claimed to have created. What is more, *Al Arqam* appeared even to be gaining large numbers of adherents within the UMNO itself.

Elites in the UMNO thus responded by denouncing *Al Arqam* as a "deviationist" cult. They then coordinated regional pressure against the organization through the ASEAN, leading to its activities being banned in other countries where it had operated, Thailand, Indonesia, and Brunei. *Al Arqam*'s leader was then deported from Thailand to Malaysia where he was arrested under the ISA. His closest followers were made to recant on public television. And the organization was officially disbanded at the end of the year. Even so, after the *Barisan*'s reelection in 1995, Mahathir announced the formation of special education camps for those in *Al Arqam* he tarred with apostasy.

And yet, despite this skilled synthesizing of coercion and patronage, various strands of Islam continued to flourish, finding their way deep into the rural Malay states, the Malay middle class of Kuala Lumpur, and even the UMNO's membership. Mahathir commissioned the Islamic Institute of Understanding in Malaysia (IKIM) to disseminate through workshops and public lectures new interpretations of Islam that were compatible with his industrializing visions. But bureaucratic agencies and state religious departments were as quickly infiltrated by revivalist elements who made more orthodox interpretations and issued stern rulings. As brief examples during this period, they inserted a new Islamic civilization subject into required university curricula, banned body-building competitions in Sarawak, and arrested beauty contestants in Selangor. Thus, during the 1990s, while economic growth seemed to ease ethnic grievances, even without awakening new class discontents, Islam – in its many guises – appeared rapidly to spread. And when finally Anwar was arrested once again, we shall see that Islam's appeal grew much stronger still.

To conclude this section, patterns of inter-elite and elite-mass relations have combined in ways that have produced in Malaysia a stable semi-democracy. This regime has been stable in that elites in the UMNO, the bureaucracy, and business conglomerates have perpetuated their cohesion, demonstrating a restrained competitiveness that is traceable to late colonial experience. And it has been semi-democratic because elites have also restrained social forces, modulating their appeals based on ethnicity, mentalities, performance, and coercion in ways proportionate to the changing tenor of participation.

More specifically, elites responded to the ethnically charged participation of May 13th by giving legal force to ethnic divisions, then unevenly rewarding the Malays and Chinese. In this situation, it became possible to open the regime in some ways while closing it in others, articulating the broad parameters for semi-democracy. Later, as the NEP encouraged more Malay participation, especially in the UMNO, elites responded first with cultural reinventions that stressed the rightfulness of Malay loyalty and organizational hierarchy. But when economic recession raised this participation to elite-level challenges, the national leader, Mahathir, responded more forcefully, purging the UMNO and tightening its rules, while broadly truncating civil liberties. In this way, semi-democracy was leveled more evenly across ethnic communities.

During the 1990s, however, economic recovery enabled elites to replenish their kit of controlling techniques, encouraging them to rely less on coercion than renewed social quiescence. Indeed, the government could again celebrate its developmental performance before broad social audiences, restoring them to private occupational pursuits. Further, because these gains were shared across ethnic communities, the government could ease its mobilization of the Malays without fear of their abandoning the UMNO, thus paving the way for the de-politicizing mentality of Vision 2020 and *bangsa Malaysia*. At the same time, though ethnic relations grew less confrontational, they rarely produced more collective political behaviors. This meant that the NGOs and trade unions that make up civil society, while in some measure vitalized by economic growth, at the same time remained stunted by lingering ethnic suspicions and arbitrary state controls. Of course, various strands of Islam made new headway during this period. But in the absence of other new galvanizing identities and themes to alloy it, political Islam remained mostly bottled up in peripheral Kelantan.

In these circumstances, the main arenas in which elites continued to compete and engage social forces were the UMNO assembly elections and general elections. The first election reaffirmed Malaysia's prime minister, while identifying a pool of UMNO elites from which he had then to recruit his top governing officials. The second election determined the size of his parliamentary majority – while revealing the extent and locations of social discontents. Of course, procedures in both arenas were restricted over time:

the rules governing UMNO assembly elections steadily tightened, while limits were placed on civil liberties prior to general elections. But these arenas have nonetheless retained enough institutional form that they have fed back to guide elite behaviors. And they have also ensured enough uncertainty in outcomes that the regime can still be classified as semi-democratic.

Contextual changes and a new elite strain point[66]

In mid-1997, Asia's financial crisis struck Malaysia, pushing down the *ringgit* by 40 per cent and Kuala Lumpur Stock Exchange indices by 80 per cent. Thus, after a decade of nearly double-digit growth, the economy suddenly contracted. As with other countries in the region, traders and fund managers focused closely on Malaysia's current account deficit, a symptom they attributed to cronyism, over-leveraging, and unproductive investments, especially in "mega-projects" and property development. Thus, they scrutinized the UMNO's many business dealings and the government's opaque forms of privatizing. Of course, one observes that Malaysia's difficulties were less severe than Indonesia's and Thailand's, enabling it to avoid appealing to the IMF. Specifically, while many firms had over-borrowed, most of them had done so locally, thus avoiding having to repay foreign loans with sharply diminished *ringgit*. Just the same, local banks were drained, causing liquidity shortages, driving up interest rates, pricking asset bubbles, and choking off business.

However, Prime Minister Mahathir refused to concede that his growth strategies of close government-business relations – what he labeled "Malaysia Inc." – were responsible. In his view, he had not favored cronies, but talented and indigenous worthies, those who had proven their managerial capacities in state enterprises and could then be nurtured to competitive entrepreneurship. But how, he asked, were they to compete in a global economy so distorted by "international manipulators," forces embodied by George Soros and Jews "who do not want to see a Muslim country do well?" He then lashed out at the currency speculators and hedge funds, blaming them for Malaysia's travails. But with Mahathir's every utterance, the currency traders and fund managers reduced their positions again, driving down the *ringgit* and stock prices further. And soon even local business elites grew weary of Mahathir, their assets having been sharply eroded. Thus, after several months, Mahathir fell silent, then turned over the levers of economic policy making to his deputy prime minister and finance minister, Anwar Ibrahim.

But Anwar, though on a lesser scale than Mahathir, had also worked through the UMNO to forge ties to business. Gomez reports in his study of Malaysia's political economy that "most influential and wealthy Malaysian businessmen by the early 1990s were also those most closely associated with

Prime Minister Mahathir Mohamad, Deputy Prime Minister Anwar Ibrahim, and government economic adviser Daim Zainuddin."[67] Indeed, Anwar battled mightily with Daim for possession of privatized assets during the mid-1990s. And with business people close to Daim evidently winning the most "lucrative privatizations," Anwar came steadily under pressure from his own business supporters.[68] Thus, we have seen the ways in which Anwar wrested control of New Straits Times Press, securing editorial support for his *wawasan* team, as well as a new source of revenue. Anwar also gained access to other media interests through Malaysian Resources Corporation and TV3. What is more, Malaysia Resources was involved in infrastructural projects, gaining from the government the much coveted status of independent power producer, then selling electricity to *Tenaga Nasional Bhd.*, the national electricity company, at high rates. Further, the *Yayasan Bumiputera Pulau Pinang*, "reputedly a political flagship of . . . Anwar," acquired divested government assets even prior to their being officially privatized.[69] Anwar also used networks centering on ABIM, thereby maintaining ties to such firms as Sapura Holdings, involved in telecommunications. And through links to Quek Leng Chan, Anwar worked closely with a major Chinese firm, the Hong Leong Group.

However, when Anwar gained a freer hand later in his tenure, he began to limit the corrupt practices of others. Thus, while serving as acting prime minister during an overseas trip by Mahathir during mid-1997, he forced the resignations of some top government officials and ordered their dealings to be investigated. And when Malaysia was gripped by economic crisis toward the end of the year, Anwar began to emerge still more clearly as a reformer. But his new policy outlooks – fueled by personal ambitions, a fresh burst of moral conviction, and a considered notion of how best to right the economy[70] – paved the way for confrontation with Mahathir. In particular, while Mahathir finally muted his rhetoric on the international stage, he continued to favor state assistance for key conglomerates.[71] He thus supported a bailout of Renong, a holding company associated with the UMNO whose director, Halim Saad, had been a protégé of Daim. And the national petroleum company, Petronas, also bought assets from an indebted shipping company, *Konsortium Perkapalan*, controlled by Mahthir's son.

Thus, just as Anwar had clashed earlier with Daim over privatized assets, so now did he resist Mahathir over bail-outs. Toward the end of the year, Anwar thus halted many infrastructural projects, then ordered an investigation into Renong. He also met with the IMF director, Michel Camdessus, then pushed an austerity program through a cabinet meeting before Mahathir arrived, cutting government spending still further.[72] What is more, at a forum in New York in April, Anwar characterized Asia's economic crisis as a blessing in disguise, one that would give rise to "creative destruction," breaking down the "perverse patronage" that characterized so much of business and politics in the region.[73] And upon his return from

New York, Anwar appears to have aborted a government bailout of Malaysian Airlines, run by another protégé of Daim, Tajudin Ramli. Of course, in adopting these contractionary policies, Anwar may have exacerbated the economic crisis, tipping Malaysia's economy more quickly into recession – in much the same way that the IMF had Indonesia, Thailand, and South Korea.[74] But these measures also enabled Anwar to gain new standing before Western governments and multilateral institutions, augmenting the already extensive personal and Islamic contacts that he had established throughout Southeast Asia and the Muslim world. One notes too that Anwar solidified these relationships with great personal charm, contrasting sharply with the irascibility of Mahathir.

The prime minister thus brooded, seeming to fear that his protégé was eclipsing him. Reports suggest, then, that by the time of the UMNO general assembly in June 1998, Mahathir had decided to drop Anwar from the government. At past general assemblies, anonymous *surat layang* ("flying letters") had often been photocopied and furtively circulated in order to besmirch various personages. But this time copies of a book entitled *Fifty Reasons Why Anwar Cannot be Prime Minister*, bearing the name of its author, a former sports writer, were inserted in the materials distributed to all 1900 assembly delegates – something that could not have taken place without Mahathir's knowledge.[75] The book was filled with detailed allegations about Anwar's corrupt practices, sexual misconduct, and even his spying for foreign countries.

But at the assembly, the UMNO Youth leader, Ahmad Zahid Hamidi, took up the cudgel on Anwar's behalf. In his Youth assembly address, Zahid denounced the "preferential treatment" given by banks to favored business people, even as small businesses struggled. Indeed, he invoked the idiom of *korupsi, kolusi, dan nepotisme* from Indonesia's democratizing experience, thus drawing parallels between Mahathir and Suharto. Next day, however, Mahathir countered by bearing ten lists of the many hundreds of persons and companies that had benefited through government contracts, privatizations, and special share allocations. While the lists contained the names of Halim Saad, Tajudin Ramli, Mahathir's three sons, and Daim Zainuddin's daughter, they also included Anwar's father, Anwar's private secretary, the secretary-general of ABIM, and, indeed, Zahid himself.[76] Thus, a chastened Anwar, in his own final address, pledged his support for Mahathir's continued leadership. And he promised also to help reflate the economy with a new fiscal stimulus package for construction and infrastructure.

Mahathir, though, was unmollified. Surely, he recollected Anwar's having pledged before the 1993 UMNO general assembly election not to contest the party's deputy presidency, only to ride a groundswell of support into the post that pre-empted a poll even being held. Accordingly, Mahathir worked now to weaken Anwar's standing. First, he brought Daim

Zainuddin into the cabinet as minister of special functions, thus augmenting the role that Daim already performed as head of the National Economic Action Council, tasked with devising a plan for recovery. Then, on September 1, Mahathir seized the reins personally, imposing controls on currency convertibility, short-term capital in-flows, and out-flows of capital gains. And in time, he would accumulate funds with which to recapitalize banks, then press them to step up their lending to conglomerates.

But most importantly, the day after imposing these controls, Mahathir confronted Anwar, ordering his deputy to resign from government or face a campaign of "humiliation."[77] Anwar refused, evidently insisting that their rift be exposed by his sacking. Mahathir duly removed Anwar from the government, then pressured the UMNO Supreme Council also to expel Anwar from the party. Shortly afterwards, the campaign of humiliation began, the government announcing that it would bring charges of sexual misconduct and corruption. Mahathir's strategists seemed to have calculated that with Anwar refusing to "go quietly," he had to be utterly disgraced in order to weaken his elite status. Though stripped of state power, Anwar would otherwise retain much charismatic appeal before his ethnic Malay followings.

Thus, the character and intensity of Mahathir's campaign against Anwar flagged new divisions in elite relations. These divisions were then signaled also by Anwar's response. Indeed, while a key indicator of elite cohesion involves the practiced under-mobilization of social constituents, Anwar now took his message of *reformasi* to the streets. Specifically, in coupling his notions of accountability with some residues of Islam and social activism, then calling openly for Mahathir's resignation, he appealed to broadly overlapping audiences of liberal Malays, intensely devout Muslims, and alienated Malay youths. In this way, during the Commonwealth Games in Kuala Lumpur in mid-September 1998, as Mahathir proudly joined Queen Elizabeth for the closing ceremonies, Anwar drew crowds of perhaps 50,000 near the city's Independence Square, the largest protest gathering ever seen in Malaysia.

Shortly afterward, Anwar was detained under the ISA through a heavy-handed police raid. Indeed, when he was presented in court nine days later on sexual misconduct and corruption charges, he appeared to have been badly beaten. The widespread indignation that followed sparked a series of weekend demonstrations, even clashes, in downtown Kuala Lumpur. And though the police reacted ferociously, the protesters persevered throughout much of October and November. But if the ISA order against Anwar was then rescinded, he was soon committed to trial on criminal charges, leading finally to a jail sentence in April 1999 of six years.[78] And after a second trial held in 2000, he was sentenced to an additional nine.

At the same time, mass action in the streets of Kuala Lumpur subsided. But they were succeeded by more sophisticated forms of mobilizing, namely NGOs and social movements, elements that in the aftermath of economic recession, greatly animated civil society. As we have seen, much of the Islamicist tone of this activity – enlivening the mosques and prompting mass defections from the UMNO to the PAS – prefigured Malaysia's rapid economic growth over the past of decade. But much of it can also be understood as a reaction against growth, while the neo-modernist form of Islam advocated by Anwar emerged from development more plainly, now resonating among Malay bureaucrats, business people, professionals, and students. In addition, broader processes of modernization equipped these forces with new organizational and technological capacity – boosted in part by Mahathir's own introduction of the Multimedia Super Corridor and information industries. In short, economic growth had created much potential for civil society, while economic crisis – by suddenly dividing elites and alienating social forces – served now to activate it.

Social resentments thus intensified over a sense of injustice committed against Anwar, the harshness of the police in putting down protesters, and the extreme partisanship of reporting by the mainstream media. Demands thus mounted for increased civil liberties and good governance. Established NGOs, like *Aliran* and *Suaram*, then articulated these demands through their journals, circulars, and internet communications. *Gerak* and *Gagasan*, two loose coalitions of political parties and NGOs, helped to aggregate different class and ethnic constituencies in broad-based opposition. Anwar's wife, Wan Azizah Wan Ismail, gave new focus to these efforts by forming a social movement, *Adil* (Movement for Social Justice). Academics, moreover, published highly critical accounts of government policies in the international press, while artists and entertainers lampooned government figures before middle-class audiences in the capital. In addition, these sentiments filtered steadily into political society, with the PAS then amplifying them through its publication, *Harakah*. At the same time, the largely Chinese DAP, motivated separately by the jailing some months earlier of one of is leaders, Lim Guan Eng, also took up the clarion call of *reformasi*. And in an attempt finally to bridge ethnic communities, *Adil* began to mediate relations between the PAS and the DAP. In consequence, social forces in Malaysia, even after easing their street demonstrations, drew closer to what O'Donnell and Schmitter have labeled the "resurrection of civil society."[79]

In a setting, then, of strained elite relations and highly mobilized social forces, Malaysia might have seemed poised for the same kind of democratic transition that Indonesia had undergone, namely, opposition-led replacement. But in Indonesia, we have seen that economic crisis denied Suharto the resources with which any longer to manage elites. And because he had never permitted elites to gain cohesion, he later stood by haplessly as they dispersed in factions, with many of them finally abandoning him. Indeed, far from perpetuating elite statuses, he was now regarded as endangering them. Mahathir was more fortunate on two counts. First, Malaysia was less affected by economic crisis, leaving intact many patronage resources.

Further, elites had long displayed patterns of cohesive behavior, leaving them collectively amenable to the patronage that Mahathir could still dispense. Indeed, they continued to view him – quite unlike elites did Suharto in Indonesia – as the leader best able to preserve their positions and fortunes. Accordingly, few joined with Anwar in confronting either Mahathir or other elites. And none joined with Anwar in mobilizing social forces. In the rest of this section, then, let us briefly investigate the ways in which after ousting Anwar, Mahathir then isolated him, thus narrowing elite divisions into a resolvable strain point. In this chapter's final section, we will examine the ways in which through general elections, elites then engaged social forces.

Mahathir began with the UMNO Supreme Council and the cabinet and chief ministerships it roughly paralleled. In particular, while most members seemed to have applauded Anwar's sacking, a few were known to have been troubled by it. They were effectively silenced, however, by their fear of losing the perquisites attached to their posts. Later, toward the end of 1998, Mahathir maneuvered more deeply in the party, convening an extraordinary general assembly through which again to amend the UMNO constitution, then roll back the assembly election scheduled for mid-1999. In this way, the trusted new deputy prime minister he appointed, Abdullah Badawi, was freed from having to contest the corresponding party position, the UMNO deputy presidency. Mahathir was thus able to avoid any recurrence of the challenge that he and Ghafar Baba, his deputy of a half-decade ago, had faced at the assembly election in 1987.

Of course, in doing this, Mahathir's arbitrariness would appear to have run counter to the UMNO's lore about its democratic procedures and grassroots character, thus alienating aspirants for the deputy presidency. But by keeping a firm grip on the UMNO machinery and its commensurate positions in government – far better than Suharto did with the *Golkar*, the DPR, and indeed, his own cabinet – Mahathir was able to gain the acquiescence of the party's elites and its rank and file. Mahathir exerted control too over other key institutions, removing those few elites still openly associated with Anwar.[80] This included top officials in Malaysia's central bank, some editorial and television offices linked to the UMNO, a key policy think tank, and the University of Malaya. He also pressed for the removal of several corporate figures – though given the great importance Mahathir attached to propping up conglomerates in the midst of crisis, few directors or top managers would have deserted him. Indeed, the cohesion that Mahathir perpetuated across business elites, both Malay and Chinese, lay in stark contrast to Suharto's situation. Put simply, there were no figures on Malaysia's business scene to perform the dissident roles of Arifin Panigoro and Sofjan Wanandi.

In sum, the region's economic crisis affected Malaysia less severely than Indonesia, preserving the worth of institutional positions through which to attract and dispense patronage. But these distributions were buttressed also by a long record of elite cohesion, enabling Mahathir more easily to keep elites on side. Indeed, he elicited new shows of loyalty within the UMNO. The party's extraordinary assembly at the end of 1998, for example, even while truncating the rights of its delegates, "served as a ringing endorsement of Mahathir" – with the party's Youth and *Wanita* even tabling a special motion of support.[81] Thus, with Mahathir perpetuating elite cohesion, let us turn now to the ways in which he engaged social forces through general elections.

The 1999 general election and more participatory society[82]

In mid-November 1999, Mahathir dissolved parliament, then arranged a hurried eight-day campaign period leading to general elections. Of course, his *Barisan* coalition made little attempt to elaborate its appeals beyond a vague mentality – as one quickly learns when perusing its manifesto. Entitled *Malaysia: Free, United, Successful*, the sixteen-page document declared the country "free" in that it had warded off "communist terrorists," "rogue currency traders," and the IMF; "united" because of the "implementation of restructuring policies," a fair distribution of wealth, and because Malaysians "idolize sports personalities regardless of race"; and "successful" because the country enjoys strong economic and financial positions without depending on foreign help."[83] The government conceded that its manifesto was "nothing exciting or dramatic," but instead enumerated plainly its developmental achievements.[84]

Hence, in appealing to social forces, *Barisan* candidates relied less on programmatic themes than pragmatic appeals, rehearsing the incumbent government's unique capacity to deliver the goods. They did little, then, to disguise the tight nexus in Malaysia between the government of the day and the organs of state, enabling them to contrast their steady conveyance of patronage with what they opined were the opposition's empty promises. Accordingly, the *Barisan* tried first to re-energize the loyalties of Malay civil servants, pledging during the campaign a 1000 *ringgit* bonus, payable in four installments that would commence that very month. The Public Service Department advised also the country's nearly 400,000 pensioners that they could soon expect higher payments. What is more, the central bank now released its estimates of 8.1 per cent growth in GDP for the third quarter of 1999, "the highest . . . since the onset of the economic crisis in 1997." This enabled PNB also to unveil a 12 per cent dividend from *Amanah Saham Bumiputera*, its unit trust, a 1.5 per cent increase over the previous year that would mainly benefit Malay shareholders. At the same time, these growth figures cheered Chinese business people, with the Associated Chinese Chambers of Commerce and Industry of Malaysia expressing its "whole-hearted support" for Mahathir. "He led the country out of the . . . economic crisis and we are grateful for the measures taken," declared the organization's spokesman.[85]

In broadcasting state patronage further afield, government ministers circulated round the country, augmenting the efforts of lesser *Barisan* candidates. Daim Zaiunuddin, while campaigning in Sabah, announced new government projects that would provide 70,000 houses. The minister of international trade and industry, Rafidah Aziz, in defending her seat in Perak, announced the government's approval of a 45 million *ringgit* bridge at Sayong – "timely," Rafidah said, because the government planned also to build a university in the town.[86] Similarly, the education minister, Najib Razak, announced a new university for his state of Pahang, while the *menteri besar* of Selangor promised a bridge to the upcountry folk of Kuala Selangor, complementing the sports complex they had received the previous year. But perhaps best encapsulating the tenor of the *Barisan*'s campaigning was the introduction given during a rally for Samy Vellu, the public works minister, by a state assemblyman: "What we want, Samy Vellu gets it for us. We have development, good roads, bridges, fly-overs. He only needs to *bisik* [whisper] to Prime Minister Datuk Seri Dr. Mahathir Mohamad and we've got it."[87]

However, as the *Barisan* celebrated its provision of patronage, the opposition parties displayed much vitality in 1999, increasing uncertainty over the government's margin of electoral victory. In particular, Wan Azizah led *Adil* and a number of other NGOs in merging as the *Parti Keadilan Nasional* (National Justice Party). The party began its political life by appealing to "liberal" Malays, usually in urban areas, those who valued the economic growth that the UMNO had fostered, but were alienated now by the government's corrupt practices and authoritarian controls. In short, *Keadilan* sought to raise the sympathy that Wan Azizah could expect over Anwar's travails into more substantive middle-class demands for good governance. *Keadilan* was shadowed too by another opposition party, the *Parti Rakyat Malaysia* (PRM, Malaysian People's Party), a small, though venerable organization that after having undergone several permutations, appeared now to focus selectively on contemplative professionals and NGO activists.

Some of this longing for good governance filtered also into the Malay states, increasing support for the PAS. *Harakah*, the PAS newspaper, thus investigated the UMNO's business activities, with villagers everywhere growing versed in the dealings of Renong and the sons of Mahathir. *Harakah*'s reporting was reinforced also by accounts downloaded regularly from the internet, photocopied, and widely disseminated across *kampung*. However, it seemed less a concern for transparency than outrage over UMNO "cruelty," signified by Anwar's beating while in police custody, that most encouraged rural Malay support for the PAS. In addition, as mentioned above, rural Malays were often less concerned with economic recovery than Islamic resurgence, mitigating the social inequalities, the fragility of families, and the waywardness of young people they viewed *Barisan* policies to have spawned. Hence, in contrast to *Keadilan*, which appealed to liberal Malays, the PAS appealed mostly to collectivist Malay sentiments.

At the other end of the opposition spectrum lay the DAP, nominally socialist and multi-ethnic, though long venting the grievances of urban Chinese over their perceptions of "second-class" citizenship. The DAP has thus campaigned stridently against the UMNO's traditional stand on Malay special rights, demanding instead a "Malaysian Malaysia." Historically, though, the DAP has been as critical of the PAS as it has been of the UMNO, viewing the prospect of an Islamic state as even more odious than Malay special rights. However, in responding to changed incentives in 1999, the DAP found new reasons to cooperate with the PAS. Specifically, with mass Malay sentiments appearing to have turned strongly against the UMNO, the DAP saw an opportunity to break what it termed the *Barisan's* "political hegemony." Accordingly, it supported *Keadilan* in calling for good governance. But it cooperated also with the PAS in order to gain electoral weight – calculating that this would never so empower its new partner that an Islamic state could finally be instituted. The DAP thus joined *Keadilan*, the PAS, and the PRM in forging a coalition that mirrored the government's own, labeling it the *Barisan Alternatif* (Alternative Front).

Accordingly, these parties reached an electoral agreement in which they put up only one candidate in each district, an understanding that was extended to the United Party of Sabah (PBS). And they produced a common manifesto, "Toward a Just Malaysia," which, while far more substantive than that of the *Barisan*, was most notable for what it left out. Specifically, there was no mention of the PAS's commitments to an Islamic state or the DAP's call for a Malaysian Malaysia. Instead, the PAS symbol of a full moon was coupled informally with the DAP's rocket, producing a popular refrain of "rocket to the moon." And with *Keadilan* serving as the linchpin, the *Barisan Alternatif* chose Anwar as its pilot, that is, its nominee for the prime ministership.[88]

In these circumstances, the *Barisan* found that merely standing on its developmental record was failing to retain constituent support. It resorted, then, to targeting the opposition with negative campaigning. Specifically, the *Barisan's* insistence on its indispensability grew much more shrill, its task having increased from advancing economic recovery to keeping fundamental social order. To this end, it mounted a media "blitz," involving many successive full-page advertisements in local dailies, often featuring scenes from the previous year's street confrontations. Voters could evidently expect a recurrence of such disturbances if they supported *Keadilan* in its push for *reformasi*. Worse, they risked ethnic riots reminiscent of May 13th if they supported the PAS and the DAP. In this way, the *Barisan* implied that strong government was necessary to contain these forces, signified by its again being given a two-thirds majority in parliament.

But in campaigning on these lines, the *Barisan* heightened precisely the fears that it had pledged to contain, deploying multiple narratives in the ethnically defined constituencies that gerrymandering makes possible. For example, while campaigning in the northern state of Terengganu, Mahathir told Malay audiences that the PAS was betraying them by making false promises of an Islamic state. "They want to do things they cannot do. They must get a two-thirds majority in Parliament," he intoned.[89] He then castigated the PAS as "a party of liars."[90] At the same time, in Chinese constituencies of Kuala Lumpur, the MCA president, Ling Liong Sik, warned that the DAP had betrayed the Chinese by aligning with the PAS. "It is very clear," he stated. "One vote for the DAP is a vote for . . . an Islamic state and *hudud* laws."[91] For good measure, the acting UMNO Youth chief, Hishammudin Hussein, criticized the DAP in Malay areas, revealing the party's "secret mission . . . to introduce Jewish ideologies among Malaysians and eventually destroy Islam." He explained that this was achieved through DAP's involvement in the Socialist International, which also included the Labour Party of Israel.[92]

Highly personalized attacks were mounted also against Anwar, with Mahathir branding his former deputy a "liar" and a "thief," secretly amassing a RM3 billion slush fund while in power.[93] Anwar was said also to have caused riots in Kedah, taken land from peasants in Penang, and approved slot machines for Sabah.[94] Moreover, it was disclosed in the press that Anwar was not the founder of Malaysia's International Islamic University, as had commonly been thought. The true founder had instead been Mahathir.[95] Photographs were published in an UMNO-controlled newspaper of Anwar dancing with "an unidentified woman" and cavorting with a singer.[96] Videotapes of Anwar's adopted brother, Sukma Darmawan, confessing to police his having committed sodomy, appeared mysteriously one morning round bus stands and market places in Kuala Lumpur and elsewhere.[97]

The *Barisan*'s negative campaigning soon took its toll, with the diverse constituencies of the opposition tugging their respective parties in quite separate directions. Most notably, the PAS edged away from the DAP, now issuing "supplementary manifestos" in Kelantan and Terengganu that revived earlier commitments to rule in close accordance with Islam.[98] Indeed, Kelantan's *menteri besar*, Nik Aziz Nik Mat, highlighted the rightfulness of Islamic punishments with a query: "The Malaysian government hangs a person for drug offenses. Under *hudud* it is just cutting off of the hand . . . Why do people get agitated over *hudud* when hundreds have died from hanging?"[99]

Such logic made it difficult for the DAP effectively to appeal to the Chinese. It thus reiterated its argument in Chinese districts – ironically, the same one conveyed by Mahathir in Malay areas – that the PAS could not win the two-thirds parliamentary majority it needed in order to impose an Islamic state. Hence, the DAP reasoned, it was safe to coalesce with the PAS in order to check the *Barisan*. However, this argument was framed too subtly for many Chinese voters. In conditions of economic recovery and ethnic peace, they could see little benefit in strengthening the PAS, even if stopping short of the brink. Nor did many Chinese appear moved by the plight of Anwar Ibrahim, seeing his ouster as an intra-Malay fight.[100] In these circumstances, the DAP leader, Lim Kit Siang, acknowledged the risk of his party's involvement in the *Barisan Alternatif*, concluding that it "could win big, or lose it all."

During the last days of campaigning, the *Barisan* diversified its strategies, perpetuating its dirty tricks, but also returning intermittently to the high road. In particular, it appealed for the "silent majority" to vote, warning against widespread complacency.[101] It reached out also to women voters and "fence-sitters," contrasting the gains made by women during the *Barisan*'s tenure with the fate they could expect under the PAS. Election day was also proclaimed for the first time a national holiday, reducing the barriers to participation. Mahathir asked voters too that when casting their ballots, they avoid emotion and sympathy, because "that's not politics." He then revisited the "Anwar factor" once more.

I realize many people grieve over Anwar's fate. I am grieving too, especially for his wife and children. But there have been many people imprisoned who have wives and children. This is what happens when you break the law.[102]

When results were reported the day after elections, the exercise appeared to have gone according to plan. The *Barisan* easily retained its two-thirds parliamentary majority, taking 148 seats. It also swept the state assemblies of Johor, Negeri Sembilan, and Sarawak, while winning extraordinary majorities in all other states of the west coast and south in Peninsular Malaysia, as well as in Sabah. Hence, in his press conference afterward, Mahathir was able to present the *Barisan* as "still the party of choice of the people of Malaysia."[103] He was then duly chaired.

But as analysts scrutinized the returns more closely, they noted that while the *Barisan* had performed adequately overall, its keystone, the UMNO, had been gravely weakened. Indeed, the UMNO lost nearly half of the Malay vote, leaving it to depend heavily on the Chinese. In these circumstances, the party's parliamentary vote total sagged some 20 per cent, leaving it with only 71 seats – and hence, for the first time fewer seats than the combined total of its non-Malay coalition partners. Four UMNO ministers and a raft of deputy ministers thus went down in defeat. Moreover, the party was routed in the state assemblies of Kelantan and Terengganu, while suffering setbacks too in Kedah, Perlis, Pahang, and

Selangor. And with its majorities eroded where even its candidates were victorious, the election was soon interpreted as an expression of deep Malay ambivalence over Mahathir's leadership.

But it is important that the UMNO's decline not be exaggerated. Indeed, some of its most formidable opponents fared even worse. In particular, *Keadilan* stumbled badly in its appeal to liberal Malays. As Chandra Muzaffar, one of the party's best known candidates lamented, "The Malays are angry with the government over a number of issues . . . but they are not angry enough to vote candidates from the opposition front into power"[104] *Keadilan* failed also into its bid to link the ethnic outliers of the opposition front by appealing to non-Malay liberals. Hence, the party's most prominent reformists, all competing in mixed districts in the Klang Valley and Melaka, were defeated by the UMNO or its coalition partners, albeit in some instances by narrow margins. Of course, Wan Azizah won in her husband's former constituency in Penang. But of the 59 seats that *Keadilan* had contested, it won only five. Thus, Wan Azizah's assessment that her party had performed well for one so newly registered must be weighed against the fact that the liberal elements she had attempted to tap had been in the making for more than a decade.[105] More specifically, neither a prolonged trajectory of rapid economic growth, nor a pattern of growth complicated by recession had prompted the middle class finally to make its participatory debut. Perhaps in anticipation of this, *Keadilan* adopted a much more Islamicized demeanor toward the end of the campaign – just as *Semangat '46* had earlier gained a more pro-Malay tone. Indeed, *Keadilan* learned in this election as *'46* had in the last one that for liberal Malays concerned with economic growth and the patronage that it offers, there can be no political life outside the UMNO.[106]

In addition, while the DAP showed some numerical improvement, raising its tally from seven parliamentary seats to 10, this election marked the party's second worst showing since 1969. Further, its most celebrated warhorses, Lim Kit Siang and Karpal Singh – so opposed to the *Barisan* that they had collaborated with the PAS – were defeated in both their parliamentary and state races. Some younger party candidates, however, more willing to conciliate the *Barisan* in order to free up constituency services, succeeded in winning seats in Penang. Nonetheless, whether collaborating with the PAS or conciliating the *Barisan*, the DAP's new orientations showed clearly that ethnicity had softened as an issue in Malaysian politics. And robbed of its opportunities to mobilize Chinese resentments, the DAP could compensate only partly by focusing on constituency services. The party made even less headway in its broader appeals for good governance pitched at the middle class. Thus, in reflecting on his involvement in the opposition front, Lim Kit Siang noted, "We did it to try and break the *Barisan Nasional*'s political hegemony to bring about justice, fair play, and ideals for a vibrant democracy. But we failed. Up to the last day I had been saying that we might either win big or lose big."[107] The DAP was thus left in something of the condition that the MCA had suffered after elections in 1969, famously diagnosed by Tun Dr. Ismail as "more dead than alive."

In sum, the UMNO-led *Barisan* was seriously challenged by neither the new middle class or traditional communalism. Instead, the UMNO's greatest opponent became the Islamicist PAS. Indeed, the PAS increased its parliamentary seats from eight to 27, now earning the right to head the opposition. And, as mentioned above, it won the state assemblies of Kelantan and Terengganu, while making deep inroads elsewhere. In consequence, Malaysia's 1999 election helped to clarify what had recently become a muddled political sociology. Most notably, the cleavage between the modernizing UMNO and the revivalist PAS, traceable to independence, then intensified during the 1980s, came now to crystallize once more.[108] It has been reinforced geographically too, with the UMNO in the peninsula's south and west facing off against the PAS in the north.

However, in thinking about how the UMNO might counter the PAS, one notes that the party can still avail itself of semi-democratic controls. Statutes can be passed through which to prohibit parties from making religious appeals, thereby denying the PAS its revivalist plank. Another redelineation could also be undertaken, finally easing the rural weightage in order to revalue Chinese votes. And with economic recovery underway, thus replenishing UMNO coffers, the party may refashion its development strategies. While starving Sabah of development funding has appeared to wear down the opposition, a similar approach in Kelantan has only intensified Islamic resentments. Accordingly, the UMNO's diverting some funding from big corporate bail-outs to small businesses in the Malay heartland would probably do much to re-energize support, thereby sparking new rivalries inside PAS constituencies. Distribution of such funding in non-partisan ways would help also to ease popular pressures in Terengganu for the PAS government to be awarded greater petroleum royalties.

To conclude, Malaysia's general election in 1999 indicated clearly the stable nature of its semi-democratic regime. Specifically, an unpopular government used semi-democratic controls in order to prolong its tenure, thus preventing the regime from unfolding in any fuller democracy. At the same time, the government did not tighten controls so much that the opposition was stopped from making new gains, thereby preventing the regime from lapsing in deeper authoritarianism. Indeed, what the UMNO-led *Barisan* lost in terms of popular votes, it may have taken back in terms of political legitimacy. In this situation, Prime Minister Mahathir, smiling broadly at his post-electoral press conference, reflected on the loss of Kelantan and Terengganu: "We will win it back next time. We accept that because ours is a democratic country."[109]

Conclusions

Malaysia's political record is distinguished by powerful historical, structural, and modernizing forces, giving rise to long continuities, as well as sharp dialectical ripostes. In particular, Malaysia's colonial legacy involved economic openness, but offered some scope for state interventions. It also divided society, juxtaposing Malay, Chinese, and Indian social identities, then rigidifying them with occupational differences and economic inequalities. Further, these ethnic divisions limited the ways in which politics could be organized, militating strongly against democracy. Nonetheless, as the British prepared to decolonize Malaysia, they introduced democratic procedures, steadily exposing local elites to elections. And the cohesion among elites they helped to foster, made manifest in the bargain, enabled these procedures to persist throughout the 1950s–60s.

But the social structure underlying this democracy remained uncongenial. And as urbanization brought ethnic communities into closer contact, it sharpened their antagonisms toward one another, as well as toward elites in the Alliance who perpetuated their inequalities. In brief, the Malays resented the barriers they encountered to the economy's modern sectors, while Chinese grievances mounted over their political and cultural statuses. This volatile setting was finally ignited by the results of the 1969 elections, with highly participatory social forces erupting in the May 13th rioting that broke democracy down.

And yet, if Malaysia demonstrates vividly the importance of contextual factors, it shows also the ways in which elites can reorganize their relations, thus earning much political autonomy. From the perspective of this book, then, what stands out is less the violence of social forces and the breakdown of democracy than the extent to which elites perpetuated their own unity, restored social quiescence, then recalibrated the regime as a semi-democracy. In brief, after May 13th, elites in the UMNO struck deeply into the economy, imposing steep NEP quotas in order to re-energize the loyalties of mass-level Malays. At the same time, if in doing this elites in the UMNO alienated mass-level Chinese and weakened MCA politicians, they entered the economy in ways that respected the statuses of Chinese business elites. In consequence, with Malay loyalties now re-energized in proportion to Chinese alienation, it grew possible to set up a semi-democracy. And with elites perpetuating much cohesion across ethnic lines, this regime could be stabilized too. In these circumstances, elites waged their competitions and engaged social forces through a pair of highly institutionalized and inter-related arenas, namely, the UMNO assembly elections and general elections. However, because this was a semi-democracy, competitions were bounded by ever tightening party rules and limited civil liberties.

But with more state power and business assets now concentrated in the UMNO, competitions in the party soon surged. Indeed, during periods when the party had more or less patronage to dispense than was usually the case, exacerbating acquisitiveness and frustrations respectively, elite struggles welled in distinct strain points. Accordingly, elite cohesion was tested at these junctures, resulting in the jailing of Harun Idris, the marginalization of Tengku Razaleigh, the ouster of Ghafar Baba, and the purging of Anwar Ibrahim. Further, where losses of patronage were rooted in deeper economic recession, these strain points were intensified by new levels of social participation, made manifest in the reform movements of the late-1980s and late-1990s. It is here that one might have expected Malaysia's semi-democracy to be destabilized, then perhaps more fully democratized. However, we have seen that in the first three of these strain points, elites drew back from their mobilization of social forces. And elites who had been vanquished in these competitions were able afterwards to regain their prerogatives. Harun Idris was pardoned, then operated UMNO enterprises. Razaleigh returned to the UMNO, then drew close to Mahathir. And Ghafar Baba, after quitting his party posts in 1993, was returned as an UMNO parliamentarian in the 1999 elections. It is only Anwar Ibrahim who awaits some restoration of his status.[110]

In making sense of this conflict between Mahathir and Anwar, one best conceptualizes it is an elite-level struggle for political paramountcy. Analyses that focus on the differences in their economic agendas appear to have been overdrawn. Specifically, while Mahathir vilified international manipulators and reacted with capital controls, he continued to value foreign direct investment as a necessary part of Malaysia's industrialization. He was, in short, no isolationist. Anwar, though criticizing crony capitalism and countermanding bail-outs, had himself engaged in money politics. It was thus difficult to think of him as a tireless reformer. But in competing for paramountcy, Mahathir and Anwar began to exaggerate their policy differences, then used their respective resources to galvanize support. Mahathir used state power, firming elite loyalties in the UMNO Supreme Council and cabinet, bureaucratic agencies, media offices, and corporate boardrooms. Indeed, by reducing interest rates, restoring equity prices, and ordering bail-outs, he won back Malay and Chinese business elites. And because these measures also preserved professional and mid-management positions, while reducing the costs of mortgages and car loans, he won back most middle-class constituencies too, especially urban Chinese already fearful of ethnic violence. Hence, in effectively using state power, Mahathir restored the loyalties – or at least gained the acquiescence – of elites and key social constituencies. He was thus able to roll back the 1999 UMNO assembly election to 2000, then arrange for the party presidency and deputy presidency to remain uncontested.

However, if Anwar was in this way denied state power and elite-level support, he possessed enough charisma and tapped enough social grievances that he was able to energize much mass-level support. In particular, while burnishing his Islamicist and activist persona, he called also for good governance which, in the context of rapid economic growth followed by recession, sparked the broad movement for *reformesi*. Malay young people thus confronted police in the streets. Malay liberals and government workers intimated their discontents. And government leaders and media outlets throughout Southeast Asia and the West declared their support for Anwar quite openly.

It has been a key argument of this book that when elites are divided, they may rapidly give way to democratic pressures from below. They may begin even to encourage these pressures themselves in order better to compete with other elites. But in Malaysia, Mahathir isolated Anwar at the elite level. Moreover, divisions appeared at the mass level among even those forces that supported Anwar. For example, because student bodies in Malaysia, in comparison to Indonesia, contain in proportional terms more "non-indigenous" students, their solidary commitments to political change are diminished. In addition, across their numbers, students in Malaysia remained far more responsive to government threats of expulsion. Put simply, Malaysia possessed a far more robust economy than Indonesia, one in which degree-holders could still reasonably expect to find their place. Further, those segments of the Malay middle class that demanded civil liberties departed from the communitarian ethos of revivalist Muslims. And Islamic revivalism, finally, stirred deeply the suspicions of most Chinese. Hence, while the parties of the *Barisan Alternatif* tried to forge new understandings, they were unable finally to unite their respective follow-ings. Indeed, in the 1999 general election, it was only the PAS that made great gains in opposition. It is difficult to see, then, how social forces, though having grown more participatory, might combine in their support for Anwar in ways that would democratize Malaysian politics.

Of course, even in these circumstances, this book has outlined a second pathway to democracy, one in which cohesive elites calculate jointly that the best way to perpetuate their statuses is by making democratic concessions to a participatory society. But Mahathir, in keeping his grip on elites, then confronting a participatory, though divided society, has remained able to refuse any greater concessions than the semi-democracy already on offer. Indeed, since the elections in 1999, Mahathir has continued his broad practice of moving resolutely the other way, arresting dissidents and clamping down on the press. At the start of the millenium, then, the only clear challenge to Mahathir's tenure remained his own mortality.

Chapter 5
Thailand

———◆———

An Unconsolidated Democracy

In Thailand, unlike the other countries in Southeast Asia we have investigated, elites have neither been cohesive or managed effectively by any paramount national leader. Instead, elites have competed for state power and business resources in unrestrained ways, often ruthlessly undermining one another's statuses while secretly mobilizing outsiders. In these circumstances, national leaders have been drawn into the fray, participating on nearly equal terms with other elite players, rather than presiding from above. And even if some, like Field Marshall Sarit Thanarat and General Prem Tinsulanond, emerged for a time to moderate elite rivalries, they never gained the paramountcy or longevity of Suharto, Lee Kuan Yew, or Mahathir.

This chapter begins by enumerating some of the consequences of this disunity, clearly distinguishing Thailand's politics, economy, and society. It then charts the organizational bases of elites and the competitive strategies they have deployed. It also investigates the ways in which elites have mobilized social constituencies – or dispersed social forces – and the ways in which these forces have responded. Next, the chapter outlines the unstable regime types that have emerged over time from these prior patterns of inter-elite and elite-mass relations, evolving finally into a democracy today. It concludes with an analysis of Thailand's general election in 2001, gauging the prospects for democracy's consolidating.

Thailand in the region

Disunity between Thailand's elites, usually unmitigated by any paramount national leader, has produced some distinctive outcomes in Thailand. First, in comparison to the other country cases examined so far in this volume, one is struck by the state's limited capacity, indicated by the quality of its economic planning and provincial administration. In particular, while state elites in Thailand have experimented periodically with import substitution since the late 1950s, they have more generally granted and withdrawn

147

contracts and licenses, then raised and lowered tariffs in ways that from a planning perspective must often be regarded as *ad hoc*, responding most strongly to the contingencies of factional competitions between elites. Only during the tenures of Field Marshal Sarit and General Prem did the state perform a more sustained developmental role, though even these leaders' strategies relied less on disciplined state interventions than releasing business from the constraints that the state itself had imposed. Consequently, in the Thai setting, one finds no grand socioeconomic or developmentalist programs like Singapore's "external wing," Malaysia's "Look East" and Vision 2020, or even New Order Indonesia's sustained commitments to *pembangunan*.

Moreover, in terms of administration, while Thailand's military and bureaucracy have been present, of course, throughout the country's provincial areas, they appear often to have been overshadowed by local business people. The military, through its anti-Communist campaigns during the 1970s and its rural development programs during the 1980s, penetrated the hinterland deeply. But in competing then for lucrative dealings – in timber concessions, weapons sales, and drug smuggling – regional commanders have often been distracted from their security and developmental tasks, miring them in dense local networks. District officers and local police have been even more seriously eclipsed, shrinking before the far greater capacity of business people to accumulate resources and dispense patronage and services, however informally. Thus, on this administrative dimension too the comparative weakness of the Thai state stands out. While in New Order Indonesia, for example, regional commanders and administrative officials certainly colluded with local business people, they maintained an upper hand, even shaking local notables down. Equally, throughout most of Malaysia's countryside, the UMNO's party apparatus, intertwined tightly with the state bureaucracy, has kept a tight grip through patronage and subtle forms of intimidation. And Singapore's PAP makes the point with still greater force, penetrating deeply the neighborhoods and public housing blocks of its island redoubt.

This disunity between elites and the commensurate weakness of the state distinguish Thailand in a second way, namely by their ceding much autonomy to private business. Put simply, elite factions in the state, seeking allies against rivals, have readily formed linkages to business elites. And business elites, in turn, in providing resources, have been able to demand more over time than mere influence and protection. Indeed, they have been able to make direct bids for state power, quite unlike their counterparts in New Order Indonesia, Singapore, and even Malaysia. More specifically, Bangkok-based conglomerates began to emerge under military and bureaucratic tutelage during the 1960s. Then, in the next decade, these conglomerates broke away from the military, forming new parties that helped to democratize politics. Finally, business people from the provinces

148

overtook big business in parliament, then pressed for more competitive elections during the late 1980s. However, lest one find in this unique progress reasons for optimism, we are reminded that the democratizing motives of business elites and their performances once in power leave room for grave doubts. One is right to be wary also of their business practices.[1]

A third feature that distinguishes Thailand from Indonesia and Malaysia involves a relatively benign social structure, one that helps also to explain the early autonomy gained by business. In particular, private business in Thailand, as in much of Southeast Asia, has been dominated by ethnic Chinese. But the Chinese in Thailand, often designated "Sino-Thais," have encountered fewer of the ethnic and religious barriers that have hindered their counterparts elsewhere in the region. Of course, this has been casually attributed by many analysts to Buddhism's possessing a more accommodative tenor than the Islamic outlooks prevailing in Indonesia and Malaysia. But even on this count, the importance of elite voluntarism remains clear. State elites in Buddhist Myanmar and Vietnam have historically conducted deep purges of Chinese business people. And in Thailand, we shall see that before World War II, governments tapped anti-Chinese sentiments in order to arouse mass support. In addition, for a decade or so after the war, Thai governments exploited Chinese business elites, stigmatizing them as "pariah entrepreneurs." Nonetheless, indigenous elites in the military and bureaucracy chose later to mute their ethnic appeals, striking up new alliances with business conglomerates based in Bangkok. In this way, Chinese business elites grew more able to operate freely, then began even to form political parties during the 1970s.

Accordingly, political parties emerged as a distinct organizational basis for elite statuses, helping to distinguish Thailand in a fourth way. Put simply, parties gained an independence that despite their internal factionalism, thin mentalities, and often temporal quality opened up a separate route to elite statuses and state power – a configuration quite in contrast to the utter fusion of state apparatuses and political parties in New Order Indonesia, Singapore, and Malaysia. In short, while national leaders in these other three countries simultaneously drew strength from their state and party hierarchies, parties in Thailand could autonomously promote their officials as prime ministers, even ones who were predominantly ethnic Chinese – an unthinkable outcome in Indonesia and Malaysia.

A fifth way in which Thailand has been distinctive is that while the country's level of development has been much lower than Singapore's or even Malaysia's, its disunity between state elites has enabled civil society to grow active much sooner. Specifically, in waging their competitions, different elite factions in the military and bureaucracy have looked beyond their alliances with Chinese business. They have sought broader social constituencies with which to undergird their statuses, or at least to precipitate mass actions that could embarrass their rivals. Hence, state elites have occasionally mobilized, instigated, or turned a blind eye to student protests, labor strikes, farmworker marches, and press criticisms. Hence, as early as the 1970s, students were able to spearhead Thailand's first democratic transition, opening the parliamentary arenas which business elites then animated with parties. During the late 1980s and again in the early 1990s, these forces were alloyed with new NGOs, youth groups, and rural migrants, enabling them to open the regime for a second and third time. No such resurrections of civil society have led to democratization in Singapore or Malaysia. And this only took place in New Order Indonesia amid severe economic crisis, finally weakening Suharto's managerial grip.

In consequence, Thailand's politics have oscillated between steep authoritarianism, full democracy, and sundry postures in between. However, sustained disunity between elites has meant that none of these regime types has stabilized, thereby distinguishing the country's record in a sixth way. Put simply, much more than any other country in Southeast Asia, Thailand's political record has been characterized by instability, punctuated by military and executive coups, counter-coups, popular upsurges in the capital, and communist uprisings in rural areas. To be sure, different elite factions have sometimes held roughly equal measures of power, producing tense standoffs. At other times, elite antagonisms have subsided, creating appearances of new equilibrium. But historically, one could find no more here than short-time accommodations, lasting only until one faction sensed weakness in its rivals, then acted on its ambitions, usually with violence.

Disunified elite relations

The monarchy in Thailand, after promoting modernization in order to stave off European colonialism, was diminished finally by the very forces it had modernized. Specifically, elements within the military and bureaucracy carried out a "revolution" against the king in 1932, then deepened the irony of their action by claiming that royal absolutism was preventing the country from modernizing further. However, after pushing the king aside, they dabbled only briefly with democratic procedures and free markets. The military and bureaucracy instead stood alone as the organizational bases for elite statuses, then reached out to rural constituents though new state enterprises, ostensibly enlarging the public sector on the farmers' behalf. In doing this, the state seized much of the rice-milling business from the Chinese, then barred the community from a fuller range of urban occupations and agricultural activities. These strategies were then legitimated by borrowing from German and Japanese models of fascist development and nationalist irredentism. Indeed, Thailand's chief ideologue, Wichit Wathakan, found great appropriateness in these models, observing that the Chinese were "worse than the Jews."[2]

During the late 1950s, Field Marshall Sarit gained the prime ministership through a pair of coups, then scaled back the state enterprises that were dominated by his rivals. He encouraged private business as the new engine of economic growth, enabling business to emerge as a third organizational basis for elite statuses. Gradually, as business in Bangkok grew stronger and more complex, it turned away from the military and bureaucracy, forming political parties during the 1970s with which directly to compete for state power. New business people from the provinces soon gained control over these parties during the 1980s, working their vehicles aggressively. Some dissident factions in the military then took the cue, forming new parties of their own. In this way, during the democratic and semi-democratic periods in which they were able to operate, political parties offered a fourth organizational route to elite standing, quickening the rise of their backers in business and the military. They became even more important with the election of Chuan Leekpai in 1992, a lawyer less connected with business or the military, thus heralding a new category of professional politicians.

In sum, the military, bureaucracy, business, and parties offer the organizational bases for elite statuses in Thailand, with preponderance shifting over time from the first pair of organized sectors to the second. But one can identify no executive office able to perpetuate leadership paramountcy, like the presidency in New Order Indonesia, the prime ministership of Singapore, the Prime Minister's Department in Malaysia, Myanmar's military cabal, or the monarchy in Brunei. Instead, elites have competed feverishly within and across these organized sectors, clearly demonstrating their disunity. And in consequence, we shall see that even as Thailand's record of regime change appears neatly to correlate with modernizing tenets – authoritarianism giving way to semi-democracy during the 1980s, followed by a fuller democracy today – this progress has been punctuated by frequent reversals and upheavals.

Military elites

For more than a half-century after the 1932 revolution, Thailand's military asserted the rightfulness of its political and economic dominance. In particular, it presented itself as a progressive and popular force, limiting royal absolutism. Thereafter, it depicted itself as unifying the nation, largely by upholding royal authority. In addition, just as Indonesia's military once justified its political role by its claim to have beaten back colonialism, the military in Thailand claimed to have staved off international communism. Accordingly, Thai generals have historically occupied or controlled indirectly the key ministerships of defense, finance, and interior. Indeed, the capstone of one's successful military career was not the supreme commander position, but the prime ministership, elaborated with company directorships.

However, while sharing this corporate sense of mission, factions in the military have confronted one another regularly over the right to fulfill it, resulting in coups, counter-coups, and the mobilization of social forces. Shortly after World War II, top officials led by Prime Minister Pridi were ousted by another faction known as the Rachakhru group, associated with the pre-war prime minister, Phibun, the police chief, Phao Sriyanon, and a top general, Phin Choonhavan. A decade later, the Rachakhru group was ousted by the Sisao Theves group, linked to a quartet of generals from the First Army led by Sarit. With the arrival of American military aid during the conflict in Indochina, the scope for rivalries widened, largely by multiplying the number of generals and power nodes in the Thai military. Then, with the withdrawal of American troops and reductions in aid, this potential was unlocked, the officer corps having swollen while its pie had shrunk.

Furthermore, as some units in the Thai military moved into the field to take up the slack in fight against communism, they came to understand better the rural grievances that fueled insurrection, thus politicizing their outlooks and inflaming factional differences. During the 1970s, then, a group of "Young Turks" emerged in the army, deeply critical of the impact on rural populations of corrupt politicians and business exploitation. A right-wing "Class 5" faction emerged in response, its members recruited from Chulachomklao Royal Military Academy's class of 1968 and key elements in the First Army, a force that had avoided upcountry action. Tracing its lineage to Sarit, Class 5 was involved deeply in business and quite uninterested in the travails of farmers or the proprieties of parliament. Finally, during the 1980s, a faction called the "Democratic Soldiers" staked out some middle ground. It emerged from the general staff, yet unlike Class 5, criticized business while expressing sympathy for poor farmers. But it avoided too the rashness of the Young Turks, preferring to use parliament to advance its aims.

In this volatile setting, military elites conspired to weaken one another's statuses. Intensity mounted during a failed coup in 1977, resulting in the killing of a staff general and the execution of its perpetrator, another top general. Pasuk and Baker observe that "this spilling of 4-star blood was unique in Thailand's coup history, and profoundly shocking for the officer elite."[3] Later that year, the Young Turks helped to oust the prime minister, Thanin Kraivixien. In 1980, they supported the "quiet coup" against Thanin's replacement, General Kriangsak Chomanan. In 1981, they tried to persuade Kriangsak's successor, General Prem Tinsulanond, to mount an executive coup, abolishing the parliament in the semi-democracy that he now operated. When Prem, backed by the king, repulsed the Young Turks, they were but momentarily subdued, mounting yet another coup in 1985. Prem blocked this one too, then exiled its leaders. And in 1991, finally, Class 5 deposed General Phin Choonhavan's son, General Chatichai

Choonhavan, who had risen to the prime ministership. Chatichai was forced from office at gunpoint and his personal assets seized.[4]

The extent of disunity between military elites is revealed also by their arousing social forces and triggering mass actions. Like the armies in Indonesia and Myanmar, it has usually been the task of Thailand's military to enforce labor discipline. But in waging their competitions, military factions have sometimes forged corporatist links to workers, especially in the public sector, then instigated mass-level unrest. Harold Crouch records that labor agitation against the Kriangsak government appeared to have been led by the Labor Council of Thailand, but was "in fact, sponsored by a rival military group."[5] Later, in mounting their coup against Prem in 1985, the Young Turks "solicited help from students and labor unions, and attempted to raise mass support."[6] Meanwhile, as the Young Turks sought support from urban dissidents, the Democratic Soldiers looked to farm-workers, advocating new development programs in the impoverished northeast.

Gradually, much of the Thai army came to value the support of farmworkers. While committed primarily, one notes, to seizing farm lands for dam projects, logging, eucalyptus plantations, and golf courses, the army tried also to harness the rural discontents that its own complicity in business had caused. Put simply, while exploiting rural populations with one hand, the army tried to recruit them with the other, offering developmental programs like Green Isarn,[7] relocation campaigns like *Khor Jor Kor*, and some opportunities for vigilante work in the Village Scouts and New Force (*Nawaphon*). And though the army was frequently clumsy in its tactics, it could occasionally smooth the contradictions between these approaches in ways that made them complementary, the army's rapaciousness increasing the need for its protection.

Bureaucratic elites

At the center of King Chulalongkorn's reforms round the turn of the century lay a new bureaucratic apparatus. As we have seen, one of his motives was to preempt external challenges, creating the functional agencies that would render redundant any modernizing mission by the colonial powers. At the same time, to obviate internal challenges, Chulalongkorn emulated the colonizers' recruitment patterns, staffing his expanding bureaucracy with indigenous aristocrats. In this way, he prevented the aristocrats' consolidating their statuses as an autonomous landowning class. But he also prevented this landowning role from falling to foreign investors. In particular, while allowing foreigners to operate commercial and financial services in the capital of Bangkok, he refused to codify their land tenure over rubber growing areas upcountry. Hence, while the arable land throughout much of colonial Southeast Asia came to be controlled by foreign plantation companies, in Thailand it was left mostly uncontrolled, an open frontier of peasant settlers until the 1950s.[8]

Chulalongkorn managed, however, only to delay the bureaucracy's internal challenge. Most monarchical prerogatives were swept away by the revolution in 1932, and his descendant, King Prajadhipok, abdicated three years later, leaving Thailand with no king in residence for a decade.[9] In these circumstances, bureaucrats began to join the military more fully in wielding state power. At the center of this nexus lay the interior ministry, "regarded as a conservative, even anti-democratic, and most intractable of bureaucratic institutions."[10] And among its many powers, this ministry, despite its demeanor, was entrusted with the task of administering elections. Accordingly, it manipulated electoral statutes and influenced rural voters, hastening the rise of candidates who then "reward[ed] the officials for their backing." Accordingly, in collaborating with the military and running elections, the interior ministry was long able to resist the demands of those who would reduce or decentralize its role.

Nonetheless, even if collectively powerful, Thailand's bureaucratic elites cannot be said to have been cohesive. To be sure, bureaucracies everywhere are marred by sharp factional battles over positions, jurisdictions, and budgetary allocations. But in the post-war period, Thailand so institutionalized these patterns that the country's politics were conceptualized by Fred Riggs as a "bureaucratic polity."[11] In this highly influential thesis, civilian and military elements in the bureaucracy were portrayed as excluding social forces in authoritarian ways. The country's political life thus mainly consisted of bureaucratic factions forming ever shifting alliances through which aggressively to compete with one another. Further, because this bureaucratic configuration was incapable of devising coherent industrial policies or productively operating state enterprises, elites reached outside the state apparatus to engage Chinese business people in a subordinate role. Specifically, factions of bureaucratic elites granted contracts and operating licenses to economically favored, but politically marginalized Chinese business people, then extracted the payments necessary for funding their intrigues.

Under Sarit's leadership during the late 1950s–60s, this bureaucratic polity was tightened and scaled back, with many state enterprises closed and private companies turned loose. But top bureaucrats persisted in competing for state spoils, while scouring for allies in business. More specifically, Suchit Bonbongkarn observes that "interior, communications, commerce, and agriculture [came] to be very powerful ministries with 'big projects' and connections with big business that [could] provide opportunities for the ministers to receive commissions, kickbacks, and other kinds of material gains."[12] In addition, during periods when Thai politics were democratized, bureaucrats extended their activities into electoral arenas, operating alongside business in all the major parties.

Over time, these bureaucratic competitions fueled new kinds of struggles, with acquisitive functionaries confronted by rationalizing technocrats. Thailand's comparatively limited state capacity has been noted. But one recognizes too that during the 1980s, Prime Minister Prem brought some technocrats to the fore who were more committed to sound monetary and fiscal policies than to opportunist microeconomic interventions.[13] Islands of technocratic expertise thus appeared within the central bank, the Bank of Thailand, as well as in what evolved over time into an oversight agency, the National Economic and Social Development Board (NESDB). To a lesser extent, one thinks here also of elements within the Ministry of Finance and the Budget Bureau. Together, these agencies contained inflation, balanced the current account, and discouraged excessive foreign borrowing. They also fashioned Thailand's tariff walls into a more coherent policy of import substitution, thus gradually nurturing dynamic new exporting manufacturers. In these circumstances, from the mid-1980s until the late 1990s, Thailand established a record of continuous growth – if not the per capita income levels of Singapore and Malaysia or the equitable distributions found in Northeast Asia.

A resurgence of factional activities forced Prem to step down from the prime ministership in 1988, however. And though Thailand's economy continued to boom for much of the next decade and its politics were steadily democratized, ruling parties began to infiltrate their partisans into the Bank of Thailand, seeking insider information and regulatory favors. The NESDB was also marginalized during this period and its governing board purged.[14] Thus, while the technocrats who remained at the Bank of Thailand began to warn during the mid-1990s of eroded expertise and declining fundamentals, they were ignored by their governor, thus creating much bitterness. The crisis that resulted in 1997 brought this factionalism to light, leading to great scandals and the governor's removal. In addition, the bank's having squandered nearly half the country's foreign reserves in a misguided effort to prop up the national currency, the *baht*, brought much recrimination that demoralized the agency.

In sum, while tensions in Thailand's bureaucracy have been less dramatic than in its military, intense struggles between bureaucratic elites have nonetheless taken place. At various junctures, this has pitted royalists against democrats, rent-seekers against technocrats, and various personalized factions against one another. Furthermore, if these factional activities were checked somewhat by Sarit and Prem, they at other times proliferated through alliances with military cliques, private companies, and political parties. During the 1990s, finally, the technocrats were eclipsed by the rent-seekers, helping plunge the country into economic crisis and regenerating bureaucratic tensions.

Business elites

Companies operated by ethnic Chinese multiplied rapidly in Thailand after World War II. During the tenure of Sarit, they were encouraged to go into banking, agribusiness, and mining, then export rubber, rice, tapioca, and tin. During the 1960s–70s, business moved from commodity exports and food processing to the production of consumer nondurables, most notably, textiles and simple appliances. And though state intervention in Thailand was less ambitious and disciplined during this period than in some other countries in East Asia, domestic markets grew protected enough that local business expanded rapidly, finally producing large conglomerates based in Bangkok. As these groups gained new competitiveness and autonomy, they also formed the cores of political parties during the 1970s through which to bid for state power.

During the 1980s, we have seen that the effectiveness of state interventions in the economy increased for a time. And as growth quickened commensurately, business conglomerates grew stronger still, enabling them to form important business associations – one each in banking, commerce, and industry – through which to consult Prime Minister Prem and technocratic agencies in finely balanced corporatist arrangements.[15] But if conglomerates prospered in Bangkok, so now did business people in the provinces, thus posing a cleavage quite unlike that found anywhere else in Southeast Asia. In the rest of the region, conflicts have often arisen between big conglomerates and small businesses, perhaps operating respectively in protected industries upstream and export manufacturing or contracting downstream. But in Thailand, Pasuk and Baker contend that fierce rivalries emerged between metropolitan and provincial business, then spilled into party arenas.[16]

Thailand's provincial business people gained a dynamism during the 1980s much greater than that of their counterparts in other Southeast Asian countries. They got their start along the highway systems that had been installed by American army forces. They took advantage of new cash-cropping opportunities around American bases, financing the planting of rice and cassava, processing the harvests, then organizing distribution, trade, and export. These business people then graduated oftentimes from agriculture into retail, local transport, property development, and textiles manufacturing. Many ventured also into gambling, narcotics, and entertainment[17] – industries that were equally encouraged by the American military presence. And new links to regional Thai army commanders and bureaucrats facilitated illegal logging and smuggling.

In this context, Pasuk and Baker observe that some of these provincial business people came from old, established families, while others were brash upstarts.[18] They record too the emergence of the *jao pho*, the local boss or godfather, and "dark influences" (*itthiphon meut*) that gained or offered protection, thereby instilling a milieu that has been far more aggressive than ordinary business competition. Indeed, provincial business activities have often shaded into gangland activities, hired gunmen, and frequent killings.[19] Moreover, in advancing their business activities, the *jao pho* began to enter politics, dispensing patronage in ways that enabled them or their surrogates to capture provincial and town council elections. They also boosted provincial business people and family members into national politics. And because 90 per cent of Thailand's parliamentary districts lie outside of Bangkok, provincial business came quickly to dominate the lower house of parliament, the house of representatives.

Accordingly, while some politicians in Bangkok recruited candidates from the provinces in order to firm up their parties, metropolitan business was generally unwelcoming. Indeed, after having been elbowed from the lower house, the conglomerates feared now that they would be challenged in their markets. Hence, metropolitan business, after siding with democratic forces during the mid-1970s as the best way to make its break from the military, would in the early 1990s acquiesce in a military coup as the best way to contain provincial business. One thus sees clearly here the ways in which disunity between different business elites exacerbated political instability.

A third kind of business elite emerged in Thailand during the late-1980s–1990s, what Paul Handley has variously conceptualized as the "new capitalists," the "new breed," "new players," and "new era political actors."[20] Amid Bangkok's booming stock market, rising property sector, and surging telecommunications industries these new business elites grew up quite independently from the old banking families, commodity producers, and manufacturers. Indeed, the new capitalists "thumb[ed] their noses at the big banks, which they saw as part of the control apparatus of the old elite."[21] Handley charts the methods by which they increased their wealth, "ramping" share prices, "chain-listing," insider trading, and a "'creative' approach to book-keeping."[22] In these circumstances, new finance companies, property developers, and media groups flourished. And as they gained prominence, stock market fluctuations became a signal to which successive governments readily responded. Accordingly, policy decisions and bureaucratic appointments were geared to unregulated growth and cheap credit, creating a heady new ethos that was "liberating." And hence, when the new Securities and Exchange Commission finally closed down several investment syndicates in 1992, one new business elite, Sia Song, responded with speaking tours, accusing "the bureaucratic elite of trying to prevent the new generation from enriching itself, [which] he argued, was totally undemocratic."[23]

In sum, in briefly surveying Thailand's business elites, one gets a sense of great dynamism, though compromised by enough cartelization and parasitic practices that the economy remained vulnerable to crisis. Of course, when finally crisis hit in 1997, many Bangkok-based conglomerates remained able to resist meaningful restructuring. Other metropolitan business elites, though, as well as most of the new capitalists suffered great setbacks, with a few reduced famously to street side vending. Similarly, while some provincial business elites benefited from the urban nature of the crisis, as well as an uptick in parts of the "illegal economy,"[24] others were forced to downsize their activities, with *jao pho* cutting loose large numbers of their "men." In addition, the disunity between these business elites, made manifest in the murderous behaviors that filtered from the provinces into the suburbs of Bangkok, was probably made worse as the economy contracted, then revived only slowly. And this disunity bore strong implications for political stability, especially when reverberating through the party system.

Party elites

Let us consider now the political parties through which many elite-level rivalries were played out. Though Thailand's parties have not generally featured ideological sophistication, complex organization, or formal mass memberships, they emerged during the 1980s as important mechanisms through which to build constituencies, wage factional battles, and ascend to elite statuses. Thailand's oldest political party still operating today is the Democrat Party. It was organized first by royalist elements in 1945, then offered mild parliamentary opposition to Phibun's government during the 1950s. During the late 1950s–60s, the Democrats succumbed to the deeper authoritarianism of Sarit and Thanom Kittikachorn, but reasserted themselves during the democratic period in the mid-1970s. Indeed, by fusing old royalist sentiments with new metropolitan business interests, the Democrats emerged as the largest party in the 1975 election. The Social Action Party (SAP) also emerged during the mid-1970s, similarly combining royalist sentiments with new business aspirations. Its leader was Kukrit Pramoj, an "enlightened" monarchist and highly critical journalist who became prime minister in 1975 after the Democrats failed in their quest to form a government. And finally, a grouping of military and bureaucratic elites that had been pushed aside by Sarit, but then sought its fortunes in business, formed the *Chart Thai* (Thai Nation) party. One of the party's founders was Chatichai Choonhavan, whose father, we recall, was linked to the Rachakhru group.

In short, these three major parties each contained traces of royalist, military, and bureaucratic elements that had been marginalized under Sarit and Thanom, motivating them now to democratize politics. They were invigorated by new Bangkok-based business elites, feeling strong enough after the economic growth of the late 1950s – early 1970s to rid their boards of military members. In turn, while some military elites cooperated with the new parties, most others resorted to intrigues, weakening each of the parties in succession as they tried to form governments. Indeed, most of the military – like most of the bureaucracy – has looked historically upon parties "with a mixture of suspicion and contempt, seeing them as illegitimate and unrepresentative."[25] Hence, after regrouping in 1976, the military closed down the new democracy. For good measure, Thanin, the new hard-lining prime minister, banned political parties outright.

However, with the political appetites of business elites now whetted and a variety of other social forces uncorked, the military found it harder to turn back the clock to the authoritarianism of Sarit. As we shall see, military elites then removed Thanin and consented to the formation of a semi-democracy for the next decade, partially restoring the party and electoral systems. The Democrats, Social Action, and *Chart Thai* quickly seized the new opportunities, and along with a new party, *Prachakorn Thai*, became the major competitors in the lower house during the 1980s. At the start of this semi-democratic period, then, the Bangkok-based business conglomerates retained the greatest weight within each of these parties. By the middle of the decade, however, provincial business had gained ascendancy, emerging first in the Social Action Party, then in *Chart Thai* and the Democrats. And after the election in 1988 that heralded change to a fuller democracy, provincial business came even to dominate the cabinet. In short, the disunity that had been evident between business elites was now reflected in, and exacerbated by, the activities of political parties, causing the misgivings of metropolitan business to deepen as the hopes of provincial business soared.

The party system was complicated, however, by the emergence also of some dissident military elements. The Democratic Soldiers formed the New Aspiration Party (NAP), with its leader, Chavalit Yongchaiyudh, now mobilizing social constituencies through the village organizations that had been set up in the northeast. During the 1990s, Chavalit twice joined governing coalitions, only to withdraw and bring them down, finally snatching the prime ministership for himself on the eve of the country's economic crisis.[26] In addition, a founder of the Young Turks, Chamlong Srimuang, organized the *Palang Dharma* (Righteous Force), enabling him to contest parliamentary and municipal elections in 1988. Moreover, Chamlong's great personal austerity and radical Buddhism seemed to resonate among Bangkok's middle class, enabling him to win the city's governorship. Lest one find in this, though, an encouraging reformism, one notes that voters later rejected Chamlong's spiritualist rigors, finding them unrealistic in the rough-and-tumble of Thai business and politics. They soon grew sceptical of his selflessness too, detecting much personal ambition in his confronting soldiers in the streets and helping trigger the violence of "Black May" 1992. The party thus began soon after to shed its idealism, then came under the leadership of a prominent "new capitalist," Thaksin Shinawatra. But as *Palang Dharma* continued to decline, Thaksin departed in order to found yet another party, *Thai Rak Thai* ("Thai Love Thai"), bolstering his bid for the prime ministership in 2001.

In this way, political parties came gradually to open a fourth route to elite statuses in Thailand. However, they did little to aggregate societal aspirations into ideologies, then mediate them effectively in parliamentary arenas. Indeed, they proclaimed only the slimmest of principles and programmatic appeals, revolving instead around personalities and patronage. Hence, during the 1970s, parties mainly offered new platforms for Bangkok-based business conglomerates. During the 1980s, they served as stripped down vehicles for provincial business people and dissident generals. And though party chairs sometimes presented a disciplined public image, secretary-generals tended to operate vigorously behind the scenes, undermining ostensible allies, encouraging defections from competitors, bringing down governments, and bargaining with rural *jao pho*. In these circumstances, censure motions in parliament became an annualized ritual. Crouch observes also the regular mobilization of outsiders, citing *Chart Thai*'s once arousing farmer activists in order to embarrass the SAP, though both parties were partners in the governing coalition.[27] And Benedict Anderson, finally, records the growing frequency of ambushes and assassinations involving parliamentarians, organized by "the victims' fellow-bourgeois political and business rivals" – an indicator, he suggests, that "the institution of MP has achieved solid market value."[28]

There can be no clearer measure of disunity between elites than the assassinations of parliamentarians that took place during the 1980s. Moreover, in the hothouse of Thailand's multi-member districts during this period, this disunity inspired much electoral violence in the hinterland too, with godfathers and local canvassers buying up votes, carrying firearms, menacing polling places, and wreaking revenge upon those who disappointed them.[29] Historically, this disunity between party elites provided a standing pretext for the military to close parliament, striking a blow – however disingenuously – against policy immobilism, business corruption, rural exploitation, and assorted social ills. And the regionalism that parties have exacerbated – with the Democrats looking mainly to Bangkok and the south, *Chart Thai* to the central plain, the NAP to the northeast – offered the interior ministry a similar pretext for resisting decentralizing reforms. One must conclude, then, that during the periods in which they have been able to operate freely, Thailand's political parties have exacerbated the pre-existing patterns of elite disunity. They have also eroded proportionately the prospects for political stability.

A no-confidence motion

In order to illustrate more closely the patterns of disunity between party elites, it is worth briefly recounting a no-confidence motion that was debated in mid-1998. This motion was filed some nine months after the economic crisis hit Thailand, forcing Chavalit's NAP-led coalition from power. Thus, the Democrat-led coalition that took up the reins, pledged to political and economic reforms, had only been in office a short time when this no-confidence motion was filed against it. Publicly, opposition parties defend censure motions in Thailand as the only mechanism by which they can hold governments accountable. But in reality they file these motions for baser purposes, namely, to lash out at enough ministers that a government might be brought down, thus forcing coalitions to reorganize and state power to be transferred.

In 1998, however, the vacuity that has often characterized no-confidence motions was revealed by the opposition's having to rummage for issues and ministers to attack. Further, its futility was shown by the refusal of Chavalit as opposition leader even to spearhead it. The task of organizing the motion, then, was left to Chavalit's former deputy prime minister, Samak Sundaravej of *Prachakorn Thai*. The opposition set up a "mailbox" to collect complaints and information from the pubic that could be used to support the motion. But Samak was outraged when members of Chavalit's NAP disclosed to the press that the box was instead filled with "hate mail," targeting the opposition for having filed the motion. Samak lamented, "It is really humiliating to ask for information because it only means we have nothing."[30]

Further, in preparing its censure motion, the opposition was unable to agree on an alternative prime minister. It thus retreated from its aim to turn out the government, claiming now that it wanted only to inform the public about the corruption of particular ministers. In releasing its 80-page "black paper," then, it focused mainly on the finance ministry, seeking to shift blame for Thailand's currency collapse from Chavalit's government to the Democrats. In particular, it claimed that the "Chuan I" government of 1992–95, by having created the Bangkok International Banking Facility in order to attract foreign lending and portfolio capital had created the conditions for later collapse. The inflow of capital had been excessive, pumping low interest loans into an asset bubble, then rudely departing, leaving the Thai economy stranded in recession. To make matters worse, said the opposition, the government had used capital from the Financial Institutions Development Fund, operated by the Bank of Thailand, to conceal the steady weakening of Thai finance companies. It was Chavalit's misfortune that these weaknesses should only have come to light during his prime ministership. The opposition then supplemented its criticisms with attacks on the ministry of agriculture over illegal logging, as well as on the industry ministry for taking bribes.

In responding, the government pushed blame for the recession back onto Chavalit, showing that it had been during his tenure that the Bank of Thailand had drained the Financial Institutions Development Fund, indeed, squandered foreign currency reserves in its ill-fated defense of the *baht*. Samak demurred, then accused the government of "wasting too much time debating economic issues."[31] The government turned next to the logging scandal, arguing convincingly that it was Chavalit who had laid the groundwork for such abuses, largely by his having so eagerly granted licenses to his allies.

Hence, with the opposition's having made little headway on substantive issues, it shifted on the second day of the debate to the government's integrity. Chavalit came forth to lead the opposition briefly, but then wilted under fierce counter-attacks. Exasperated, he protested that "this is not a no-confidence debate against the opposition."[32] Samak retook the floor, though astonished his opposition partners by admitting the frivolousness of the no-confidence motion. He stated that the only reason for the opposition's having mounted the debate was to "vent its frustration at being blamed for the economic crisis. . . . We want the people to know that politics is like this. . . . The vote is not important."[33] Accordingly, when after four days of debate the motion was finally voted upon, it was defeated by 208–177.

During debate over the no-confidence motion, a marked absence of collegiality became clear. Parliamentarians ridiculed one another as "puppets" and "lepers," while roundly accusing their foes of vote buying, corruption, narcotics trafficking, faking university degrees, and committing *lese majeste* against the king. Allegations were made about illegal land dealings involving Chuan's wife. Former Prime Minister Chatichai Choonhavan, now heading the *Chart Pattana*, was sarcastically dismissed as an "old man," prompting him to walk out of the chamber. Further, if one examines the periods before and after the debate, these personalist attacks and the mobilization of outsiders are brought into even sharper relief. For example, a spokesman for the NAP claimed to have received death threats over his pager, then accused the Democrat's secretary-general and interior minister.[34] Another NAP parliamentarian complained that the police were being used by the government to intimidate him, searching his house and declaring his four wheel drive vehicle – much prized by parliamentarians – to have been smuggled from neighboring Malaysia, an act that carried a penalty of ten years imprisonment.[35] Meanwhile farmers from the northeast were mobilized in "rowdy" demonstrations outside the agriculture ministry, hurling bags of waste into the compound. Members of the Isan Farmers Assembly were assembled outside Government House, then advised by speechmakers that Prime Minister Chuan, on an official visit to the United States at the time to seek economic support, "care[d] more about President Bill Clinton than them," prompting the demonstrators to break through police formations and again hurl bags of waste, food leftovers, and betel juice."[36] Next, the demonstrators carried their attack to the National Assembly building as parliament debated the no-confidence motion inside. Upon losing the debate, the NAP threatened to organize mass rallies throughout the northeast "as part of its effort to keep a close check on the government's performance."[37]

After the NAP leveled its threat, the police responded by declaring to the press that still more NAP parliamentarians had been found in possession of smuggled vehicles. One of the accused promised to retaliate by naming members of the government who also owned luxury cars "of dubious origin." Next, the police threatened to arrest a key NAP parliamentarian on charges of taking payments in exchange for fixing police promotions. The parliamentarian responded by billing himself a "kamikaze politician," then declared "all-out war against the government."[38] Police investigations widened to several other NAP parliamentarians, raiding their businesses and seizing equipment. The interior ministry also authorized a mass transfer of provincial governors belonging to the NAP.[39] Prime Minister Chuan denied, however, that the NAP was being harassed for having mounted the no-confidence motion. It was, Chuan said, simply "a matter of law enforcement."[40]

Explaining elite disunity

This longstanding disunity between elites in Thailand, mitigated only intermittently by any paramount national leadership, has perpetuated political instability. As such, Thai politics conform to what Burton and Higley have identified as the "modal pattern" of developing countries.[41] In their view, so long as elites find that their unrestrained warring offers at least temporal gains for some of them, they will continue to engage in it. Indeed, individual elite persons and factions have little choice, recognizing that any forbearance they might show will quickly be construed by their rivals as weakness.

However, while elite disunity and political instability may constitute a modal pattern, Thailand is the only country examined in this volume that has failed mostly to avoid it. On this score, Burton and Higley identify a variety of ways through which elite disunity can be remedied by cohesion. A first route originates in crisis, one that so severely diminishes the worth of organizational positions and resources that elites are momentarily sobered. Recognizing that only by sharing power can they in some measure keep power, elites grow motivated to reorganize their relations in more cohesive ways.[42] This process, involving face-to-face negotiations marked by secrecy and conciliation, has been conceptualized by Burton and Higley as a "settlement."

Elite settlements are rare events, however, and in democracy's third wave they have probably occurred only in Spain and Taiwan.[43] We find none in the political record of Southeast Asia. In Indonesia, though, what we do find is that the political crisis of 1965 enabled Suharto to galvanize military elites and Muslim elements in eliminating communist leaders and their constituencies. And in then stabilizing the economy, he gained the consensus of generals and top bureaucrats for liberalizing reforms. Moreover, he used the paramountcy he gradually established if not to unify elites, at least to manage them through careful distributions of patronage and sanctions. In this way, Suharto perpetuated a record of political stability for some three decades.

In Thailand, however, no such motivating crisis has ever taken place – at least until 1997–98. The country's economy has traditionally been buoyed by commodity exports, especially rice, more recently by foreign investment and export manufacturing. The economy thus even coped with the surges in oil prices during the early 1970s, then boomed for a decade from the mid-1980s. In addition, we have seen that Thai society has mostly been spared the ethnic and religious tensions found in neighboring countries. And though the country faced a class-based challenge during the 1970s, this uprising was kept separate from urban labor discontents, then denied its rural base. Finally, to the extent that Thailand has faced security threats from abroad, its role as a frontline state during conflict in Indochina brought it much American aid and infrastructure development, thereby converting its military vulnerability into a market advantage.[44]

To be sure, Thailand's military coups and street-level confrontations might be interpreted as critical events. But they pale alongside Indonesia's mass slayings in 1965–66, Singapore's expulsion from the Malaysian federation in 1965, and Malaysia's May 13th rioting in 1969. Moreover, though incidents in Thailand have sometimes demanded mediation by the king, Bhumibol Adulyadej, he has only intermittently managed elites, while demonstrating uneven commitments to regime types. During the 1950s, the king strongly endorsed Sarit's authoritarian rule, clearly reciprocating for Sarit's having propped up his monarchical standing. In 1973, however, he forced Sarit's successors into exile, clearing the way for a democratic transition. Three years later, he sanctioned the military coup that brought authoritarianism back. During the 1980s, he supported Prem against coups by the Young Turks, thereby helping to perpetuate a semi-democracy. In 1991, he appeared quietly to support a coup led by General Suchinda Kraprayoon, contributing to democracy's collapse. And in 1992, he chastized both Suchinda and Chamlong Srimaung, helping once more to democratize Thai politics. The king is portrayed as a constitutional monarch. Yet he has dismissed written constitutions as "foreign implants." He is popularly characterized as generous and caring. Yet he has railed sharply against social welfare.[45] It would appear that the king is less a paramount national leader, able astutely to balance elites and stabilize politics, than a source of endorsement that competing elites sometimes bid for.

In these circumstances, elite-level warring in Thailand has continuously circulated winners and losers, rather than threatening them all in one go with collective ruin. However short their tenures, elites have found the positions they acquired held value, providing them with a burst of state power and access to business opportunities. And their factional conflicts, then, unfolding against a backdrop of comparatively benign structural and external factors, never accumulated in such severe political crises that they were motivated to reach a comprehensive settlement. Instead, elites in Thailand, viewing their competitions as perilous, but fruitful, have preferred to take their chances.

A second way identified by Burton and Higley through which elite cohesion can be gained involves favorable colonial rule, usually coinciding with a gradual introduction to democratic procedures. Myron Weiner has developed this argument more fully, showing how specifically British colonial "tutelage" imparted meritocratic norms of bureaucratic advancement and electoral practices as guidelines for elite-level competitions.[46] Arend Lijphart then elaborated this thesis in multiethnic settings, citing the importance of a "tradition of elite accommodation" for sustaining a consociational approach to democracy.[47] He concluded his study by showing how in Malaysia, British officials convened a series of meetings on the eve of independence that encouraged cohesion between local elites.

This tradition of elite accommodation was similarly extended by the British to Singapore, while in the Philippines, we will see that American colonial officials did much to promote elite cohesion and at least formal democratic commitments. To be sure, there have been significant deviations from these patterns over time, with strain points marring elite relations in Malaysia, Lee Kuan Yew truncating democracy in Singapore, and Marcos carrying out an executive coup in the Philippines. But enough accommodative traditions have survived among elites, traceable to the colonial period, that some level of elite cohesion and democratic procedures has been perpetuated or revived. Indeed, we shall see in our examination of the Philippines that Marcos's legacy of abuses probably helps to shore up democracy today, even as the quality of political leadership and economic performance deteriorated sharply under Corazon Aquino and Joseph Estrada.

Thailand, for its part, has surely derived benefits from its having avoided the indignity of formal colonization. Unbroken lineages of "Thai-ness" can thus regularly be celebrated, useful for undertaking the tasks of nation-building. Indeed, Anderson speculates that precisely because Thailand was never colonized, no external power manipulated ethnic sentiments in a cynical process of divide and rule.[48] But it means also that in the absence of profound crisis, Thailand has found no alternative pathway to elite cohesion. And hence, if fissures between elites have enabled local democratic pressures to emerge earlier in Thailand than in many other countries in Southeast Asia, the democracies that have resulted have remained unconsolidated. Accordingly, Thai politics conform closely to the modal pattern of instability.

Quiescent, but sceptical social forces

While elites in Thailand, in confronting one another, have resorted often to stoking social forces, they have sought more generally to enforce mass quiescence. In doing this, state ideologues have constructed some "traditional" themes, then integrated them into a mentality of "Nation, Religion, and Monarchy." They have reinforced this by asserting a long record of *phatthana* (development), thereby seeking performance legitimacy too. More substantively, some corporatist bonds have historically been imposed upon labor, while more diffuse populist programs and clientelist appeals have been extended to farmers. One notes, however, that labor activists and farmworkers who have spurned this embrace have sometimes been coerced. And rarely has this involved even the legalist forms found in Singapore, Malaysia, and to a lesser extent in New Order Indonesia. Rather, troublesome activists, when not useful to elites in waging their own struggles, have simply disappeared.

While the military and bureaucracy carried out a revolt against the monarchy in 1932, greatly diminishing its role, Field Marshall Sarit, after closing the parliament, rediscovered the monarchy as a legitimating tool. Indeed, the king was portrayed now as the fount of authority from which the military and bureaucracy could draw. Further, as the state grew more committed to economic development during the late 1950s, made manifest in the freeing of Chinese business, the king gradually proved useful in easing social costs. Indeed, King Bhumibol emerged as a foil, declaring the state's concern about the rapacity of capital and its effects on farmers. Thus, while circulating between his upcountry palaces, he has advised on new agricultural techniques, inaugurated new irrigation schemes, and consoled desolate hill tribes. These activities have been duly recorded on the army's television station and disseminated by the Public Relations Department.[49]

To underpin the traditional social order more deeply, Sarit took control of the Buddhist *sangha* (monkhood) in Thailand through the *Sangha* Act of 1962. Administered, then, by the Department of Religious Affairs, the *sangha* has encouraged through its temple networks steeply hierarchical, anti-liberal, and nationalist interpretations of Buddhism. More specifically, Peter Jackson notes the state preference for karmic Buddhism and Brahmanism, teaching that social inequalities, now rapidly widening, are justified by different amounts of merit accumulated in earlier life cycles.[50] Inequalities could only be remedied, then, in later cycles, not through social action. State ideologues have worked tirelessly to refine these doctrines. Pasuk and Baker describe, for example, the Department of Fine Arts "rehabilitating" an ancient text during the 1970s, enumerating the cosmos's 31 levels of social standing.[51] Such refinements were politically timely, firming the social order during this period against a tide of new student activism. A prominent monk then drove the point home by advising that Buddhists could gain merit by killing communists.[52]

From within the Prime Minister's Office, the National Identity Board has prescribed the collectivist nature of Thai-ness, positing it strongly against liberal behaviors. In doing this, the board has relied mostly upon the trusty old tenets of nation, religion, and monarchy, thus devising "a largely backward and inward-looking interpretation of national identity."[53] It has advocated feudalist notions of obligation through the semi-deification of King Chulalongkorn, for example, while proclaiming the rightfulness of mass-level servitude. And it has celebrated Thai farmers as the "backbone of the nation" – evidently a timorous backbone, though, for the board attested through a published survey that "villagers have little ambition to change their lifestyles."[54]

While the state has enshrined in its mentalities the stalwart qualities of Thai society, it has also contained society through some baser strategies. Put simply, with Thailand's rapid industrialization dependent on cheap labor, the state has historically suppressed workers. In some measure, this has involved a fairly primitive approach, using the military to incorporate labor in sporadic and top-down ways. But the state has also relied more imaginatively on the disunity of labor leaders themselves. Andrew Brown shows how the state's granting labor a limited right to organize has succeeded in disorganizing labor, with union leaders competing to form their own congresses and federations, then earning high positions in official bodies like the National Advisory Council for Labor Development and the Labor Court.[55] Thus, if the disunity of state elites has sometimes allowed social pressures to rise, the disunity of labor leaders has facilitated state control. In addition, where the state's control strategies run short, business deploys its own, hiring young women workers for its assembly lines, offering short-term contracts, closing troublesome factories in order selectively to rehire workers, and resorting finally to intimidation and disappearances. In consequence, the orthodox assessment made of labor in Thailand is – as in the rest of Southeast Asia – that organized industrial labor remains quite weak.

In approaching farmworkers, the military tried much more fervently to mobilize constituent support, though with uneven success. In brief, during the 1970s, the military attempted to win back the countryside from the communist insurgents, introducing the development schemes outlined above.[56] But as dissidents in the military gravitated into parliamentary politics, they attempted to energize rural support for their new parties. We recall General Chavalit's reactivating his ties forged through village organizations in order to gain a voter base for his NAP in the northeast. The parties that were formed by business people did likewise in other parts of the country, exploiting their provincial bases and market resources. In this way, widespread vote buying at election time, reinforced tactically between elections with pork barrel projects, became the mainstay of provincial politics.[57]

In short, elites in Thailand have tried to enforce mass quiescence. But owing to their own disunity, their record has been ambiguous. Hence, through the interstices in their relations and the gaps in their mentalities, one finds social resistances, even popular upsurges. Analysis begins with the rapid expansion of tertiary education during the 1960s, producing the first generation of students pondering careers outside the state bureaucracy. And during the 1970s, like students elsewhere in the region, they grew critical of state power and authoritarian rule. But unlike their counterparts in Indonesia and Malaysia who met with crackdowns on civil liberties, students in Thailand were able to rise up and democratize politics, forming alliances with newly freed business interests. And even after military elites recovered enough unity that they were able to close the regime again, students fled to the rural areas to invigorate the communist uprising.

Throughout Southeast Asia, farmworker grievances intensified during this period. Population increases put pressures on the land at precisely the moment that new greening technologies made large farming populations redundant. Thus, the discontents that had roiled the region after World War II were now reactivated in Thailand, as well as in the Philippines and in some measure Malaysia. In consequence, rural insurgency erupted in Thailand, inspired by a profound sense of deprivation, disciplined by Marxian doctrine, articulated by students, and – despite the military's counter-insurrection and populist campaigning – given vent through a yawning elite disunity. This insurgency was, of course, finally suppressed. But later, during the boom years of the 1990s, grievances surged anew in disputes over land use and resources. And toward the end of the decade, they were amplified by the economic crisis, giving rise to new forms of organization like the Assembly of the Poor and the Peasant Federation of Thailand. Gaining a new militancy and organizational know-how, farmers shut down development projects that threatened their livelihoods, blocked major highways, and marched on Bangkok.[58] In addition, though students retreated from the countryside back to the cities, the NGOs they formed articulated new modes of village-level cooperation and self-sufficiency. And after the economic crisis of 1997–98, they advocated a new "localism" in order to resist global capital.[59]

With respect to the region's new middle class, analysts have rightly contended that it has not consistently supported democracy. But in Thailand, middle-class elements have nonetheless contested the weaker idioms in the state's authoritarian mentalities. Where symbols have plainly been spurious, the middle class has dismissed them. But where they still resonate, they have been reinterpreted. For example, while surely valuing rapid economic growth, the middle class has sharply challenged "official" notions of development. For example, through the Bangkok Forum and a broader network called Civicnet, it has organized the "urban lawn movement" (*larn khon muang*), opposing the construction of mega malls that overshadow small shopkeepers and erode communitarian ethics.[60] On a cultural plane, the worth of the state's Buddhist appeals has lately depreciated, their relevancy eroded by the their deadening conservatism, their sanctity dimmed by some appalling scandals in the *sangha*.[61] But in still valuing Buddhism, many members of the middle class have sought new understandings. They have turned, then, to schools like *Santi Asoke*, then discovered new avenues for political participation. Chamlong Srimaung, for example, the monk-soldier-politician who led *Palang Dharma*, broadened his appeals to the middle class through his association with *Santi Asoke*.

However, in analyzing middle-class demands for more fundamental political change, one finds that ambivalence prevails. To be sure, much is made of middle-class participation in the events of Black May in 1992 when the military attempted at least indirectly to regain power. And we will see that middle-class elements also rallied in support of constitutional reforms after the 1997 economic crisis. But the middle class had failed earlier to support a transition to fuller democracy under Prem in 1988. Nor did it much mind when his elected successor, Chatichai Choonhavan, fell victim to a military coup. During the 1990s, the middle class grew deeply disillusioned with the electoral system that brought provincial politicians to power and provided poor governance. And after the economic crisis hit, many middle-class elements despaired when even a reformist government was unable to hasten economic recovery, prompting calls for the deliberate and systematic spoiling of ballots during the 2001 election, organized under the refrain of "elect to not elect."

In sum, Thai society can historically be classified as quiescent, blanketed with legitimating mentalities, corporatist controls, divide-and-rule strategies, deadly coercion, and indeed, its own debilitating ambivalence. The middle class, though educated and increasingly participatory, remained limited in size and concentrated in Bangkok. And despite the intermittent surges of militancy in the rural areas, a leading English-language newspaper assessed recently, "there are as yet few articulate village-born leaders capable of challenging the government."[62] Nevertheless, with Thailand's elites habitually disunified, even mild participation by social forces has succeeded periodically in democratizing the country's politics. Consolidation, however, has remained problematic.

Regime outcomes

These patterns of disunified elites and generally quiescent, though sometimes participatory social forces have produced great fluctuations in Thai politics. To be sure, a broad and indeed, commonplace progress can be detected in the post-war period, marked first by the dominance of military and bureaucratic elites, later by the emergence of business parties, and recently by the stirrings of civil society. But this record has been highly nuanced. Accordingly, in attempting to track the regime types that have emerged, we find an unstable authoritarianism from 1947–73, an unconsolidated democracy from 1973–76, a semi-democracy from 1977–88, and an unconsolidated democracy once again from 1988 to the present, though punctuated by a brief military interlude.

Unstable authoritarianism

In 1947, after a coup against the Pridi group, General Phibun was restored to the prime ministership. And though allowing parliament at least nominally to operate, Phibun was perhaps more conspicuous for his recycling the statist and anti-Chinese appeals that he had made during the late 1930s. However, the Rachakhru group that had brought Phibun back was less convinced now about the capacity of the state to generate wealth. Its members were instead more impressed by the new dynamism of Chinese business groups, having prospered during the war as European companies departed. Of course, the military continued to operate some state enterprises, and it even set up its own holding companies. But it also injected large amounts of cash from the Ministry of Commerce into the ethnic Chinese-owned Bangkok Bank, quickly making it into the largest financial institution in Thailand. Accordingly, Bangkok Bank was able to finance new businesses, then order them into syndicates of artisans, retailers, transporters, and loggers. These syndicates then returned the favor, rewarding the military with fees, bonuses, and "special shares."[63]

It was in this context, then, with political competitiveness kept inside the state and coercion meted out to society that Riggs developed his bureaucratic polity model. During the late 1950s, however, Field Marshal Sarit tightened the regime's authoritarian features, closing down parliament, political parties, and trade unions in the name of anti-communism, then began to liberalize the economy. Social forces thus remained quiescent in the dense mentality of nation, religion, and king. And where they dared still to organize, they were harshly repressed. Indeed, under Sarit, urban labor leaders disappeared, rural activists in the northeast were publicly executed, and Muslim separatists in the south were crushed. Sarit's successor, Thanom, permitted a small amount of political openness a decade later, but this too was quickly pared back through a coup in 1971.

In this way, the preeminence of the military and bureaucracy grew more pronounced under Sarit and Thanom than it had been under Phibun. And Sarit, aspiring now to industrializing Thailand more rapidly, began to raise tariff walls. However, we have seen too that he closed down many state enterprises, noting that they were the redoubts of his factional rivals. And he eased controls over the Chinese, thus distinguishing private business more clearly as the engine of growth. But during this period, generals and top bureaucrats began also to set up their own businesses. And with no greater cohesion between them, their factional struggles widened. Crouch thus records that rivalries swelled beyond statist cliques to involve large "military-sponsored empires."[64] During the early 1970s, then, analysts identified on one side the prime minister, Thanom, his deputy prime minister and army chief, Praphat, and his son, Narong, who even while heading some key state agencies sat on the boards of 40 different companies. Most notably, Narong directed a variety of anti-corruption bodies "which were used to harass competing factions within the army and to ensure that contracts and other favors passed to members of the Thanom-Praphat following."[65] On the other side stood elites committed to the army commander-in-chief, General Krit Sivara. Krit would soon emerge as a soft-liner, finally breaching the boundaries of the authoritarian regime.

These rivalries unfolded during the early 1970s against a backdrop of commodities exports, import substitution policies, and partnerships with foreign capital, thus puffing up business confidence. But there was also a hint now of uncertainty, with domestic markets nearing saturation and international currency systems unsettled by the break up of the Bretton Woods system. In these circumstances, business pondered democratization as a way of freeing itself from military board members and rent payments. As early as 1973, then, it began organizing the political parties enumerated earlier in this chapter. Furthermore, their efforts were paralleled by students who, after a decade of rapid expansion in tertiary education, began protesting strongly against military rule. In late 1973, then, students clashed with riot police near Thammasat University, resulting in the deaths of more than 100 demonstrators.

It was at this juncture that General Krit fulfilled his soft-lining role, refusing government orders to suppress students further. A humiliated Thanom then resigned as prime minister, and he, Praphat, and Narong were pressed by King Bhumibol to leave the country. Indeed, during a complex transition that lasted a year, the king emerged now as a democratizing "swing man," convening consultative conventions and various committees that produced a new constitution and parliament. In short, Thailand departed sharply from the authoritarian undertow of the "reverse wave" of the 1960s–70s identified by Huntington, its elites interacting in ways that gave rise to a democracy. However, elites remained disunified, while the king's support for democracy later waned, thus preventing the new regime from stabilizing.

Unstable democracy

In 1975, national assembly elections took place. And while the Democrat Party won a plurality, it was unable to form a government. The SAP then formed a cabinet under Kukrit Pramoj, one that included prominent business people like Boonchu Rojanastien of Bangkok Bank, as well as some disgruntled military elites and royalist bureaucrats. But the SAP and the parties in its coalition were mostly new parties, and hence, they lacked social followings. Kukrit tried desperately, then, to find new constituencies, resorting finally to populist appeals. He promised new developmental programs, minimum wage increases, medical care, low-cost housing, and free bussing for the poor, for example.[66] And he promised to relax political controls on communist organizing too, then expel American troops from the country within a year.

In making these appeals, Kukrit began seriously to alienate other elites. In particular, while business had only recently helped to democratize politics, it grew doubtful now about Kukrit's aims and indeed, about the worth of democracy. And, as has been its habit in moments of doubt, business contemplated a new partnership with the military. At the same time, the military and bureaucracy cooperated in mounting new efforts against communism, organizing the Internal Security Operation Command and sponsoring widespread vigilantism. In a reign of terror that picked up steadily toward the election in 1976, shadowy groups assassinated leftist academics, party officials, and labor organizers in Bangkok, while murdering rural leaders "at the rate of roughly one per week."[67] Kukrit's house was attacked too – though significantly, not by vigilantes who offered some plausible deniability, but rather, quite openly by police.

Amid these great pressures and new military machinations, Kukrit's coalition fell apart. He thus called an election in early 1976, but was constrained from contesting it effectively. Meanwhile, Kukrit's former coalition partner, *Chart Thai*, with its extensive links to business, made plain its new loyalties by adopting the slogan "Right Kill Left."[68] And though it was the Democrats that finally won a plurality, taking all the seats in Bangkok, the military then weakened this party too, largely by encouraging different factions. Finally, in October, vigilante groups and riot police again attacked student demonstrators at Thammasat, this time killing around 1300. The military promptly stepped in, appointing a new prime minister, then the entire cabinet. And royal family members showed their approval, consorting publicly with generals and vigilante leaders. Hence, just as Thailand's democratic transition had begun in great violence at Thammasat, so now did democracy break down there. And if the king had earlier swung the gate open for democracy, he now helped firmly to close it. As with earlier regime changes in Thailand's political record, however, this latest one did more to signal elite disunity than to alleviate it.

Semi-democracy

After Thailand's democratic breakdown in 1976, the military tried at first to operate a regime that while steeply authoritarian, was outwardly civilian. It was led by Thanin Kraivixien, a former supreme court judge. The military's own disunity persisted, however, indeed, crystallizing in the factional loyalties of the Young Turks, Class 5, and Democratic Soldiers. Furthermore, the military had to accommodate business elites on more favorable terms than it had under the bureaucratic polity – even if business too was divided, gradually pitting the Bangkok-based conglomerates against provincial business people. On the other hand, the military steadfastly refused to engage students, especially with so many student leaders having fled after 1976 to join the communists in the countryside.

Amid these rivalries, Thanin was ousted by a coup in 1977 and replaced by General Kriangsak. A new constitution was introduced in 1978 whose power sharing arrangements and formal institutions amounted to what have been conceptualized in this volume as a semi-democracy. Briefly, it safeguarded the interests of military and bureaucratic elites, yet accommodated business. And while limiting civil liberties, it permitted some elections. Of course, the institutional terms of this semi-democracy were specific to the patterns of inter-elite and elite-mass relations that they reflected in Thailand. But the regime still resembled in important ways the kind of semi-democracies we have seen in Singapore and Malaysia. And in partially masking the prior elite disunity that persisted, it seemed also to yield in Thailand the same kind of stability.[69]

More specifically, the military and bureaucracy retained control over the ministries of defense, finance, and interior. They also held most seats in the appointed senate, enabling them to veto the security, budgetary, and appointment proposals made in the house of representatives. And even after announcing the end of the communist insurrection during the early 1980s, the military retained its role in rural development. Thus, in sharing control with the bureaucracy over top ministries, the senate, and most rural administrative outposts, the military protected its vital stakes in business. What remained of cabinet positions and policy making, however, was conceded to the lower house, steadily dominated by provincial business after its having wrested the parties from the Bangkok-based conglomerates. It was in the lower house too that electoral activity was conducted, enabling provincial business to tap its rural networks of *jao pho* and canvassers.

At the same time, if the conglomerates were edged out of their old parties, they were compensated with a direct corporatist line to the government, the Joint Public and Private Sector Consultative Committee (JPPCC). Indeed, it was through this conduit that metropolitan business was able to maintain influence, even in positive ways, persuading the government to shift from its haphazard policies of import substitution to providing more systematic incentives for export oriented industrialization. Anek Laothamattas shows how metropolitan business first sought support in the gemstone and tourist industries, then textiles, electronics and automotive parts.[70] In addition, the middle class that emerged from this new economic dynamism was treated to glittering opportunities in careers and consumerism, especially after the mid-1980s. But more than a passive recipient, the middle class was empowered also by an increasingly free print media. As one might expect in semi-democracy, then, the army retained control over television and radio outlets, while the middle class gained voice through a critical and independently owned print media.

But institutional designs mostly reflect – and only lightly reinforce – the prior configurations of elites and constituents. Causality flows more strongly, then, from elites to the regime types they operate. And elites in Thailand, first in the military, gradually in business and political parties, grew dissatisfied with the power sharing terms of their semi-democracy. We have seen that the Young Turks were involved in coup attempts in 1980, 1981, and 1985. The army chief, General Arthit, threatened also a coup in 1984 over a currency devaluation he deemed "unpatriotic." The parties that were controlled by business forced elections in 1983, 1986 and 1988, though less to provide popular representation than to capture more ministerships.

However, the prime minister during the 1980s, Prem Tinsulanond, used the institutions and procedures of semi-democracy astutely. In a conflict that at base pitted the military against provincial business, he remained outside the parliament and refused generally to take sides, but then intervened tactically to prop up whichever side might have weakened. In doing this, he also gained support from the king, then eventually from mainstream elements in the military. He then allocated institutional positions and resources in the ways enumerated above, enabling him to manage coup attempts and to survive elections. His performance led the prominent political analyst, Chai-anan Sumadavanija, to label Thai politics during the 1980s a "stable semi-democracy."[71]

Fuller democracy, breakdown, and redemocratization

Despite semi-democracy's appearance of stability, it is worth underscoring that while political regimes can take on something of a life of their own, the elites that precede them carry greater causal weight. And as Thailand's economy started to "boom" during the mid-1980s,[72] business people tested the military's grip on state power, and hence, the limits posed by semi-democracy. Specifically, after some normal party jockeying weakened the ruling coalition, Prem called another election in 1988. But this time, business people mostly from the provinces rose up to take two-thirds of the seats in the house of representatives. And the largest party, *Chart Thai*, now demanded much more than the right to form a government. Tapping the sentiments of a revitalized civil society, it insisted also that the prime minister be an elected member of the lower chamber. The king and the military, though wary, remained silent. And Prem, rather than suffering the indignity of a no-confidence vote, resigned, thereby paving the way to Thailand's "second-try" democracy.[73]

After the election in 1988, the *Chart Thai* leader, Chatichai Choonhavan, formed a ruling coalition and assumed the prime ministership. However, while the parties he had mustered and the provincial business interests they represented had helped to promote Thailand's democratic transition, their subsequent behaviors negated the prospects for stability. First, they profoundly alienated elites in the military and bureaucracy. We recall that Chatichai was the son of a Rachakhru leader, the faction that had been pushed aside by Sarit in 1957. And now, as if to retaliate, he led a broad assault on military and bureaucratic prerogatives. He began by snatching away the ministerships of defense, finance, and interior, then shared them with his civilian coalition partners. The new ministers then promptly trimmed military budgets, scrutinized procurements, and took control over state contracts. In addition, business people were given direct access to the bureaucracy, even becoming managers of state enterprises. They then discarded the JPPCC, their old consultative arena. Meanwhile, permanent civil servants and provincial officials were transferred or retired in large numbers. And as the terrain continued to shift, organized labor and farmworkers resurfaced.

In addition, the ruling parties alienated metropolitan business elites and much of the new middle class. As we have seen, these parties were not complex bourgeois organizations, geared primarily to defending property rights from the state, yet requiring also that the state impartially adjudicate commercial disputes and provide public goods. Nor did they articulate liberal or egalitarian ideologies before mass electorates. On the contrary, these parties were less interested in limiting state power, rationalizing administration, and aggregating social aspirations than in crudely seizing cabinet portfolios, pocketing state resources, then passing a cut to their *jao pho* and canvassers in the provinces. In consequence, amid this frenzied pork barreling and atomized vote buying, ideologies and programmatic appeals were scant. Moreover, many analysts have observed that in adopting these strategies, the ruling parties went so far as to politicize the Bank of Thailand with cronyist appointments, and they marginalized the NESDB. It was during this period, then, that Thailand's technocratic agencies were first seriously degraded, their topmost technocrats sheared clean away.

The corruption of *Chart Thai*'s coalition, then, in its exclusivity and inefficiency, alienated the military and bureaucracy on one side, big business and the middle class on the other. However, so long as General Chavalit led the army, a coup could be avoided, largely because he gauged that after retiring, he too could use the parliament as a sure route to the prime ministership. Meanwhile, the middle class, though frustrated by its vote totals paling before those of the provinces, found that its discontents softened amid the boom conditions of late 1980s. Middle-class *desencanto* thus dissolved quietly in cynicism, rather than fueling any greater insistence on good governance.

However, the disunity between elites, the *desencanto* of the middle class, and the instability of democracy gradually gained force. In 1990, Chavalit left the army in order to start his political career. He was promptly awarded the ministership of defense. However, his successor as military commander, General Suchinda, the leader of Class 5, mounted a coup in early 1991, one that in its aims and strategies was patterned after the experiences of Sarit.[74] Suchinda closed the parliament, replacing it with a junta called the National Peace Keeping Council (NPKC). He then sought support from the Bangkok-based business elites, coalescing with them against the provincial business people. Hence, Anand Panyarachun, an executive with the Saha Union textile conglomerate, was recruited to act as prime minister until an election could be held. By contrast, politicians linked to provincial businesses were investigated for "unusual wealth," while the names of *jao pho* were publicly revealed. In tracing these new alignments, one finds that the middle class generally welcomed the coup, while most labor unions were outlawed.

But relations between the military and metropolitan business soon grew uneasy. Anand took up where Prem had left off, rationalizing the economy further in order to promote exports. He thus withheld ministerial appointments from the military and renegotiated contracts with its companies. At the same time, the parties representing provincial business people abandoned Chatichai in order to make new overtures to the military. Indeed, after the military wrote a new semi-democratic constitution, then formed a political party, *Sammakhitham* (Unity), in order to contest the next election, provincial business people joined in great numbers. One sees clearly here the great fluidity with which rivalries and alliances shift in the Thai context. It is perhaps only the tensions between metropolitan and provincial business interests that remain constant.

A parliamentary election was held in March 1992, and with the *jao pho* and canvassers suitably reoriented, *Samakkhitham* emerged as the largest party. *Samakkhitham*'s leader, Narong Wongwan, a provincial businessman from the far north, then prepared to take up the prime ministership – until it was disclosed that he had once been refused an American visa because of suspicions over narcotics trafficking. With Narong forced to withdraw, Suchinda resigned from the military in order to take the prime ministership himself, despite having pledged earlier that he would not. Demonstrations broke out immediately against Suchinda, then gained leadership from Chamlong Srimaung, the one-time Young Turk member who now headed *Palang Dharma*. A series of violent confrontations then erupted between army units and protesters in Bangkok, an upheaval known as Black May in which hundreds were killed. Thus, with elites now severely divided, Thai society, at least in Bangkok, grew highly participatory.

At this point, King Bhumibol intervened, evidently fearing another bloodletting like that at Thammasat in 1976. He summoned Suchinda and Chamlong to his palace for a dramatic televised meeting. They appeared respectively in a business suit and farmer's outfit, while appropriately contrite on their knees. Shortly after the meeting, Suchinda resigned from the prime ministership. And Chamlong, blamed for having behaved recklessly, would gradually lose favor with the electorate. The king then recalled Anand Panyarachun as acting prime minister. And Anand bravely saved the next government much difficult work, replacing commanders involved in the violence of Black May with more avowedly professional officers. A parliamentary election was then scheduled for September.

As the election approached, parties were classified by the media as "devils" and "angels," the first having rushed to join *Sammakkhitham* in government and the latter having kept their distance. Provincial business people were associated unambiguously with the devil parties. Bangkok-based business conglomerates, however, were more difficult to plot. While they had eventually fallen out with the military, finding coups to weaken their investment ratings and juntas to blacken their tourist ventures, they had earlier accepted Suchinda's offers to join his cabinet. The middle class too, while having finally opposed Suchinda's taking office, had at first welcomed his coup. And it is difficult to know also how to make sense of middle-class participation in Black May. While executives and professionals were often depicted in the media as participating in the demonstrations – carefully parking their BMWs out of harm's way, then coordinating their street actions over hand phones and pagers – they were plainly given disproportionate attention. More measured accounts showed that the demonstrations were organized by elements at the margins of the middle class – students and NGO activists – and that they were mostly attended by disaffected workers, rural migrants, and youths.

In the next section, we will analyze more fully the implications of this popular upsurge. It is enough to say here that a Democrat-led government was brought to power through an election held in 1992, one that was classified as "angelic" and committed initially to reforms. However, while the military lay chastened, offering a moment in which to deepen democratic reforms, the new government failed mostly to seize it. The prime minister, Chuan Leekpai, displayed a "legalistic and plodding decision making style."[75] His coalition thus faded slowly before the "devilish" opposition which, in league with the senate that had been appointed by the NPKC, thwarted proposals to reduce the power of the upper house to delay legislation. Proposals to elect provincial officials directly and to reduce military budgets were also defeated. Little was finally achieved, then, in terms of closing the reserve domains held by the military and bureaucracy – an outcome reminiscent, as we shall see, of President Aquino's government after democratization in the Philippines.

The Democrat-led coalition unraveled finally over a scandal involving land reform. It was revealed in parliament that the Democrats, less angelic after three years in power, had used the reforms as much to reward provincial business elites as to benefit village constituents in need of land titles. In an election that was held in July 1995, then, *Chart Thai* was returned with a new plurality. We recall that *Chart Thai* had itself been brought down by the military four years earlier, yet had later joined the *Samakkhitham* in government, marking it as a devil party from the start. In addition, its new leader, Banharn Silpa-archa, was widely characterized as a "classic" provincial business elite. He bargained to cobble together an unwieldy coalition of seven parties which, while enabling him to take power, prevented him from effectively using it. In addition, the military began also to stir once again, its army chief, General Wimon Wangwanit, described as "grudging in his acceptance of Banharn as the new premier."[76] The middle class despaired too over the quality of leadership that elections were producing. Banharn thus labored continuously to fend off personal and party scandals, while struggling to hold his coalition together.

Finally, after barely a year-and-a-half in office in office, the *Chart Thai* coalition was abandoned by the New Aspiration Party. Meanwhile, Chavalit, the NAP leader and interior minister, continued to plot his rise to the prime ministership. Hence, when the opposition filed a no-confidence motion again Banharn, Chavalit agreed not to vote against him, but only on condition that Banharn resign shortly afterwards. An election was then held in November 1996, and Chavalit's NAP, swollen with parliamentarians poached from other parties, emerged as the biggest party. In this way, Chavalit at last gained the top office, forming Thailand's third government since redemocratization in 1992. He would soon come undone, however, amid the country's economic crisis.

Democratic consolidation

In surveying Thailand's record of elite relations, we find a tilt in state power from military and bureaucratic elites to business and party elites, a pattern corresponding with broad regime changes from authoritarianism to semi-democracy, then to fuller democracy today. In this section, we will focus on the political effects of Thailand's economic crisis, the transfer of power from the NAP-led ruling coalition to a Democrat-led coalition, and finally, the parliamentary election held in 2001. The aim is to gauge the extent to which Thailand's new democracy can be assessed as consolidated – a question first broached in our analysis of Indonesia.

Unlike democratic transition, the notion of consolidation remains contested. As Omar Encarnacion observes, the study of transitions has been guided by consensus that democracy is best understood in the minimalist procedural terms of polyarchy.[77] But with many of the democracies that emerged during the third wave now marked by low quality, the study of consolidation has split between analysts who maintain their minimalist focus on democracy's persistence and those lifting their normative gaze to include the rule of law, greater government responsiveness, popular participation, and sundry forms of social equality. In the first camp are analysts concerned with the attainment of elite unity, political stability, formal civil liberties, and the peaceful waging of elections.[78] In the second camp focusing on reforms and democratic deepening, one finds those assessing appropriate institutional designs of presidential and parliamentary rule, administrative decentralization, effective party systems, enhanced citizenship, and class compromises.[79] In addition, if the first camp still celebrates the centrality of elite voluntarism, the second dwells more pessimistically on structural and institutional impediments, most notably, authoritarian legacies, sectarian rivalries, non-hierarchical militaries, and unusable bureaucracies.[80]

Encarnacion also contends that this debate over consolidation is unlikely to be resolved, largely because basic inquiry into what constitutes democracy, until recently privileging the procedural understanding, has now been reopened. In his view, "the mere survival of democracy does not signal that it is consolidated. . . . [I]t seems pointless to place upon [low quality democracies] the label of 'consolidated' when the political system fails to meet the aspirations of large sections of the population and when considerable space remains for democratic maturing and deepening."[81] However, by this more demanding criteria, the consolidation of any democracy grows problematic, evinced by the low rates of "confidence" and "trust" in many advanced industrial democracies today,[82] even if masking significant *desencanto* by compulsory voting. Thus, it is not difficult to see why this latter camp of consolidologists is marked by greater pessimism than the first.

Given this impasse over how best to understand consolidation, the most fruitful way to proceed may involve separate examinations of persistence and quality, with high levels of both necessary to reach consolidation. To be sure, these dimensions are each fraught with operationalizing difficulties. How long must a democracy persist before it can be regarded as stable? Does a breakdown suggest that however lengthy a prior record of persistence might have been, democracy never really did gain equilibrium? How robust must a democracy's institutions and policy outputs grow in order for it to be classified as high-quality? At what point is quality so eroded through executive abuses, reserve domains, electoral cheating, and social disparities that a democracy slips into a lesser category of semi- or pseudo-democracy? On these issues too no absolute thresholds can be specified.

What one can do, however, is measure each dimension for progress, a strategy that permits us to assess them individually, as well as the degree of interplay. For example, a democracy that persists may establish a track record that becomes in some degree self-perpetuating. A democracy that gains quality may set the precedents for additional reform and renewal. Further, where these dimensions intersect, they may either reinforce or weaken their respective progresses. Democratic stability may help to bolster quality, extending the opportunities for regular increments of reform. Alternatively, democracy may be threatened with breakdown, with quality fast dissolving in "backsliding." This causal sequencing can also be reversed, with similarly ambiguous implications. Institutional designs and programs that raise democracy's quality may enhance the prospects for stability. Conversely, stability may be eroded by increases in quality.[83]

This last permutation of reverse sequencing, with efforts to deepen democracy proportionately diminishing its capacity to persist, can hardly be understood in real-world terms as benign. It remains, however, analytically intriguing. In this scenario, social forces may have grown participatory enough that elites have responded by democratizing their regime. But elites then operate a low quality democracy, studded with enough delegative practices, reserve domains, and hollow electoralism that their tenures remain secure. Accordingly, O'Donnell observes that in the Latin American setting new democracies characterized by low quality have been the ones most likely to persist.[84] It may follow that efforts to raise democracy's quality – vitalizing procedures and producing equitable policy outcomes – may prompt elites to resist in a variety of ways, to the point of testing the new democracy's stability.

To illustrate democracy's failure to consolidate in this way, this section focuses on Thailand's new democracy. Among Southeast Asia's democratic regimes, Thailand's record of persistence is surpassed only by the Philippines. At the same time, since the region's economic crisis in 1997, Thailand has stood out as the country most committed to extending reforms. Hence, in circumstances of democratic newness, poorly regulated business dealings, and great social disparities, much tension exists between the two dimensions that characterize consolidation, with reforms perhaps threatening persistence. To be sure, top military commanders in Thailand have pledged greater professionalism, making it unclear how democracy might finally be destabilized.[85] But a new bid by business elites for access to state power – reverberating in the bureaucracy, amplified through the parties, and resonating among social followings – may demonstrate that democracy's persistence is in some measure contingent on elites finding ways to circumvent reforms. Put differently, where elites are cornered by democracy's rising quality, they may respond in ways that challenge its stability, even if calling upon security forces only indirectly. As an entryway for analysis, this section briefly reviews Thailand's democratic experience during the 1990s, then addresses the lower house election held in 2001.

Thailand's democratic record

Thailand's most recent democratization began in 1992. And in keeping with O'Donnell and Schmitter's celebrated dictum, we have seen that this process involved a break-up of an authoritarian coalition, with divisions between military classes, rivalries among top business persons, and a frenzied jockeying among party leaders leaving the collectivity vulnerable to popular upsurge amid a more widely resurrected civil society. Indeed, through the violent upsurge of Black May, the military was forced from power in ways that correlate most closely with bottom-up "replacement." Further, because such replacement promises far-reaching reforms that threaten the "inviolable" interests of military and business elites, we recall its having been diagnosed by Huntington as the mode of transition least likely to stabilize.[86]

As path-dependent theorists would predict, elections held in Thailand at the end of 1992 produced a Democrat-led government that began work on constitutional reforms. But several factors combined to prevent – or at least delay – any authoritarian backlash. First, the military appears to have been disheartened by its ineptitude in managing, however briefly or indirectly, an increasingly sophisticated political economy.[87] It had also been chastened by the intensity of monarchical and middle-class recrimination that had resulted. The military thus retreated humbly to the barracks, though retained a compensatory presence in some key state enterprises and corporate boardrooms.

Second, though many of Thailand's Bangkok-based business elites had supported the military while in power, they were once again counterpoised by provincial businessmen who lent their weight to the democratic transition. Indeed, shadowing the resurrection of civil society was a resurgence of provincial business – especially as Thailand entered its economic boom. However, if provincial business favored formal democracy as a way to establish conduits to parliament and state power, it afterward obstructed the reform process in order to keep its new entryways open. Indeed, provincial business soon flourished even within the Democrat Party, enabling it to dampen the reformist impulse. In sum, pressures for authoritarian backlash were offset by the weakness of the military, then made redundant by the capacity of provincial business to limit democracy's deepening.

Hence, with business as usual, the Democrat-led government collapsed eventually in the land scandal mentioned above. An election held in mid-1995 produced a new government led by *Chart Thai*, but one that was harnessed still more plainly to the interests of provincial business. And this government soon collapsed too, foundering in disagreements over which local *jao pho* should gain the interior ministership, while key regulatory agencies were run down.[88] Hence, through elections in late 1996, the NAP came to power under Chavalit, alloying its base in provincial business with more direct mobilizations of farmers in the country's impoverished northeast, a strategy made possible by the prime minister's old ties to the military and its rural security networks.

Of course, even as an authoritarian backlash was avoided in these ways, the social forces that had sparked the transition by replacement continued to pursue democratic reforms. Indeed, they were helped in this by the economic crisis of 1997–98, imbuing the reform process with a greater sense of urgency, while subduing elites in a new mood of forbearance. Thailand's economic crisis thus appeared to have multiple positive effects, advancing progress on consolidation's twin dimensions of stability and quality.

More specifically, in early 1997 the Constitutional Drafting Assembly was convened, mainly involving metropolitan business elites who sought to contain their provincial rivals, as well as academics, lawyers, and NGO leaders trying to deepen democratic reforms.[89] And in reaching a "subtle compromise," these elements drafted a "people's constitution" that as we shall see promised greatly to enhance democratic quality. Accordingly, when the charter was presented to parliament for adoption, it met with resistance from the NAP-led government, still linked tightly to provincial business.[90] The government was also joined by a powerful roster of allies, including elements in the military that feared additional limits on their prerogatives, the interior ministry whose control over elections and provincial appointments stood to be reduced by a new independent commission and local-level contests, and most ruling coalition party members and provincial businessmen whose collaborative activities would be exposed by new forms of oversight. On the other side, the Democrats supported the draft constitution, having partly rid themselves while in opposition of provincial businessmen in order to take on a more technocratic guise. The Democrats thus led a tactical and temporal alliance made up of the metropolitan business elites and political activists enumerated above.

As political confrontation deepened, Thailand was struck in the middle of the year by its economic crisis.[91] After a 40-year run of nearly continuous growth, Thailand watched now as its currency collapsed, prompting massive capital flight, pushing down stock values, and plunging financial institutions and corporations into insolvency. Indeed, among the East Asian countries hit by the crisis, only Indonesia fared worse. However, these events, in discrediting old ways of conducting business and politics, gave new impetus to Thailand's reform process. More elites were thus motivated to cooperate in passing the new constitution. On this count, we recall Burton and Higley having mapped the ways in which disunified elites, when confronted by pivotal crises, may be encouraged to reorganize their relations along more conciliatory lines, even reaching a settlement on their most fundamental differences. To review, crises diminish the worth of high positions and assets, prompting elites to recognize that only by sharing power can they hope in some degree to retain it. In these conditions, a regime may gain new stability. Further, Burton *et al* contend that in reasonably developed settings, elites may be induced to share power also with social forces that have grown participatory.[92] In these circumstances, a regime may be democratized too.

These insights give grounds for optimism over the consolidation of Thailand's democracy. As popular pressures mounted for the constitution's passage, largely taking the form of middle-class protests, a harried NAP-led government contemplated a state of emergency. The military refused to oblige, however, favoring a broader configuration of elite cooperation and restraint – an important milestone in democratic persistence.[93] Chavalit then relented on the constitution, thus signaling also a sharp increase in reform. Shortly afterward, he resigned, and when his coalition was unable to agree on a successor, it peacefully transferred power to the Democrats. In consequence, new elite cooperation brought progress in terms of democratic stability. New accommodations with social forces raised democratic quality. What is more, the new Democrat-led government's political reforms were paralleled by reforms in the financial sector, promising improved corporate governance, while winning the acclaim of multilateral agencies.

To sum up this section, Thailand's democratizing progress appears to correlate with a rough composite of theoretical insights, though with important qualifications. A breakup of the authoritarian coalition, coinciding with popular upsurge, heralded a democratic transition. Further, because this amounted to a transition by replacement, one could anticipate far-reaching reforms, thus jeopardizing persistence. Rising quality, we remember, threatens stability. However, this outcome was delayed by the depth of the military's retreat, made bearable to the officer corps by its retaining some of its most cherished domains. In addition, the collectivity of business elites was split, with important elements of provincial business regaining their preeminence in political parties, enabling them to circumvent or dampen reforms. A humbled military and a divided bourgeoisie, important sections of which were back in the saddle, were thus unlikely to deliver the expected authoritarian backlash, at least any time soon.

Shifting to the social level, this hiatus in the causal sequence was also extended by the rapid economic growth that Thailand continued to enjoy, even as its export manufacturing mutated into a pernicious asset bubble. Thus, while social forces matured steadily into civil society, even helping to produce a new constitution, many of their grievances were tempered by new opportunities for urban careerism and consumerism. Moreover, if economic crisis later invigorated social forces, it also encouraged restraint among elites, thus auguring well for democratic stability. And with elites finally consenting to the reformist constitution, then peacefully transferring power to the Democrats, they also raised democratic quality. Thus, a transition that had begun with the break-up of an authoritarian coalition drew closer to consolidation, rooted in elite moderation, the accommodation of civil society, new institutional designs, and the promise of more efficient and equitable policy outputs.

But under what conditions might the tensions associated with transition by replacement recur and intensify, with increases in democratic quality finally testing stability? Many analysts surveying East Asia during its economic crisis concluded that where it was practiced, democracy showed great resilience, with peaceful changes of government in Thailand, the Philippines, and South Korea contrasting with the violent demise of the New Order in Indonesia and the popular upsurges in Malaysia.[94] Still unexplored, however, are questions about democracy's fate after subsequent governments prove unable to restore rapid economic growth. In short, while crisis may moderate elite behaviors, its prolongation or partial resolution may rekindle the disunity between once stunned, now fully conscious elites. And as these elites again grow restless, thus resuming their probes and maneuvers, they may bump up against democracy's new reforms, with some elements finally pondering actions that threaten persistence.

In Thailand, the Democrat-led government that had taken over from the NAP completed the full term of parliament, the first government ever to do so. And throughout its time in office, the Democrat Party conducted its affairs in ways that mostly conformed to the new constitution. Indeed, when the party's secretary-general and deputy prime minister, Sanan Kachorn-prasart, was found by the National Counter Corruption Commission (NCCC) to have behaved corruptly, he promptly resigned, an unprecedented action that was hailed as a challenge to Thailand's elite-level "culture of impunity."[95] And yet, while largely committed to reforms, the Democrats made compromises over time may have stunted the country's economic recovery. Stephan Haggard notes, for example, that in order to extend its tenure, the government accepted a new member, *Chart Pattana*, into its coalition, then awarded ministerships to the party's provincial politicians, despite "their less than sterling reputation.[96] And in swiftly reverting to old practices, *Chart Pattana* then used its ministerial posts and seats in the senate to ward off reform measures that impinged on its leaders' business dealings.

Likewise, metropolitan business elites, though still loosely associated with the Democrats, mounted rearguard resistances to any significant restructuring of their banking and business activities. Further, at the social level, workers from state enterprises demonstrated against the privatizations that the government undertook, while those in the corporate sector reacted to retrenchments with violence. Farmer groups from the impoverished northeast marched on Government House, providing the opposition with new opportunities for the censure motion, backed by mass-level mobilizations discussed above. In these circumstances, the government relaxed it economic reforms, shifting from financial sector restructuring to low interest rates, and from deregulatory measures to social safety nets, however scant.[97] Accordingly, though Thailand appeared to emerge slowly from its crisis in 1999, it economy was not projected to regain its pre-crisis size for several more years. Growth rates remained approximately half what they had been during the boom.

Hence, in thinking about the conditions in which the hypothesized tradeoff between persistence and reform might resume, one needs to remove from the matrix of variables Thailand's extraordinary economic boom, followed by utter collapse, that distorted the country's "normal" socio-political trajectory. On this count, one observes that the Democrat-led government helped to lift the economy to modest levels of probably sustainable growth, but regenerated neither the great prosperity that gladdens elites, nor perpetuated the crisis that tames them. Further, if the economic crisis had given pause to the country's long record of elite rivalries, there is no evidence of any lasting elite settlement or even any sectional pact-making. Instead, the refusal of the military to intervene in politics when invited by the NAP, though obviating an outright coup, simply masked more subtle, but ongoing tensions in elite-level relations. Hence, the ending of crisis coupled with shortfalls in growth poses finally the parameters in which elites, their surging ambitions running against democratic reforms, may find their earlier acceptance of new democratic quality slipping now into a contingent semi-loyalty.

The 2001 national assembly election

As Anek Laothamattas observes, studying elections in institutionalized democracies fails to interest most comparativists.[98] Elections in these circumstances are dismissed as a matter of transient winners and losers and ephemeral party platforms, remaining inside the bounds of well-trodden regimes. Anek notes also, however, that in less institutionalized settings, elections can provide meaningful insights into a regime's prospects for continuity and change. In Thailand, the lower house election in January 2001 marked the first to be waged by the terms of the new constitution. It also took place in a context of quite modest economic recovery. Accordingly, the election affords opportunities for an early examination of the extent to which elites might recoil from democratic quality, then jeopardize stability, once again extending the causal pathway that began in transition by replacement. Let us start by reviewing some of the constitutional reforms that elites encountered.

The "people's constitution"

Thailand's new charter, the so-called people's constitution, encouraged horizontal accountability, with independent state agencies now checking government activities. Most notably, the judiciary was strengthened through the introduction of a constitutional court, possessing powers of judicial review, and an administration court to oversee bureaucratic affairs. Further, an election commission was set up, thus taking over the interior ministry's electoral role, while the existing NCCC was vastly strengthened. Greater vertical responsiveness was shown too by new provisions for a human rights commission, an ombudsman, and a freedom of information act.

The constitution also posed deep changes to the national assembly and its electoral procedures, chiefly designed to strengthen the party system and improve governance. The number of seats in the house of representatives was increased to 500, with 400 of them elected from single member districts, newly converted from multi-member constituencies in order to encourage party cohesion and greater voter equality. The remaining 100 seats were to be filled through a party list system, thereby strengthening party leadership, but also forcing regional parties to broaden their appeals. In addition, barriers were placed on party hopping and the collection of "transfer fees," with individuals required to be members for 90 days before they could stand as their party's candidate. They were also subjected to new educational standards, with candidates required to possess university degrees. Further, once elected, parliamentarians would henceforth be barred by Article 111 from influencing appointments, promotions, and transfers in the civil service and police, long a reliable means for their exchanging favors. And their no-confidence motions, so perfunctorily introduced in the past, had now to be supported by 200 representatives and accompanied by a serious nomination of an alternative prime minister.

In addition, those who aspired to ministerial posts would be required to stand for election through the party list system, then resign from the assembly, thus sparing them the demands of constituency pork barreling, while enhancing their loyalties to the prime minister. They would also have to declare their personal assets as a condition for their entering the cabinet. Meanwhile, the 200 seats in the senate, a body used habitually by entrenched interests to check lower house measures, would for the first time be directly elected, rather than appointed by the prime minister as in the past. Moreover, in contesting the senate elections, candidates would be barred from holding bureaucratic positions or even party memberships, thereby weakening deleterious old links between politics and business. On this score, one notes that when senate elections were held in March 2000, the constitution's relevant provisions were faithfully implemented, to the point of annulling the victories of 200 candidates tainted by vote buying and organizing four additional rounds of elections, a process requiring five months.[99] Finally, local-level officials, previously appointed by the interior minister, would henceforth be directly elected too, thus commencing the process of decentralization.

The people's constitution also ranged widely across the social terrain, obliging the state to provide national health care, welfare, and twelve years of public schooling.[100] Other clauses called for consumer rights, gender equality, protection from domestic violence, and consultations with relevant NGOs over projects having environmental impact. In consequence, the charter's sweeping reforms promised to do much in raising the quality of Thailand's democracy. But because it so profoundly challenged the attitudes and behaviors of many elites, one could speculate that in the post-crisis setting, either loopholes would be found or democracy's persistence would be tested.

The campaign

Thailand's Democrat-led government dissolved the assembly in November 2000, within the timeframe specified by the new constitution. The election commission then scheduled the lower house contest for January 6, 2001. Nearly 3800 candidates from 37 parties competed for the 500 seats on offer.[101] Public commitment was regarded as high, with an approximately 70 per cent turn-out recorded among the country's 44 million eligible voters.

Though the Democrats had steadily advanced political reforms during their tenure, their modest economic performance and social policy aloofness now alienated most constituencies. Many metropolitan business elites had grown impatient with the government's placing greater store on deregulating the financial sector than restarting the real economy. And though the government gradually shifted its attention to mild kinds of subsidies, metropolitan business elites grew increasingly distant. In addition, provincial business elites were frustrated by the government's reining in expenditures on public works. Similarly, the rural *jao pho* with whom provincial business elites were frequently allied watched haplessly as many of their illegal enterprises contracted. Bangkok's middle class too, while having earlier been gratified by the passage of the new constitution and the ascendancy of the Democrats, now despaired over the economy's lassitude. And organized labor and farmer groups, deriving little from the government's deregulatory measures save industrial sector retrenchments and rising rural debt, grew steadily more militant. Thus, the Democrat Party, in alienating many urban and rural constituencies alike, then mounting a campaign assessed as stale and defensive,[102] appeared to retain only its most committed middle-class constituencies in Bangkok and its traditional supporters in the south.

Into the breach stepped Thaksin Shinawatra, frequently billed as "Thailand's richest man." Thaksin had gained some hurried, though high-level political experience during the mid-1990s, serving briefly as foreign minister, then twice as deputy prime minister, as he revolved through a variety of parties and governments. His background was more distinguished, however, by his business dealings, commencing with an exclusive contract to supply the police department with computers during the early 1980s, then using his new revenues to form the Shinawatra group of companies.[103] And in deepening links to top politicians, Thaksin's companies won government concessions to operate the country's tele-communications satellites and mobile phone and pager networks, enabling him rapidly to expand his wealth. It was reported too that unlike Thailand's other business elites, Thaksin was unaffected by the economic crisis, having been forewarned of the *baht's* flotation by the NAP finance minister at the time, enabling him safely to hedge his dollar borrowings.[104]

Historically, of course, many Bangkok-based business elites had increased their holdings through government connections. But never had they gone on to bid directly for the prime ministership. Only provincial businessmen had done this successfully, drawing upon their local machines and *jao pho* networks. It was these behaviors, we recall, that had antagonized metropolitan business elites, prompting them to support the constitutional reforms. Hence, Thaksin, in using government connections to build up his metropolitan business interests, then using his wealth as a springboard to the prime ministership, introduced new permutations into the bases for elite statuses and the conduct of Thai politics.

After abandoning *Palang Dharma* in 1996, Thaksin founded a new political party, *Thai Rak Thai* ("Thai Loves Thai"). And over the next two years, he used his vast wealth to attract a large bloc of sitting representatives from other parties, a practice known locally as "*duut*" (the suck).[105] In its last stages, this recruitment was made possible by the election commission's suspending the no-hopping rule in order to hasten the extinction of small parties. In consequence, a decision meant to strengthen the party system served instead to highlight the system's weaknesses, enabling a two-year-old vehicle untested by elections to claim a *de facto* plurality in parliament through mass defections. Further, through the "transfer fees" this involved, the *duut* contributed to what finally was estimated to be Thailand's most expensive election, despite its taking place amid new electoral rules and a moribund economy.

In readying his new party for electoral victory, Thaksin fashioned a series of appeals conceptualized by many analysts as populist, mostly because of the fiscally dubious programs that he proposed for the poor. Populism is often dismissed as an analytically imprecise term, evoking disparate experiences ranging from rural American politics at the turn of the century to urban politics in South America and southern Europe during the inter-war period.[106] Populist mobilization also produces ambiguous outcomes, in some cases invigorating democratic procedures, at other times unleashing authoritarian pressures, with some variants even shading into fascism. However, populist experiences do display commonalities, namely, a charismatic leader who forges a cross-class coalition, one that links elements of sullen big business, insecure small proprietors, and alienated mass audiences, then binds them together in wounded nationalist pride. In addition, the leader usually promises quick statist solutions for failing free markets, offering government funding for industrialists who cooperate and redistributive schemes for the dispossessed.

With the opportunities afforded at this juncture by Thailand's political and structural conditions, Thaksin chose strategies that indeed correspond to the notion of populism. Of course, in his most boisterous appeals, Thaksin called for aggressive entrepreneurism, declaring it of higher priority than political reforms, given the country's economic travails. But in later embroidering his message with populist themes, he proposed less entrepreneurial ruggedness than public assistance. Specifically, Thaksin canvassed a national asset management company, relieving big banks of their non-performing loans, while easing the terms of restructuring for corporate debtors. He also outlined new equity funds, then intimated some vague forms of protection from global competition. Further, in attempting to bridge the gap between metropolitan and provincial business, he promised a new bank geared to small- and medium-sized enterprises. But most notable were Thaksin's pledges to farmworkers, involving a three-year moratorium on debt repayments to the bank from which they had mostly borrowed, the state-owned Bank of Agriculture and Agricultural Co-operatives (BAAC), a revolving credit scheme of one million *baht* for each of the country's 77,000 villages, and a generous state subsidy for medical treatment.

Hence, alongside the Democrat's dull commitments to austerity, *Thai Rak Thai*'s platform shimmered with populism. The new party thus won over metropolitan business elites who, even if doubting the wisdom of restoring close government-business relations with the intrinsic risks of moral hazard, were keen to be associated with a winner.[107] A prominent example was Dhanin Chearavonont, head of Charoen Pokphand, Thailand's largest conglomerate. Meanwhile, big banks still encumbered by bad loans, in particular, Bangkok Bank and Bank of Ayudhya, stood to benefit more concretely, drawing upon the proposed asset management company.[108] Thus, the chairman of Bangkok Bank, Chatri Sophonpanich, opined, "Mr Thaksin is someone who can make decisions quickly, someone who I believe is suitable for helping address the problems we face now."[109] At the same time, *Thai Rak Thai* appealed to some provincial business people, though less strongly, as Thaksin was likely to require their forfeiting some local autonomy to the center. Accordingly, where *Thai Rak Thai* was unable to work through local potentates, it simply bypassed them, its offer of debt relief resonating profoundly with a vast clientele of farmworkers below.[110]

Days before the election, however, the NCCC again bared its teeth, recalling the earlier episode involving the Democrat's secretary-general,

Sanan. After months of investigation, the commission determined that Thaksin, while serving as deputy prime minister in 1997, had shifted equity holdings into the hands of relatives and servants in order to avoid the full disclosure of assets that was required by the new constitution. In an 8–1 decision, Thaksin was indicted, and his case was forwarded to the constitutional court. Based on Sanan's case, proceedings were expected to take four-to-six months. Hence, if Thaksin gained the prime ministership during the interim and the court found against him, he would be ordered to step down, then barred from contesting political office for a further five years.

In these circumstances, much of the Bangkok-based media called for Thaksin to withdraw, arguing that the Thai economy could not withstand the uncertainty created by his occupying the prime ministership. Thaksin responded defiantly, belittling the corruption commission's findings and spurning the media, arguing that he was duty bound to remain as head of *Thai Rak Thai* and vie for the prime ministership. "My spirit is about holding on to my responsibility to the country," he intoned.[111] However, he later revealed more personalist motivations: "Making all [economic] problems go away is certainly graceful, and you will be remembered forever. Abandon the post and people will applaud for five minutes and forget you forever."[112] A provincial *jao pho* who had been recruited to *Thai Rak Thai*, Piya Angkinand from Petchaburi, portrayed the commission's findings in more electorally upbeat and indeed, analytically illuminating terms: "More people will vote for us because they feel sympathy for our leader, given the judgment. . . . The people have been watching TV and understand everything clearly."[113]

While the reformist Democrats and the populist *Thai Rak Thai* continued to duel on the political foreground, a third aggregation – provincial businessmen, the *jao pho*, and some old-time machine politicians – continued to operate across the hinterland and even in some constituencies in Bangkok. Many of them remained apart from *Thai Rak Thai*, either because their notoriety was so great that they were unwanted, or because they were determined to defend their local bailiwicks and dynasties. Examples included a former deputy interior minister, Chalerm Yubamrung, whose sons contested on the NAP ticket in the capital, the Asavahame family of the *Rassadorn* party in Samut Prakan province, and the Chidchob family of *Chart Thai* in the northeastern province of Buri Ram. In waging their campaigns, these elements sometimes showed new sophistication in weaving their appeals for traditional loyalties with some studied rebuttals of *Thai Rak Thai*'s policies.[114] And some of them tried also to project their images on the national scene, contesting through the party list system in order to qualify for ministerships. Indeed, their plotting to take their parties after the election into a ruling coalition that would doubtless be led by *Thai Rak Thai* revealed some easy synergies in policy content and style. Put simply, one could conceptualize the up-market and centralizing populism of *Thai Rak Thai* as paralleling on a higher plane the rough and fragmented clientelism found in the urban machines and poor provinces.[115]

Election outcomes

Though the election commission delayed its release of official results, owing to complaints of campaign violations against many winning candidates, the exit polling conducted by media organizations and observer groups quickly revealed that unofficially *Thai Rak Thai* had won easily. Indeed, while the party's victory had been expected, its margin proved so great that it claimed a majority of seats in its own right, the first party ever to do so in Thailand's political record. And, in making its majority more comfortable still, boosting its unofficial tally from 256 to beyond 300 in order to preempt any censure motions later, *Thai Rak Thai* contemplated taking on only one, perhaps two coalition partners, rather than the customary half-dozen. Further, it proposed firm conditions, claiming all the economics ministries for itself, while rebuffing parties that laced their entreaties with demands for portfolios. Hence, after the previous days of uncertainty about Thaksin's leadership that the NCCC's indictment had caused, the prospect of a strong government now gave a shot in the arm to local stock prices, especially in the banking and telecommunications sectors.

Meanwhile, the Democrat Party, in retaining the grudging support of Bangkok's middle class and its traditional constituencies in the south, won an unofficial total of 126 seats.[116] But with half the total of *Thai Rak Thai*, it readied itself to go into opposition. Further, the traditional provincial politicians and machine figures, especially those who had gambled on the party list, "lost *en masse*." In part, they fell victim to the new electoral reforms, banning the singers, whiskey, and feasts that had traditionally been staples of campaign entertainment. Even more important, though, was the introduction of centralizing vote counting stations that greatly enhanced ballot secrecy.[117] Specifically, while local potentates attempted still to buy votes – albeit in stealthier ways given the new vigilance of the Election Commission – rural electorates, after taking the money, abandoned their local patrons for the grander populism of *Thai Rak Thai*.[118] In addition, the party list system, far from enabling small parties to extend their appeal, merely conveyed at the national level the anonymity of their candidates. Thus, the former *Chart Thai* prime minister, Banharn Silpa-archa, often regarded, we recall, as a prototypical provincial politician, expressed great disappointment over the results.[119] A leader of the Asavahame family's *Rassadorn* party lamented, "I will wash my hands of politics. Our era is over."[120] In sum, the Democrats, having risen to power in economic crisis, were now brought low by the crisis's partial resolution. And many of the local potentates were weakened by electoral reforms and the greater populist appeal of *Thai Rak Thai*.

To be sure, despite the enhanced powers of the electoral commission, much vote buying had taken place, cumulating finally in the customary "howling night" on the eve of the election.[121] Doubts thus arose over the commission's resolve, its five members often unable during the campaigning to reach the unanimity necessary for disqualifying errant candidates. Accordingly, though evidence was presented against many candidates by sundry poll monitoring groups, most notably PollWatch and P-Net (People's Network for Elections in Thailand), the election commission dared issue only a few of the "red cards" that disqualified candidates, preferring instead the milder yellow strain that while standing candidates down, permitted them to run again in a subsequent round. Moreover, after the election had been held, vote counting and reporting were marred by local protests and violence, apparently instigated by losing politicians and elements in the bureaucracy, the latter acting less to discredit the outcomes of particular races than to undermine the more fundamental process of democratization.[122] One notes too that these events were played out against a customary backdrop of gun men and bodyguards, bullet proof vehicles, convoys and safe houses. Indeed more than 40 canvassers were murdered, with Pasuk advising that "the culture of violence has penetrated into the top ranks of the Thai political elite."[123] She notes also that amid the private sector's continuing languor, "the competition to get access to government budgets is becoming more fierce." And with a parallel increase in illegal activities, politicians became more able to sell protection to what she portrays as "gangster-businessmen."

Nonetheless, the conduct of Thailand's election in 2001 demonstrates that significant gains were made in terms of raising democratic quality. The ban on campaign entertainment injected a new note of seriousness into many campaign rallies. Further, though vote buying appears not to have been reduced by the election commission's power to disqualify candidates, it was rendered less salient by centralized counting. And after the election, the commission grew more responsive to the complaints that were lodged by poll monitoring groups, thus ordering a new round of elections in 63 constituencies. Finally, violence among canvassers, though occurring at unacceptable levels, seemed to stem less directly from election campaigning than the shady business activities with which local politics often overlapped.

However, this evident increase in quality, made manifest in electoral reforms, did not prompt Thaksin to resort to the hypothesized destabilization of Thailand's new democracy. Indeed, to the extent that the new reforms appeared to take hold, they redounded mostly to the benefit of *Thai Rak Thai*, negating the crude vote buying strategies of the party's local challengers, but leaving untouched its own systematic recruitment of parliamentary defectors before the election and its promise of populist pay-offs afterward. And hence, while the election commission finally annulled the victories of 32 *Thai Rak Thai* candidates, with five of them red-carded and hence, prohibited from contesting again, most of the rest found that their party's populist message still held, enabling them to win once more in a second electoral round, held at the end of January.[124] In these circumstances, *Thai Rak Thai* suffered a net setback of only eight seats which, while costing the party the slim parliamentary majority that it had unofficially won, enabled it still to forge the three-member coalition that had originally been envisaged. Thus, after negotiations in early February, the party coalesced with the NAP and *Chart Thai*, gaining 350 seats. And in early February, the assembly duly selected Thaksin as prime minister.

Thai Democracy 2001: the flight from quality

One thus concludes that in terms of electoral reforms, the quality of Thailand's democracy was raised, but not so much that the ambitions of Thaksin and *Thai Rak Thai* were seriously checked. One must examine the electoral process more broadly, then, to find a good test of elite attitudes toward democratic quality. More specifically, because the election commission finally endorsed Thaksin's rise to the prime ministership, he had no reason to counter it. But if the constitutional court tries later to remove him from the post, his conduct during the election campaigning gives reasons for thinking that he may in these circumstances react more aggressively. Indeed, Thaksin made plain during the campaign his disrespect for the new independent agencies and courts that have heightened democratic quality. For example, after the NCCC indicted him, he simply dismissed the agency and the horizontal accountability it imposed. Anticipating winning the prime ministership, he claimed, "I am still in. . . . I can legally hold a political post and perform duties because the inquiry process is not yet finished.[125] And when the NCCC's findings were later forwarded to the constitutional court, Thaksin predicted that the case would bog down in complexities, "so there should be no problem about me staying in office for years."[126] And if the court does eventually find against him, he suggested in a press interview that by that time, his five-year ban on holding office would have expired.[127] What is more, even if somehow forced from the prime ministership, Thaksin advised that "I would remain in charge of my party, pick someone to replace me, and I would support him." So startling an incarnation as *eminence grise*, in going well beyond the executive abuses associated even with delegative democracy, would serve essentially to divert state power into Thaksin's own reserve domain, thus marking a sharp diminution of democratic quality.

But more than circumventing the constitutional court, stratagems have been canvassed by *Thai Rak Thai* that confront the institution head on. A high-level party official has warned that "soon, the normal courts will challenge the power of independent bodies set up under the constitution."[128] Analysts have speculated also about *Thai Rak Thai*'s drawing upon its great popular mandate and parliamentary numbers to amend the constitution, perhaps abolishing the new institutions outright. As one indicator of *Thai Rak Thai*'s readiness to make swift and substantial changes in law, we note that shortly after the election, well before results had been made official, party leaders proposed undoing many of the financial reform measures passed by the Democrat-led government, loosening banking regulations that had been raised to international standards, while diverting state funding to favored sectors.[129] Indeed, Thaksin came to refer to himself as "Thailand's chief executive officer," equipped with a "war room" through which to pursue his new policy directions.[130] In a press interview, he took on an even more forceful guise as a "Genghis Khan type of manager."[131]

This analysis argues, however, that if ascendant elite factions are unable to roll back democratic quality, they will respond in ways that test stability. It attributes this outcome to the transition by replacement, a regime change through which reforms are advanced to the extent that they challenge entrenched interests, finally provoking an authoritarian backlash. Let us speculate briefly about the ways in which this might occur in Thailand's politics today, while scouring for early indicators.

Paradoxically, Thaksin himself can be construed as having acted to raise democratic quality, though of a kind that is in tension with other kinds of quality, as well as with the requisites for stability. More specifically, by the reckoning of those who find consolidation in social egalitarianism, Thaksin's policies must be assessed as more favorable than those of the Democrats, paralyzed while in office by their fears that social welfare yields little but inefficiencies and corruption. But as we have seen, in trying to secure the prime ministership in order to advance his populist aims, Thaksin may run afoul of the agencies and courts that promote horizontal accountability. What is more, his populism may threaten other elites, finally setting the conditions in which democracy may be destabilized.

This process may derive from budgetary constraints faced by Thaksin's populist policies, fracturing his cross-class coalition over time. Estimates produced by Standard Chartered Bank indicate that *Thai Rak Thai*'s spending programs, if fully carried out, would raise public debt to an unsustainable 100 per cent of the country's GDP.[132] Thus, in their haste to gain access to their respective programs, business elites and farmworkers may clash over limited resources, prompting Thaksin to rein in one side or the other. Indeed, just days after the election, some major corporate debtors, characterized in the local press as "delighted" by the prospect of a new asset management company, suspended negotiations with their banks over loan restructuring.[133] On the other side, farmers began to refuse payments on their loan installments to the BAAC, leaving the institution "seriously affected."[134] The United Front of Northern Farmers went further, calling the proposed moratorium insufficient and demanding debt write-offs, then threatening to rally farmers throughout the north "to show their force."[135] In this situation, the BAAC's branch managers were instructed in some districts to inform borrowers that "it was not yet certain" that the debt relief program would be implemented. Similarly, many farmworkers and urban poor, believing that *Thai Rak Thai*'s health scheme had come into effect immediately upon the party's victory, began approaching hospitals to demand subsidized treatment. Besieged hospital officials thus implored *Thai Rak Thai* to explain more fully the time tabling for its scheme. Party officials complied, stating that the budget for 2001 was already in place and next year's already drafted, thus preventing the subsidies from being introduced until 2003.[136]

Accordingly, one gets a sense of which way *Thai Rak Thai* will tip when its cross-class coalition comes under strain. And with the party having raised democratic quality in terms of egalitarian social policies, it perhaps must itself administer the authoritarian backlash, defending the interests of Bangkok-based business elites over those of the farmworkers and urban poor. Moreover, because this would probably involve new restrictions on civil liberties, rather than mere curbs on horizontal accountability, the flight from democratic quality would threaten stability, shifting the regime into a distinct, though lesser category of semi- or pseudo-democracy. As we have seen, one finds in this configuration the marked diminution of civil liberties, in particular, freedoms of communication and assembly. And elections, though regularly held, are proportionately distorted.

Hence, as tensions appear in *Thai Rak Thai*'s cross-class coalition, the party's populist policies, or its attempts to retreat from those polices, sharply betraying its new farmworker followings, may attract strong criticisms from the media. In these circumstances, it is easy to imagine a *Thai Rak Thai*-led government curbing press freedoms, a course that during the recent campaigning Thaksin showed a willingness to undertake. When a popular new media outlet, *iTV*, attempted to air reports that were critical of his party, Thaksin's Shin Corporation, a major shareholder, issued "telephone orders" to the editorial staff banning the broadcasts[137] – an action reminiscent of the "telephone culture" in Suharto's Indonesia. Shin Corporation also overruled the station's planned coverage of a Democrat Party campaign rally, while managerial pressure forced several staff members to resign. In this way, Thaksin clearly violated Article 41 of the new constitution that guarantees the editorial independence of media organizations from state agencies and owners. And hence, as political tensions and press criticisms intensify during his prime ministerial tenure, whatever its duration, Thaksin may react by legislating tighter guidelines for "responsible" reporting.

At the same time, one can anticipate the intensification of Thailand's recent record of farmworker organizing and militancy. We recall that under the Democrats, who undertook little but market liberalization, farmers grew increasingly confrontational. But with their expectations dramatically raised by *Thai Rak Thai*, perhaps only to be dashed, confrontation may burst into widespread rural violence. Of course, irrespective of social upheavals, it is unlikely that the military in its current temper would try directly to take power. But the government could well call upon the security forces to contain the NGOs and social movements that are associated with farmers, thus sharply curbing freedoms of assembly. To be sure, Thaksin has so far given no clues of his willingness to react to the demands of farmers in these ways. But during the recent election campaign, when one of his canvassers was shot in the northern province of Phrae, Thaksin declared that if he won the prime ministership, he would "take over the National Police and stamp out all political influence – starting with Phrae."[138] His rapport with the police force in which he once was a lieutenant-colonel, inspiring his campaign plea that police officers support "one of their own," makes Thaksin's canvassing the use of coercion quite credible.

Finally, in delivering any authoritarian backlash, Thaksin could draw from a deep and congenial wellspring of elite-level sentiments. Indeed, in seeking to uncover democracy's enemies in Thailand, one can readily identify some conservative, even royalist elements who, in the name of decisional efficiencies, social harmony, cultural appropriateness, or resistance to globalization call today for a "democratic" or "constitutional pause."[139] As their model, they look nostalgically upon the semi-democracy that Thailand operated under General Prem during the 1980s.[140] These elements consist of mid-ranking officers in the military, less able than top generals to perpetuate their prerogatives, officials in the interior ministry and the police who resent the new independent agencies and courts, and sundry ex-senators, constitutional lawyers, and talk show hosts.[141] Their policy aims may not square with Thaksin's. But they may nonetheless collaborate with him in any regime closure he undertakes in order to restore their own privileges. Alternatively they may keep their distance, quietly awaiting, perhaps even inciting, the tensions in *Thai Rak Thai*'s unfundable populism and cross-class coalition. Either way, in a context of greater democratic quality, critical weight is lent to destabilizing pressures.

In evaluating the twin dimensions of democratic consolidation, this analysis has argued that in the contemporary setting of Thai politics a high-quality democracy is unstable, a stable democracy must be low quality. Hence, if elites are unsuccessful in significantly rolling back democratic reforms, they may shift to another, more fundamental dimension, thus testing democratic persistence. More specifically, with Thaksin Shinawatra, Thailand's new prime minister, having in some ways increased democratic quality through his egalitarian policies, the contradictions in his cross-class coalition, inflamed by budgetary constraints, may force him to recoil in ways that destabilize democracy. In brief, by withdrawing his populist offerings, certainly to farmworkers, but perhaps also to business elites, he will have so antagonized his followings that he must respond by curbing civil liberties of communication and assembly. Here, one finds a great irony. Though our expectations about the consequences of transition by replacement will in this way have been fulfilled, the same national leader who raised democratic quality will have delivered the blow to stability, an unanticipated conflation of roles.

In this situation, even if regular elections continue to be held, the abrogation of civil liberties marks the advent of a different regime type, namely, semi-democracy. Such change would signal clearly that Thailand's democracy had been undermined, finally closing our causal sequence. There are empirical precedents in Thaksin's recent performance and Thailand's longer political record for this kind of outcome. There are also some theoretical grounds, derived largely from a process of transition by replacement that began nearly a decade ago. Hence, the assessment made by Suchit shortly before the 2001 election still stands: "conditions for consolidation have not yet been met in Thailand."[142]

Conclusions

Thailand's political record has been marked by sustained disunity between elites, the consequences of which have been distinctive in the region. First, divisions between elites in the military and bureaucracy have eroded state capacity, sharply limiting developmental planning and administration. Second, these weaknesses have in turn ceded much autonomy to business, based both in Bangkok and the provinces. Third, business elites in these circumstances have been involved in forming political parties, thus opening up a new conduit by which to increase their access to state power. Further, this strengthening of business and parties has in recent decades been unimpeded by any ethnic or religious barriers, with competing elites in the state apparatus choosing to mute their anti-Chinese appeals in order to forge alliances with different conglomerates and parties. Fifth, with elite disunity so evident in the competitions that have raged across the military, bureaucracy, business, and parties, civil society has sooner grown active than in other countries in Southeast Asia. But with elites failing still to gain cohesion, neither the democracies that have emerged or the different kinds of authoritarianism into which the regime has thereafter lapsed have gained stability.

Viewed from another perspective, Thailand's political record is distinctive in that it has displayed no clear hierarchy of institutions. Instead, four organizational pillars have supported elite statuses – the military, bureaucracy, business, and parties – and political power has tilted over time from the first pair to the latter. The regime has changed correspondingly, evolving from different kinds of authoritarianism to a semi-democracy, then finally to a fuller democracy today. In part, these institutional configurations and their shifting relationships can be attributed to historical, structural, and cultural factors. Thailand was never formally colonized, but replicated the bureaucratization it observed in neighboring territories precisely in order to avoid their fate. And in doing this, it recruited aristocrats, just as the Dutch did in Indonesia and the British in Malaysia. But unlike these other territories, Thailand, in organizing its own security apparatus also built up a local military much sooner. And in league with bureaucrats and middle-class elements, the military overturned the monarchy in 1932, then tightened its grip on state power toward the end of the decade. In addition, perhaps guided by notions of Buddhist accommodation, the military and bureaucracy engaged Chinese business elites in ways that enabled business to gain much organizational autonomy. This was quite unlike New Order Indonesia, its business terrain scored by Suharto's personalist web works, and Malaysia, marked by the NEP's reverse discrimination. Hence in Thailand, as business grew more powerful – both in Bangkok and the provinces – it sought to open its own pathways to state resources through powerful, though ever-shifting, party coalitions.

Clearly, then, historical, structural, and cultural factors have done much to forge the context in which Thai politics have unfolded. But elite-level choices and relations have also mattered. For example, despite Buddhism's accommodative qualities, Phibun derived political gains by ostracizing the Chinese, laying the groundwork for their long-time status as pariah entrepreneurs. Indeed, one of the most distinctive features of Thailand's elite collectivity is that in comparison to the other countries we have examined, elites have perpetuated deep divisions. They have never been disciplined by deep crisis, even during 1997–98. And they have gone unmanaged by paramount leaders. Sarit's tenure was too short, and Prem's, despite his great skill, was pocked by a number of coup attempts. In these conditions of elite disunity, then, social forces were able to act on their participatory impulses much sooner than in Suharto's Indonesia, Lee Kuan Yew's Singapore, and Mahathir's Malaysia. Their popular upsurges thus gave rise to an early and home-grown democratization during the mid-1970s, rural insurgencies during the late-1970s, the Black May confrontation of 1992, and the demonstrations against Chavalit in 1997.

Nonetheless, while new institutional designs and mass attitudes may help to vitalize Thailand's democracy today, one must remain sceptical of the behaviors of elites. Under the new constitution, they will at most exercise greater caution, showing much cunning in circumventing its strictures. But if finally constrained by democracy's new quality, they will respond by testing stability. Of course, this is not to suggest that Thailand will lapse back into military rule. The army has been much discredited by the violence of Black May, to the degree that it no longer seeks a preeminent role. And rationalist authoritarianism is clearly beyond the bureaucracy's grasp, as shown by the performance during the crisis of even its top macroeconomic agencies. Hence, the danger for Thailand's democracy arises not from deliberate plots against it, but simply from the semi-loyal commitments of many elites, readily fragmented by their everyday warring. We are reminded that it was social forces, not business or party elites, that re-democratized Thai politics in 1992. It was again social forces that after prolonged economic growth, followed sharply by recession, raised democracy's quality five years later. But with elites still lacking cohesion, the new democracy remains unconsolidated.

Chapter 6

The Philippines

━━◆━━

Stable, but Low Quality Democracy

In important respects, the Philippines completes our progression of cases. The country not only underwent a democratic transition during the mid-1980s, but stabilized its democracy during the early 1990s. Further, this persistence evokes elites who are cohesive and a society that is participatory, attitudes reinforced through formal institutions. However, even if the Philippines closes this volume, one should not think of it as offering the last word on political development or any normative optimality. While the country may have succeeded in stabilizing its democracy, grave doubts persist about quality. Thus, in significant ways, the Philippines poses the mirror image of Thailand, the latter's new democracy displaying increases in quality, but incurring commensurate challenges to persistence.

This chapter begins by placing in regional context some key features of Philippine politics. As with Thailand, we will discover stark contrasts between the Philippines and the first three countries examined in this volume. Indeed, for many observers, the Philippines seems in terms of its colonial legacies and social structure to be more at home analytically in Latin America. However, by deploying our framework of inter-elite and elite-mass relations, we can shed comparative light on the case, thus helping not only to account for its departures from the Southeast Asian setting, but also to reveal its similarities. Next, this chapter examines the organizational bases for elite statuses and the contours of elite unity. It explores also the appeals that elites have made to their social constituents, first perpetuating quiescence, later managing participation. It then charts the regime types and changes that these relations have produced: a stable, but low quality democracy after World War II, an unstable period of authoritarianism under Marcos during the 1970s–80s, and finally a stable democracy today – though again, of doubtful quality. On this score, because so many analyses of the Philippine democratic transition have recently been published, it seems most fruitful to give emphasis in this chapter to questions about quality, addressing issues of leadership behaviors, social participation, and electoral practices. One way to begin doing this is to give close attention to the general election of May 1998.

The Philippines in the region

Many analysts have suggested that because of its colonial experience, first under the Spanish, then the United States, the Philippines is best studied using frameworks based on Latin American data. Accordingly, its political economy has been scrutinized through the lenses of neo-colonialism, dependency theory, and bureaucratic authoritarianism. Of course, the country's indigenous populations have been constructed socially as Malay, the involvement of Chinese in business has pricked ethnic resentments, and Islam has continued to roil on the southern island of Mindanao, thus imparting to the Philippines at least some of the features and dynamics that mark it indelibly as Southeast Asian. But analysts have been more generally impressed with its sugar-growing *hacendados*, the pervasiveness of Roman Catholicism, the intrusiveness of U.S. diplomacy, and even the ubiquity of everyday *machismo*, factors that have conditioned the economy and society in ways that more obviously approximate Latin America. Indeed, for many analysts, the Philippines highlights the spuriousness of relying upon geographic propinquity as an organizing principle.

One aim of this chapter, then, is to show that while the Philippines is in many ways distinctive, its politics can nonetheless be compared to other Southeast Asian cases in nontrivial ways. For example, in terms of national leadership, one finds similarities in the paramountcy and ruling style exercised by President Marcos and Suharto. During their tenures, patronage was highly centralized, then dispersed through familism, cronyism, and populism. Further, in examining the broader record of elite relations, the Philippines resembles the Malaysian experience of cohesion punctuated by strain points. In particular, the electoral fraud of President Quirino in 1949 strained elite understandings, with the defeated candidate, Jose Laurel, threatening to "turn off the light and start shooting."[1] The machinations of President Marcos in the 1969 election equally tested elite patience. And after declaring martial law in 1972, Marcos proceeded more seriously to disrupt patterns of elite unity and recruitment, with repercussions blemishing even the presidency of his successor, Corazon Aquino. However, despite these tensions, cohesion between elites was each time reasserted, most clearly made manifest in the sharing – or alternating – of state positions and resources, practices that have amounted to a roughly contested, but still stable politics.

Further, in more deeply examining the matrices of state capacity, business elites, social structures, and political practices, one finds clear parallels between the Philippines and Thailand. In brief, state capacity in the Philippines has remained limited, its colonial legacies inhibiting developmentalist policies in the way that elite disunity has in Thailand. And in these circumstances, the political role enjoyed by business elites has surged inversely, with the "Chinese *mestizo*" segment of the business community operating in politics as the functional equivalent of Thailand's Sino-Thais. What is more, with political parties poorly institutionalized and standing ideologically for little, business elites have used them as personalist vehicles with which to gain access to state power. They have also relied on informal institutions to mobilize voter support, either exploiting the patrimonialist ties that once bound their haciendas, or working through mediary networks of rural *caciques* (chieftains), machine bosses, and ward *liders* – the rough counterparts to Thailand's provincial *jao pho* and canvassers. Finally, in anchoring these relations, social forces have generally been mired in dense clientelism, enabling us to characterize them as quiescent. Periodically, however, society has grown more participatory, with middle-class "people power" foreshadowing Black May, the *Hukbalahap* rebellion and the New People's Army articulating the same rural discontents as the Communist Party of Thailand, and Muslim separatist movements in Mindanao loudly echoing the tensions found in Thailand's southern provinces.

These sets of variables have combined in the Philippines and Thailand to produce the region's longest standing democracies. An intriguing difference, however, is found in their varying inversely in terms of the twin dimensions of democratic consolidation. Specifically, we have seen that in Thailand's quest to raise quality, the stability of its democracy may be tested. By contrast, democracy in the Philippines, while failing to gain quality, has remained stable, at least for the past decade. In explaining this Philippine pattern, James Putzel attributes democratic persistence to the "illegitimacy of alternatives, with the experience of Marcos's authoritarian crony capitalism a significant disincentive to abandoning the democratic framework."[2] There is no such instructive legacy available in Thailand. At the same time, Putzel attributes the low quality of Philippine democracy to a "mismatch" between formal and informal institutions, with the latter involving a pernicious set of "mental models" in which "big man" populism and clan-based patronage are able to flourish.[3] To be sure, Thailand is equally burdened with such attitudes and behaviors. But the country underwent an economic crisis during the late 1990s that the Philippines did not, one that subdued elites, emboldened social forces, and permitted dramatic new political reforms to be put in place.

Accordingly, in terms of a number of variables and causal sequences, enough similarities exist between the Philippines and other countries examined in this volume that meaningful comparisons can be made. One important way, though, in which the Philippines is clearly incongruous involves the traditional sources of sociopolitical power. In brief, the country's Spanish colonial experience imparted a rare organizational basis for elite statuses, namely, large landholdings. The U.S. colonial experience perpetuated this outcome, favoring landowning elites, while democratizing politics, thus weakening the state and rendering it an easy mark. More specifically, in contrast to the Dutch in Indonesia and the British in Singapore and Malaysia who built powerful colonial bureaucracies, American officials gave greater attention to nurturing a political party system and elections.[4] And hence, in the region's post-colonial political economies, while one can in many Southeast Asian countries identify a "bureaucratic capitalism" in which the state retains primacy over business, Paul Hutchcroft detects in the Philippines a "booty capitalism" in which state resources are "grabbed by groups with an economic base *outside* the state."[5] In short, the centrality of the state in New Order Indonesia, Singapore, Malaysia, and even in Thailand until the mid-1980s stands in sharp contrast to the preeminence of business elites in the Philippines, rooted initially in large landholdings, later in protected industries.

Nonetheless, we will see that if the state in the Philippines has acquired less capacity than its counterparts elsewhere in the region, it has remained an essential armature for social power. Put simply, state positions and resources have been significant enough that landed and business elites have competed vigorously for them. We will see also that while the state's ministries have readily been captured, it has gained over time some autonomous capacity to extract, raising some revenues locally, but more importantly, attracting overseas developmental assistance. Thus, even while reinforcing the prior statuses of business elites, the state has recently been shown by John Sidel to offer conduits through which internally to promote new kinds of elites.[6] In consequence, if a major trend in Southeast Asia today involves a steady gravitation of power from military and bureaucratic elites to business and parties, the Philippines may be undergoing a reverse progress, however partial and nuanced, thus offering some points of convergence and bases for comparison.

Another way in which the Philippines appears distinct in the region involves its comparative economic performance. Put simply, with the state's developmental capacity limited, the country was unable until very late in the day to attract and coordinate the large inflows of foreign capital that once buoyed Southeast Asia. The state was unable to set up much infrastructure, evinced by Manila's electrical brownouts. It was unable to create efficient approval agencies, thus discouraging foreign direct investment. What is more, the country's business conglomerates were so degraded by Marcos that they were unable for a time even to operate effectively as joint venture partners. And hence, because the Philippine economy began only slowly to rise from its sickbed, it avoided the worst of the economic crisis that suddenly brought down much of the rest of the region.

But if this record of economic performance serves again to differentiate the Philippines in Southeast Asia, it must separate it cleanly too from the Latin American setting into which so many analysts seek to place it. As

Mark Thompson notes, even when at its peak under Marcos, state capacity fell far short of any bureaucratic-authoritarian model[7] – surely the qualification needed for entering into meaningful comparisons with Latin America's political economy during the 1960s–70s, as well as for addressing tangential issues of indebtedness, democratic transition, and consolidation during the 1980s–90s. Instead, relations between state and business elites in the Philippines – bristling with monopoly licenses, untendered state contracts, and preferential loans – give the country's business scene a Southeast Asian texture. And when finally the Philippine economy began to recover, it was achieved through new liberalization, the "strategic retreat" that had been pioneered in the region by Indonesia.[8]

In sum, in examining constellations of national leaders, elite relations, mass attitudes, some major structural factors, and democratic outcomes, we can discover the analytical basis for comparing Philippine politics in a regional context. Let us investigate more fully, then, the ways in which the country's political dynamics have unfolded.

Elite relations

In analyzing regime types in Southeast Asia, we have characterized politics as state-centered. The region has thus featured high executive offices, ruling party apparatuses, massive bureaucracies, and modernizing militaries. And in different combinations, these institutions have underpinned state elites, who, in then dominating national politics, have penetrated deeply into economic sectors and social structures. In Malaysia, though, we have seen that after the state promoted business elites, some were able to work back and influence politics through party positions and personalist networks. Further, in Thailand, business elites rising up outside the state – first in Bangkok during the 1970s, later in the provinces during the 1980s – took more formal political control through electoral processes.

In the Philippines, these processes began sooner and advanced much further. Business elites, often tracing their dynastic lineages to colonial agriculture and social structures, have possessed greater autonomy from the state. And they have perpetuated greater unity, helping usually to stabilize their democracy. In addition, in using democratic procedures, these elites have sought more than to protect their property from the state. They have sought directly to occupy key parts of the state in order to get more property still. Put plainly, in using their economic bases to win electoral offices, they have looted state assets and abused regulatory authority. In consequence, for many observers, what stands out in the Philippines is not only its democracy, but the utter impotence of its state, softly pliable and tapped easily for largesse.[9]

However, in his recent studies, Sidel warns against overdrawing this portrait of state "decay."[10] Specifically, while the state has doubtless been denied much administrative and developmental strength, it has nonetheless possessed a mean capacity to extract. There should otherwise have been nothing for business elites to loot. Hence, the state has been kept strong enough that it has been able to renew itself at least in primitive ways, either by fixing local monopolies or attracting overseas developmental assistance. What is more, this capacity has enabled some elites to originate within the state, rather than outside in business, even if they soon supplement their statuses with the business opportunities that the state's extractive capacity allows. These state elites, then, rising through municipal councils, mayorships, congressional districts, and governorships, pursue commensurate levels of personal business, often illegal, thereby reversing the directionality of plunder. In sum, though Philippine politics cannot be depicted as tightly state-centered, the state has hardly slipped from the stage. While often captured by business elites, it has been important in then extracting the resources with which to solidify elite statuses. Its extractive capacity has been able to promote internal elites too, those who underpin their statuses by working back into business. Thus, the country's political patterns can be understood by plotting them well ahead on a continuum that they share with the rest of Southeast Asia, though one along which they have in some instances backtracked, establishing points of convergence.

Finally, if the Philippines is furthest along this continuum, the organizational bases for its elites are clearest. We need not give attention to so broad and differentiated an elite spectrum as Thailand's, for example, which, amid the country's ongoing transition, still rumbles with competing segments in the military, bureaucracy, business, and parties. Instead, it is an economic base that matters most in the Philippines, today derived mostly from business and commerce, but earlier from landholdings. However, in regularly exercising the state's extractive capacity, business elites have built up state bodies able also to generate elites internally. Thus, as Sidel reminds us, business elites are not the end of the elite register. While bounding into the congress, they have triggered a quieter – though no less abusive – reverse flow of state elites into business. Let us investigate the historical and organizational bases for these two kinds of elite statuses more closely.

Business and government

The emergence of business elites outside the state, but able to gain state power, has much to do with Philippine historical legacies. In particular, Spain's remoteness from its colonial possession, as well as its ambition to move still further afield in Christianizing China,[11] meant that *de facto* control over administration and the economy was given in the Philippines to the Catholic Church. And in these circumstances, the religious orders prospered, carving out haciendas and patterns of landholding that were unique in the region. During the 19th century, these patterns were extended by the up-country migrations of Chinese *mestizos*, the descendants of unions between ethnic Chinese and indigenous Malays. Finding themselves unable to compete in small business and trade with the Chinese migrants who arrived after them, the *mestizos* moved from the ports to the rural interior, then acquired their own large landholdings on which to plant sugar and rice. In this way, they transcended the mediating role in rice sales performed by their Sino-Thai counterparts. And they avoided the slow decline endured by the *peranakan* in Indonesia and the Straits Settlements of Malaya. Indeed, they gained ownership over many of the new sugar lands in central Luzon and the Visayas, then grew rich with the returns on their exports.

At the turn of the century, through conflict with Spain, the United States became involved in the Philippines, first ousting the Spanish, then harshly suppressing a local bid for independence. But while then claiming the territory as a colony for itself, the United States left the *mestizo* landowners undisturbed. Indeed, it greatly bolstered their economic standings. Instead of absorbing their lands for American plantation companies or redistributing them locally (as it would later encourage in South Korea and Taiwan), U.S. officials helped to enlarge them, purchasing haciendas from the friars and making them available for local auction.[12] In addition, unlike the British and the Dutch in their colonies nearby, the United States never constructed a powerful colonial state, one elaborated with highly rationalist agencies that favored imperial interests over local ones. Indeed, as early as 1913, U.S. officials yielded control over the bureaucracy to local personnel, only keeping a hand in the education departments. Local security forces were left similarly undeveloped, amounting to no more than the Philippine Constabulary. In consequence, the bureaucracy and military in the Philippines were granted much less capacity and prestige than in other Southeast Asian countries. During the colonial period, it was large landholdings that formed the organizational bases for elites.

In short, the United States did much to reinforce the *mestizo* landowners' social power with economic resources. It increased their holdings, left their modes of production unruffled by any colonial state apparatus, shielded them from American plantation companies, yet gave their sugar exports free access to American markets (thereby preempting a challenge too from any pre-war impulse to industrialize). In return, while these landowners nominally supported calls for independence, they remained more content to collaborate with the United States. And U.S officials, thus finding the landowners trustworthy and pragmatic in their judgements, now aided them politically too, setting up a local parliament in 1907 known as the Philippine Assembly, a bicameral legislature in 1916, and finally a commonwealth presidency in 1935. Of course, it was the *mestizo* landowners who were best placed to exploit this new democratic openness, organizing the *Nacionalista* party with which to contest the presidency and seats in the assembly. And in doing this, they appeared able to count on the habitual support of their tenants, drawn from a fragmented and quiescent society.

The Philippines formally gained independence in 1946. And over the next decade, while plantation agriculture remained important, industrialization began also to take place. Indeed, through import substitution, the Philippines developed a manufacturing base and engineering sector that during the 1950s were the most advanced in the region. Two points must be made, however. First, this industrialization signaled no increase in the administrative or developmental capacity of the state – of a kind being acquired at the time by new bureaucratic pilot agencies in Japan and a decade later in Korea, Taiwan, and Singapore. Instead, it was the upshot of Quirino's having drawn so heavily on Philippine foreign currency reserves during his presidential campaign in 1949 that he sparked a balance of payments crisis.[13] It was thus simply to avoid exacerbating trade deficits – rather than strategically to undertake any primary phase of ISI – that tariffs were imposed against imported goods, inadvertently creating the vacuum in which industrialization might occur. Second, one notes that landed elites were not squarely challenged by this industrialization. On the contrary, using their agricultural surpluses, many large landowners participated in the industrializing drive. The Lopez family, for example, heading the "sugar bloc" from its redoubt in Iloilo, went into power generation, publishing, and manufacturing. And if critical weight then tilted slowly from agriculture to industry, it was those families with a foot in both haciendas and manufacturing that came now to spawn Philippine business elites.

To enhance their private holdings, business elites competed for high public offices. As we have seen, the state possessed little developmental capacity. It could, however, extract resources from society. And thus, at the national level, elites wanting to unlock these resources tried to capture the presidency. Specifically, the president had strong budgetary powers – far stronger than his American counterpart. And with the congress legislating more programs and appropriating more funding than revenues could support, the president typically impounded the funds, largely in the name of fiscal responsibility.[14] But then, he could selectively release them, favoring some cabinet secretaries, representatives, and their constituents over others – thereby easing them into clientelist postures. In addition, through a precedent set by Manuel Quezon during the 1930s, the president could "transfer" budgetary allocations, shifting them unaccountably across departments and programs. And the only real way for the business elites in the congress to check these powers was to refuse to attend legislative sessions, preventing the quorum that was needed to pass spending bills in the first place. The bureaucracy, for its part, possessed even less defense, blackmailed by the president and congress alike into puffing itself up with patronage appointments, lest it suffer retaliatory budget cuts.[15] Thus, within the state, only the senate seemed able to resist the president, largely by nurturing the ambitions of its members to replace him.

Accordingly, with the presidency having gained strong budgetary powers, it helped greatly in solidifying, indeed, enhancing the statuses of those business elites who controlled it. Further, the house of representatives offered seats from which to receive and distribute the resources that the president might release. And the senate served as a platform from which incumbents could contemplate replacing the president. But in gaining this capacity, the state not only enhanced the statuses of business elites, it was able also to buoy up elites from within. Ramon Magsaysay, president during the 1950s, was plucked from the defense ministry by U.S. officials, then coached in charisma and thrust to the top. Ferdinand Marcos was a lawyer, then entered the senate before winning the presidency in 1964. Fidel Ramos, before ascending to the presidency in 1992, had been commanding general of the armed forces. And Joseph Estrada rose from the mayorship of San Juan to the vice-presidency under Ramos, then finally to the presidency in 1998.

In tracing this progress to its local roots, Sidel has argued that across the archipelago, figures who possessed no landed wealth, but much individual "prowess," were able to win council seats, mayorships, governorships, and congressional seats. And by exploiting the regulatory powers and enforcement agencies attached to their offices, they penetrated the world of business, awarding themselves licenses, franchises, and concessions in milling, mining, bus services, ferry routes, inter-island shipping, and the like, while arranging protection for a myriad of illegal activities. And then, by working the "mutually reinforcing nexus of political and economic power,"[16] they heaved themselves up the next political rung.

Finally, in characterizing relations between Philippine elites, one can assess them as cohesive, at least apart from the Marcos period. Elites have competed vigorously, but not interminably or at all costs. Hence, in waging their campaigns, they have stopped short of seriously eroding one another's statuses and inflaming social grievances. Further, in elections, though often protesting the vote counts that have gone against them, they have accepted the victories of their rivals. These patterns were tested during Quirino's presidency in the late 1940s, and disrupted more seriously by Marcos during the 1970s–80s. Indeed, as we will see, after gaining paramountcy as national leader, Marcos proceeded so deeply to disunify elites and disillusion social constituents that he destabilized his authoritarian regime, unleashing a popular upsurge coined locally as "people power." But after Marcos's ouster, Philippine elites gradually restored their unity and again stabilized their democracy. However, before turning to patterns of regime continuity and change that resulted, it is necessary to assess a second causal dimension, namely, the relations between elites and their social constituents.

Elite-mass relations

In trying to energize constituent support – or alternatively, to perpetuate social quiescence – elites in the Philippines have confronted distinct challenges. Owing in part to the state's limited capacity, they were never able to institute the kind of corporatist arrangements that we encountered in New Order Indonesia and Singapore. State weakness meant also that the Philippines never achieved the "miracle" rates of economic growth that other countries in Southeast Asia did, thus offering little scope for performance legitimacy. Indeed, since the 1950s, the Philippine economy has been mainly in decline, belying any claims made by elites to managerial effectiveness. Hence, what few surpluses have been available for rural development and populist schemes have mostly taken the form of particularized pork barreling by congressmen.

In addition, if appeals based on developmentalism have been precluded, so too have cultural reinventions and legitimating mentalities rooted in ancient kingships, empires, and grand civilizations. More specifically, while Suharto drew upon *Majapahit* and *Mataram* greatness, the UMNO upon the *Melaka* sultanate, and the king of Thailand and the sultan of Brunei upon their lengthy royal lineages, elites in the Philippines have possessed little heritage to tap and mythologize. In short, the country possesses no record of precolonial majesty that can be mined for legitimacy.[17] In addition, while nationalist forces emerged in opposition to Spain, then waged a guerrilla war against early American occupation, they fought no successful war of independence like Indonesia's "people's army" did against the Dutch and Vietnam's peasant army did against a succession of interlopers.[18] Indeed, Philippine elites were more often noted for their closely accommodating their colonial overlords.

What is more, elites have been discouraged from articulating even the base grievances of indigenous populations against ethnic Chinese – a strategy used historically in Malaysia, episodically in Thailand, and implicitly in New Order Indonesia. They have avoided this first, because so many of them are themselves Chinese *mestizos*, and second, because alarming the Chinese-Filipino community would put further at risk the country's perennially fragile economy. Of course, in the past, *mestizo* politicians have quietly squeezed their distant ethnic kin for campaign contributions and sundry immigration fees. But Marcos appeared to diminish even these possibilities, relaxing the terms for Philippine citizenship in hopes of motivating Chinese entrepreneurism and investment.

What, then, has cemented elite-mass relations in the Philippines, enabling elites to energize constituents or perpetuate quiescence? One of the ways in which elites have attempted to mobilize support has been by making "moral" appeals, declaring before mass audiences their commitments to democracy and good governance, then denouncing their opponents as authoritarian and corrupt.[19] In the 1998 presidential election campaign, for example, a spokesman for the new *Reporma* party explicitly invoked "moral forces" against the leading candidate, Joseph Estrada, warning that his party's opponent "was surrounded by underworld characters like drug and gambling lords. . . . [A]n Estrada victory would bring '*Sindikato* Inc.' to Malacanang."[20] The morality of these appeals could also be deepened by gaining endorsements from Catholic Church leaders and evangelical groups. Thus, while Estrada's personal habits had strongly alienated Jaime Cardinal Sin, he labored still to gain the blessing of priests in San Juan, the city neighboring Manila where he had earlier been mayor, a position to which his son succeeded him.[21] Estrada managed also to get the endorsement of *El Shaddai*, the country's largest Catholic charismatic group, and the *Iglesia ng Kristo*. His chief opponent, Jose de Venecia, however, gained endorsements from important "born-again" Christian organizations, the Jesus is Lord Ministry and the Jesus Miracle Crusade.

How effective have elites been in using these moral, even impassioned, appeals based on democracy, clean government, and religion? Whether democracy in the Philippines has been placidly oligarchical or run crudely through machines, its ideals seem still to resonate with many Filipinos. Indeed, as society has evolved from quiescence to a more participatory posture, many cases have emerged of ordinary Filipinos taking great risks for democracy, either challenging local bosses to keep elections honest, or even directly confronting President Marcos over his despotism. In a recent interpretation of the meaning of Philippine elections, Ben Kerkvliet offers some examples.[22] In the 1969 congressional elections, much manipulated by Marcos, teachers who had served as poll station clerks "def[ied] threats against their lives" by testifying before investigators after having been forced by gunmen to falsify tally sheets. In 1982, elections were held for village heads, the first since martial law had been declared. But when an incumbent in a village in Nueva Ecija used his links to Marcos's political party to prevent an opponent's filing candidacy papers, two-thirds of the villagers bravely boycotted the election – or voted for the opposing candidate despite his disqualification. In 1988, a volunteer movement arose to monitor the gubernatorial election in Ilocos Norte, keeping "the counting and reporting process honest" enough that an unpopular, but well-connected incumbent was dislodged. In sum, as Kerkvliet records, there is much evidence in the Philippines of "people trying to preserve or create some integrity and honesty in elections and turn them into expressions of actual sentiments or evaluations of candidates and issues."

Mark Thompson counters, however, that it is only when social forces hold grievances that are unusually intense – as in the Marcos years – that moral appeals based on democracy gain sway. And endorsements offered by religious leaders, further, have failed to deliver up reliable followings. For example, while the Catholic Bishops Conference issued a pastoral letter on the eve of the 1998 election imploring their flock to choose "anyone but Erap," Catholic voters nonetheless turned in large numbers to Estrada.[23] Voters were untroubled too by the renewed prospects for lax governance and cronyism under Estrada, asking what good had it done them to elect "brainy" and principled presidents in the past.[24] Thompson thus bluntly concludes that while moral appeals have often been used by elites in the Philippines, "they were secondary to the bread and butter of 'normal' Philippine politics: patronage."[25] Accordingly, despite the counsel dispensed regularly by the Catholic Church and the media, vote buying during the during the 1998 election campaign remained rampant.[26]

Thus, with elites in the Philippines lacking tight corporatist controls, legitimating mentalities, a developmentalist record, and even – except during the Marcos years – a reliable means of applying coercion, how then have they moved beyond the infirmity of their moral appeals to perpetuate social support or quiescence? Many analysts have declared the centrality of clientelism in the Philippines, networks of personalized obligation and exchange that while steeply unequal, are nevertheless braced by affection and a timeless sense of hierarchy. Patrons informally pass down protection, employment, and ceremonial favors. Clients loyally perform their labors, then vote in elections as their patrons instruct. These outlooks prevail, of course, in most settings at low levels of economic development, cumulating in societies that can be characterized as quiescent. But they have been reckoned to be especially intense in the Philippines, owing to the patterns of large landholdings and hacienda-based agriculture.

To be sure, this same system of labor repressive agriculture has sometimes so alienated peasants they have broken their patterns of deference and surged with great militancy. In consequence, the Philippines has experienced the most serious peasant rebellions to be found in Southeast Asia, including the *Hukbalahap* uprising in central Luzon that grew first in opposition to the Japanese occupation, then afterward turned against landowners. Further, the Philippines spawned a powerful Communist party which, in alliance with the New People's Army, perpetuated the region's longest-running rural insurgency. And in spreading from Luzon to the Visayas, it abutted a series of Muslim secessionist movements in Mindanao. But less dramatically than open rebellion, researchers have also discovered small acts of resistance – insolence, vandalism, and pilferage – among even those peasants who have remained tied to their hacienda.[27] In addition, as peasants were later dispersed by the green revolution, such clientelism as existed mutated into "bossism," with traditional obligations dissolving in more instrumentalist codes of exchange and coercion. In short, elites turned increasingly from clientelist loyalties to patronage machines in order regenerate constituencies and shore up their statuses. Elections were now won, in the Philippine refrain, through "guns, goons, and gold."

In sum, elites in the Philippines, in managing social forces, have never possessed enough state capacity to institute corporatist controls. Nor have they had capacity enough to expand the economy in ways that would have earned them performance legitimacy. Further, without a record of ancient kingships and empires or sustained anti-colonialism, they have had no traditions or lore to reinvent, thus denying them the wherewithal also for legitimating mentalities. Nor with so many elites constructed as possessing Chinese ancestry have they risked appeals to indigenous resentments. In this situation, elites have used moral appeals, invoking the idioms of democracy, good governance, and religion that appear at least sometimes to resonate with constituents. But more potent than this has been the clientelist posture of social forces, grounded in unique Philippine patterns of land ownership. Of course, this clientelism has been challenged by open rebellions and secretive resistance. But patterns of social deference appear still to persist in the Philippines. Moreover, even as these outlooks have been tested over time by urbanization, they have been reproduced on the cityscape through machine politics and bossism. Once concludes, then, that despite the increasingly participatory attitudes of Philippine society, cumulating famously under Marcos and Estrada in people power, enough quiescence has remained that elites in business and politics continue to oversee steep social hierarchies.

Regime outcomes

Inter-elite and elite-mass relations, set in a context of distinctive colonial legacies and socioeconomic structures, have produced in the Philippines greater experience with democratic procedures than in any other Southeast Asian country. They have also instigated one of the most notorious authoritarian hiatuses. Thus, after Philippine independence in 1946, we find a stable, but low quality democracy until 1972, a personal dictatorship until 1986, and stable democracy today, though again, of low quality. In this section, we will briefly review the first democracy period, the Marcos interlude, and a process of redemocratization. This chapter then concludes with an extended analysis of the 1998 general election, gauging the new democracy's quality.

Stable democracy

After gaining independence in 1946, the Philippines possessed a democratic regime, though one introduced to elites through colonial tutelage, rather than demanded by participatory society. Of course, without this tutelage, local elites would doubtless have been slower to adopt democratic procedures. But once in place, they discovered these procedures could be operated in ways that met their interests, enabling them peacefully to share access to state positions and resources. They were encouraged in this too by Philippine society remaining quiescent. While rural uprisings took place, ethnic sentiments never hardened like in Indonesia and Malaysia. In addition, at junctures in which elite relations grew strained, the United States continued to pose managerial interventions. Most notably, after President Quirino's fraudulence and violence during the campaign of 1949, U.S. officials recruited a new figure, Manuel Roxas, to break away from the *Nacionalistas* in order to form the Liberal Party. They also introduced an election commission (COMELEC) and a poll watching organization, the National Citizens Movement for Free Elections (NAMFREL).

Thompson offers a concise schema by which to understand the ways in which elites in the *Nacionalista* and the Liberal parties then cooperated over the next two decades.[28] First, they avoided all ideological appeals that might have heightened their differences. They then collaborated in marginalizing any third parties that might have offered policy alternatives. Finally, they contested vigorously against one another in general elections, though in ways that remained bounded by understandings. More specifically, the *Nacionalistas* and the Liberals each tried to capture the presidency while maximizing their senate seats, enabling them to gain control over budgetary processes, pork barrel expenditures, bureaucratic hiring, bribe taking, and license selling. Further, once a party emerged victorious, its elites took care to observe the principle of the minimum winning coalition, accepting enough members into their uppermost ranks to hold power, but not so many as to dilute the rewards of high office. Nonetheless, even some elites who had been rewarded inevitably felt shorted. And they could then be wooed by the party in opposition, aspiring to greater rewards in the event of government turnover. In this way, political weight shifted gradually from the ruling party to the opposition, enabling a transfer of power to take place. As Thompson notes, "no party ever won the presidency for a third consecutive four-year term."[29] And hence, as Kerkvliet observes, elections offered "a process by which elites rotate[d] among themselves access to public coffers."[30] Indeed, during the 1950s–60s, the *Nacionalistas* and the Liberals exchanged resources in much the same way that intra-party factions of elites had throughout the colonial period.

Of course, when a democratic regime is operated in this way, doubts arise about quality. Indeed, at low levels of development, elites may perpetuate democratic procedures because, while peacefully exchanging state positions and resources, they have little fear of intrusion by quiescent social forces. In these circumstances, even large landowners, the practitioners of a labor repressive agriculture that is cast universally in the literature as the enemy of democracy, can become democracy's advocate. It is for these reasons that Philippine democracy has frequently been dismissed by its critics as "oligarchical" democracy – raising questions about what benefits might accrue to social forces beyond their escaping the grossest and most arbitrary forms of state coercion. Further, as modernization works its well-known effects, elites who had happily operated their democracies amid quiescent societies, now rediscover old virtues in authoritarian rule.

Unstable authoritarianism

In 1969, Ferdinand Marcos won re-election, gaining a second term as president. But the ferocity with which he contested this election signaled that even a second term would not satisfy him. Indeed, as his tenure neared its end, he proposed that his wife, Imelda, run as *Nacionalista* candidate for the presidency in 1973 – a stratagem that while commonly deployed at the provincial level, was regarded as unacceptable on the national scene. Thus, he struck even more audaciously, summoning a constitutional convention (ConCon) through which to introduce a parliamentary system. In this way, Marcos could gain the prime ministership, neatly skirting the term limits on presidents. However, while Marcos softened up the delegates with bribery, then won them over with false promises of seats in an interim national assembly, they labored slowly, if obediently, in drafting the new charter. Hence, with the end of his presidency approaching, Marcos feared the loss of incumbency, loosening his grip on the delegates. It was in these circumstances that he declared martial law in 1972 – though he was careful to cite the Communist disturbances in central Luzon as his reason.

It is important to note, though, that in suspending Philippine democracy, Marcos was not opposed by most elites. Their acquiescence thus revealed their practice of democracy to have been conditional – subject to their constituents remaining quiescent as they staidly rotated state positions and resources. But recently, social quiescence had been tested. During the 1960s, the mechanization of agriculture had quickened, causing the haciendas to shed tenants and workers. Landed elites, then, in contesting elections, found affect-laden clientelist bonds to have weakened. Consequently, they now had to mobilize support more actively, employing machines to fix bureaucratic favors, mediate vote buying, and apply coercion. In these circumstances, David Wurfel observes that "elite[s] began to question the utility of rising costs, because their control seemed to be slipping anyway, and many elite politicians were becoming tolerant of a suspension of elections."[31] In addition, they were unnerved by the Communist insurrection in the countryside and the growing militancy of students – even if Marcos was himself funding the students in order secretly to increase their militancy. Further, his declaring martial law soon intensified the Communist insurrection, while giving an early boost also to the Muslim separatist movements in Mindanao.

This period of martial law, forming a clear break in the Philippine record, reminds us that elites who are cohesive can carry out regime closures, as well as perpetuate democracies. Indeed, it could even be argued that democracy in the Philippines had been exposed as functionally premature, the product of American imposition rather than social participation. And, as social forces began finally to stir, elites responded by forming a regime type more typical of those at their country's level of development, one through which they were able to cooperate politically in demobilizing society. It was only a decade later, then, after Marcos had divided elites and precipitated a popular upsurge that the Philippines would be restored to democracy.

But early in his tenure, Marcos demonstrated also that if elites could be cohesive in operating an authoritarian regime, social forces could be placated too. In short, while society had become less quiescent during the 1960s–70s, it was not yet participatory, leaving it receptive to benefits dispensed from top-down. Marcos thus promised in patrimonialist fashion what most Philippine elites would not, namely, land reform. Of course, Marcos sidestepped the haciendas of most landowning elites, taking care to avoid alienating them. And he avoided carving up most of the sugar plantations too, leaving them geared to exports. Instead, he focused mostly on land that was used for growing rice and corn, convertible to small holdings for subsistence and local markets. And though the owners who were affected were able sometimes to resist, blocking the reform process in the courts or the bureaucracy, Marcos's "accomplishment was, nevertheless, greater than in any previous administration."[32] Indeed, Marcos's relative success could be measured by the New People's Army finding it difficult during the early years of martial law to recruit new fighters. Thus, one observes that in shoring up elite statuses, placating social forces, and more broadly restoring order, Marcos was able to perpetuate his authoritarian regime.

In this way, Marcos emerged from the elite collectivity as paramount national leader. And he adopted a ruling style whose patterns we recognize as neo-patrimonialist – thereby inviting comparisons with President Suharto. First, the patrimonialist dimension of Marcos's rule was made clear by the utter arbitrariness of his actions. He made little distinction between public and private funds, taking full control over the national budget, then helping himself to state coffers – either directly to enrich his family members and cronies or to deepen the loyalties of his social constituents. Under martial law, congress was closed and the *Nacionalista* and Liberal parties soon withered, their legislation supplanted by presidential decrees and instructions. Provincial governors and municipal leaders were equally circumvented, the president now concentrating patronage in his own hands, then "lavish[ing] pork barrel directly on the *barrio*."[33] Indeed, the local *barrios*, renamed *"barangay"* in 1974, "became the basis of a personal, nationwide political machine," with each *barangay* organized into groups of solicitous small business people, farmers, workers, and the like. In addition, "integrity boards" were formed to open up feedback loops, carrying complaints about public officials up from the *barangay* directly to the president. Surveying these linkages, Wurfel suggests that Marcos "aspired to be the *padrino* of all Filipinos."[34] And even as his health declined, Marcos's aspirations were pursued more fully by his wife, Imelda. As minister of human settlements, she set up "the largest patronage machine in the country," building roads, schools, and housing projects, all "displaying a prominent plaque bearing the name of Imelda Marcos."[35]

The "*neo-*" component of Marcos's ruling style was conveyed through two images, a technocratic one generated by financial departments in the bureaucracy and a pseudo-democratic one associated with representative institutions. The technocratic guise was essential for gaining assistance from international agencies and donors, replenishing the state coffers that Marcos continuously looted. Marcos thus appointed Cesar Virata, the much respected Philippines representative on the World Bank's board of governors, to serve as finance secretary throughout the 1970s. He also appointed Virata as prime minister in 1984 after dual executive positions had been introduced. But while Virata managed to keep the loans flowing, he was never able seriously to restrain Marcos's patrimonialist dealings.

Further, if this false technocratic image was useful for gaining funding, pseudo-democracy could be helpful in winning legitimacy. Marcos, with his background as a lawyer, remained attentive to the legalist forms of limited government and representative institutions. He began modestly, first bribing the ConCon in order to fashion a new constitution. He also packed the judiciary with loyalists, but left its complex structures intact. In this way, Marcos was able to christen his martial law regime one of "constitutional authoritarianism." Further, after delivering the press into the hands of his cronies, Marcos permitted it to resume reporting. He also organized regular referenda. And while withdrawing the ones he sensed would go against him, the rest highlighted public approval for martial law and constitutional changes. Finally, in 1976, Marcos set up a national assembly, the *Batasang Pambansa*, heralding new rounds of legislative and local elections. He thus created a new party too, the New Society Movement (KBL, *Kilusan Bagong Lipunan*). And he promoted this vehicle as embracing the interests of all existing parties. Indeed, if the KBL had been more explicitly corporatist, and had its appeals been ordered more systematically into a "mentality," Marcos's KBL and New Society might have matured along lines matching Suharto's *Golkar* and New Order.

The *pseudo-* character of Philippine democracy, however, involving limits on civil liberties and electoral fairness, meant that many interests were left unrepresented, hence requiring some harsh repression. Indeed, dissidents were routinely arrested, tortured, even "disappeared" through a curiously named process of "salvaging." In 1977, five years after martial law had been declared, an estimated 70,000 Filipinos were held as political prisoners.[36] To carry out this coercion, Marcos built up the military, doubling its personnel during the mid-1970s, and giving it a prominence that it had never before possessed. Its budgets, salaries, and promotional opportunities were all greatly increased. It was also given a new role in business, running electricity and telephone companies, waterworks, railways, and steel plants. To oversee this expanded military, Marcos filled top positions with officers recruited from his home province of Ilocos Norte, including the commanding general of the Philippine Constabulary, Fidel Ramos, and the head of the Presidential Security Command, Fabian Ver. Ramos and Ver held additional familial qualifications, one notes, by virtue of their being Marcos's cousins. Finally, to regain control over the police – long decentralized, indeed, absorbed into the private armies of landowners and bosses – they were integrated into a national force under the defense department. They were augmented also by new formations of vigilantes, in particular, the Civilian Home Defense Forces, which through their ill-disciplined actions, earned great notoriety. Indeed, one of the reasons that Marcos had so dramatically to enlarge the military was that his patrimonialist strategies were eroding its professionalism and battle-readiness.

In sum, by declaring martial law, Marcos transformed the Philippine political regime. However, at least at the start of this authoritarian hiatus, he perpetuated unity among most elites by respecting their statuses. And he placated social forces by undertaking some land reforms. In addition, he implemented these strategies in patrimonialist ways, then masked his arbitrariness with technocratic appointments and pseudo-democratic procedures. And what little dissent remained was suppressed by the rapidly expanding armed forces. However, what elites did not foresee was that in allowing Marcos to emerge as national leader, he would soon use his paramountcy to exaggerate his standing further while diminishing theirs. Over time, Marcos thus divided the elite collectivity, then began openly to confront some factions. In addition, his land reforms soon sputtered, disillusioning many mass-level supporters. In these circumstances, we will see that Marcos so alienated elites and social forces that they finally combined in bringing him down.

Disunifying elites

In clinging to the presidency, Marcos "disregarded the iron law of pre-martial law politics: orderly presidential succession."[37] And not only did he monopolize the office, he greatly enhanced it, closing the congress in order personally to control patronage flows to local officials. As we have seen, many elites were at first unperturbed, believing that Marcos would respect their statuses. A few, however, began immediately to oppose him, raising a pole of resistance around which other elites would rally over time. Most notably, Senator Benigno Aquino who, through his marriage into the Cojuangco clan had become a large landowner, began after Marcos's reelection in 1969 to experiment with armed strategies. Aquino formed a large private army and cultivated ties to the Huks, still operating during this period as bandits. He permitted these forces to train on his hacienda, then mediated their cooperating with the Communist Party in helping form the New People's Army.[38] Aquino's aim was to instigate rural guerrilla actions that would check Marcos's power.

After martial law was imposed in 1972, Aquino abandoned his armed strategies, but started to denounce Marcos more openly. Marcos responded by jailing Aquino, and a military court sentenced him to death, though the order was later rescinded. Marcos next attacked Aquino's organizational bases, ordering that his opponent's landholdings be redistributed and business interests sold. However, while Aquino's resources were in this way diminished, sympathy for him began to mount. Thus, when Marcos at last called elections for the *Batasang* in 1978, he tried to gain credibility by allowing Aquino to contest. Indeed, Aquino was even permitted to form a party, the LABAN (*Lakas ng Bayan*, or People Power). Of course, Marcos left many restrictions in place, while refusing also to release Aquino from prison. And during the election, Marcos again cheated vigorously, relying on "prestuffed ballot boxes, phony registration, 'flying voters,' manipulated election returns, and vote buying"[39] Thus, after the election was over, official results showed that despite the rising popularity of LABAN, not one its party's candidates were successful in winning a seat in the *Batasang*.

The harsh treatment given Aquino and the flagrant electoral cheating raised new doubts among elites about Marcos. Thus, after Marcos officially lifted martial law in 1981 and again called elections, this time for the presidency under the new dual executive system, a growing opposition movement refused to oblige him. Indeed, many politicians organized demonstrations urging voters to boycott. Marcos then sent COMELEC teams to tour the country, warning of the penalties for refusing to vote. The military gave these admonitions force, shooting five boycott marchers in one incident, while arresting many others attending rallies. Finally, Marcos managed to coax a general out of retirement to stage an opposition campaign, then soundly beat him. This exercise only disunified elites further, however, and hardened the attitudes of key factions against him.

While trying to deal with the landed elites and politicians who opposed him – breaking up their haciendas and tightening political outlets – Marcos worked also to contain business elites. The best example involves the Lopez brothers, Fernando, who was also Philippine vice-president, and Eugenio, publisher of the *Manila Chronicle*. We recall that the Lopez family had long been involved in sugar growing, but then expanded during the 1950s into business. And during the early years of martial law, they, like most elites, had firmly supported Marcos. But when Marcos later denied them important opportunities in petrochemicals and other industries, they began to criticize him in the press.[40] Marcos struck back in familiar ways, seizing their media interests, redistributing their lands, and forcing them to sell their electric power generating utility to Imelda's brother at a steeply discounted price. For good measure, the family scion, Eugenio, was imprisoned for allegedly plotting to assassinate Marcos – effectively muting the Lopez's criticisms while accelerating the sale of their assets.

Business assets that were confiscated in these ways were then operated by the state or by Marcos's family members and cronies. More specifically, after Marcos observed the state enterprises that had been set up by some other countries in East Asia, he commenced his own interventions, ostensibly with developmental aims. Accordingly, by 1982, there were nearly 100 state enterprises in the Philippines with 120 subsidiaries,[41] some of which, as we have seen, were run by the military. But more importantly, Marcos introduced a range of new business cronies, nurturing them with seized assets, state contracts, cheap credit, and operating licenses. The most favored cronies were given sure-fire monopolies over commodity exports. Eduardo "Danding" Cojuangco, for example, the estranged cousin of Aquino's wife, was given control over the coconut industry – the country's largest export earner. And after levying a steep tax on coconut farmers, Cojuangco accumulated enough revenues that he was able to purchase the United Coconut Planters Bank from two important Spanish *mestizo* families, the Sorianos and the Zobels, then use the institution to stash the additional levies he collected.[42] Then, in further confusing public revenues with private wealth, Cojuangco borrowed from his bank in order to buy a controlling stake in the San Miguel Corporation, the best known company in the Philippines. Similarly, Robert Benedicto took control of much of the sugar industry, while Antonio Floriendo dominated the banana market. At the same time, a second cohort of cronies was given protected access to manufacturing. Herminio Disini gained a monopoly on imported filter materials, thus enabling him to take over most cigarette manufacturing. Ricardo Silverio assumed control of the automobile parts industry. And Rodolfo Cuenca received most major contracts for government construction projects.

During the late 1970s, then, a few business elites grew so alienated by Marcos's crony capitalism that they turned violently against him, resorting even to urban terrorism. Eduardo Olaguer, vice-president of *Business Day* magazine and a professor at the Asian Institute of Management (a school associated with the Eugenio Lopez Foundation), organized a small circle that came to be known as the "Light-a-Fire Movement" (LAFM).[43] The group made contact with Aquino's forces and the Catholic Church. An in-law of the Lopez family reportedly supplied arson materials. The LAFM then targeted business premises that were associated with Marcos's family members and cronies, especially their hotels and casinos. It managed also to set fire to the building occupied by COMELEC, the body seen to have sanctioned Marcos's cheating in the 1978 election. And though Olaguer was finally arrested, he was succeeded by the April 6th Movement, which then bombed the Manila Convention Center during an international gathering of travel agents, gaining worldwide attention.

Of course, while many business elites had grown resentful of the favors that Marcos had lavished on his cronies, they remained much less militant than Olaguer. Still, as the Philippine economy deteriorated after the second petroleum price shock in 1979, then worsened again when a major business figure, Dewey Dee, fled the country, leaving behind many millions of dollars in debt, their doubts intensified. And when during the early 1980s Marcos used large amounts of state bank funding to bail out the faltering construction firm of Rodolfo Cuenca, their alienation peaked. Business elites, then, began to tilt collectively away from Marcos. It only required a crisis to unite them in confronting him.

In addition, Marcos alienated not only landed and business elites, but elites in the state apparatus he had built up. In particular, with his patrimonialist dealings now eroding the economy, tensions emerged among technocrats in the bureaucracy. On the one hand, Marcos wished genuinely to attain the economic growth rates that he witnessed elsewhere in East Asia. To this end, he organized a pilot agency, the National Economic Development Authority (NEDA). He also introduced the Integrated Reorganization Plan, streamlining the bureaucracy in ways favoring the technocrats. And he opened up channels that bypassed his department heads, increasing the number of officials reporting directly to him – a strategy strongly reminiscent of his contemporary in South Korea, Park Chung Hee. But if corrupt practices and inefficiencies were at first reduced by this shortening in the chain of command, they quickly surged to new levels – making clear the risks of setting up developmental states in uncongenial settings. As Wurfel notes, "reports of 'squeeze' by the president and the First Lady, and their agents, amounting to tens and even hundreds of millions of pesos, were rife in Manila."[44] Economic growth then slipped proportionately from 6 per cent during the early years of martial law to 2 per cent near the end, "the poorest performance of any ASEAN country."

The technocrats were dismayed by this corruption, most of it traceable to crony monopolies, Imelda's prestige projects, and the quadrupling of military budgets. But whenever the technocrats tried to rein in these enterprises, Marcos overrode them. Thompson records that while Cesar Virata had sometimes bailed out cronies in difficulty, the coconut levy was more than he could tolerate. However, when he abolished it in 1981, Marcos promptly restored it – after a word from Conjuangco. In that same year, the head of the NEDA, Gerardo Sicat, was dropped, apparently for having attempted too seriously to liberalize the economy. And earlier, in 1975, the executive secretary, Alejandro Melchor, was forced out for having tried to restrain military spending.[45] In short, Marcos relied on the technocrats to create an appearance of reform, enabling him to lure in developmental assistance from overseas. But he denied them any substantive policy influence, causing them much frustration.

Similarly, while relying on coercion to prop up his government, Marcos's patrimonialist dealings weakened the armed forces, thus breeding tensions between military elites, as well as more deeply in the ranks. The most critical rivalry involved Fabian Ver, Fidel Ramos, and the defense minister, Juan Ponce Enrile. As Marcos's health declined during the early 1980s, he sought a new armed forces chief to safeguard his leadership. But in making his appointment, he chose not the respected, highly professional Ramos, a graduate of West Point, but Ver, the head of the presidential guard and a close friend of Imelda's. Then, to increase tensions further, Marcos also passed Enrile over for promotion, even dropping him later as defense minister. Enrile had once been close to Marcos and his crony business elites. He had been especially involved with Eduardo Cojuangco, heading the state agency, the Philippine Coconut Authority, that collected the coconut levy on Cojuangco's behalf. But now, it was made plain to Enrile that he had fallen from favor, causing him even to fear that he might be assassinated by Ver.

In seeking to protect himself, Enrile turned to some informal groupings of mid-ranking officers that had cropped up, the Reform the Armed Forces Movement (RAM) and the Young Officers Union (YOU). These officers had been sharply alienated by Marcos's patrimonialism and its effects on military leadership and competence. However, while their declared aim was to restore the professionalism and fighting effectiveness of the Philippine military, they helped paradoxically to erode its hierarchy further. In particular, they were approached by Enrile, given heavy weapons, and recruited to act as his bodyguard. And then, during the early 1980s, Enrile joined with the RAM in plotting a coup through which to impose a military junta. General Ramos, for his part, seems not to have been involved in this plotting. But a crisis would nonetheless prompt him finally to cooperate with Enrile against Marcos.

In sum, while Marcos was doubtless "a master of spreading dissension among his opponents,"[46] he was unable to balance the factions that he produced. In promoting some, he seriously alienated others, rather than putting them effectively at loggerheads in a posture of mutual negation. Landed and business elites, then, while initially supporting Marcos, grew alienated over his refusal to rotate the presidency and share state resources. They were further antagonized by his confiscating assets and promoting new cronies. Moreover, within the state, Marcos appointed top technocrats, but then frustrated them deeply by rejecting their reforms. And though building up the military, he undermined its professionalism, breeding personal animosities at the peak and deep resentments in the ranks, thus planting the seeds for challenges to his leadership.

Comparing leaderships: Marcos and Suharto

In order to understand better how Marcos alienated elites, it is useful to compare the challenges he encountered and the strategies he adopted with the record of President Suharto. In many ways, these paramount national leaders displayed striking similarities in their ruling styles. Marcos and Suharto both concentrated state power in the presidency, extended patrimonialist ties to business and society, forged some technocratic and pseudo-democratic cover, then laced up the edifice with decrees made binding by the military. However, what profoundly distinguishes these leaders is that while Suharto used his paramountcy to manage the elite collectivity, designating factions and artfully balancing them, Marcos disunified, then alienated many elites, crudely running down some factions while conjuring up new cronies. Thus, while Suharto succeeded in perpetuating his authoritarian regime until confronted by economic crisis, Marcos destabilized his by eroding elite relations.

In enumerating the different strategies that these leaders adopted, we recall that Suharto, in starting his ascent in 1965, faced an essentially clean slate. He was thus unchallenged by any landed elites. On the contrary, Suharto made free use of timber concessions, mining contracts, and development projects to raise up new elites who would support him. Similarly, he faced few established business elites. While under Sukarno's guided economy some cronies had emerged, they were mostly swept away after 1965. Hence, far from being constrained by preexisting business elites, Suharto was able to promote a new collectivity from scratch, recruiting ethnic Chinese tycoons, his own family members, and a few indigenous bureaucrats and entrepreneurs.

In gaining paramountcy over these elites, Suharto was also able to set up a highly centralized state apparatus. Of course, within the state's financial agencies, Suharto, like Marcos, was obliged to install technocrats in order to attract foreign investors and donors. But during the late 1960s, then again during the 1980s, Suharto demonstrated too that he was able to make good use of these technocrats, calling upon them to liberalize the economy in ways that advanced industrialization. Of course, Suharto also bracketed their periods of ascendancy with economic nationalism, pitting them against the technologues, while roiling the waters also with ordinary rent-seekers. But in this way, he ensured that bureaucratic elites confronted one other, rather than collectively opposing him. Likewise, within the armed forces, Suharto promoted, rotated, and purged different factions of military elites, skillfully staving off challenges to his leadership. Yet he preserved enough professionalism that the military could enforce his rule, harshly disciplining labor and preventing secessions.

In consequence, elites in Indonesia, whether based in business or the state apparatus, never acquired any expectations about rotating the presidency or

223

decentralizing patronage. Suharto was thus able to dominate the office and assert its powers, using them effectively to manage elites. He took particular care to prevent the emergence of those who possessed political ambitions and talent, thereby obviating any credible successors to whom loyalties might shift. In these circumstances, Suharto held elections regularly, fabricated large majorities, and perpetuated his authoritarian regime.

By contrast, as Marcos sought paramountcy, he faced landed and business elites who were well established and culturally assimilated. At the same time, he enjoyed less access to natural resources with which to promote new elites, with coconuts and sugar paling alongside the timber, minerals, and petroleum that Suharto controlled. Hence, in confiscating assets from traditional elites in order to subsidize new ones, Marcos gradually inflamed elite relations. And in these circumstances, he proved less able than Suharto to manage the factions that resulted. Indeed, rather than divide and artfully balance elite factions, he alienated large segments of this collectivity. What is more, Marcos was unable to manage elites in the state apparatus. In the bureaucracy, he appointed technocrats, yet overrode or rashly dismissed them when they attempted to rein in his activities. He thus failed utterly to deploy them in ways that promoted economic growth. In addition, Marcos divided elites in the military, to the point where some of them feared assassination at the hands of their rivals. Thus, despite his expanding the armed forces, he steeply eroded their hierarchy and professionalism, leaving them unable to contain rural uprisings and secessionist movements. Instead, military factions were encouraged finally to plot against Marcos.

Moreover, in confronting more established elites than Suharto did, and in managing them less skillfully, Marcos was less able also to institutionalize a pliable party system and legitimating election schedule. Instead, his record consisted of irregularly timed contests, randomly chosen offices, clumsy referenda, and *ad hoc* modes of cheating. He thus sometimes triggered organized boycotts, at other times fierce opposition. And as elites began gradually to rally around Benigno Aquino, they confronted Marcos with an opposition leader of far greater caliber than any that Suharto had permitted to emerge. And, as we shall see, it was the assassination of Aquino, followed by an effort to steal a presidential election from his widow that set in train the events finally bringing Marcos down.

Redemocratization

In disunifying elites, then alienating key factions, Marcos destabilized his regime and put his leadership at risk. And as politicians got wind of rifts in the military, their hopes of ousting him surged. Thus, when Marcos announced that elections would be held for the *Batasang Pambansa* in 1984, elites ended their boycott in order to contest them. Benigno Aquino prepared to run too, returning from the United States where he had gone for medical treatment.

The transition to democracy in the Philippines is well enough known that only a brief sketch is needed here.[47] Marcos had allowed Aquino to go to the United States for medical care, but counted upon this amounting to exile. Thus, when Aquino attempted to return in August 1983, he was shot immediately upon disembarking at Manila airport, an action evidently planned by Imelda Marcos and General Ver.[48] Indeed, in its ruthless and maladroit nature, the shooting bore their unmistakable stamp. It also provided the crisis that alienated still more business elites, then began uniting them in opposition. Thompson observes that "Aquino's murder . . . shattered the self-assurance of the privileged . . . [T]he wealthy were shocked that one of their own could be killed on government orders."[49] Equally, at the mass level, much of Philippine society was outraged, marking the assassination as a milestone toward society growing more participatory. However, rather than erupting in violence, as occurred in Thailand in 1992 and Indonesia in 1998, elites and their constituents renewed their commitments to contesting the following year's *Batasang* election. Indeed, business leaders and Catholic Church workers cooperated in forming a poll watchers group, naming it NAMFREL after the original organization formed by the U.S. officials during the early 1950s.

However, if the 1984 election reduced the KBL's majority in the *Batasang*, business elites remained unenthusiastic about the opposition figure who had fared best, Salvador Laurel. As a traditional politician steeped in great personal ambition and clientelist ways, it seemed wasted effort to advance him as Marcos's replacement. Business elites thus formed a convenor group, then pushed past Laurel in order to recruit Aquino's widow, Corazon, as their candidate for president. And after a million signatures were gathered in her support, she agreed to stand whenever Marcos should again call an election for the top office.

Marcos called a snap presidential election for early 1986, though more to gain approbation from the Americans than legitimacy among Filipinos. And at the start of his campaign, he seemed confident that the KBL's machinery and command of patronage resources would secure his reelection once more. Aquino, however, while only dimly outlining any social reforms, made moral appeals that galvanized mass audiences. Her representatives also made contact with Enrile and the RAM, who in turn communicated with Catholic Church officials. Gradually, Marcos grew aware of the seriousness of the challenge. He thus began preparing for elections more assiduously, altering voting lists, moving polling stations, paying off voters, and finally tampering with the counting. But this time, in an action displaying great courage, computer operators hired by the COMELEC revealed the padding of Marcos's tally, then walked out. The *Batasang Pambansa* quickly took over the counting and declared Marcos the winner.

Aquino responded by mobilizing her constituents in a campaign of civil disobedience. And Enrile and the RAM reacted by at last mounting their coup, which, when discovered by Ver, prompted them to retreat to a military base in Manila, then turn to Aquino for protection. Aquino recognized, of course, that Enrile did not seek her election as president, but instead, to impose his own military junta. She calculated also, though, that if her constituents protected him, Enrile could help first in forcing Marcos's ouster, then be obligated to support her for the presidency. As it turned out, Aquino calculated rightly. Behind the barricades formed by her many thousands of supporters, Enrile was able to win over Fidel Ramos, then persuade most of the rest of the armed forces to defect. And while Enrile and the RAM were thus greatly strengthened, they found that it was too late to oppose Aquino openly. The United States then carried Marcos overseas, and Aquino was named president.

This transition to democracy, marked by flower brigades, food columns, and nuns on the front line, gave rise to a persuasive image of "people power." And indeed, Marcos's refusal to negotiate with opposition leaders left him unable to save anything of his leadership position, and he fell precipitously from power. Accordingly, in providing a rigorously documented account of the transition, Thompson is right to conclude that this was not a state-led "transformation" of the kind seen in Spain ten years beforehand and throughout much of Latin America.[50] It was instead a process of what Huntington has termed "replacement," a regime change imposed by the opposition.[51]

However, in probing more deeply in the Philippines this notion of replacement, one finds that more is at work than autonomous social forces. One must ask what enabled these forces to gain the causal momentum that they did? And why did they act peacefully, rather than with the violence seen in Jakarta? In answering these questions, it is best to begin with the disunity between elites. In particular, with Marcos refusing to share state power, many elites grew alienated, preventing their cooperating any longer in demobilizing society. On the contrary, elites who were respectively aligned to Marcos and Aquino now competed in mobilizing their constituencies, the first promising patrimonialist benefits and the latter moral rightness. And it was these competitive mobilizations, rather than any spontaneous societal upsurge, that drew up constituents through the fissures between disunified elites.

But as these constituents were activated, what prevented their turning violent? Part of the answer has to do with what Thompson calls "street parliamentarians,"[52] figures who had grown skillful in helping to marshal mass actions. In contrast, there were few such sentinels on hand in Indonesia in 1998, the lid on the country's political life having for so long been fitted tightly, then abruptly prised off. But the comparative discipline shown by constituents in the Philippines must also be ascribed to the strongly moral appeals made by Aquino, a message grounded in her effectively conveying her husband's martyrdom and her own sense of loss. Catholic Church leaders also worked to mobilize their followings, yet contain violent surges. In sum, while the transition to democracy was different in the Philippines from many other cases in the third wave, it cannot be understood without reference to elites. Though doubtless Philippine society had by now grown participatory enough that it sought to democratize politics, it was only able to act on its sentiments because elites were divided and competed for its support. And in this competition, Aquino was able to out-mobilize Marcos.

However, while the transition to democracy was advanced in the Philippines by Aquino's gaining the presidency, stabilization was thwarted by her coalition's unraveling. Put simply, despite Aquino, Enrile, Ramos, and the RAM having cooperated in ousting Marcos, their relations stopped short of any settlement. In particular, Enrile was unconstrained by any sense of loyalty, either to Aquino or to the democracy she had helped create. Of course, he was unable to act openly so long as the memory of people power was still fresh. But he began quietly to ferret out allies with whom he could later mount coups.

During the first years of her presidency, Aquino made Enrile's work easier, delivering many elites into his hands as she responded to the expectations of her constituents. Put simply, Aquino attempted to raise the quality of the new Philippine democracy. For example, she closed the tainted *Batasang* and purged local offices, thus angering many politicians, indeed, encouraging them to turn the tables by denouncing her as undemocratic. She also prepared to resume land reforms. And though the measures she proposed were modest ones, they nonetheless spurred landed elites to reconvene their private armies. Further, in attempting to sequester crony fortunes and dismantle the trading monopolies that been accumulated under Marcos, many of the cronies who had survived Marcos, as well as the new elites who had inherited the monopolies, turned squarely against Aquino. And finally, in seeking to investigate human rights abuses and negotiate with the Communists, Aquino seriously antagonized the military. Indeed, it was in this context that Enrile and the RAM, sometimes in concert with landowners and other elites who had been alienated, mounted seven major coup attempts during 1986–89.

Thus, in order to restore elite cohesion and perpetuate democracy, Aquino scaled back her reforms. She left in place, of course, the formal procedures for which her constituents had sacrificed. But she tilted her substantive policy outputs back heavily toward elites. Hence, after Aquino delivered a new constitution in 1987 and then held elections, she allowed many politicians associated with Marcos to align their impromptu party vehicles with her LABAN, then to regain their offices at both national and local levels. Indeed, Thompson records that "Aquino went so far as to endorse many of the governors and mayors she had replaced upon taking power, including some unsavory 'warlords.'"[53] Consequently, there was a resurgence too of many familiar family clans, prompting analysts to suggest that democratic politics under Aquino were beginning to look very much like they had during the period before Marcos, even if an unstructured multiparty system had displaced the earlier two-party arrangement. In addition, Aquino ceased all serious attempts to reform land ownership and trading monopolies, helping to calm landed and business elites. And she appointed Fidel Ramos as armed forces commander, restored military budgets, and resumed military action against the Communists, thus halting the many coups. In these ways, Aquino was able peacefully to serve out the rest of her term. And at its end, she rewarded Ramos once more, supporting his successful bid for the presidency in 1992. One observes that his victory was a close one, though, based on plurality of 23.5 per cent in a field of seven candidates. Eduardo Cojuangco came in third with better than 18 per cent and Imelda Marcos fifth with more than 10 per cent.

It is at this point that Philippine democracy can probably be evaluated as stable. With Aquino abandoning her social reforms, she reassured elites that their core interests would be protected even as politics were democratized. And her social constituents, though their respective interests were proportionately sold out, seemed content with the civil liberties and electoral opportunities left to them.[54] In brief, though benefiting from few changes in economic distributions or social structures, they celebrated their political democracy through an impressive range of NGOs and high electoral turnouts. One notes also that these procedures were formally enshrined in the 1987 constitution. In addition, some hierarchy was restored to the military. And at least parts of the bureaucracy remained "useable," providing the technocratic advice that Ramos was prepared later to take. Accordingly, democracy in the Philippines appeared to meet the stability requirements of consolidation as specified by Linz and Stepan – elite and societal agreements, a hierarchical military, and a useable bureaucracy – thereby emerging in their oft-quoted refrain as "the only game in town." In addition, this new democracy passed Huntington's two-turnover test, featuring an electoral transfer of power from Marcos to Aquino (even if her margin could only be estimated), and from Aquino to Ramos (however thin his plurality). However, in falling short on a second dimension of quality, democracy in the Philippines, though stable, must be assessed as unconsolidated.

Democratic quality[55]

Debates over democracy's quality have been stimulated by the collapse of most other regime types. Indeed, with its negative referents removed, democracy's inability to deliver all the benefits that had been anticipated by democratic theorists and activists during the 1980s has been made more glaring. But because this discussion is new, there are no firm benchmarks yet by which to gauge democracy's worth. Rather, there stands only a "vast corpus of normative democratic theory and . . . the expectations of a vast majority of normal democratic citizens."[56] Juan Linz has recently provided some more substantive measures, focusing on the leaders and politicians that collectively make up what he terms the "political class." His indices include the extent to which this class regards politics as a vocation, rather than simply as a way of making a living; its willingness to compete actively through parties for programmatic gains, but not at all costs; its minimizing corrupt practices; and its refusal to "play with or use the disloyal opposition, revolutionary extremists or putchists against opponents."[57] Further, at the societal level, Jon Elster and James Bohman have begun to explore institutional designs for enhancing popular participation, conceptualized as deliberative democracy.[58]

This growing discussion over democratic quality has centered on the established democracies of North America and northern Europe and the new democracies of Latin America and eastern Europe. This book, in extending discussion to Southeast Asia, examined in the last chapter the ways in which Thailand has tried to raise quality. In this section, we will observe the ways in which the Philippines has avoided it. As Thompson notes, "the Philippines meets the minimal criteria generally used to define democracy without achieving what most observers would consider good government."[59] He then catalogues democracy's disappointing record in the country: political corruption, sustained human rights abuses by the armed forces, and an unreformed social structure. Of course, one can qualify these criticisms. Since redemocratization in 1986, responsiveness appears to have improved in several important government departments, like the Department of Economic and Natural Resources.[60] Local government has sometimes improved, too, with city administration in Olongapo near Subic Bay and Naga City in Camarines del Sur emerging recently as exemplars.[61] In terms of the economy, Fidel Ramos introduced some liberalizing reforms during his presidency, burnishing his country's performance enough that it was welcomed, however briefly, as Southeast Asia's latest "tiger cub." Moreover, even if the military still violates human rights, the extent of its abuses has necessarily been scaled back by the collapse of the New People's Army, its primary target. And finally, the failure to carry out social reform should hardly be surprising. This was the price for Corazon Aquino's gaining the oligarchical consent that was necessary for maintaining democracy during her tenure, then peacefully transferring state power to Ramos.

Nonetheless, Thompson's judgement of low quality still stands, particularly in terms of electoral procedures. To see this, we will examine the Philippine general election of May 1998, using it as one indicator by which to assess the country's democracy more broadly. However, because this election is a discrete event, its worth cannot be finely gauged by Linz's more open-ended measures. This analysis thus proposes some alternative measures that appear more appropriate for a single electoral contest. Specifically, it examines the extent to which former President Ramos and the candidate he chose to succeed him respected electoral rules during campaigning and vote counting. It next investigates the quality of campaign appeals and debate, as well as the extent and meaningfulness of mass participation. It concludes by monitoring the level of political violence during the election. Of course, these are rough measures by which to gauge electoral quality. It is difficult to specify exact thresholds of presidential rule bending and political killings, for example, beyond which democratic quality must be rated as low. But these measures nevertheless enable us to make some judgements based on widely shared norms about the acceptability of different political behaviors.

The 1998 Philippine general election

In the Philippine general election of 1998, 64,000 candidates stood for 17,510 positions: the presidency and vice-presidency (the latter elected independently from the president); half the 24-seat senate; all 260 seats in the house of representatives (80 per cent from single member districts, 20 per cent from a new party list system); provincial governorships, mayorships, and *barangay* captaincies, and a range of provincial, city, and municipal council seats. These contests were regulated in important ways by the 1987 constitution. Specifically, candidates for the presidency were eligible only for a single term of six years; those contesting lesser positions could serve for three terms of three years each (a reform that, though designed to discourage the formation of political dynasties, appears to have quickened the pace with which offices are bequeathed to spouses, siblings, and offspring). By stimulating turnover in these ways, even if principally among family members, the constitution helped to enliven the Philippine elections. Finally, while there were some elements of American political culture in the campaigning, there was also much indigenous dynamism, producing a rich local vocabulary of "presidentiables," "re-electionists," party "bets," and "black propaganda," as well as a three-day ban on alcohol sales and cockfighting.

The observance of electoral rules

In extending their study of democracy's consolidation from stability to quality, Linz and Stepan note that presidents, while technically observing democratic procedures, may nonetheless bend rules in order to lengthen their tenure, win policy successes, or gain corrupt pay-offs. As examples, they document the political behaviors of several Latin American presidents, including Argentina's Carlos Menem and Peru's Alberto Fujimori.[62]

In the Philippines, Fidel Ramos has often been lauded as the best president the country has ever had. In recognizing the limited developmental capacity of the state, Ramos scaled back the state's capacity to extract, largely by deregulating state monopolies and privatizing state assets. In turn, foreign investors began to rediscover the Philippines as a favorable site for export-oriented industrialization. During the mid-1990s, then, industrial parks sprouted around Manila Bay and in the Visayan city of Cebu, boosting average annual growth rates to nearly 5 per cent throughout Ramos's term.

But Ramos appeared then to read these achievements as signifying his indispensability. He began advocating that the constitution be changed in order that he could stand for reelection in 1998 (a so-called "cha-cha," i.e., charter change), first mounting a "people's initiative," then trying to convert the congress into a constituent assembly.[63] However, he was stoutly resisted by former President Aquino and Jaime Cardinal Sin. Reactivating people power, the two held a great prayer rally in Luneta Park, with audiences solemnly opposing any tampering with the constitution. Finally, the supreme court ruled that in any event, the charter could not be amended by means of a signature campaign. Observers then watched Ramos intently to see how the former general would react. But in confirming once more that democracy in the Philippines had reached equilibrium, Ramos accepted the court's decision, setting his personal ambitions aside and allaying fears of *continuismo* – that is, "the reappearance of the [authoritarian] past in new guises."[64]

Hence, in the short time left before the 1998 election, Ramos began looking for a successor who would support the economic reforms that he had put in place. He settled on the speaker of the house of representatives, Jose de Venecia, whose mastery of congressional dealings indeed had secured passage of many of Ramos's bills. But this mastery also had led de Venecia to become widely vilified in the press as "the worst *trapo*" (i.e., traditional politician, also *Tagolog* for "dirty rag") then operating on the country's political scene.[65] As speaker, he had relied heavily on pork barreling through which to forge a rainbow coalition of support. For the purpose, the Countrywide Development Fund had been organized by the Congressional Appropriations Committee, dispensing 18 million *pesos* to each senator and 12 million *pesos* to each representative annually.[66] The funds were ostensibly dedicated to necessary infrastructural projects. However, they often seemed to result only in modest community halls and so-called "waiting sheds," their painted inscriptions brightly proclaiming they had been delivered by the local congressman. The difference between the funds that were allocated and the costs of constructing these projects (generally estimated by finance officials at 40 per cent) was then returned by contractors to the relevant congressman.[67]

But if corruption damaged de Venecia's credibility among journalists, it probably did not affect his standing more generally.[68] Nonetheless, de

Venecia's endorsement by Ramos still failed to generate much enthusiasm – attributable at least partly, perhaps, to the economic reforms he was pledged to uphold.[69] Specifically, while Ramos's reforms had benefited most Filipinos in absolute terms, they also had made relative disparities worse than they had been in 1985, even before politics had been redemocratized and the economy had recovered.[70] And when the region's economic crisis began finally to affect the Philippines – slowing down annual GNP growth to 2.5 per cent during the first quarter of 1998, the lowest rate in five years[71] – the benefits that had sifted through to the mass level appeared to be at risk. Thus, while approval levels of Ramos's presidency remained quite high, a large part of the electorate called for policy changes.[72] Indeed, as early as 1996, survey data indicates that the personal quality most desired in presidential candidates was that they be "pro-poor," followed by their being "approachable."[73]

In these circumstances, though Ramos campaigned vigorously for de Venecia, he appeared to doubt the prospects of his "anointed one." Some analysts have contended, then, that Ramos felt that de Venecia should be "'helped' to do well."[74] Hence, they allege that Ramos resorted to bending severely, without finally breaking, the country's electoral rules. Most notably, he appointed what was assessed as a weak slate of COMELEC officials, figures who would perhaps countenance the behaviors that would bolster de Venecia's chances.[75] For example, the COMELEC refused to reorganize old voter lists or issue identification cards, thus leaving the door open for so-called "flying voters" (i.e., those who vote more than once). Using the courts, it tried to block exit polls, essential for preventing the manipulation of returns. And it quarreled with NAMFREL when trying to carry out quick counts, much valued because of the many weeks that the election commission would take in carrying out its own counting processes. Commenting on the situation in an editorial, the *Philippine Daily Inquirer*, probably the country's most important daily, intoned, "With its officials barely able to conceal their political colors, the COMELEC's crediblity is in tatters."[76]

Shortly before the election, a commission member, Manolo Gorospe, predicted publicly that the election would be derailed by violence, especially in the southern island of Mindanao.[77] And in the event of such an "election failure," Ramos would be permitted to remain in office until a new election could be organized. A candidate for the presidency, Miriam Defensor Santiago, who had claimed after the 1992 election to have been cheated by Ramos, responded that the COMELEC's behavior was "part of Malaca-nang's last-ditch effort to perpetuate President Ramos in power."[78] A much respected former president of the senate, Jovito Salonga, noted too that Ramos would be the "beneficiary" of any election failure, though he suggested that a military takeover was also possible.[79] In turn, Jaime Cardinal Sin warned the military against "'collusion' . . . in any such fraudulent intervention," promising the resurgence of people power.[80] And the Young Officers Union (YOU), involved, we recall, in sundry coup attempts during the late 1980s, firmly admonished those "people with intentions to sow trouble or to cheat. Don't attempt it because the YOU is watching."[81]

As the election drew nearer, President Ramos took still more controversial actions. First, he appeared to harass the candidate who had emerged as de Venecia's most serious competitor, his own vice-president, Joseph Estrada. Ramos ordered state security agencies to investigate reports of Estrada having tried to assassinate him on four different occasions during 1992 – reports that were widely dismissed as baseless. In addition, a week before the election, Ramos abruptly issued an executive order to release the so-called "coco fund," the revenues that had been levied by Eduardo Cojuangco on coconut farmers during Marcos's presidency, but ordered sequestered by the courts after Marcos's ouster. Ramos claimed that the fund at last would be made available to the farmers as livelihood loans in order to rehabilitate their industry. However, while this decision might normally have been applauded, its eleventh-hour timing instead raised suspicions in the press that "the coco levy monies [were] being used shamelessly to court the 1.4 million coconut farmers' vote." Cojuangco, supporting Estrada, may have been correct, then, in claiming that Ramos's real intention was to build "the largest presidential war chest ever."[82] Cojuangco's counsel thus charged that Ramos had "reversed a decision of the supreme court and usurped legislative powers,"[83] and he succeeded in blocking the lifting of the sequestration order through a special anti-graft court.

Finally, after the elections had been held and the vote counting began, suspicions arose once more over the very slow pace with which COMELEC officials proceeded. COMELEC protested the allegations, attributing delays to the difficulties of tallying votes for the new party list system. Further, when it at last reported the results, they correlated more closely than in past elections with the estimates made by NAMFREL and Social Weather Stations (SWS), indicating that electoral cheating had indeed subsided, at least at the presidential and congressional levels.[84] This did little to allay doubts over the COMELEC's independence, however. In taking stock of the elections, Joel Rocamora, director of the Institute for Popular Democracy, writes that "it appears that de Venecia people prepared to cheat,"[85] but their candidate trailed Estrada by so great a margin that any fabricated results would have been quite implausible.[86] In these circumstances, then, amid continuing distrust, the restraint shown finally by the incumbent president and his chosen successor did little to build confidence in the quality of Philippine democracy.

Level of campaign appeals

Another measure of democratic quality involves the appeals that candidates make to voters. Substantive appeals addressing serious issues and inviting constituent debate can, of course, make election campaigns meaningful. Conversely, candidates who rely on entertainers, sports celebrities, and evangelists probably diminish a campaign. In the Philippines, after the COMELEC had culled some nuisance entrants, a field of 11 candidates stood for the presidency in 1998. And during the two-month campaign period, they made appeals of uneven quality.

With Jose de Venecia's political record consisting largely of deal making, he began by advocating little more during his campaign than pushing ahead with Ramos's agenda. However, with the Philippine *peso* having recently lost a quarter of its value, causing inflation and joblessness to rise, the appeal of deregulation already had begun to fade. De Venecia thus turned to asserting his religiosity, calling upon born-again Christian groups to mount campaign rallies. The Jesus is Lord Ministry and Jesus Victory Crusade obliged him, with the leader of the latter group even declaring that "if Joe de Venecia loses, I'm willing to be shot before a firing squad."[87] At the same time, de Venecia operated more sedately through the *Lakas-NUCD* (Strength-National Union of Christian Democrats) which, while offering little ideology, was thought to be able to dispense patronage through its party machinery and control over pork barrel. Never, though, did he or his party take up issues of poverty, unemployment, or the environment, a decision that would prove pivotal: he finished the presidential race a very distant second, gaining less than 16 per cent of the popular vote.

Meanwhile, a pair of third force candidates appeared, crafting more imaginative appeals that whittled away at the top end of de Venecia's upper- and middle-class constituencies. Raul Roco, a lawyer and senator who possessed no party machine, outlined a high-tech vision for Philippine economic renewal. And even if it appeared that Roco was ahead of his time in a country still struggling with land tenure issues and food shortages, he nonetheless placed third in the vote count with nearly 14 per cent, thus raising his stature and positioning him for the next election. In addition, Emilio Osmena, the governor of prospering Cebu, offered a decentralized, province-based economic plan for the country. He promised to "abolish income taxes, since they don't work anyway" and proposed introducing consumption taxes instead.[88] But even as he pledged to middle-class audiences that he would be a business-oriented president, he made populist appeals to the masses of poor farmers in the provinces who often gravitated to Manila slums. However, though articulating his themes with eloquence, Osmena was unable to maintain much mass-level support beyond the Visayas, thus confining him to fourth place in the polls.

In contrast to the aforementioned candidates, a trio of law-and-order and anti-corruption figures seemed to drive the quality of campaign appeals back down. Alfredo Lim, the mayor of Manila and former chief of police, focused solely on crime issues. His dispensing of rough justice in the capital had earned him the sobriquet "Dirty Harry," ennobling him to some voters but greatly alarming others. In particular, during his tenure as mayor, he personally had led teams of police in sealing and signposting the houses of suspected drug dealers. Corpses were sometimes found in Manila's streets, bearing messages in *Tagolog*: "I'm a drug pusher. Don't follow."[89] Interestingly, Lim gained the endorsement of Corazon Aquino. But rather than winning him any new support, it seemed instead to erode Aquino's own standing, leaving her remaining supporters to wonder what had ever become of people power. The second candidate was Miriam Defensor Santiago. Still striking the indignant posture against corruption that had nearly won her the election in 1992, she evidently fatigued the voters this time around. Christening her campaign "The Return of the Jedi" and erecting a billboard that depicted her wielding a laser sword, she slumped to seventh in the polls and gained less than 3 per cent of the vote. Finally, the *Partido Bansang Marangal* (National Dignity Party) candidate for president, former Philippine Sweepstakes and Lotto Manager Manuel Morato, harped solely on the moral shortcomings of Joseph Estrada in his campaign. He wound up in last place as a result of this narrow focus, achieving less than 1 per cent support.

Finally, among a cohort of minor candidates one found Imelda Marcos, heading the KBL. In campaigning, she promised to "use the wealth" of her late husband to revive the economy – thereby disclosing this wealth's existence.[90] She also reviewed the virtues of her husband's direct grants to *barangay* and the promise of aquaculture. Still, she managed only to inspire a small band of loyalists. And upon recognizing the futility of her bid, she pledged to withdraw, passing on her voters to Joseph Estrada. Indeed, Estrada was well-known for his admiration of Ferdinand Marcos, even pledging now that the former president's body would at last be shifted from its glass, air conditioned crypt in the Marcos family mansion at Batac to the resting place of national heroes, the *Libingan ng mga Bayani Filipino*. But whatever Estrada might do, Imelda still found herself in a terrible bind over her decision to quit. On the one hand, she reasoned, "I withdrew because I did not want to be a party to the COMELEC-predicted bloody elections. On the other hand, my supporters are threatening to kill themselves if I pursue my withdrawal."[91] But she only formally withdrew two days before the election, too late to remove her name from the ballot or to shake off her small followings.

Hence, in campaigning for the presidency in 1998, these candidates mainly addressed ways to halt the economic decline or to ameliorate its effects on law and order. However, Joseph "Erap" Estrada, heading the

Struggle of the Nationalist Filipino Masses (LaMMP) ticket,[92] went further, focusing intently on the needs of the urban and rural poor. His campaign slogan was straightforward – *"Erap para sa mahirap"* (Erap for the poor) – thereby eclipsing Osmena's more nuanced appeals. Of course, Estrada offered even fewer programmatic details about his populism than Thaksin Shinawatra would do later in Thailand. Instead, he spoke vaguely of the need to promote "food security" in a country afflicted by El Niño while perhaps doing something for small business, too.[93] But his concerns were nonetheless given force by his roles as a film star during the 1950s–60s, portraying figures that were street smart and crime busting yet moved by the plight of poor city dwellers. It must be pointed out, however, that in real life Estrada was not a member of the poor. He has instead been depicted as a "'black sheep' of the elite," a drop-out from Ateneo National University, one of the country's leading tertiary institutions.[94] The films he made after leaving Ateneo made him wealthy and paved the way for his entry into politics – first as mayor of San Juan, later as senator, then as the Philippine vice-president under Ramos. One notes, too, that his wife, Loi Ejercito, a psychiatrist trained at the University of Santo Tomas, was regarded as a key figure in Manila's social set.[95] Estrada's populist appeals, then, were necessarily cross-class. But they gave him the lead over other candidates, one that grew ever larger as election day neared and enabled him finally to win the presidency with nearly 40 per cent of the vote. His LaMMP also gained a plurality of 110 seats in the house of representatives, soon bumped up to a majority after mass defections from de Venecia's *Lakas-NUCD*.

The limited substance in Estrada's campaign appeals made it difficult to know what precisely Estrada would offer the poor.[96] And confusion only deepened as analysts began scrutinizing the highly eclectic make-up of his advisory team.[97] In brief, Estrada outlined some redistributive schemes, pledging state assistance for sectors that had been neglected under Ramos, agriculture and small business in particular. But Estrada evidently wished also to retain the confidence of international investors and aid donors. Thus, like de Venecia, he stated that he would preserve Ramos's reforms, and he recruited some economists from the University of the Philippines to provide technocratic advice. Further, to reassure local business people, Estrada brought in some prominent bankers, selecting one of them, Edgardo Espiritu, to be finance secretary. On the other hand, he also maintained ties to some Marcos-era business people, seemingly through the Zamorra brothers, Ronaldo, whom he tipped as his executive secretary, and Manuel, his campaign treasurer. The Zamorras were linked in turn to Eduardo Cojuangco and Lucio Tan.[98] Finally, speculation mounted over Estrada's even darker ties to the Chinese-Filipino underworld of drug traffickers and illegal lottery operators who, it was alleged, had provided the LaMMP with a long credit line for vote buying.[99]

Given this mixed bag of advisors, questions arose over which factions would prevail – and whether Estrada would really assert much personal influence over outcomes. Indeed, there were hints that some of these groups, especially the technocratic ones, had only chosen to join Estrada because of the populist cover he could offer them during troubled economic times. One University of Philippines professor stated, "What endears us to Erap is that he listens to what we say, and seems to be open to ideas as long as you can explain these to him. . . . He has been known to talk openly against things like liberalization and open trade, but he really has no hard line position."[100] Thus, while these different factions coalesced uneasily during Estrada's campaigning, it was possible their conflicts would resume once he was in office.

Hence, in the interlude after the elections that Estrada was now projected to win, some candidates dwelled publicly on the contradictions among Estada's advisors and then focused intently on the crime syndicates. De Venecia complained of vote buying funded by the syndicates and warned, "I will not recommend 'People Power' at this time because we want to review the situation. But it could lead to that if there is truly nationwide vote buying, nationwide cheating, and nationwide use of Mafia money, drug lord money, underworld money. We cannot allow a Mafia structure to take hold of the government."[101] However, de Venecia also let it be known that try as he might to restrain them, his born again Christian supporters might spontaneously begin to mount protest rallies. Furthermore, Miriam Defensor Santiago tried to substantiate de Venecia's claims, even specifying a figure of at least 900 million *pesos* that had been spent by Estrada's LaMMP to buy votes.[102] She then demanded that all election returns be submitted to the senate for inspection, thus delaying the proclamation of the next president until after the June 30 inauguration date. She also stated that while she was aware that this would trigger a constitutional crisis, with Ramos ineligible to remain as caretaker, she would nevertheless press her case.

Accordingly, one concludes that, even if still observing formal democratic procedures, de Venecia and Santiago formed a marriage of distinct convenience, then together rehearsed scenarios that augured poorly for democratic quality. To be sure, their suspicions of Estrada were in retrospect well founded, enabling them to make appeals that could be likened to those of Peruvian President Fujimori. Specifically, they asserted the need to suspend democracy in order to save it, even if this provoked a constitutional crisis. But after Santiago had so critically attacked de Venecia during the campaigning, one doubted their motivations in coming together now to block Estrada's rise to the presidency. In consequence, far from cleansing the electoral process, their collaboration seemed to diminish its quality further.

In sum, the level of campaign appeals for the presidency in 1998 must be assessed as mixed. Raul Roco and Emilio Osmena appeared to heighten the campaign's quality by generating proposals for economic renewal. Other candidates diminished it, however, invoking appeals tinged with religious fundamentalism, anxieties over crime, and nostalgia for Marcos. Meanwhile, Estrada came up with the winning issue, namely, addressing the plight of the poor. But in refusing to discuss seriously how his populism might be implemented, then deepening uncertainties by recruiting an eclectic band of advisers, his appeals did little to raise the campaign's tenor.

Quality of mass participation

One is quickly impressed in the Philippines with the depth of political knowledge possessed by many activists and their commitments to safeguarding democratic procedures. One clear manifestation of this is the many organizations that research – and act upon – political and social issues. These take the form of university study centers, NGOs, social movements, neighborhood associations, church groups, and the like. Teachers' Village, in particular, a subdivision of the Philippine capital, Quezon City, bristles with cause-oriented groups in rented suburban homes and shop fronts. In total, more than 14,000 secular voluntarist organizations operate in the country.[103]

But in the 1998 election, it was the Catholic Church that seemed to do most in raising the quality of mass-level electoral participation. VoteCare, overseen by the Catholic Bishops' Conference of the Philippines, provided voter education about candidates, issues, and electoral mechanics (much in contrast to the COMELEC that did little to elucidate the new party list system). The Parish Pastoral Council for Responsible Voting organized poll watching across the country. And NAMFREL, directed by Jaime Cardinal Sin, carried out Operation Quick Count. These three organizations, together with the Integrated Bar of Philippine Lawyers, which provided legal assistance, coalesced for the first time in 1998 under the banner of HOPE, or "honest, orderly, and peaceful elections."[104] In addition, Social Weather Stations provided objective and accurate voter surveys throughout the campaign, while sundry other agencies were commissioned by media outlets to carry out exit polls.

These organizations were confronted by different forms of electoral cheating, many of them highly refined during the long Philippine experience with democracy. They included stuffing ballot boxes before polling stations were opened, circulating "flying voters" through multiple precincts, vote buying (or more commonly, paying voters *not* to vote), *lanzadera* (paying a voter to submit an already completed ballot, then return with the empty ballot so that it can be filled out and submitted by the next voter), and the infamous *dagdas-bawa* ("shaving" votes from one candidate's totals, then using them to pad another's, thus leaving the total return unchanged). But in the 1998 election, despite high voter turnout of 75–80 per cent, the incidence of cheating appeared to have been moderated, at least at the national level.[105]

Thus, in observing the participatory nature of the Philippine electorate – and the infrastructure provided by civil society through which to make that participation meaningful – one finds reasons for celebrating the political maturity of the people. However, a noted Manila-based columnist, Belinda Olivares-Cunanan, cautioned that during elections in 1998, this maturity "ha[d] to be qualified." Specifically, she tallied the number of media celebrities, actors, and sports stars elected to office, especially in the senate, then asked, "Was it mature to have elected [a] basketball star[,] Robert Jaworksi, despite his open admission that he'd only be a part-time senator?"[106] Even more worrisome was the willingness of voters to elect convicted criminals. In the province of Nueva Ecija, for example, five members of the Joson family were elected to various local offices, despite two of them having campaigned from prison where they were serving life sentences for having murdered their political rivals. Similarly, in Zamboanga del Norte, Romy Jalosjos overwhelmingly won reelection to congress, notwithstanding his imprisonment for raping and killing an 11-year old girl. And while voters had rejected Imelda Marcos as their president, they elected her son, Bongbong, as governor of Ilocos del Norte, and her daugher, Imee, as congresswoman. However, the Philippine electorate is not necessarily committed to entertainers, jailbirds, and the progeny of dead dictators. Olivares-Cunanan cites a SWS survey showing that 45 per cent of the electorate was willing to sell its vote in 1998 to the highest bidder, irrespective of celebrity status.

Rocamora counters, though, that mass-level voters should not be dismissed simply as starstruck or shamelessly selling their votes. Despite Estrada's film personage, voters had few illusions about what his presidency might achieve. Indeed, they had learned generally to expect little from state institutions, impelling them earlier in Philippine political experience to seek aid from patrons and bosses, today from NGOs. In Rocamora's view, the voters' election of such candidates represented faintly reasoned but nonetheless meaningful mass actions that served effectively to taunt elites.[107] In terms of the analysis made in this chapter, though, even if meaningful, such actions did little to put qualified politicians in office.

Political violence

Philippine elections have historically been notorious for high levels of violence, surely diminishing their quality. Of course, we have seen that because political elites have, apart from the Marcos period, adhered to some tacit understandings about the acceptability of different behaviors, they have limited their violent actions against one another. And during the 1998 general election, violence appeared to be relatively limited at the mass level too, resulting in a comparatively low figure of 50 or so deaths. Still, for uninitiated observers, the level of violence seemed unacceptable. Candidates at the local level were assassinated in many districts during the campaign, prompting the COMELEC to declare hot spots that were directly overseen by its officials. The most conspicuous of these involved the race for the mayorship of Makati, the capital's central business district, where thugs associated with the incumbent – seeking now to ensure the election of his wife – killed two of his challenger's campaign workers inside city hall. In addition, one notes that if families sometimes perpetuated lengthy dynasties in the Philippines, they at other times erupted in deadly feuds. As one example, in Samar, the last-term mayor of Matuguinao, Celso de la Cruz, was shot dead in front of 200 supporters. The killing was blamed on the mayor's younger brother, running against the slain mayor's wife.[108] Finally, at the *barangay* level, shootings were widely reported, especially in volatile Mindanao.

Political violence did not end once the campaign period was over. Indeed, in a country where the local wisdom holds that there are only two kinds of candidates – those who win and those who have been cheated – it must be expected that protests would take place while ballots were counted, causing the violence to surge anew. COMELEC seemed to bear some of the blame, confusing precinct workers over how they should make their returns known to NAMFREL at a time when officials were trying to perform quick counts. And amid this uncertainty, supporters of local favorites who appeared to be losing assaulted polling stations, either making off with ballot boxes or barricading the stations so that returns could not be delivered. Such violence surrounded even the contest for the mayorship of Quezon City. One concludes, then, that while the 1998 Philippine election was more peaceful than in previous years, it could not yet be evaluated on this score as high quality.

This section has used the Philippine general election of May 1998 as a means by which to gauge the quality of the country's democracy. It suggests that while civil liberties are respected and elections held regularly, minimalist procedures that evoke stability, the ways in which the most recent election were conducted show also that quality remains low. Accordingly, Philippine democracy, like Thai democracy, cannot be regarded as consolidated, though the specific shortcomings of these two regimes appear in some measure to vary inversely.

To be sure, a democracy that is consolidated, possessing stability, but also high quality, does not promise good government. It ensures only that governments can be held accountable and peacefully changed. By contrast, there are reasons for thinking that a low quality democracy correlates closely with particular outcomes, namely, poor leadership and bad governance. If a leader acquires power through processes marred by crude campaigning, rule bending, and violence, it can be expected that he or she will perpetuate and exercise power in the same way.

The leadership of Fidel Ramos posed a partial exception to this pattern. Though hardly freeing politics of corruption, he liberalized the economy enough that it began finally to expand, albeit unevenly. His successor, however, Joseph Estrada, conformed to the pattern closely. Early in his presidency, it was hoped that Estrada's populist imagery would ease the social grievances sparked by uneven economic expansion, enabling technocrats quietly to deepen Ramos's reforms. But Estrada's personal corruption and poor policy making, aptly symbolized by his fondness for "midnight cabinets" and his creaming off funds with which lavishly to support pork barreling activities and mistresses, soon brought the economy to ground. His behaviors also precipitated a long series of political scandals.

Of course, if Estrada had dispensed patronage in ways that placated or artfully balanced elites, he could probably have clung to power. But his distributions were unskilled, finally alienating key allies. Most notably, when Estrada shifted control over new franchises in the country's illegal lottery from Governor Luis Singson of Ilocos Norte to others, the governor retaliated by publicly revealing Estrada's involvement in protecting the racket. And though rumors about Estrada's activities had long circulated, these latest revelations were given force by their coming from an "insider." Tensions thus reverberated through the congress. Thus, as public sentiment began to mount against Estrada, the house of representatives voted for impeachment in November 2000, while many of his cabinet ministers resigned – actions that were hailed as signaling new quality in Philippine democracy.[109] Put simply, procedures conforming to the constitution were being put in place by which peacefully to remove the president for corruption, thereby allowing for democracy's renewal.

The senate began its trial of Estrada at the end of the year. But suspicions soon grew that Estrada had succeeded in delivering enough patronage that he retained the support of a slight majority. Indeed, when new evidence appeared of Estrada's corruption that would have made acquitting him difficult, the senate voted in January 2001 to bar it, prompting resignations by the prosecutors and bringing the impeachment proceedings to a halt. Soon afterward, however, large groups mobilized by middle-class NGOs, the Catholic Church, and trade unions gathered in the streets of Manila. They gained expressions of support from Corazon Aquino and Ramos, as well as from many business elites.[110] In addition, top military commanders, evidently fearing that the armed forces would split over questions of loyalty to Estrada, declared that they no longer regarded the president as their commander-in-chief.[111] They favored instead the transfer of power to Estrada's vice-president, Gloria Macapagal-Arroyo.

Hence, through a sequence of events that many analysts claimed paralleled the uprising against Marcos in 1986, thus earning the sobriquet "people power II," Estrada was forced from the presidential palace, while many of his crony associates fled overseas.[112] And though Estrada refused formally to resign, he was succeeded peacefully by Arroyo.[113] Surely, this marked an increase in the quality of Philippine national leadership. But the senate's failure to facilitate this transfer of power, causing it to be upstaged by the military, suggested that there was no commensurate increase in the quality of procedures. And an effort by the supreme court to give constitutional sanction to these outcomes instead raised questions about its own role. As William Overholt reflected, "the message coming through is that they cared about getting Estrada out, not the rule of law."[114]

Conclusions

One aim of this chapter has been briefly to map the colonial legacies, social structures, and record of economic failings that so distinguish the Philippines from the other countries we have investigated. But this chapter has also argued that many similarities exist – the centrality of the state apparatus and business as conduits to elite statuses, the role of ethnic Chinese in business, a business scene tinged with regional forms of cronyism, and long contours of rural-based insurgencies and secessionist movements, the latter inflamed by revivalist Islam. Moreover, despite the country's having the greatest democratic experience in the region, it spawned also a long period of personal dictatorship, finally coming undone through a process of transition by replacement – creating patterns that correspond to the paramount leaderships and opposition-led regime changes that have figured prominently across Southeast Asia. In short, enough similarities can be found that comparisons between the Philippines and other Southeast Asian countries can be usefully made through which to elucidate differences in regime outcomes. Put simply, Philippine politics have been stable for long periods, owing to an elite cohesion punctuated by strain points that we encountered also in Malaysia. And after the Philippines gained a paramount leader who disunified elites, the regime was destabilized, then democratized by social pressures in ways that set precedents for Thailand in 1992 and Indonesia in 1998.

But the more important aim of this chapter has been to move beyond questions of democratic transition and persistence in order to analyze democracy's quality. In doing this, it has outlined some indicators based on the conduct of elections, namely, the attitudes toward electoral rules of incumbent leaderships, the character of campaign appeals and debates, the quality of political awareness and participation displayed by an electorate, and the amounts of political violence. In then using these indicators to analyze the 1998 Philippine general election, it concluded that while democracy may be stable, it remains low quality, with doubts emerging over the behavior of Ramos late in his tenure as well as that of top members of the election commission. Though these figures remained committed to formal democracy, they tested its rules. Indeed, they would perhaps have tested them more seriously had de Venecia not been so far behind Estrada that a stolen election would have lacked all credibility. Regarding the voters perhaps casting their ballots for frivolous candidates, how else might they have responded to campaign appeals that amounted to what one columnist labeled a "political burlesque?"[115] And Joseph Estrada, who though addressing the concerns of the poor, did so only in the sketchiest terms, mouthing slogans of food security and small business, yet giving no hint as to how they might be put into practice. And political violence, finally, while perhaps low by the electoral standards of the Philippines, still occurred at unacceptable levels.

In sum, while democracy in the Philippines has reached equilibrium, its quality – as measured by the 1998 election – remains compromised. The Estrada presidency that followed, in its leadership and policy outputs, probably diminished quality further. And the manner in which this presidency was changed, even if introducing better leadership, perpetuates our doubts about procedures.

Chapter 7

Southeast Asia

————

Uncovering State Elites and the Business Connection

A key methodological aim of this book has been simply to demonstrate the comparability of five important countries in Southeast Asia. Though the region is generally understood as highly diverse, one finds enough similarities in terms of contextual factors to make meaningful comparisons about political regime forms. First, state apparatuses in Southeast Asia originated in conditions of Western colonial dominance – or in the case of Thailand, through the government's replicating the state building it observed in neighboring territories in order to ward off its formal colonization. This legacy was then made manifest after independence in large, highly interventionist state apparatuses in Indonesia, Singapore, and Malaysia. A less efficacious, though still large state apparatus endured also in Thailand, reaching its apogee in the bureaucratic polity. And even in the Philippines, though the state displayed little capacity for productive economic or social interventions, it gained significant ability to extract.

Second, with the colonial powers having heavily geared their territories toward commodity production and exports, they recruited much migrant labor. In this way, plural societies emerged, featuring communities constructed in the region as Overseas Chinese. Moreover, after independence, the Chinese then used their networks to gain ascendancy over many business activities. To be sure, such merchant minorities have existed in many national settings. But in Southeast Asia, the disparity between the Chinese community's demographic size and its role in local business has been glaring. And the collaborative patterns that have emerged between Chinese owners of conglomerates and indigenous elites in the state have given the region's business dealings a distinctive styling. Further, these patterns have aroused mass-level resentments, especially in Islamic Indonesia and Malaysia, but also episodically in Thailand. And in the Philippines too, the alien status held by Manila-based Chinese has left them vulnerable to various forms of low-level state predation.

A third basis for comparison lies in the timing of these countries' late-industrialization, delineating Indonesia, Malaysia, Thailand, and the

Philippines as the *ASEAN 4*. During the first decade of independence, their commodity exports tended to discourage industrialization, but thereafter funded a primary phase of import substitution. Indeed, high petroleum prices during the 1970s enabled Indonesia and Malaysia even to proceed to industrial deepening. During the 1980s, however, the decline of oil prices, deregulation, and the search by Japan for cheap production sites offshore converged in new patterns of foreign investment. This buoyed up the labor intensive industries of Indonesia, Malaysia, Thailand, and to some extent the Philippines, thereby earning at least the first three countries new World Bank rankings as lower-middle or middle income. During the mid- to late 1990s, though, over-investment, capital flight, and currency collapses – doubtless exacerbated by Southeast Asia's distinct business practices – plunged these countries into economic crises from which they are today emerging at varying rates.

Finally, prominent state apparatuses, ethnically divided societies, and late, but rapid industrialization have done much to delay the formation of civil society in Southeast Asia. One observes that NGOs have proliferated across the region, dedicated to sundry issues of sectional and public interest. And trade unions have long engaged in organizing workers. These entities remain weak, however, in comparison to those in Northeast Asia and Latin America, confined mostly to performing a consultative role with relevant ministries over environmental and development issues. Of course, at a few critical junctures, NGOs have been able to go further, helping coordinate pressures for democratic change in the Philippines in 1986 and in Thailand in 1992 and 1998. And they contributed also to the formation of an important opposition party in Malaysia in 1999. But the kinds of democracies that then emerged in the Philippines and Thailand have been more responsive to business elites than to the social forces that NGOs represent. And in Malaysia, NGOs have as yet brought about no increase in democracy at all. In sum, in taking a broad view of Southeast Asia's political record, we find that colonial legacies, generally large and interventionist, but often undisciplined state apparatuses, plural societies, distinctive patterns of government-business relations, the timing and character of late, though rapid industrialization, the severity of recent economic crisis, and the relative weakness of civil society all provide a basis in the region for more than trivial comparisons.

At the same time, upon this common ground, one remains mindful of many finer differences. For example, though all the countries analyzed in this volume have been strongly affected by Western colonialism, the nature of their experiences has varied. In Indonesia, the Dutch emphasized bureaucratic control and resource exploitation, then decolonized in ways that involved violent confrontation. In Malaysia and Singapore, the British also emphasized bureaucratization and commodity markets, yet offered democratic tutelage as part of a peaceful decolonizing process. In the

Philippines, while the United States provided the state with some administrative form, it was dedicated far more to democratizing politics, subsidizing modest economic development, and reinforcing old social structures. By contrast, the government in Thailand emulated colonial state building, but incurred few of the constraints of a formal colonial presence, thus enabling its military to expand, indeed, to seize power as early as the 1930s.

In addition, despite the social pluralism of these countries, their configurations of ethnic, religious, and linguistic affiliation have evolved in distinctive ways. Malaysia has historically been marked by a bi-polar face-off, pitting the Muslim Malays against the Chinese. In Indonesia too anti-Chinese sentiments have been strong, but recent waves of social conflict indicate patterns of much more complex ethnic and regional fragmentation. In Thailand and the Philippines, though anti-Chinese sentiments have periodically surged, Buddhism and Catholicism have permitted the Chinese more easily to assimilate. Indeed, because religious and cultural barriers have been lower, the Chinese have been able to operate relatively freely in business, then to gain direct access to state power. National leaders have thus emerged in Thailand and the Philippines who possess Chinese ancestry, a rise to prominence that is difficult to imagine in Malaysia and Indonesia.

But despite these different progressions, these countries also display strong similarities in terms of regime outcomes. In brief, we find stable pseudo- or semi-democratic regimes in New Order Indonesia, Singapore, and Malaysia. The Philippines also operated a pseudo-democracy during the Marcos period, while Thailand was a semi-democracy during the 1980s. In addition, where transitions to fuller democracy have taken place in the Philippines, Thailand, and Indonesia, they have nearly always involved opposition-led replacements – clearly distinguishing this region from the state-led or state-negotiated processes of transformation and trans-placement that more commonly occurred elsewhere during the third wave. Given the long-standing patterns in Southeast Asia of leadership prerogatives and interventionist state powers, few soft-liners appeared to bargain with the opposition – in the way that top politicians and generals often did in Northeast Asia, Latin America, and Southern Europe. Thus, as Mark Thompson observes in the Philippines, "Marcos had to be brought down because he would never step down . . . [T]he personal character of his rule meant that he had no outside interests that could be retained if he relinquished authority."[1] The same could be said of Suharto and to lesser extent, the Thai military in 1992 as it tried to reclaim its privileges.

Accordingly, a great irony of democratic transitions in Southeast Asia involves their execution by quiescent social forces aroused in brief flashes of democratizing fury, after which societies return to quiescence. An important exception to this pattern involves Prem Tinsulanond's agreeing to democratize Thailand's politics in 1988, more a response to pressures from provincial business elites than to participatory social forces. Thailand's earlier democratization in 1973 and its "third try" democratization in 1992 conform better to regional trends. However, if opposition-led replacement has been the modal form of transition in Southeast Asia, outcomes have remained uncertain. New Order Indonesia and Thailand possess unstable democracies today, while democracy in the Philippines, though stable, is marked by doubtful quality.

Thus, despite the great differences in these countries' contextual factors – though not so different that meaningful comparisons cannot be made – we find some similar patterns of regime types and change. Indeed, demonstration effects have reverberated powerfully throughout the region, helping to deepen these similarities. The national leaders of New Order Indonesia, Singapore, and Malaysia collaborated in authoring the notion of Asian democracy. In turn, social forces in Indonesia borrowed the Philippine concept of people power. And the reform movement in Malaysia borrowed from Indonesia a galvanizing refrain of *korupsi, kolusi, dan nepotisme*.

Explaining these disjunctures between bounded contextual diversity on one side and similar political outcomes on the other has been this book's second major concern. In doing this, structuralist, modernizationist, and culturalist accounts were all briefly canvassed. We learned that these approaches helped to make sense of contextual factors, but that much could still go awry *en route* to regime types and change. More specifically, the structuralist theories most relevant to Southeast Asian politics have focused on the evolving requirements of maturing capital, motivating big business to break the patrimonialist ties associated with authoritarianism in order more freely to compete in a liberalized economy, probably buttressed by democracy. In Indonesia, however, most big conglomerates remained aligned to Suharto until finally his practices helped to ruin them, demonstrating a dysfunctionality and reversal with which straightforward structuralist accounts seem unable to cope. In Thailand, provincial business sought democracy in order to gain a political edge against the conglomerates based in Bangkok, not to discover some greater international competitiveness. And in the Philippines, big business sought democracy in order to recapture the rents that had been confiscated by Marcos's new cohort of cronies. We shall explore these motivations more fully later.

Modernization theory has focused historically on the middle class as a democratizing agent. And indeed, this thesis is at least partly borne out by the experiences of Thailand and the Philippines. But Indonesia's recent democratization, while involving middle-class activists and students, was most forcefully driven home by urban mob rioting – certainly a side effect of modernizing processes in developing countries, but hardly the kind of medium envisioned by modernization theorists. Further, the middle classes in Singapore and Malaysia, while in proportional terms the largest in

Southeast Asia, have remained quite indifferent to democracy. In Singapore, the middle class appears to have been depoliticized first through educational methods and curricula, later through its bureaucratic employment. In Malaysia, the middle class remains ethnically segmented, with many middle-class Malays similarly dependent on the state for bureaucratic employment. Middle-class Chinese, in turn, have found that their best defense lies in private wealth accumulation, overseas connections, and displays of support for the ruling *Barisan* coalition, rather than open campaigns for democratic reform.

The correlations drawn by modernization theorists between economic growth and middle-class activism have also been tested by the recent economic crisis. Put simply, more often than lineal patterns of growth, steep crisis has aroused middle-class interest in democracy – and less for the intrinsic joy of participation than for fear of losing their hard-won statuses. Hence, an important lesson emerging from the crisis suggests that the effectiveness with which national leaders responded had much bearing on whether social forces demanded democratization, strengthened social support for an existing democracy, or renewed support for authoritarianism.[2] Suharto and Chavalit performed poorly and hence, were ousted, quickly precipitating democratic change in Indonesia, while invigorating democracy in Thailand. In Malaysia, Mahathir at first performed rashly, but then capably imposed capital controls, thereby cheering the middle class and blunting the pressures for reform. In Singapore, the government similarly retained the confidence of the middle class, leading one to speculate that the crisis afflicting the country may even have strengthened local support for authoritarianism. And in the Philippines, finally, while its escaping the worst of the crisis permitted an electoral transfer of electoral power, the quality of leadership provided by President Estrada triggered a belated economic slowdown.[3] In sum, Southeast Asia's recent economic crisis helps to elaborate the modernizing context in which politics are transacted. But it has worked no straightforward impact on middle-class outlooks and democratic change. One must instead consider an important intervening variable of leadership choices and effectiveness.

Finally, though Singapore, Malaysia, and the Philippines gained early exposure to democracy through colonial tutelage – or in the case of Indonesia, through demonstration effects, Western influence, and the lack of any contemporary alternatives – their democratic regimes soon withered. In Indonesia, democracy broke down amid policy immobilism, Outer Island rebellions, and reckless national leadership. In Singapore, democracy was eroded by competing elites, in Malaysia by elite-level responses to ethnic upheavals, and in the Philippines by an avaricious leader amid much mass-level apathy. In explaining these closures and breakdowns, culturalist theories emphasize the weakness of social forces, their patterns of deference rooted in ethnic loyalties and agrarian clientelism. Further, even as modernization takes place, governments remain able to reinvent cultural traditions in order to prolong social quiescence. And yet, one recollects that Southeast Asia has also been the locus of great peasant-based insurgencies, galvanized by Communist appeals. It has recently been the site also of thunderous student mobilizations, spontaneous labor confrontations, and Islamic militancy that hardly square with culturalist assumptions of deeply engrained fatalism and political indifference.

These approaches, then, in confronting ambiguous contextual factors, are unable to trace clear causal pathways to the forms regimes take. Hence, in addressing the gap between contexts and outcomes, this book has given much attention to mediating forms of agency – conceptualized in terms of the ways in which elites engage one another while managing social forces. A simple explanatory schema thus emerged. Where elites are cohesive (respecting mutual statuses and avoiding competitive social mobilizations), they can stabilize their regime, thus avoiding the executive and military coups or mass uprisings that are the hallmarks of inequilibrium. In addition, where they preside over social forces that are quiescent, they can operate their regimes in authoritarian ways, even where colonial experience has bequeathed formal democracy. By contrast, where elites are disunified and social forces grown participatory (perhaps enlivened by the kinds of processes charted by structuralist and modernization theorists or freed from the attitudinal bonds noted by culturalists), a democratic transition may take place.

More specifically, where factions of soft-lining elites appear, calculating that by trading off some security of tenure they can retain other vital prerogatives, a process of state-led or negotiated regime change may unfold. This was the pathway most commonly taken in Northeast Asia, Latin America, and southern Europe. By contrast, where elites divide into factions, but none consent to bargain with the opposition, bottom-up replacements may occur. As we have seen, apart from Thailand's democratization in 1988, this has been the most common pattern in Southeast Asia, an outcome attributable to the great unwillingness of Southeast Asia's leaders and elites to cede state power, even when weakened by intense rivalries.

Finally, this book has investigated the organizational bases upon which elite statuses have been fixed. Owing to the varied and complex ways in which contextual factors have played out, the registries of resource-rich organizations change greatly across countries. However, they everywhere contain organizations within the state apparatus and, with the partial exception of Singapore, the world of private business. In New Order Indonesia, it was the presidency that was most important, enabling a paramount national leader to manage elites in the military, bureaucracy, and big business conglomerates. In Malaysia, the UMNO merged almost seamlessly with the bureaucracy and the conglomerates, thus elevating the Prime Minister's Department, the party's Supreme Council, and top corporate boardrooms as key arenas. In Thailand, the military and bureaucracy were historically preeminent, but have gradually been over-shadowed by business – whether Bangkok-based conglomerates, provincial operations, or "new capitalists" – as well as the party organizations into which business has gravitated. In the Philippines, land ownership, business conglomerates, the presidency, and the senate have been most important, their relative weightings shifting over time. And in Singapore, finally, the PAP and the bureaucracy have been preeminent, peaking in the party's central executive committee and cabinet.

To be sure, the causal weight possessed by elites in different organizations is an empirical question, to be investigated in respective settings. But in disentangling different organizational matrices, analytical gains can be made by focusing explicitly on relations between state and business elites. As we have seen, structuralist approaches address the nexus between government and business in order to explain new democratizing pressures. But in thinking less in terms of the voluntarism of elites than the ineluctable rise of capital, they are unable to account for cases of authoritarian persistence and democratic breakdown. Others kinds of approaches illuminate business elites more clearly, though less to explain democracy than to monitor rent seeking and competitiveness, respectively made manifest in particularistic cronyism and the more productive forms of lobbying carried out by business associations.[4] Accordingly, the rest of this chapter focuses on relations between state and business elites, examining the implications for democratic transitions.

Pivotal business elites

In a context of late industrialization, state elites in many developing countries have promoted business elites, forging relations that can be characterized as balanced and consultative or top-down and managerial. However, in some of these cases, state elites have withdrawn their patronage, closing down patrimonialist or corporatist channels, thus alienating business sharply. State elites may be motivated by new preferences for state-owned enterprises or foreign investors. Alternatively, they may be tempted by base opportunities for predation, or they may be simply afflicted by incompetence, causing the business climate to deteriorate in inflation, recession, and crises. Indeed, it is the "exclusion of business elites from policymaking during economic hard times" that appears most often to threaten, and hence to alienate the business community.[5] In this situation, with elite relations now strained, business elites sometimes retaliate by destabilizing the regime. As Eduardo Silva and Francisco Durand conclude from their investigations of business elites in Latin America,

[T]he literature has long recognized that in market economies, business' support for a form of government – whether democratic, authoritarian, or intermediate forms – is vital for stability. At its roots, business' power stems from its capacity to influence public functions of employment and investment. The decisions of business elites, then, significantly affect economic stability, which in turn, is central for the health of governments. If they find a particular form of government intolerable, they may exacerbate economic crises in order to bring down a government.[6]

Lee Payne and Ernest Bartell then record the ways in which business elites can bring pressure to bear: concentrating on speculative investments, engaging in capital flight, limiting production and laying off workers.[7] What is more, business elites can help to mobilize participatory social forces, their pronouncements "sway[ing] the foreign sector, middle classes, and even elements of the poorer classes to [their] side."[8] Finally, business elites can coordinate their activities by coalescing in business associations, gaining a new sectional unity that reveals a broader configuration of disunified elites.

In the Latin American setting, recent investigations have focused less on the circumstances in which state elites have withdrawn their patronage than on cases in which business elites have spurned state protectionism in order to liberalize economies. Business motivations have included the failure of industrial policies, the comparative success of free market strategies, the disappearance of socialist alternatives, and international pressures for change.[9] But more than this, researchers have begun to take a new look at the conditions in which business elites might lend their weight also to democratizing politics. Of course, as Silva and Durand remind us, "businesspeople have no intrinsic allegiance to either authoritarianism or democracy."[10] The first loyalty of business, quite plainly, is to capital accumulation. But just as economic liberalization can sometimes be more profitable than state protectionism, so too can democracy be more profitable than authoritarian controls. Indeed, Silva and Durand suggest optimistically that democracy can reinforce economic liberalization, thus quickening the pace toward economic buoyancy.

To be sure, pressure by business elites for economic liberalization and political democratization, even if sporadic, has been more advanced in the Latin American setting than in Southeast Asia. On this score, Myanmar demonstrates clearly how it is possible for state elites still to extinguish business elites, then seize the commanding heights of the economy themselves. Specifically, through the Union of Myanmar Economic Holdings (UMEH), the Myawady Bank, a variety of joint ventures with Thai and Western companies, and dealings with opium warlords, state elites have doubled as business elites.[11] In this way, they have operated a primitive economy, but surely a stable form of authoritarianism.

At the other end of Southeast Asia's spectrum, however, more distinct, even autonomous business elites have emerged. To guide our analysis, we can develop a short, subsidiary schema. Where state elites promote, incorporate, or effectively suppress business elites, the regime remains stable and authoritarian, most likely taking the form of a pseudo- or semi-democracy. Our roster here includes New Order Indonesia, and Singapore. But where business elites have in some measure been promoted, then excluded and sharply alienated, those who can readily energize social constituencies may press for democracy. This may amount to a brief democratic surge, as in Malaysia during the late 1980s, or cumulate in transformative pressures, as in Thailand, the Philippines, and even Indonesia during the late 1990s. Of course, this tells us little about the consolidation of any democracy that results. Nor, in partial contradistinction to Silva and Durand, does it guarantee anything about the subsequently competitive or productive behaviors of business. It is simply that where the breakup of an authoritarian coalition involves the alienation of business elites, the likelihood of a democratic transition increases. As O'Donnell and Schmitter observe, "one class condition which does seem unavoidable for the viability of the transition is that the bourgeoisie, or at least important segments of its, regard the authoritarian regime as 'dispensable.'"[12]

Government and business in Southeast Asia

As elsewhere in the developing world, state elites in Southeast Asia have often promoted business elites. They have done this for a variety of reasons: to lay the infrastructure or pursue the import substitution that commence or deepen industrialization (as the Chinese *cukong* were encouraged to do in New Order Indonesia, especially during the 1970s); to redress the material and status imbalances that fester between ethnic groups (thus uplifting Malaysia's *korporat Melayu*, for example, during the 1970s and 1980s); to compete with existing business elites whose loyalties have grown doubtful (as Marcos's new cronies did in the Philippines); or simply to reward presidential in-laws, offspring, and cronies (like the Romualdezes in the Philippines and the children of Suharto). Of course, while emphasizing one aim, state leaders can alloy them with others, thereby bonding with business elites even more closely. Surely, Marcos was gratified when his friend, Lucio Tan, succeeded in mixing his rent-seeking with his profitably operating Philippine Airlines, at least for a time.[13]

Where state elites have been able, though, they have acted selectively, taking care to promote business elites who, while duly enriched, have been prevented by their origins or acquired statuses from finally shaking free and mounting political challenges. Specifically, these business elites have been curbed by their sometimes holding organizational bases within the state apparatus (like state enterprise managers in Singapore), their gaping ethnic vulnerabilities (like the Chinese in Indonesia, Malaysia, and in Thailand under Phibun), or their memberships in stifling first families or tight clientelist networks (like in Indonesia under Suharto, in Malaysia under Mahathir, and in the Philippines under Marcos).

By contrast, business elites less encumbered by their origins – and thus better able to launch political challenges – have been commensurately under-promoted by state elites. One thinks here of *pribumi* contractors in New Order Indonesia, Chinese-educated bankers, traders, and property developers in Singapore, a rival "team" of *bumiputra* business people in Malaysia, blackened during the late 1980s by its factional disloyalties, and land-owning oligarchs under Marcos. Even in Thailand, though the bureaucracy's low level capacity does much to explain the state's under-promotion of indigenous business people, it is still striking that within the indigenous community, the only prominent conglomerate is King Bhumibol's Crown Property Bureau.

Finally, sooner than promoted business elites, it is these lesser, under-promoted elements that help to determine transitions to democracy. In brief, where they are skillfully contained by state leaders – given enough that they are unwilling to risk political challenges, but not so much that they are able to – authoritarian regimes persist for long periods. But where these lesser elements are systematically excluded, they may grow so alienated that they do mount such challenges, helping to energize their social constituencies in pursuit of democracy. Let us illustrate these variable postures and outcomes more fully.

Managing business elites

New Order Indonesia

In New Order Indonesia, Suharto neatly segmented business elites, then skillfully promoted some while under-promoting others. More specifically, Suharto promoted Chinese business elites, then later his own children, knowing that while they all took state contracts and grew personally wealthy, their ethnic origins or filial loyalties would discourage their mobilizing mass constituencies and challenging him politically. Figures like Liem Sioe Liong, Bob Hasan, and Prajogo Pangestu thus carried out Suharto's developmental projects – milling commodities, building cement plants, and processing plywood. Further, his sons, Bambang and Tommy, and his daughter, Tutut, fulfilled his parental hopes, acquiring state assets and stacking up great conglomerates. In consequence, while ethnic Chinese constitute a small minority, we have seen that they controlled most of the business scene. But amid this ethnic distortion, Bambang's holding company, *Bimantara Citra*, was gauged still to be the country's fifth largest.

However, these business conglomerates, whether operated by the Chinese or the president's children, were politically checked, the first by the social grievances they sparked, the latter by their deep economic dependence. Liem's bank, for example, Bank Central Asia, was bombed repeatedly by Islamicists during the 1980s, thus requiring state protection. Tommy Suharto's national car project, *Timor Putra Nasional*, was sustainable only with generous state financing and tariff exemptions. At the same time, other *pribumi* business elites, holding indigenous statuses, yet residing outside the Suharto family, could more readily mobilize social constituencies. Accordingly, Suharto modulated closely – though never cut off – the state contracts on which they too depended. Indeed, through the State Secretariat's Team 10, he consented during the 1980s to the promotion of a few *pribumi* contractors, in particular, Aburizal Bakrie, Fadel Muhammad, and Ponco Sutowo. One notes, however, that much of this promotion was reserved for Bambang's *Bimantara Citra*.

In sum, despite the many social pressures that roiled New Order Indonesia – ethnic antagonisms, Islamic resurgence, new labor and gender grievances, an uprooted peasantry, and bleak urban anomie – its pseudo-democracy persisted for more than three decades. Further, this record of pseudo-democratic stability can partly be attributed to an absence of democratizing business elites, those socially empowered enough and economically alienated enough that they were willing to break with the national leader. Instead, by promoting ethnically vulnerable Chinese, then under-promoting indigenous *pribumi* – though without granting them so little they contemplated defecting – Suharto neatly contained Indonesia's business elites. Other societal forces, then, though they may have called for democratization, were left largely to languish.

Of course, in Chapter Two, we saw also how economic crisis finally robbed Suharto of the resources with which any longer to manage business elites. In these circumstances, some confronted him openly, like Arifin Panigoro and Sofjan Wanandi. Indeed, Arifin joined Amien Rais, with his denunciations of Suharto resonating with indigenous social forces, while his personal wealth provided logistical support for student protesters. Many Chinese business elites, meanwhile, shifted what capital they retained overseas. However, after democratization commenced, some Chinese elites began to return, acquiescing in the gradual transition undertaken by Suharto's successor, B.J. Habibie. And in part because of this gradual pace, they were spared much painful restructuring and bankruptcy, enabling them in most cases still to operate their conglomerates, even if greatly devalued. Thus, just as alienated business elites helped to precipitate a democratic transition under Suharto, so has their acceptance first of Habibie's leadership, later that of Abdurrahman Wahid, boded well for democratic stability. We await their reaction to Megawati.

Singapore

In Singapore, we have seen that the state has historically neglected private local business. Instead, the state has nurtured its own brand of public sector entrepreneurism, recruiting personnel who are English-educated, then promoting them swiftly through the bureaucratic apparatus. On this count, one notes the government's Economic Development Board (especially its Projects Division), the Development Bank of Singapore (involved in shipping, transportation, tourism, and real estate), the Ministry of Finance (which, through the Central Provident Fund, has accumulated great equity holdings), and a vast spectrum of profitable statutory boards and government linked corporations.[14] In consequence, analysts often observe that the country's most vital business activity beats deeply in its bureaucracy. Further, much of this dynamism has involved partnerships with foreign capital, luring in transnational companies through efficient approval systems, disciplined labor, industrial estates, and infrastructure. And though these transnationals have then mostly hoarded their technologies and repatriated their profits, they have left behind a thick residue of tax revenues, executive salaries, and factory wages that have enriched Singapore.

In short, state elites have promoted a category of what analytically can be understood as business elites, but then lodged it in the bureaucracy, enrolled it in the PAP, and tamed it with fine lifestyles – rendering business elites, indeed, the middle class more generally, quite indifferent to democracy. But even if the perspectives of these business elites change, they would find it difficult to act: their bureaucratic positions and English-language education have left them far more attuned to transnational capital than to the Chinese-educated business community and the broader social forces pining below. Indeed, while English-educated elites have been promoted, their Chinese-educated counterparts have been neglected, left to forage in slim local markets.

In part, Singapore's state elites have neglected local Chinese business because they have doubted its industrializing prowess – its marked lack of capital, technology, and modern management techniques. Historically, state elites also doubted this category's political loyalties – whether linked to old-time British interests or, if more nationalist, tinged probably with socialism. However, while Chinese-educated business elites may have been neglected, they have never been excluded outright. They have instead been left to their lending, small trading, and modest property developments. Hence, if in elections today Chinese-educated workers oppose the PAP, there is no evidence they are joined by Chinese-educated business elites. And if state leaders fret over small dips in their electoral standings, their semi-democratic elections have never unseated them. They have too deftly segmented and calibrated business elites, promoting English-educated bureaucrats who are disembodied from social constituencies, then neglecting – but not seriously alienating – Chinese-educated business people who are better grounded.

Alienating business elites

Structuralist approaches often argue that beyond some developmental threshold, the functional requirements of capital must change, posing finally some challenges for authoritarian regimes. Specifically, as capital matures and economies grow complex, business elites try to break with the state that has promoted them. Indeed, their personal longings for organizational autonomy and their discovery of finer product lines and growth engines are said to require it. To this end, business elites demand new limits on the prerogatives of state elites. They demand also, however, that the state impartially referee their inter-firm dealings. Here, discussion turns to bureaucratic transparency, the sanctity of contracts and property rights, impartial legal systems and commercial codes – principles of good governance said best to flourish in democracies. This heartening sequencing can even be extended. Economic growth – by empowering business elites and diversifying civil society – favors democracy. And democracy – by freeing, yet disciplining business dealings and consumerism – renews economic growth. One thus sees why a mutual reinforcement between free markets and democratic politics is so often assumed.[15]

In Southeast Asia, however, it has not been once promoted, now mature business elites who have pressed for regime change. It has instead been once promoted, now excluded elites – a disjuncture that has historically made business dealings in Southeast Asia most difficult to undertake. In this debate, the region's business elites have been ranged analytically on a continuum, sloping upward from "parasites" and "pariahs" to "promoters" and "paragons."[16] More specifically, their exchanges with state leaders and elites have been conceptualized as state-led and patrimonialist (as they once were between Suharto and top Chinese *cukong*, and as they remain between Mahathir and designated *korporat Melayu*), socially weighted and oligarchic (as they have historically been in the Philippines), more evenly consultative (as in Thailand under Prem), or abstracted and structural (as they were between Suharto and vital downstream exporters). But however Southeast Asian capitalism is understood and whatever the competitiveness of those who practice it, most business elites have perpetuated their elite statuses through their ties to the state, forming a dependence that some may have raised to more productive symbiosis, but that few have escaped altogether. Thus, it is when business elites are denied promotion – rather than their outgrowing the need for it – that they may seek to break with the state. In these circumstances, a category of once promoted, now excluded business elites, while having little resonance with social forces, can destabilize the authoritarian regime by withholding investment. And a category of once under-promoted, though now similarly excluded business elites may energize social constituencies in pressing for democracy.

Malaysia

In Malaysia, we have seen that quite in contrast to Indonesia, state elites have long promoted indigenous business elites, hoping that they might one day compete with the Chinese. This promotion, christened the New Economic Policy (NEP), commenced during the early 1970s, shortly after Malay resentments over ethnic disparities had erupted in the May 13th rioting. The UMNO thus tightened Malaysia's regime into a semi-democracy, accumulated more state power, then struck deeply into the economy. And armed with a grab bag of mechanisms – state enterprises and contracts, cheap credit, forced restructurings, secret share offers, and a steady hum of insider information – the UMNO rapidly promoted a new category of *korporat Melayu*.

In doing this, however, state elites made it clear that in promoting, then excluding business elites who were socially empowered, pressures for new leadership, indeed democracy could increase – precisely the progress that Suharto had feared most. During the 1970s, much of this promotion in Malaysia was associated with Tengku Razaleigh, then the finance minister and, through his family companies and property holdings, a business elite in his own right. But during the 1980s, this was overseen by his successor, Daim Zainuddin. A long-time confidant of Mahathir, Daim facilitated the rise of his proteges, breeding a cohort that came to be known as "Daim's boys." It included Halim Saad, first of *Hatibudi*, later Renong, Wan Azmi Wan Hamzah of Land and General, and Tajudin Ramli of Malaysia Airlines.[17] During the mid-1980s, however, as the price of petroleum fell and Malaysia slipped into recession, much of this promotional activity became unaffordable. Thus, while Mahathir held the NEP broadly "in abeyance," Daim reined in much of his patronage. Daim did this selectively, though, continuing to promote the *korporat Melayu* closest to him, while abandoning more ordinary contractors.

In Chapter Four, we encountered in Malaysia's political record a number of strain points, one of which took place during the 1980s. And in involving business elites, it produced one of the country's greatest surges in democratizing pressure. To summarize, business elites who had once been promoted under the NEP were now excluded and deeply alienated by Daim. They thus gravitated to Tengku Razaleigh who, amid declining elite cohesion, challenged Mahathir for the presidency of the UMNO at the 1987 assembly election.[18] Though Mahathir won, his victory was narrow, thus prompting Razaleigh to pursue his "team" challenge in the media, the judiciary, and finally, the 1990 general election. In this situation, Razaleigh broke with the UMNO in order to form a new party, the *Semangat '46*. Accordingly, while broadening his support among alienated business elites,[19] Razaleigh was able to appeal also to middle-class Malays and trade unions. Further, he joined with Chinese and Kadazan parties, thereby creating an alliance which, while Malay-centered, was clearly multi-ethnic, paralleling closely the UMNO's own coalition. Public excitement intensified – detectable in universities, middle-class meeting places, and open air coffee shops – as prospects mounted for semi-democratic elections now stunning state elites, and the country's single-party dominant system reequilibrating as a competitive two-party democracy.

The UMNO retaliated, however, against business elites who opposed it. After having earlier cut state contracts, the UMNO quietly ordered now that state bank loans be called in, promptly ruining many business elites associated with Razaleigh.[20] But more than this, the UMNO's most potent weapon turned out to be economic recovery. Indeed, as global markets brightened during the late-1980s, foreign investment returned to Malaysia, enabling the UMNO again to promote the business elites it had alienated. Hence, when general elections finally took place in 1990, they fell well short of replacing the UMNO-led *Barisan*, or even diminishing its two-thirds majority in parliament. We recall also that in the years that followed, remnants of the '46 crept back to the UMNO, finding the meager deals they were now offered better than any principled spell in the wilderness. And during the UMNO party election in 1996, Razaleigh himself dissolved the '46 and returned to the fold. One must conclude that *bumiputera* business elites had all along been keener on promotion and sharing in boom cycles than democratizing their country's politics. Indeed, Mahathir's capacity to retain business loyalties later in the decade helped him to win the general election in 1999 by a more comfortable margin than he had gained in 1990.

Thailand

In Thailand, we have seen that under the bureaucratic polity of the 1940s–50s, elites in the military and bureaucracy promoted Chinese in business, providing the licensing and funding with which to generate returns, a great portion of which could be extorted. Further, with the stigma of pariah entrepreneurs still lingering, state elites could perpetuate these arrangements without fear of the Chinese converting their earnings into autonomous political power. However, after Sarit became prime minister, state elites rationalized their authoritarianism, thus enabling Chinese business people to operate more freely. It is during this period, then, that the great banking families and business conglomerates based in Bangkok emerged. Further, during the mid-1970s, "the fragmentation and instability among the top military echelons made military patronage less productive and less reliable for private companies. The military-bureaucratic presence on the boards of large corporations thus declined."[21] In these conditions, business elites supported democratization in 1973, then quickly found their place in political parties, the parliament, and cabinets. Indeed, Anek observes that after elections in 1975, business people made up 35 per cent of the house of representatives, the largest occupational bloc and thus greatly overshadowing those with a bureaucratic background. They also formed more than half the cabinet of Prime Minister Kukrit.[22]

But the military, after easing its divisions, struck back with a coup in 1976. And during the 1980s, it settled into an equilibrium in which the national leader, Prem, forged new understandings with business elites, helping to perpetuate a semi-democracy. Representatives of the government and key business associations thus met in the new Joint Public and Private Sector Consultative Committee, with meetings often chaired by the prime minister.[23] With the stigma of Chinese-ness finally softening, it remained safe during this period to cooperate with business. Factional and cross-organizational ties thus persisted amid family relationships, personal friendships, and long-standing business dealings that were mutually profitable.

However, as economic growth quickened during mid-1980s, business elites who were less well incorporated appeared in the provinces. And these provincial business elites, in confronting barriers to their further enrichment posed by the links between the state and big business, began to press now for democracy. Prem obliged them, permitting an election to take place in 1988 that brought *Chart Thai* to power, leading a coalition of mainly rural-based parties. The military and bureaucracy grew resentful, though. And as the new *Chart Thai* government squeezed their prerogatives, the military responded in 1991 by mounting yet another coup. Next, the military set up the National Peace Keeping Council, then took power more directly after elections in March, while the Bangkok-based conglomerates quietly applauded this setback for provincial business. Indeed, big business elites sat as readily in the new cabinet of General Suchinda as they had that of Prime Minister Chatichai.

But soon, what Paul Handley has identified as the "new capitalists," made rich during the late 1980s by a flourishing stock market, rising land prices, and booming export production, "now risked their newfound wealth and security to take a political stand and support the May demonstrations" of 1992, thus helping to drive the military back out.[24] They also supported the Democrat and *Palang Dharma* parties in the election held in September, helping to bring Chuan Leekpai to power. However, the new capitalists were afterward disappointed with Chuan, as the Securities and Exchange Commission closed several of the share manipulations syndicates upon which they depended.[25] They appear also to have been neglected by the Banharn government, which was linked much more closely to provincial business. And during Chavalit's prime ministership, Thailand's stock market finally collapsed, greatly weakening the new capitalists as a political force. It remains, however, that these new capitalists had participated in Thailand's redemocratization in 1992. And the big conglomerates, in competing with provincial business, helped to invigorate democracy in 1997, made manifest in Chavalit's replacement by the Democrats. Indeed, the new Democrat finance minister, Tarrin Nimmanhaeminda, tasked with reforming the banking system, was himself a former commercial bank president, and hence, "seen to be part of the 'old elite.'"[26] Finally, one notes that the prime minister today, Thaksin Shinawatra, heading a *Thai Rak Thai* coalition government, gained the start-up capital for his telecommunications empire while a police official selling computer systems to law enforcement agencies. Plainly, pressures for democracy in Thailand have had much to do with the outlooks of business elites.

The Philippines

In the Philippines, the search for alienated business elites begins with the "oligarchic families," those whose statuses are traceable to old land holdings and early import substitution. Initially, these elites had benefited from Marcos's declaring martial law in 1972, gaining "political stability, docile unions, and rapid economic growth."[27] However, as martial law wore on, Marcos attempted to centralize more tightly the country's patrimonialist dealings. He thus wrested large assets from the likes of the Lopez, Osmena, Jacinto, and Aquino families, bringing them under his own control or shifting them to his new cronies. Marcos took over much of the sugar industry, for example – even imposing land reform on the Aquino family's hacienda – then used its surpluses to fund "the personal and political needs of the First Family."[28] He also shifted the media interests of the Lopez family to his favorite, Roberto Benedicto, and to his in-law, Benjamin Romualdez. Further, he set up monopolies on coconut milling and exporting for Eduardo Cojuangco and Ponce Enrile, import licenses and tax breaks for Herminio Disini's cigarette filter company, and some favorable tariffs, for Ricardo Silverio's auto assembly operations. And finally, when many of these newly promoted business elites managed still to go broke during a credit squeeze in 1981, Marcos resuscitated them with a government bail-out – causing much anger among those business elites who had been excluded.

Specifically, Hutchcroft records that the "massive Central Bank bail-out of failed crony firms provoked a great deal of resentment, and a suprafamilial elite coalition ... developed among 'nonfavored' and 'less-favored' business people. The most prominent business organization seeking political change was the Makati Business Club, formed in 1982."[29] Further, we recall Thompson's observation that the assassination of Benigno

Aquino in the following year "shocked" and thus galvanized "the wealthy."[30] Accordingly, business elites responded by mounting a "confetti revolution" in the Makati district, paving the way for weekly rallies that accumulated later in people power. Thompson notes also that while business elites boycotted the 1984 legislative elections, they were gradually convinced that Marcos could be challenged. Accordingly, they organized a Convenor Group to select a candidate. And after meeting in the Cojuangco Building in Makati in 1984, they selected Corazon Aquino, then boosted her candidacy by organizing the Cory Aquino for President Movement.

President Marcos, under pressure from the United States, called a snap presidential election in 1986. He rigged it in pseudo-democratic ways, however, budgeting some $500 million for vote buying, still more to distort vote counting, especially in the rural areas beyond international scrutiny. He also removed some 12 per cent of the voters from the electoral rolls, then deadened the campaign period with state terror.[31] And apparently satisfied with his work, Marcos is described by Thompson as having been quite confident of victory. Nonetheless, the voting turned strongly against the president. He thus attempted some last-minute "padding," but triggered instead a walk-out by election commission workers, finally laying bare his many machinations. And when the military refused to overturn the results, and the United States promised no more than exile – prompting Marcos to lament to an American emissary, "I am so very, very disappointed"[32] – rigged elections became stunning ones, thus paving the way for Aquino's rise to the presidency and the democratization of Philippines politics.

Business elites and democracy

One way of assessing the motivations of business elites who call for democracy, of course, is to monitor their behaviors in cases where they have attained it. And what one finds oftentimes is that after democratization has taken place and governments have been changed, elites connect quickly with new incumbents – perhaps even gaining an upper hand or assuming the role of state elites themselves. In short, they waste little time in piercing democracy's thin barriers round conflicts of interest, revealing them as less interested in a limited or impartial state than in restarting their promotion.

Let us consider the two Southeast Asian countries that have established the longest records of democratic politics, Thailand and the Philippines. In Thailand, after the country's many regime changes, business has joined governments regardless of regime type. Thus, as noted above, business elites slipped as easily into the cabinets of General Prem and General Suchinda under authoritarian regimes as they did those of Chatichai, Banharn, Chavalit, and Chuan in more democratic settings. And in finding their place under each of these leaders, business continued to engage extensively in corruption. Indeed, even senior politicians in the Democrats and *Palang Dharma* were linked to share manipulation syndicates,[33] with Chuan's first government collapsing in a land scandal. Accordingly, in assessing the political behaviors of Thailand's "new breed" politicians, Handley concludes that their "wealth committed its owners to a path that was little different from that of previous generations. . . . When their new source of wealth was threatened, the result was conservative and old-style responses."[34]

What is more, in the Philippines, though alienated business elites helped to oust Marcos, they afterward filled the presidency with one of their own, re-entered the Congress, and recaptured state agencies. They then thwarted the land reforms that had been mooted, as well as new deregulatory measures that threatened the Marcos-era monopolies they had inherited.[35] In consequence, there can be little doubt about why among Southeast Asian countries, Marxian analyses have been pushed deepest in Thailand and the Philippines, the countries whose business elites have been assessed as the most autonomous in the region, yet whose democracies – when in place – have respectively been dismissed as "bourgeois" and "oligarchic." In the Marxian view, then, business elites have debased in quite predictable ways the democracies they helped to bring about. One awaits outcomes in newly democracized Indonesia, keeping a close watch on the activities of Megawati's businessman husband, Taufik Kiemas.

Conclusions

This book has argued that inter-elite relations – set amid contextual factors mediated by social forces – are the principal determinant of regime types and change. This final chapter has extended this argument, focusing more closely on relations between elites in the state and business. In brief, where state elites have promoted business elites who lack social bases, and where they have skillfully under-promoted business elites who are better grounded, their pseudo- and semi-democracies have remained stable. Accordingly, in New Order Indonesia, the national leader unevenly promoted Chinese and *pribumi* business elites. Likewise, Singapore's state elites have distinguished between English- and Chinese-educated business elites, promoting the first in the bureaucracy, while neglecting the latter in a comparatively sparse private sector. By contrast, in countries where state elites promoted, then excluded business elites, business has been alienated. In these circumstances, business elites without social bases ceased their investing, helping to destabilize authoritarian regimes. Those who were better connected energized social constituencies, advancing democratic transitions. Thus, in Malaysia, a "team" of alienated business elites contested the UMNO assembly election in 1987, then the general election in 1990. In Thailand, Bangkok-based business elites helped to democratize the regime in 1973, provincial business elites redemocratized politics in 1988, and the new capitalists lent their weight to a third process of democratization in 1992. And finally, in the Philippines, our most exemplary case, Marcos's exclusion of the oligarchic families, indeed, the state sanctioned assassination of one of their leaders, tilted them strongly toward democracy during 1983–86.

In sum, this chapter has highlighted the democratizing role of business elites. But in the literature on transitions, one is struck by how little attention business has been given – a lament heard even among Latin Americanists.[36] In the third wave, investigation has focused instead on elite factions within state apparatuses and their bargaining with opposition politicians, namely, Catholic Church figures, charismatic trade unionists, human rights lawyers, even artists. Business elites have largely been dismissed as aloof or timid in the Latin American cases, waiting for the chips to fall before placing their own. In profitless eastern Europe, moreover, business was usurped by state managers – only figuring in transitions with the return of those millionaires who had made good in the West and aspired now to high office in their motherland.

But historically, business elites have been viewed as pivotal for democracy's prospects. In Barrington Moore's succinct and once widely cited remark: "No bourgeoisie, no democracy."[37] Indeed, whether confronting the state (as the structuralist theorists predicted) or prodding the state onward to do their bidding (as the neo-Marxists once intoned), business elites were identified as key democratizing agents. In most of the transitions literature, however, business appears to have lost causal weight. Hence, at end of this wave, in the eddy of Southeast Asia, some of its democratizing importance can perhaps be rediscovered. Here, in a region that once lagged far behind Latin America and eastern Europe, yet until recently was industrializing rapidly, business elites have been thrown sharply into relief, even amid a rapidly changing political terrain. More broadly, one recognizes that in gauging democracy's prospects in Southeast Asia today, regional trends of rapid industrialization, sudden and steep crisis, tepid recovery, and renewed economic stagnancy by themselves tell us little. Indeed, most recent studies have concluded that there is no direct correlation between Asia's economic crisis and democracy. Instead, what matters is the ways in which state and business elites interact while responding to crisis, thus reminding us of the significance of voluntarism.

Notes

Preface

1 Barbara Geddes, "What do We Know About Democratization After Twenty Years?" *Annual Review of Political Science*, no. 2 (1999), p. 118.

1 Comparing Politics in Southeast Asia

1 See, e.g., Andrew MacIntyre, "Business, Government, and Development: Northeast Asia and Southeast Asian Comparisons," in Andrew MacIntyre, ed., *Business and Government in Industrializing Asia* (St. Leonards: Allen and Unwin, 1994); and Richard Doner and Gary Hawes, "The Political Economy of Growth in Southeast and Northeast Asia," in Manochehr Dorraj, ed., *The Changing Political Economy of the Third World* (Boulder: Lynne Rienner, 1995).

2 See Kunio Yoshihara, *The Rise of Ersatz Capitalism in South-East Asia* (Singapore: Oxford University Press, 1988); Ruth McVey, "The Materialization of the Southeast Asian Entrepreneur," in Ruth McVey, ed., *Southeast Asian Capitalists* (Ithaca: SEAP, Cornell University, 1992); Peter Searle, *The Riddle of Malaysian Capitalism: Rent-seekers or Real Capitalists* (St. Leonards: Allen and Unwin, 1999).

3 See Richard Robison and David S.G. Goodman, eds., *The New Rich in Asia: Mobile Phones, McDonalds, and Middle-class Revolution* (London and New York: Routledge, 1996); Garry Rodan, Kevin Hewison, and Richard Robison, eds., *The Political Economy of Southeast Asia* (Melbourne: Oxford University Press, 1997); and Tadashi Yamamoto, ed., *Emerging Civil Society in the Asia Pacific Community* (Singapore: Institute of Southeast Asian Studies, 1995).

4 See, e.g., Kevin Hewison, Richard Robison, and Garry Rodan, eds., *Southeast Asia in the 1990s: Authoritarianism, Democracy, and Capitalism* (St. Leonards: Allen and Unwin, 1993); Adi Sasono, Dewi Fortuna Anwar, and Moh Jumhur Hidayat, eds., *Democratization Trends in Southeast Asia: Sectoral Groups' Involvement in Mainstream Politics* (Jakarta: CIDES, 1994); Clark D. Neher and Ross Marlay, *Democracy and Development in Southeast Asia: The Winds of Change* (Boulder: Westview Press, 1995); Donald K. Emmerson, "Region and Recalcitrance: Rethinking Democracy in Southeast Asia," *Pacific Review*, vol. 8, no. 2 (1995), pp. 223–48; Anek Laothamatas, ed., *Democratization in Southeast and East Asia* (Singapore: Institute of Southeast Asian Studies, 1997). Southeast

Asian case studies are also featured in Larry Diamond, Juan J. Linz, and Seymour Martin Lipset, eds., *Democracy in Developing Countries: Asia* (Boulder: Lynne Rienner, 1989); James Morley, ed., *Driven by Growth: Political Change in the Asia-Pacific Region* (Armonk: M.E. Sharpe, 1993); Daniel A. Bell, David Brown, Kanishka Jayasuriya, and David Martin Jones, *Towards Illiberal Democracy in Pacific Asia* (London: Macmillan, 1995); and Gary Rodan, ed., *Political Oppositions in Industrializing Asia* (London: Routledge, 1996).

5 Jacques Bertrand, "Growth and Democracy in Southeast Asia," *Comparative Politics*, vol. 30, no. 3 (April 1998), p. 368.

6 Important case studies of the economic crisis in Southeast Asia are offered by Manuel Montes, *The Currency Crisis in Southeast Asia* (Singapore: Institute of Southeast Asian Studies, 1998); H.W. Arndt and Hal Hill, eds., *Southeast Asia's Economic Crisis: Origins, Lessons, and the Way Forward* (Singapore: Institute of Southeast Asian Studies, 1999); Jomo K.S., ed., *Tigers in Trouble: Financial Governance, Liberalization, and Crises in East Asia* (London: Zed Books, 1999); Karl D. Jackson, ed., *Asian Contagion: The Causes and Consequences of a Financial Crisis* (Boulder: Westview, 1999); T.J. Pempel, ed., *The Politics of the Asian Economic Crisis* (Ithaca: Cornell University Press, 1999); Richard Robison, Mark Beeson, Kanishka Jayasuriya, and Hyuk-Rae Kim, *Politics and Markets in the Wake of the Asian Crisis* (London: Routledge, 2000); and Stephan Haggard, *The Political Economy of the Asian Financial Crisis* (Washington D.C.: Institute for International Economics, 2000).

7 See Amitav Archaya, "Southeast Asia's Democratic Moment," *Asian Survey*, vol. 39, no. 3 (May/June 1999), pp. 418–32.

8 Samuel P. Huntington, *The Third Wave: Democratization in the Late Twentieth Century* (Norman: University of Oklahoma Press, 1991).

9 In a press conference in London, February 7, 1999, Mahathir stated, "I was looking forward to resigning last year. But now, I will not resign. I will stay here unless somebody shoots me." Quoted in bungaraya@listserv.net-gw.com, posted February 9, 1999.

10 Myron Weiner, "Empirical Democratic Theory," in Myron Weiner and Ergun Ozbudun, *Competitive Elections in Developing Countries* (Durham: Duke University Press, 1987), pp. 3–34.

11 Stephanie Lawson, "Conceptual Issues in the Comparative Study of Regime Change and Democratization," *Comparative Politics*, vol. 25, no. 2 (January 1993), pp. 183–205; and Mattei Dogan and John Higley, "Elites, Crises, and Regimes in Comparative Analysis," in Mattei Dogan and John Higley, eds., *Elites, Crises, and the Origins of Regimes* (Lanham: Rowman and Littlefield 1998), pp. 20–23.

12 The debate over consolidation – especially with reference to democracy – is now extensive. See Guillermo O'Donnell, "Illusions About Consolidation," *Journal of Democracy*, vol. 7, no. 2 (April 1996), pp. 34–51; and Richard Gunther, P. Nikiforos Diamandouros, and Hans-Jurgen Puhle, "O'Donnell's 'Illusions': A Rejoinder," *Journal of Democracy*, vol. 7, no. 4 (October 1996), pp. 151–59.

13 For some early typologies, see Juan J. Linz, "Totalitarian and Authoritarian Regimes," in Fred I. Greenstein and Nelson W. Polsby, eds., *Macropolitical Theory* (Reading: Addison Wesley, 1975); Guillermo O'Donnell and Philippe Schmitter, "Tentative Conclusions about Uncertain Democracies," in Guillermo O'Donnell, Philippe C. Schmitter, and Laurence Whitehead, eds., *Transitions from Authoritarian Rule: Prospects for Democracy*, vol. 4 (Baltimore: Johns

Hopkins University Press, 1986), pp. 6–14; Larry Diamond, "Introduction," in Larry Diamond, Juan J. Linz, and Seymour Martin Lipset, eds., *Democracy in Developing Countries: Asia* (Boulder: Lynne Rienner, 1989), pp. xvi–xviii; Michael Burton, Richard Gunther, and John Higley, "Introduction," in John Higley and Richard Gunther, eds., *Elites and Democratic Consolidation in Latin America and Southern Europe* (Cambridge: Cambridge University Press, 1992), pp. 3–8. See also David Collier and Steven Levitsky, "Democracy with Adjectives: Conceptual Innovation in Comparative Research," *World Politics*, vol. 49, no. 3 (April 1997), pp. 430–51.

14 Robert Dahl, *Polyarchy: Participation and Opposition* (New Haven: Yale University Press, 1971).

15 Burton, Gunther, and Higley, "Introduction," p. 2.

16 O'Donnell and Schmitter, "Tentative Conclusions," pp. 9–11.

17 Dahl, *Polyarchy*; Samuel P. Huntington, *The Third Wave*, p. 7.

18 Linz and Stepan, *Problems of Democratic Transition: Southern Europe, South America, and Post-Communist Europe* (Baltimore: Johns Hopkins University Press, 1996), pp. 67–69.

19 Juan J. Linz, "Some Thoughts on the Victory and Future of Democracy," in Axel Hadenius, ed., *Democracy's Victory and Crisis* (Cambridge: Cambridge University Press, 1997), pp. 421.

20 Amid the controversy that emerged after Malaysia's prime minister, Mahathir Mohamad, ordered the arrest of his deputy, Anwar Ibrahim, in 1998, the *Far Eastern Economic Review* (hereafter *FEER*) opined in an editorial, "Malaysians have democracy. [T]his isn't a country where people can't vote or where UMNO is assured of winning. Dr Mahathir is no despot and Malaysia isn't Indonesia." November 26, 1998, p. 110. Similarly, a columnist in the *Australian Financial Review* wrote, "Mahathir may be aggressive and lack Anwar's PR skills, but Malaysians are free to vote again at the next general election if they so choose." Michael Backman, "Keeping Out of Charm's Way," *Australian Financial Review*, January 8, 1999, p. 21.

21 Joseph Schumpeter, *Capitalism, Socialism, and Democracy* (London: Allen and Unwin, 1943).

22 Huntington, *The Third Wave*, p. 55.

23 For an extended discussion of political legitimacy in Southeast Asia, see Muthiah Alagappa, ed., *Political Legitimacy in Southeast Asia: The Quest for Moral Authority* (Stanford: Standford University Press, 1995), especially Chapters 1–3.

24 Huntington, *The Third Wave*, p. 313.

25 Theda Skocpol, *States and Social Revolutions* (1979), p. 294, quoted in Mark I. Lichbach, "Social Theory and Comparative Politics," in Mark Irving Lichbach and Alan S. Zuckerman, eds., *Comparative Politics: Rationality, Culture, and Structure* (Cambridge: Cambridge University Press, 1997), p. 253.

26 Harold Crouch, *Domestic Political Structures and Regional Economic Co-operation* (Singapore: Institute of Southeast Asian Studies, 1984).

27 Jomo Kwame Sundaram, *A Question of Class: Capital, the State, and Uneven Development in Malaya* (New York: Monthly Review Press, 1988).

28 Alvin Rabushka and Kenneth Shepsle, *Politics in Plural Societies: A Theory of Democratic Instability* (Columbus: Charles E. Merrill, 1972).

29 David Brown, *The State and Ethnic Politics in South-East Asia* (London: Routledge, 1994).

30 Richard Robison, Kevin Hewison, and Garry Rodan, "Political Power in Industrializing Capitalist Societies: Theoretical Approaches," in Kevin Hewison,

Richard Robison, and Garry Rodan, eds., *Southeast Asia in the 1990s: Authoritarianism, Democracy, and Capitalism* (St. Leonards: Allen and Unwin, 1993), p. 24.

31 Robison *et al*, "Political Power," p. 29.

32 Lichbach, "Social Theory," p. 258.

33 Clark D. Neher, "Political Succession in Thailand," *Asian Survey*, vol. 32, no. 7 (July 1992), pp. 601–2.

34 Michel Camdessus, "Globalization and Asia: The Challenges for Regional Cooperation and the Implications for Hong Kong," address to conference on *Financial Integration in Asia and the Role of Hong Kong*, Hong Kong, March 7, 1997, at http://www.imf.org/external/np/sec/mds/1997MDS9703.htm, quoted in Mark Beeson, "Indonesia, the East Asian Crisis and the Commodification of the State," *New Political Economy*, vol. 3, no. 3 (1998), p. 358.

35 *From Miracle to Meltdown: The End of Asian Capitalism?*, conference co-hosted by Asia Research Center, Murdoch University and Center for International Studies, Yonsei University, Freemantle, Western Australia, August 20–22, 1998.

36 S.M. Lipset, *Political Man: The Social Bases of Politics* (Garden City: Doubleday, 1960).

37 Samuel P. Huntington, *Political Order in Changing Societies* (New Haven: Yale University Press, 1968).

38 The literature on the developmental state is voluminous. For recent renditions, see Linda Weiss, *The Myth of the Powerless State* (Ithaca: Cornell University Press, 1998); and Meredith Woo-Cumings, ed., *The Developmental State* (Ithaca: Cornell University Press, 1999).

39 See Tun-jen Cheng, "Is the Dog Barking?" *International Study Notes*, vol. 15, no. 1 (Winter 1990), pp. 10–17; Tun-jen Cheng and Eun Mee Kim "Making Democracy: Generalizing the South Korea Case"; and Heng Lee, "Uncertain Promise: Democratic Consolidation in South Korea," in Edward Friedman, ed., *The Politics of Democratization: Generalizing East Asian Experiences* (Boulder: Westview Press, 1994), pp. 125–47 and 148–60. See also studies on correlations between economic growth, democratic transition and consolidation by Larry Diamond, "Economic Development and Democracy Reconsidered," *American Behavioral Scientist*, vol. 35, no. 4/5 (March/June 1992), pp. 450–99; Adam Przeworski and Fernando Limongi, "Modernization: Theories and Facts," *World Politics*, vol. 49, no. 2 (January 1997), pp. 155–83; and Adam Przeworski and Fernando Limongi, "Democracy and Development," in Axel Hadenius, ed., *Democracy's Victory and Crisis* (Cambridge: Cambridge University Press, 1993), pp. 163–94.

40 Huntington, *The Third Wave*, p. 65.

41 Ibid., pp. 67–68.

42 See Robison and Goodman, *The New Rich in Asia*; Garry Rodan, "The Growth of Singapore's Middle Class and its Political Significance," in Garry Rodan, ed., *Singapore Changes Guard: Social, Political, and Economic Directions in the 1990s* (New York: St. Martin's Press, 1993), pp. 52–71; Francis Loh Kok Wah, "Introduction: Fragmented Vision," in Joel S. Kahn and Francis Loh Kok Wah, eds., *Fragmented Vision: Culture and Politics in Contemporary Malaysia* (St. Leonards: Allen and Unwin, 1992); Richard Tanter and Kenneth Young, eds., *The Politics of Middle Class Indonesia* (Clayton: Monash University, 1990).

43 Dietrich Rueschemeyer, Evelyne Huber Stephens and John D. Stephens, in *Capitalist Development and Democracy* (Oxford: Polity Press, 1992), argue that

even in the West, the middle class role in democratization was a limited in one. At most, the middle class entered into a coalition led principally by the working class.

44 Harold Crouch and James W. Morley, "The Dynamics of Political Change," in James V. Morley, ed., *Driven by Growth: Political Change in the Asia-Pacific Region* (Armonk: M.E. Sharpe, 1993), p. 277.

45 MacIntyre, "Business, Government, and Development," p. 16.

46 Robison and Goodman, *The New Rich in Asia*, p. 8.

47 John A. Hall, "In Search of Civil Society," in John A. Hall, ed., *Civil Society: Theory, History, Comparison* (Cambridge: Polity Press, 1995), pp. 1–31.

48 Lester M. Salamon, "The Rise of the Nonprofit Sector," *Foreign Affairs* (July/ August 1994), pp. 108–22, as quoted in Tadashi, *Emerging Civil Society*, p. 4.

49 Tadashi, *Emerging Civil Society*, p. 13.

50 Philip J. Eldridge, *Non-Government Organizations and Democratic Participation in Indonesia* (Kuala Lumpur: Oxford University Press, 1995), pp. 134–37.

51 Nicos Mouzelis, "Modernity, Late Development and Civil Society," in Hall, ed., *Civil Society*, p. 225.

52 Tadashi, *Emerging Civil Society*, p. 46.

53 Lim Teck Ghee, "Malaysia: Nongovernmental Organizations in Malaysia and Regional Networking," in Yamamoto, ed., *Emerging Civil Society*, p. 167.

54 Garry Rodan, "Theorizing Political Opposition," in Gary Rodan, ed., *Political Oppositions in Industrializing Asia* (London: Routledge, 1996). p. 22.

55 Karen R. Remmer, "Theoretical Decay and Theoretical Development: The Resurgence of Institutional Analysis," *World Politics*, vol. 50, no. 1 (October 1997), p. 45. In this same vein, Mehran Kamrava and Frank O. Mora argue that among the conditions necessary for civil society organizations to "become agents of political liberalization" is "the existence of social actors able and willing to mobilize various constituents for specific goals that may be local or even national in scope." "Civil Society and Democratization in Comparative Perspective: Latin America and the Middle East," *Third World Quarterly*, vol. 19, no. 5 (1998), p. 896.

56 Clifford Geertz, *The Interpretation of Cultures* (New York: Basic Books, 1973).

57 Benedict R. O'G. Anderson, *Language and Power: Exploring Political Cultures in Indonesia* (Ithaca: Cornell University Press, 1990). See also *Imagined Communities: Reflections on the Origins and Spread of Nationalism* (London: Verso, 1983).

58 James C. Scott, *Weapons of the Weak: Everyday Forms of Peasant Resistance* (New Haven: Yale University Press, 1985).

59 Michael R.J. Vatikiotis, *Political Change in Southeast Asia: Trimming the Banyan Tree* (London: Routledge, 1996), pp. 42 and 60–61.

60 Neher and Marlay, pp. 16 and 19. See also, Clark D. Neher, "Asian Style Democracy," *Asian Survey*, vol. 34, no. 11 (November 1994), pp. 949–61.

61 David Martin Jones, *Political Development in Pacific Asia* (Cambridge: Polity Press, 1997), pp. 16–20. See also David Martin Jones, "Democratization, Civil Society, and Illiberal Middle Class Culture in Pacific Asia" *Comparative Politics*, vol. 30, no. 2 (January 1998), pp. 147–69.

62 R.H. Taylor, ed., *The Politics of Elections in Southeast Asia* (New York: Cambridge University Press, 1996) attempts to move "beyond culture," using a political economy approach to gauge the meaning of elections in different Southeast Asian settings. But in reviewing the book, Philip Kelly concludes "the approach taken . . . is very much a cultural analysis, as the symbolic, contested importance of the electoral process is evaluated across the region." In *Pacific Affairs*, vol. 70, no. 3 (Fall 1997), p. 461.

63 Marc Howard Ross, "Culture and Identity in Comparative Political Analysis," in Lichbach and Zuckerman, eds., *Comparative Politics*, p. 44.

64 Linz, "Totalitarian and Authoritarian Regimes," pp. 26–29.

65 Jones, *Political Development*, e.g, pp. 21, 26, 27, 42, 47.

66 *New Straits Times*, October 11, 1996, pp. 14, 16–17.

67 *New Sunday Times*, November 26, 1995, p. 1.

68 Robison *et al*, "Political Power," p. 15.

69 See Michael van Langenberg, "The New Order State: Language, Ideology, Hegemony," in Arief Budiman, ed., *State and Society in Indonesia* (Clayton: Monash University, 1992), pp. 121–49.

70 Crouch and Morley, "The Dynamics of Political Change," p. 299. See also David Brown, who writes, "It is elite cohesion which generates political stability; not the other way round. Elite cohesion itself must be created, deliberately and repeatedly, by elites themselves." "The Search for Elite Cohesion," *Contemporary Southeast Asia*, vol. 15, no. 1 (June 1993), p. 112.

71 Donald K. Crone, "State, Social Elites, and Government Capacity in Southeast Asia," *World Politics*, vol. 40, no. 2 (January 1988), pp. 252–68; "States, Elites, and Social Welfare in Southeast Asia," *World Development*, vol. 21, no. 1 (1993), pp. 55–66.

72 Crone writes, "the state in Southeast Asia has been vital to both economic growth and political stability. Despite some liberal economic policies, the weight of state intervention has been heavy and consistent." "State, Social Elites, and Government Capacity," p. 268.

73 Ibid., pp. 260–61.

74 John Higley, Michael G. Burton, and G. Lowell Field, "Revolutions as Elite Transformations," paper presented American Sociological Association meeting, San Francisco, August 12, 1989.

75 Eva Etzioni-Halevy, *The Elite Connection: Problems and Potential of Western Democracy* (Cambridge: Polity Press, 1993), p. 25.

76 Robert D. Putnam, *The Comparative Study of Political Elites* (Englewood Cliffs: Prentice-Hall, 1976), pp. 121–22; Giuseppe Di Palma, *The Study of Conflict in Western Societies: A Critique of the End of Ideology* (Morristown: General Learning Press, 1973); G. Lowell Field and John Higley, *Elitism* (London: Routledge and Kegan Paul, 1980).

77 Eric A. Nordlinger, *Conflict Regulation in Divided Societies* (Cambridge: Harvard University Press, 1972); Arend Lijphart, *Democracy in Plural Societies: A Comparative Exploration* (New Haven: Yale University Press, 1977). For a recent discussion of elite cooperation amid divided ethnic constituencies in a variety of democratizing contexts, see Robert Hislope, "Ethnic Conflict and the 'Generosity Moment,'" *Journal of Democracy*, vol. 9, no. 1 (January 1998), pp. 140–54.

78 O'Donnell and Schmitter, "Tentative Conclusions," p. 19.

79 Ibid., p. 16.

80 Ibid., p. 21.

81 Etzioni-Halevy, *The Elite Connection*, especially Chapter 3.

82 Michael G. Burton, "Elite Settlements," *American Sociological Review*," vol. 52, no. 3 (June 1987), pp. 295–307; Terry Lynn Karl, "Petroleum and Political Pacts: The Transition to Democracy in Venezuela," in Guillermo O'Donnell *et al*, *Transitions from Authoritarian Rule*, Part 2, pp. 196–219; Giuseppe Di Palma, *To Craft Democracies: An Essay on Democratic Transitions* (Berkeley: University of California Press, 1990).

83 Huntington, *The Third Wave*, pp. 142–51.

84 Thomas S. Kuhn, *The Structure of Scientific Revolutions* (Chicago: University of Chicago Press, 1970).

85 Larry Diamond, *Developing Democracy: Toward Consolidation* (Baltimore: Johns Hopkins University Press, 1999), especially Chapter 2.

86 Linz and Stepan, *Problems of Democratic Transition and Consolidation*, Chapter Four.

87 O'Donnell and Schmitter, "Tentative Conclusions," p. 18.

88 For a discussion of the comparability of these countries in terms of their economic characteristics, see Alasdair Bowie and Danny Unger, *The Politics of Open Economies: Indonesia, Malaysia, the Philippines, and Thailand* (Cambridge: Cambridge University Press, 1997), pp. 14–16.

89 See Carl A. Trocki, ed., *Gangsters, Democracy, and the State in Southeast Asia* (Ithaca: SEAP, Cornell University, 1998).

90 For a concise overview of Southeast Asia from a democratic perspective, see Kevin Hewison, "Political Space in Southeast Asia: 'Asian-style' and Other Democracies," in Peter Burnell and Peter Calvert, eds., *The Resilience of Democracy: Persistent Practice, Durable Idea* (London: Frank Cass, 1999), pp. 224–45.

91 Emmerson, "Region and Recalcitrance."

92 Carl A. Trocki, "Democracy and the State in Southeast Asia," in Trocki, ed., *Gangsters, Democracy, and the State*, p. 8.

2 Indonesia

1 R. William Liddle, "Suharto's Indonesia: Personal Rule and Political Institutions," *Pacific Affairs*, no. 58 (Spring 1985), pp. 68–90.

2 Harold Crouch, "Patrimonialism and Military Rule in Indonesia," *World Politics*, vol. 31, no. 4 (July, 1979), pp. 571–87.

3 See Dwight King, "Indonesia's New Order as a Bureaucratic Polity, a Neopatrimonialist Regime or Bureaucratic Authoritarian Regime: What Difference Does it Make?" in Benedict Anderson and Audrey Kahin, eds., *Interpreting Indonesian Politics: Thirteen Contributions to the Debate* (Ithaca: Cornell Modern Indonesian Project, 1982), pp. 104–16.

4 Harold Crouch, "Democratic Prospects in Indonesia," in David Bourchier and John Legge, eds., *Democracy in Indonesia: 1950s and 1990s* (Clayton: Centre of Southeast Asian Studies, Monash University, 1994), p. 123.

5 R.William Liddle, *Leadership and Culture in Indonesian Politics* (St. Leonards: Allen and Unwin, 1996), p. 13.

6 Robert Elson, *The Tragedy of Modern Indonesian History* (Nathan: Griffith University inaugural professorial lectures, 1998), pp. 6–7.

7 See M.C. Ricklefs, *A History of Modern Indonesia* (Houndmills: Macmillan Education, 1981), pp. 225–44.

8 Herbert Feith, *The Indonesian Elections of 1955* (Ithaca: SEAP, Cornell University, 1971).

9 The classic account of Indonesia's Guided Democracy period, as well as the origins of the New Order remains Harold Crouch, *The Army and Politics in Indonesia* (Ithaca: Cornell University Press, 1978).

10 Damien Kingsbury, *The Politics of Indonesia* (Melbourne: Oxford University Press, 1998), p. 60.

11 Much uncertainty persists over the so-called "coup attempt." For an assessment of the different accounts, see Crouch, *The Army and Politics*, Chapter 4. "Gestapu" was an acronym coined later by New Order ideologues that meant

30th of September Movement (*Gerakan Tigapuluh Setember*), the forces that had killed the generals.

12 See Robert Cribb, ed., *The Indonesian Killings of 1965–1966* (Clayton: Center of Southeast Asian Studies, Monash University, 1991).

13 See John Bresnan, *Managing Indonesia: The Modern Political Economy* (New York: Columbia University Press, 1993), p. 145.

14 Jamie Mackie, "Indonesia: Economic Growth and Depoliticization," in James Morley, ed., *Driven by Growth: Political Change in the Asia-Pacific Region* (Armonk: M.E. Sharpe, 1993), p. 80.

15 For a good account of mismanagement in Pertamina, see Bresnan, *Managing Indonesia*, pp. 164–93.

16 The most concise listing of Suharto's powers as president are found in Richard Robison, "Indoneisa: Tensions in State and Regime," in Kevin Hewison, Richard Robison, and Garry Rodan, eds., *Southeast Asia in the 1990s: Authoritarianism, Democracy, and Capitalism* (St. Leonards: Allen and Unwin, 1993), pp. 39–74.

17 For extensive analyses of Team 10's activities, see Jeffrey A. Winters, *Power in Motion: Capital, Mobility, and the Indonesian State* (Ithaca: Cornell University Press, 1996).

18 "Yayasan Menyimpang, Soeharto Dijerat," *Forum Keadilan* (Jakarta), vol. 7, no. 18 (December 1998), pp. 82–85.

19 See Robert Cribb, *Gangsters and Revolutionaries: The Jakarta People's Militia and the Indonesian Revolution, 1945–49* (Honolulu: University of Hawaii Press, 1991).

20 Bresnan, *Managing Indonesia*, p. 209.

21 For a concise overview of economic development under the New Order, see Hal Hill, "The Economy," in Hal Hill, ed., *Indonesia's New Order: The Dynamics of Socio-economic Transformation* (St. Leonards: Allen and Unwin, 1994), pp. 54–122.

22 See Richard Robison, *Indonesia: The Rise of Capital* (Sydney: Allen and Unwin, 1986), and *Power and Economy in Suharto's Indonesia* (Manila: Journal of Contemporary Asia Publishers, 1990); Michael R.J. Vatikiotis, *Indonesian Politics Under Suharto* (London: Routledge, 1993), Chapter 8; and Adam Schwarz, *A Nation in Waiting: Indonesia in the 1990s* (St. Leonards: Allen and Unwin, 1994), Chapter 6.

23 Andrew MacIntyre, "Politics and the Reorientation of Economic Policy in Indonesia," in Andrew J. MacIntyre and Kanishka Jayasuriya, eds., *The Dynamics of Economic Policy Reform in South-east Asia and the South-west Pacific* (Singapore: Oxford University Press, 1992), pp. 142–43.

24 Schwarz, *A Nation in Waiting*, p. 28. See also Christopher Barr, "Bob Hasan, the Rise of Apkindo, and the Shifting Dynamics of Control in Indonesia's Timber Sector," *Indonesia*, no. 65 (Cornell SEAP: April 1998), pp. 1–36.

25 Schwarz, *A Nation in Waiting*, p. 99.

26 Ibid., pp. 153–57.

27 Richard Robison, "Politics and Markets in Indonesia's Post-oil Era," in Garry Rodan, Kevin Hewison, and Richard Robison, eds., *The Political Economy of Southeast Asia*, p. 45. However, despite these opportunities, the Suharto family seems not to have exploited them effectively, thus racking up much less than the $30 billion they were estimated at the time to have held. See "Suharto Family Missed Out on a Fortune," *Asian Wall Street Journal*, January 4, 1999, p. 1.

28 For good overviews of New Order legitimation, see Micahel van Langenberg, "The New Order State: Language, Ideology, Hegemony," and David Reeve,

"The Corporatist State: The Case of *Golkar*," both in Arief Budiman, ed., *State and Civil Society in Indonesia* (Clayton: Center of Southeast Asian Studies, Monash University, 1992), pp. 121–49 and pp. 151–76. See also Niels Mulder, "The Ideology of Javanese-Indonesian Leadership," in Hans Antlov and Sven Cederroth, eds., *Leadership on Java: Gentle Hints, Authoritarian Rule* (Richmond: Curzon Press, 1994), pp. 57–72.

29 R. William Liddle, "A Useful Fiction: Democratic Legitimation in New Order Indonesia," in R.H. Taylor, ed., *The Politics of Elections in Southeast Asia* (Cambridge: Cambridge University Press, 1996), p. 40.

30 Richard Tanter, "The Totalitarian Ambition: Intelligence Organizations in the Indonesian State," in Arief Budiman, ed., *State and Civil Society in Indonesia* (Clayton: Southeast Asia Studies Center, Monash University, 1992), p. 214.

31 Tanter, "The Totalitarian Ambition," p. 220.

32 See Kingsbury, *The Politics of Indonesia*, Chapter 8.

33 For a discussion of the legal restrictions on NGOs, see Philip J. Eldridge, *Non-government Organizations and Democratic Participation in Indonesia* (Kuala Lumpur: Oxford University Press, 1995), Chapter 3.

34 Andrew MacIntyre, *Business and Politics in Indonesia* (North Sydney, Allen and Unwin, 1991), p. 25.

35 Stefan Eklof, "The 1997 General Election in Indonesia," *Asian Survey*, vol. 37, no. 12 (December 1997), p. 1191.

36 Ed Aspinall, "What Price Victory? The 1997 Elections," *Inside Indonesia* (July–September 1997), pp. 4.

37 Stefan Eklof, "The 1997 General Election," p. 1192.

38 Bresnan, *Managing Indonesia*, p. 221.

39 There are reasons for thinking that these attacks were mounted by the military in order to discredit Islamic forces. Robert Cribb, personal communication.

40 Douglas E. Ramage, *Politics in Indonesia: Democracy, Islam, and the Ideology of Tolerance* (London: Routledge: 1995), p. 95.

41 See Ed Aspinall, "What Happened Before the Riots," *Inside Indonesia* (October–December 1996), pp. 4–8.

42 Ed Aspinall, "What Price Victory? The 1997 Elections," *Inside Indonesia* (July–September 1997), pp. 2–4.

43 Human Rights Watch Asia, "The Horror in Kalimantan," *Inside Indonesia* (July–September 1997), pp. 9–12.

44 Eklof, "The 1997 General Election," p. 1189, fn. 21.

45 In January, Apkindo ordered its member companies to deposit Rp50,000 (US$5) with the organization for every cubic meter of plywood they exported. It demanded also that exports be shipped through Karana Lines, controlled by Bob Hasan. *The Sunday Observer*, March 22, 1998, p. 3.

46 Hadi Soesastro, interview, March 10, 1998. Hadi further characterized Suharto's new recklessness as "gambling the whole thing." Center for Strategic and International Studies, Jakarta.

47 *Far Eastern Economic Review* (hereafter *FEER*), January 21, 1999, p. 59.

48 Guillermo O'Donnell and Philippe Schmitter, "Tentative Conclusions About Uncertain Democracies," in Guillermo O'Donnell, Philippe Schmitter, and Laurence Whitehead, eds., Transitions from Authoritarian Rule: Prospects for Democracy, Part 4 (Baltimore: Johns Hopkins University Press, 1986), p. 19.

49 Stephen Haggard and Robert R. Kaufman, *The Political Economy of Democratic Transitions* (Princeton: Princeton University Press, 1995), p. 32.

50 See Margaret Scott, "Indonesia Reborn?" *New York Review of Books*, August 13, 1998, pp. 43–48.

51 Ibid., p. 43.

52 *FEER*, January 8, 1998, p. 18.

53 *Jakarta Post*, December 2, 1997, p. 12. Djiteng's outrage was sparked by Suharto's decision in early November 1997 to reauthorize eight private power projects that two months earlier been put under review. One power station, Tanjung Jati A, involved Suharto's middle daughter, "Titiek," while another, Tanjung Jati B, involved eldest daughter, "Tutut." Java's grid was already 50 per cent oversupplied, however. Thus, the "PLN faced the prospect of choking to financial death on excess capacity." *FEER*, December 4, 1997, p. 79. See also "PLN yang Bangkrut Disetrum Intervensi," *Forum Keadilan*, December 29, 1997, pp. 12–14.

54 *Jakarta Post*, December 2, 1997, p. 12.

55 See "Nyanyian 'Suksesi' dari Luar Gelanggang," *Forum Keadilan*, January 26, 1998, p. 15.

56 *Forum Keadilan*, January 26, 1998, p. 16.

57 Samuel P. Huntington, *The Third Wave: Democratization in the Late Twentieth Century* (Norman: University of Oklahoma, 1991), p. 144.

58 O'Donnell and Schmitter, "Tentative Conclusions," p. 27.

59 Interview with U.S. embassy official, Jakarta, March 19, 1998. For a profile of Arifin, see *Forum Keadilan*, May 23, 1999, pp. 36–40.

60 "Merancang Kudeta di Pertemuan Terbuka," *Forum Keadilan*, March 23, 1998, p. 22. See also *FEER*, April 2, 1998, p. 23.

61 *FEER*, February 19, 1998, pp. 46–50. See also "Kontroversi Sofjan Setelah Ledakan," *Forum Keadilan*, February 23, 1998, pp. 12–17.

62 *FEER*, February 19, 1998, p. 50.

63 *FEER*, March 5, 1998, pp. 18–19.

64 *Jakarta Post*, March 16, 1998, p. 7.

65 Ibid., p. 1.

66 For a good discussion of student communication, mobilizing, food distribution, and the like, see "Romantika Laskar, Penngerak Moral," *Forum Keadilan*, January 11, 1999, pp. 40–44.

67 *Jakarta Post*, March 17, 1998, p. 2.

68 O'Donnell and Schmitter, "Tentative Conclusions," pp. 48–49.

69 Ibid., p. 48.

70 *Jakarta Post*, March 14, 1998, p. 2.

71 See interview with Karlina Leksono, *Detektif dan Romantika*, March 14, 1998, pp. 34–37.

72 *Jakarta Post*, March 13, 1998, p. 2.

73 *FEER*, May 14, 1998, p. 22.

74 Ibid., p. 21.

75 O'Donnell and Schmitter, p. 54.

76 Marcus Mietzner, "From Suharto to Habibie: The Indonesian Armed Forces and Political Islam During the Transition," in Geoff Forrester, ed., *Post-Soeharto Indonesia: Renewal or Chaos* (Bathurst: Crawford House Publishing, 1999), pp. 78–79.

77 Susan Berfield and Dwi Loveard, "Ten Days that Shook Indonesia," July 24, 1998, *Asiaweek On-line*, at http://www.pathfinder.com/asiaweek. John McBeth, "Shadow Play," *FEER*, July 23, 1998, pp. 23–27. Eyewitness accounts are reported in *Tajuk* (Jakarta), September 1–3, 1998, pp. 23–27.

78 In an interview in early May, Amien Rais suggested that the military would never shoot student demonstrators: "It would be the most stupid act imaginable. The reaction from the people would be huge and devastating. It would give a

tremendous push to the people to further resist the government." *FEER*, May 14, 1998, p. 28.

79 Michael Vatikiotis and Adam Schwarz, "A Nation Awakes," *FEER*, June 4, 1998, p. 22.

80 John McBeth, *FEER* correspondent in Jakarta, "Indonesia Up-date Conference," Australian National University, September 25–26, 1998, Canberra.

81 Haggard and Kaufman, *The Political Economy*, p. 7.

82 See Ed Aspinall, "Opposition and Elite Conflict in the Fall of Suharto," in Geoff Forrester and R.J. May, eds., *The Fall of Soeharto* (Bathurst: Crawford House Publishing, 1998), pp. 130–53. On transition paths, see Huntington, *The Third Wave*, Chapter 3.

83 Huntington, *The Third Wave*, p. 276.

84 Harold Crouch, "Wiranto and Habibie: Military-Civilian Relations since May 1998," in Arief Budiman, Barbara Hatley, and Damien Kingsbury, eds., *Reformasi: Crisis and Change in Indonesia* (Clayton: Monash Asia Institute, 1999), p. 135.

85 See Stefan Ekof, "Megamania," *Inside Indonesia* (January–March 1999), pp. 18–19. Mega's party faction came to be labeled "PDI *Perjuangan*" (PDI Struggle).

86 See Irawati, "Bersikap Lunak kepada Debitor Kakap" ("Soft Attitude Toward Large Debtors"), *Forum Keadilan*, May 16, 1999, p. 71; and Dan Murphy, "Play Now, Pay Later," *FEER*, May 27, 1999, pp. 40–41.

87 This section borrows from William F. Case, "Revisiting Elites, Transitions and Founding Elections: An Unexpected Caller from Indonesia," *Democratization*, vol. 7, no. 4 (winter 2000), pp. 51–80.

88 Guillermo O'Donnell, "Delegative Democracy," in Larry Diamond and Marc F. Plattner, eds., *The Global Resurgence of Democracy* (Baltimore: Johns Hopkins University Press, 1996), pp. 94–108.

89 See Juan Linz and Arturo Valenzuela, eds., *The Failure of Presidential Democracy* (Baltimore: Johns Hopkins University Press, 1994).

90 Crouch, "Wiranto and Habibie," p. 140.

91 National Democratic Institute Assessment Team, *The New Legal Framework for Elections in Indonesia* (National Democratic Institute for International Affairs), February 23, 1999.

92 Adam Przeworski, "Some Problems in the Study of the Transition to Democracy," in O'Donnell and Schmitter, eds., *Transitions*, Part 3, esp. pp. 58–61.

93 The main criterion was that qualifying parties should have branches in at least nine provinces, thus discouraging particularistic regional parties (Sumatra has eight). Robert Cribb, personal communication.

94 Lea Jellinek and Bambang Rustanto, "People Want New Leader Who Cares," *Jakarta Post*, June 17, 1999, p. 4.

95 O'Donnell and Schmitter, "Tentative Conclusions," p. 62.

96 John McBeth, "Balancing Act," *FEER*, November 4, 1999, p. 19.

97 See Larry Diamond, *Developing Democracy: Toward Consolidation* (Baltimore and London: Johns Hopkins University Press, 1999), pp. 112–16.

98 Larry Diamond and Svetlana Taslik, "Size and Democracy: The Case for Decentralization," in Larry Diamond, *Developing Democracy: Toward Consolidation* (Baltimore: Johns Hopkins University Press, 1999), pp. 117–60.

99 See *Tempo*, July 31-August 6, 2000, pp. 18–19; August 7–13, 2000, pp. 20–26; October 9–15, 2000, pp. 20–22.

100 Juan J. Linz and Alfred Stepan, *Problems of Democratic Transition and Consolidation: Southern Europe, South America, and Post-Communist Europe* (Baltimore: Johns Hopkins University Press, 1996), pp. 66, 88, 115.

101 See *Indonesia Briefing, Indonesia's Maluku Crisis: The Issues* (Jakarta/Brussels: International Crisis Group, July 19, 2000), pp. 3, 7–8.

102 *Tempo*, September 24, 2000, p. 22.

103 *Tempo*, September 10, 2000, p. 31.

104 *Tempo*, July 30, 2000, p. 21.

105 For an overview, see Foreign Affairs, Defence and Trade Group, *Indonesia's Future Prospects: Separatism, Decentralisation and the Survival of the Unitary State*, Current Affairs Brief No. 17 (Canberra: Department of the Parliamentary Library, Information and Research Services, 1999–2000).

106 *Indonesia's Crisis: Chronic But Not Acute*, (Jakarta/Brussels: International Crisis Group, May 31, 2000), pp. 12–17.

107 Personal communication, R.E. Elson, August 30, 2000.

108 *FEER*, October 19, 2000, pp. 76–79.

109 *Tempo*, September 17, 2000, pp. 116–18.

110 Ibid., p. 117.

111 Marcus Mietzner, *Abdurrahman's Indonesia: Political Conflict and Institutional Crisis*, unpublished manuscript.

112 Ibid., p. 17.

113 R. William Liddle, "Pemilihan Presiden dan Primordialism" ("Presidential Elections and Primordialism"), *Tempo*, August 27, 2000, p. 52.

114 Calvin Sims, "U.S. Braces for Trouble in Indonesia as Relations Rupture," *New York Times on the Web*, http://www.nytimes.com, posted October 30, 2000.

3 Singapore

1 W.G. Huff, "Turning the Corner in Singapore's Developmental State?" *Asian Survey*, vol. 34, no. 2 (March/April), 1999, p. 215.

2 See Stephan Haggard, *Pathways from the Periphery: The Politics of Growth in the Newly Industrializing Countries* (Ithaca: Cornell University Press, 1990), pp. 114–15.

3 See William F. Case, "Can the 'Halfway House' Stand? Semidemocracy and Elite Theory in Three Southeast Asian Countries," *Comparative Politics*, vol. 28, no. 4 (July 1996), pp. 437–64. See also Chan Heng Chee, "Democracy: Evolution and Implementation, An Asian Perspective," in Robert Bartley, Chan Heng Chee, Samuel P. Huntington, and Shijuro Ogata, *Democracy and Capitalism: Asian and American Perspectives* (Singapore: Institute of Southeast Asian Studies, 1993), pp. 1–26.

4 Natasha Hamilton-Hart, "The Singapore State Revisited," *Pacific Review*, vol. 13, no. 2 (2000), pp. 195–216.

5 For a good summary discussion of insulation and coherence as the twin dimensions of state strength, see Andrew MacIntyre, "Business, Government and Development: Northeast and Southeast Asian Comparisons," in Andrew MacIntyre, ed., *Business and Government in Industrialising Asia* (St. Leonards: 1994), pp. 1–28.

6 "Economic Indicators," *Far Eastern Economic Review*, April 15, 1999, pp. 88–89.

7 Garry Rodan, *The Political Economy of Singapore's Industrialization* (Petaling Jaya, Malaysia: Forum, 1991), pp. 71–72.

8 Ooi Can Seng, "Singapore," in Wolfgang Sachsenroder and Ulrike E. Frings, eds., *Political Party Systems and Democratic Development in East and Southeast Asia, Volume 1: Southeast Asia* (Aldershot: Ashgate, 1998), p. 363.

9 James Cotton, "Political Innovation in Singapore: The Presidency, the Leadership and the Party," in Garry Rodan, ed., *Singapore Changes Guard: Social, Political and Economic Directions in the 1990s* (Melbourne: Longman Cheshire, 1993), pp. 10–11.

10 Hamilton-Hart, "The Singapore State Revisited," pp. 206–8.

11 Garry Rodan, "Singapore: Economic Diversification and Social Divisions," in Garry Rodan, Kevin Hewison, and Richard Robison, eds., *The Political Economy of South-East Asia: An Introduction* (Melbourne: Oxford University Press 1997), p. 161.

12 Garry Rodan, "Preserving the One-Party State in Contemporary Singapore," in Kevin Hewison, Richard Robison, and Garry Rodan, eds., *Southeast Asia in the 1990s: Authoritarianism, Democracy, and Capitalism* (St. Leonards: Allen and Unwin, 1993), p. 100; and Jon S.T. Quah, "Public Housing," in Jon S.T. Quah, Chan Heng Chee, and Seah Chee Meow, eds., *Government and Politics of Singapore* (Singapore: Oxford University Press, 1985), p. 248.

13 Chris Leggett writes, "Non-confrontational, if not harmonious, labor-management relations may be said to have been achieved in Singapore by the end of the 1970s." "Singapore's Industrial Relations in the 1990s," in Rodan, ed., *Singapore Changes Guard*, p. 61.

14 David Brown, *The State and Ethnic Politics in South-East Asia* (London: Routledge, 1996), pp. 67–78.

15 Chua Beng Huat, "Racial Singaporeans: Absence after the Hyphen," in Joel S. Kahn, ed., *Southeast Asian Identities* (Singapore: Institute of Southeast Asian Studies, 1998), p. 37.

16 Linda Lim, Pang Eng Fong, and Ronald Findlay, "Singapore," in Ronald Findlay and Stanislaw Wellisz, eds., *Five Small Open Economies* (New York: Oxford University Press, 1993), p. 104.

17 Chua Beng Huat, "Racial Singaporeans," p. 39.

18 Asian democracy spawned a large literature during the mid-1990s. For a critique of the concept, see Yung-Myung Kim, "Asian-Style Democracy: A Critique from East Asia," *Asian Survey*, vol. 37, no. 12 (December 1997), pp. 1119–34.

19 Garry Rodan, "State-Society Relations and Political Opposition in Singapore," in Garry Rodan, ed., *Political Oppositions in Industrialising Asia* (London: Routledge, 1996), pp. 106–14.

20 David Martin Jones, *Political Development in Pacific Asia* (Cambridge: Polity Press, 1997), p. 144.

21 Garry Rodan, "The Internet and Political Control in Singapore," *Political Science Quarterly*, vol. 113, no. 1 (Spring 1998), p. 70.

22 Ooi, "Singapore," p. 392.

23 Ibid., p. 374.

24 Garry Rodan, "Class Transformations and Political Tensions in Singapore's Development," in Richard Robison and David S.G. Goodman, eds., *The New Rich in Asia: Mobile Phones, McDonalds and Middle-class Revolution* (London: Routledge, 1996), p. 26.

25 Ooi, "Singapore", p. 366.

26 Haggard, *Pathways from the Periphery*," pp. 114–15.

27 See Dietrich Rueschemeyer, Evelyne Huber Stephens, and John D. Stephens, *Capitalist Democracy and Development* (Cambridge: Polity Press, 1992), pp. 50, 59.

28 Rodan, "State-Society Relations," p. 102.
29 Ooi, "Singapore", p. 367.
30 See Rodan, "One-Party State," pp. 87–91.
31 *Straits Times*, September 16, 1995, quoted in Ooi, "Singapore," p. 388.
32 Garry Rodan, "Elections Without Representation: The Singapore Experience under the PAP," in R.H. Taylor, ed., *The Politics of Elections in Southeast Asia* (Cambridge: Cambridge University Press, 1996), p. 83.
33 Ooi, "Singapore", p. 355.
34 *Straits Times*, January 2, 1997, quoted in Ooi, "Singapore", p. 394.
35 Ooi, "Singapore", pp. 386, 386.
36 Rodan, "One-Party State," p. 84.
37 "Singapore's Voters Get a Choice: Slums or the Ruling Party," *New York Times*, December 31, 1996, quoted in Huff, "Turning the Corner," p. 234.
38 N. Ganesan, "Entrenching a City-State's Dominant Party System," in *Southeast Asian Affairs 1998* (Singapore: Institute of Southeast Asian Studies, 1998), pp. 23–31.
39 Garry Rodan, "Singapore: Emerging Tensions in the 'Dictatorship of the Middle Class,'" *Pacific Review*, no. 5 (1992), p. 377.
40 Garry Rodan, "Introduction: Challenges for the New Guard and Directions in the 1990s," in Rodan, ed., *Singapore Changes Guard*, p. xix.
41 Cotton, "Political Innovation," p. 10.
42 Rodan, "Introduction," pp. xx–xi.
43 David Martin Jones and David Brown, "Singapore and the Myth of the Liberalizing Middle Class," *Pacific Review*, vol. 7, no. 1 (1994), pp. 79–87.
44 Cho-oon Khong, "Singapore: Political Legitimacy Through Managing Conformity," in Muthiah Alagappa, ed., *Political Legitimacy in Southeast Asia: The Quest for Moral Authority* (Stanford: Stanford University Press, 1995), p. 135.
45 Huff, "Turning the Corner," p. 239.
46 "Asian Economic System Still Strong," *Straits Times Weekly*, December 20, 1997, quoted in Huff, "Turning the Corner," p. 240.
47 Rodan, "The Internet and Political Control," p. 64.

4 Malaysia

1 Stefan Eklof, "The 1997 General Election in Indonesia," *Asian Survey*, vol. 37, no. 12 (December 1997), p. 1190.
2 See Donald M. Nonini, *British Colonial Rule and the Resistance of the Malay Peasantry, 1900–1957* (New Haven: Yale University Southeast Asia Studies, 1992), especially Chapter 5.
3 Jomo Kwame Sundaram, *A Question of Class: Capital, the State, and Uneven Development in Malaya* (New York: Monthly Review Press, 1988), pp. 169–70.
4 Ibid., p. 145.
5 See Rajah Rasiah, "Class, Ethnicity and Economic Development in Malaysia," in Garry Rodan, Kevin Hewison, and Richard Robison, eds., *The Political Economy of Southeast Asia: An Introduction* (Melbourne: Oxford University Press, 1997), pp. 121–47.
6 For one of the fiercest critiques, see Colin Abraham, "Manipulation and Management of Racial and Ethnic Groups in Colonial Malaysia: A Case Study of Ideological Domination and Control," in Raymond Lee, ed., *Ethnicity and Ethnic Relations in Malaysia* (Urbana-Champaign: University of Illinois, 1986).
7 See David Brown, *The State and Ethnic Politics in South-East Asia* (London: Routledge 1994), pp. 205–15.

8 Alvin Rabushka and Kenneth Shepsle, *Politics in Plural Societies: A Theory of Democratic Instability* (Columbus: Charles E. Merrill, 1972).

9 Jomo K.S., "Elections' Janus Face: Limitations and Potential in Malaysia," in Robert Taylor, ed., *The Politics of Elections in Southeast Asia* (Cambridge: Cambridge University Press, 1996), p. 92.

10 See William Case, *Elites and Regimes in Malaysia: Revising a Consociational Democracy* (Clayton: Monash Asia Institute, 1996), pp. 74–84.

11 Gordon Means, *Malaysian Politics* (London: Hodder and Stoughton, 1976), pp. 125–34.

12 Samuel P. Huntington, *Political Order in Changing Societies* (New Haven and London: Yale University Press, 1968).

13 *Straits Times*, May 9, 1969, quoted in Leon Comber, *13 May 1969: A Historical Survey of Sino-Malay Relations* (Kuala Lumpur: Heinemann Asia, 1983), p. 64; and David Brown, *The State and Ethnic Politics in South-East Asia* (London: Routledge, 1994). p. 239.

14 The best account is provided by Karl von Vorys, *Democracy without Consensus: Communalism and Political Stability in Malaysia* (Princeton: Princeton University Press, 1975).

15 Jomo, *A Question of Class*, p. 252.

16 Quoted in von Vorys, *Democracy without Consensus*, pp. 373–74.

17 See Diane K. Mauzy, *Barisan Nasional: Coalition Government in Malaysia* (Petaling Jaya: Marican and Sons, 1983).

18 John Funston, *Malay Politics in Malaysia: A Study of the United Malays National Organization and Party Islam* (Kuala Lumpur: Heinemann Educational Books, 1980), p. 89.

19 Jomo, *A Question of Class*, p. 254.

20 Brown, *The State and Ethnic Politics*, p. 235.

21 Harold Crouch, *Government and Society in Malaysia* (Ithaca: Cornell University Press, 1996), p. 163. In 1978, the *bumiputera* quota was reduced to 65.5 per cent.

22 Crouch, "Government and Society," pp. 208–11.

23 James V. Jesudason, *Ethnicity and the Economy: The State, Chinese Business, and Multinationals in Malaysia* (Singapore: Oxford University Press, 1989), p. 160.

24 Zakaria Haji Ahmad writes, "[T]he post-1971 Malaysian political system is one in which there is political dominance by one communal group but also room for the accommodation of other communal interests." "Malaysia: Quasi Democracy in a Divided Society," in Larry Diamond, Juan J. Linz, and Seymour Martin Lipset, eds., *Democracy in Developing Countries: Asia* (Boulder: Lynne Rienner, 1989), p. 372.

25 Quoted in Zakaria, "Malaysia," p. 349.

26 Larry Diamond, *Developing Democracy: Toward Consolidation* (Baltimore: Johns Hopkins University Press, 1999), p. 228.

27 The phrase is Chandra Muzaffar's.

28 This section borrows extensively from William Case, "The 1996 UMNO Assembly Election: 'Two for the Show,'" *Pacific Affairs*, vol. 70, no. 3 (Fall 1997), pp. 393–411.

29 Jaehyon Lee, "The UMNO 2000 Party Elections: Stability and the Post-Mahathir Era," *Asiaview* (July 2000), p. 4.

30 A high-level UMNO official and cabinet minister stated that upon becoming a branch leader, "one comes close to power. Party dignitaries passing through call upon you, sit next to you at dinner, etc. [But for divisional heads,] the sky's the limit." Interview, Kuala Lumpur, January 1990.

31 There are a total of 44 seats in the UMNO Supreme Council, with the 19 non-elected seats either *ex officio* ones or appointed by the party president. There are also five vice-presidencies in the party, three of them elected and two held as *ex officio* positions by the leaders of the UMNO Youth and *Wanita*.

32 Crouch, *Government and Society*, p. 39.

33 Symbolized, perhaps, by the Petronas twin towers, brooding on K.L.'s skyline and linked critically by a "skybridge." For background on the formation of the *UMNO Baru*, see Gordon P. Means, *Malaysian Politics: The Second Generation* (Singapore: Oxford University Press, 1991), Chapters 7–8.

34 *Far Eastern Economic Review* (hereafter *FEER*), April 25, 1996, p. 24.

35 See the contrasting interpretations made by Harold Crouch, "Authoritarian Trends, the UMNO Split and the Limits to State Power," and Khoo Kay Jin, "The Grand Vision: Mahathir and Modernization," in Loh Kok Wah and Joel Kahn, eds., *Fragmented Vision: Culture and Politics in Contemporary Malaysia* (Sydney: Allen and Unwin, 1992), pp. 21–43 and 44–76. See also James V. Jesudason, who, while analyzing Malaysia's broader coalition of government forces, asserts strongly the UMNO's "syncretic" ideological content. "The Syncretic State and the Structuring of Oppositional Politics in Malaysia," in Garry Rodan, ed., *Political Oppositions in Industrializing Asia* (London: Routledge, 1996), pp. 128–60.

36 Gordon P. Means writes that the "UMNO remains the most vital and democratic party in either Malaysia or Singapore." "Soft Authoritarianism in Malaysia and Singapore," *Journal of Democracy*, vol. 7, no. 4 (1996), p. 104.

37 Harold Crouch, "The UMNO Crisis," in Harold Crouch, Lee Kam Hing, and Michael Ong, eds., *Malaysian Politics and the 1978 Election* (Kuala Lumpur: Oxford University Press, 1980), p. 17.

38 For good accounts of the 1987 UMNO general assembly election, see Shamsul A.B., "The Battle Royal: The UMNO Elections of 1987," in M. Ayoob and Ng Chee Yuen, eds., *Southeast Asian Affairs 1988* (Singapore: Institute of Southeast Asian Studies, 1988), and Khoo Kay Jin, "The Grand Vision: Mahathir and Modernisation," in Kahn and Loh, eds., *Fragmented Vision*, pp. 44–76.

39 The best analysis is *Tangled Web: Dissent, Deterrence, and the 27th October 1987 Crackdown* (Haymarket: Committee Against Repression in the Pacific and Asia, 1988).

40 For details on the desperate bid to stop the high court's ordering new UMNO elections, see *Asiaweek*, February 19, 1988, pp. 8–10.

41 A thorough overview is provided by Mohamed Salleh Abas (with K. Das), *May Day for Justice: The Lord President's Version* (Kuala Lumpur: Magnus, 1989).

42 See Jomo K.S., ed., *Privatizing Malaysia: Rents, Rhetoric, Realities* (Boulder: Westview, 1995).

43 *New Straits Times* (hereafter *NST*), November 4, 1993, p. 2.

44 Sanusi Junid, quoted in *New Sunday Times*, November 7, 1993, pp. 1–3.

45 The opposition normally wins 30–40 per cent of the vote, translating into roughly 20 per cent of the seats.

46 See Harold Crouch, "Malaysia: Do Elections Make a Difference?" in R.H. Taylor, ed., *The Politics of Elections in Southeast Asia* (Cambridge University Press: 1996), pp. 114–35. Rural development did not include land reform, however, for fear of antagonizing Malay landowners in the UMNO.

47 Harold Crouch, "Malaysia: Neither Authoritarian nor Democratic," in Kevin Hewison, Richard Robison, and Garry Rodan, eds., *Southeast Asia in the 1990s: Authoritarianism, Democracy, and Capitalism* (St. Leonards: Allen and Unwin, 1993), pp. 138–39.

48 Edmund Terence Gomez, "Malaysia," in Wolfgang Sachsenroder and Ulrike E. Frings, eds., *Political Party Systems and Democratic Development in East and Southeast Asia, Volume I: Southeast Asia* (Aldershot: Ashgate 1998), p. 267.

49 Gomez, "Malaysia," p. 266.

50 Harold Crouch, "The Politics of Economic Growth and Social Restructuring in a Communally Divided Society" (unpublished manuscript).

51 For a good overview, see James Chin, "Politics of Federal Intervention in Malaysia, with Reference to Sarawak, Sabah and Kelantan," *Journal of Commonwealth and Comparative Politics*, vol. 35, no. 2 (July 1997), pp. 96–120.

52 Probably the best account of this episode is offered by Muhammad Kamlin, "The Storm before the Deluge: The Kelantan Prelude to the 1978 General Election," in Crouch, Lee, and Ong, eds., *Malaysian Politics*, pp. 37–68.

53 Jomo, "Elections' Janus Face," p. 91.

54 Gordon P. Means, "Malaysia," in Robert N. Kearney, ed., *Politics and Modernization in South and Southeast Asia* (New York: John Wiley and Sons, 1975), p. 167.

55 Ibid., p. 170.

56 Hari Singh, "Tradition, UMNO and Political Succession in Malaysia," *Third World Quarterly*, vol. 19, no. 2 (1998), p. 243.

57 Bridget Welsh, "Attitudes Toward Democracy in Malaysia: Challenges to the Regime?" *Asian Survey*, vol. 36, no. 9 (September 1996), pp. 882–903.

58 Jesudason, "The Syncretic State," pp. 150 and 153.

59 For a thorough analysis of Malaysia's increasingly vital civil society, see Meredith L. Weiss, *The Politics of Protest: Civil Society, Coalition-Building, and Political Change in Malaysia*, Ph.D. thesis, Yale University, September 2001.

60 Jesudason, "The Syncretic State," p. 151.

61 Ibid., p. 144.

62 Rajah Rasiah, "Free Trade Zones and Industrial Development in Malaysia," in Jomo K.S., ed., *Industrializing Malaysia: Policy, Performance, Prospects* (London: Routledge, 1993), pp. 130–31.

63 K.S. Jomo and Ahmad Shabery Cheek, "Malaysia's Islamic Movements," in Kahn and Loh, eds., *Fragmented Vision*, p. 99.

64 Ibid.

65 For a good account, see David Camroux, "State Responses to Islamic Resurgence in Malaysia: Accommodation, Co-option, and Confrontation," *Asian Survey*, vol 36, no. 9 (September 1996), esp. pp. 863–65.

66 This section borrows from William Case, "Politics Beyond Anwar: What's New?" *Asian Journal of Political Science*, vol. 7, no. 1 (June 1999), pp. 1–19.

67 Edmund Terence Gomez and Jomo K.S., *Malaysia's Political Economy: Politics, Patronage, and Profits* (Cambridge: Cambridge University Press, 1997), p. 99.

68 Ibid., p. 112.

69 Ibid., p. 96.

70 For an excellent attempt to disaggregate Anwar's different motivations in confronting Mahathir, see Hari Singh, "Democratization or Oligarchic Restructuring? The Politics of Reform in Malaysia," *Government and Opposition*, vol. 35, no. 4 (2000), pp. 520–46.

71 For a concise discussion of proposed bail-outs during Malaysia's economic crisis, see Stephan Haggard, *The Political Economy of the Asian Financial Crisis* (Washington DC: Institute or International Economics, 2000), pp. 162–71.

72 *Business Week*, November 9, 1998, p. 26.

73 Ibid., p. 28. Anwar's notion of "creative destruction" paralleled the insights of Haggard and Kaufman in "crisis transitions," ones in which "economic circumstances provide opportunities for executives to seize the initiative and launch wide-ranging economic reforms." Stephen Haggard and Robert R. Kaufman, *The Political Economy of Democratic Transitions* (Cambridge: Cambridge University Press, 1995), p. 14.

74 Jeffrey Sachs, "Missing Pieces," *FEER*, February 25, 1999, p. 11.

75 *Business Week*, November 9, 1998, p. 29.

76 Santah Oorjitham, "Who's Who on the List," *Asiaweek On-line*, July 3, 1998 issue, http://www.pathfiner.com/asiaweek. The complete lists were made available at this site.

77 *Business Week*, November 9, 1998, p. 29.

78 For details, see William Case, "The Anwar Trial and its Wider Implications," in Colin Barlow and Francis Loh Kok Wah, eds., *Malaysian Economics and Politics in the New Century* (London: Edward Elgar, forthcoming).

79 Guillermo O'Donnell and Philippe Schmitter, "Tentative Conclusions in Uncertain Democracies," in Guillermo O'Donnell, Philippe Schmitter, and Laurence Whitehead, eds., *Transitions from Authoritarian Rule: Prospects for Democracy* (Baltimore: Johns Hopkins University Press, 1986), Part 4, pp. 53–56.

80 Leslie Lopez, "Political Connections Carry a New Cost in Malaysia," *Asian Wall Street Journal*, November 20–21, 1998, p. 1.

81 Sangwon Suh and Santha Oorjitham, "Tried and Tested Ways," *Asiaweek Online*, December 25, 1998 issue, http://www.pathfinder.com/asiaweek.

82 This section borrows from William Case, "Malaysia's General Elections in 1999: A Consolidated and High-Quality Semi-democracy," *Asian Studies Review*, vol. 25, no. 1 (March 2001), pp. 35–55.

83 *Malaysia: Free, United, Successful* (*Barisan Nasional* Headquarters: Kuala Lumpur, 1999).

84 "No Pie in the Sky," *NST*, November 23, 1999, p. 2.

85 "Support from Chinese Businessmen," *NST*, November 25, 1999, p. 2.

86 "Bridge for Kampung Sayong," *NST*, November 23, 1999, p. 15.

87 "Sungei Siput's Tireless Rep," *The Star*, November 24, 1999, p. 14.

88 Anwar, though long an UMNO member and associated now with *Keadilan*, remained acceptable to the PAS. "He used to be with us. We take him back," stated the editor of *Harakah*, Zulkifly Sulong. Discussion, November 23, 1999, Kuala Lumpur.

89 "Dr M: Time to Discard PAS," *The Star*, November 27, 1999, p. 2.

90 "Dr M: PAS has Lied to the People About Setting Up an Islamic State," *NST*, November 27, 1999, p. 1.

91 "A Vote for DAP 'is a Vote for PAS,'" *The Star*, November 25, 1999, p. 4.

92 "DAP's 'Secret Mission' Revealed," *NST*, November 24, 1999.

93 Sangwon Suh, "A Popularity Contest," *Asiaweek*, November 26, 1999, p. 21.

94 "Anwar Approved Gaming Licenses," *NST*, November 27, 1999, p. 1.

95 "Dr M founded IIU, Says Former Deputy Rector," *The Star*, November 27, 1999, p. 9.

96 "Many Faces of Anwar," *Utusan Malaysia*, November 27, 1999.

97 "Keadilan Lodges Report Over Lewd Video Tapes," *The Star*, November 26, 1999, p. 3.

98 "PAS Islamic Plan," *The Star*, November 26, 1999, p. 1.

99 "Nik Aziz: It's Hudud Law if PAS Wins," *NST*, November 23, 1999, p. 5.

100 Discussions with MCA state assemblyman and campaign manager, Selangor, December 2, 1999.

101 "Wooing Silent Majority," *NST*, November 23, 1999, p. 1.
102 "Dr M: Vote Wisely," *New Sunday Times*, November 28, 1999, p. 1.
103 "Better than in 1995, Says Dr M," *The Sun*, December 1, 1999, p. 4.
104 *"Keadilan* Deputy Chief: Anwar Will Be Forgotten," *NST*, December 1, 1999, p. 4.
105 "'Victory of the People,' Says Wan Azizah," *The Sun*, November 30, 1999.
106 Nonetheless, Wan Azizah showed new grit and independence by remarking after her victory, "I'm very happy to win, but sad that Anwar is not here to share it with me. I will be busy in the next two weeks and will not be able to bring the good news personally to him at Sungai Buloh Prison. "DAP 'Top Guns' Fire Blanks," *The Star*, November 30, 1999, p. 3.
107 "Writing was on the Wall for DAP," *The Star*, November 30, 1999, p. 4.
108 Shamsul Akmar, "UMNO's Worst Fears Come True," *The Star*, November 30, 1999, p. 2. It is important to note, however, that when campaigning in the Malay heartland, the UMNO highlighted its commitments to Islam. Conversely, when campaigning in Kuala Lumpur, the PAS appealed to Muslim business people and professionals, citing its candidates who hold MBAs.
109 Quoted in "BN Wins," *The Sun*, November 30, 1999, p. 1.
110 One notes, though, rumors abound of the government's dispatching emissaries to meet with Anwar, there amid his relatively comfortable terms of incarceration.

5 Thailand

1 See Michael Backman, *Asian Eclipse: Exposing the Dark Side of Business in Asia* (Singapore: John Wiley and Sons, 1999), especially Chapter 8.
2 Quoted in Pasuk Phongpaichit and Chris Baker, *Thailand: Economy and Politics* (Kuala Lumpur: Oxford University Press, 1995), p. 258.
3 Ibid., p. 325.
4 Ibid., p. 354.
5 Harold Crouch, *Domestic Political Structures and Regional Economic Co-operation* (Singapore: Institute of Southeast Asian Studies, 1984), p. 66.
6 Pasuk and Baker, *Thailand*, p. 327.
7 See Shane P. Tarr, "The Nature of Military Intervention in the Countryside of Surat Thani, Southern Thailand," *Bulletin of Concerned Asian Scholars*, 23 (July–September 1991), p. 44.
8 Pasuk and Baker, *Thailand*, p. 33.
9 John L.S. Girling, *Thailand: Society and Politics* (Ithaca: Cornell University Press, 1981), pp. 55–56.
10 Surin Maisrikrod and Duncan McCargo, "Electoral Politics: Commercialisation and Exclusion," in Kevin Hewison, ed., *Political Change in Thailand: Democracy and Participation* (London: Routledge: 1997), p. 133.
11 Riggs, Fred W., *Thailand: The Modernization of a Bureaucratic Polity* (Honolulu: East-West Centre Press, 1966).
12 Suchit Bunbongkarn, "Thailand's Successful Reforms," *Journal of Democracy*, vol. 10, no. 4 (October 1999), p. 68, fn. 4.
13 Michael T. Rock, "Thailand's Old Bureaucratic Polity and Its New Semi-democracy," in Mushtaq H. Khan and Jomo K.S., eds., *Rents, Rent-Seeking and Economic Development* (Cambridge: Cambridge University Press), pp. 182–206.
14 Pasuk and Baker, *Thailand*, p. 350.
15 Anek Laothamatas, "From Clientelism to Partnership: Business-Government Relations in Thailand," in Andrew MacIntyre, ed., *Business and Government in Industrializing Asia* (St. Leonards: Allen and Unwin, 1994), pp. 195–215.

16 Pasuk and Baker, *Thailand*, pp. 332–40.
17 Pasuk Phongpaichit, Sungsidh Piriyarangsan, and Nualnoi Treerat, *Guns, Girls, Gambling, Ganja: Thailand's Illegal Economy and Public Policy* (Chiang Mai: Silkworm Books, 1998).
18 Pasuk and Baker, *Thailand*, p. 333.
19 See James Ockey, "Crime, Society, and Politics in Thailand," in Carl A. Trocki, ed., *Gangsters, Democracy, and the State in Southeast Asia* (Ithaca: Cornell Southeast Asia Program, 1998), pp. 39–53.
20 Paul Handley, "More of the Same? Politics and Business, 1987–96," in Hewison, ed., *Political Change in Thailand*, pp. 94 and 98.
21 Ibid., p. 98.
22 Ibid., p. 100.
23 Ibid., pp. 104–5.
24 Pasuk *et al*, *Guns, Girls, Gambling, Ganja*.
25 Duncan McCargo, "Thailand's Political Parties: Real, Authentic, and Actual," in Hewison, ed., *Political Change in Thailand*, p. 115.
26 Ibid., p. 129.
27 Crouch, *Domestic Political Structures*, p. 66.
28 "Murder and Progress in Modern Siam," in Benedict Anderson, *The Spectre of Comparisons: Nationalism, Southeast Asia and the World* (London: Verso, 1998), p. 188.
29 Maisrikrod and McCargo, "Electoral Politics," p. 135.
30 *Bangkok Post*, March 12, 1998, p. 4.
31 *Bangkok Post*, March 19, 1998, p. 1.
32 Ibid.
33 *Bangkok Post*, March 20, 1998, p. 1.
34 *Bangkok Post*, March 12, 1998, p. 4.
35 *Bangkok Post*, March 23, 1998, p. 1.
36 *Bangkok Post*, March 17, 1998, p. 1. See also *Bangkok Post*, March 19, 1998, p. 11, where it is noted that while farmer protests in front of Government House had become "a permanent feature in Thai politics . . . it had never gone so repulsively overboard." The article linked the demonstration directly to Auychai Watha of the NAP.
37 *Bangkok Post*, March 23, 1998, p. 3.
38 *Bangkok Post*, April 2, 1998, p. 3.
39 Ibid., p. 4.
40 *Bangkok Post*, March 27, 1998, p. 2.
41 Michael Burton, Richard Gunther, and John Higley, "Introduction: Elite Transformations and Democratic Regimes," in John Higley and Richard Gunther, eds., *Elites and Democratic Consolidation in Latin America and Southern Europe* (Cambridge: Cambridge University Press, 1991), p. 13.
42 Michael Burton and John Higley, "Political Crises and Elite Settlements," in Mattei Dogan and John Higley, eds., *Elites, Crises, and the Origins of Regimes* (Lanham: Rowman and Littlefield, 1998), pp. 47–70.
43 Richard Gunther, "Spain: The Very Model of the Modern Elite Settlement," in Higley and Gunther, eds., *Elites and Democratic Consolidation*, pp. 38–80. John Higley, Tong-yi Huang, and Tse-min Lin, "Elite Settlements in Taiwan," *Journal of Democracy*, vol. 9, no. 2 (April 1998), pp. 148–63.
44 See Richard Stubbs, "War and Economic Development: Export-Oriented Industrialization in East and Southeast Asia," *Comparative Politics*, vol. 31, no. 3 (April 1999), pp. 337–55.
45 See Kevin Hewison, "The Monarchy and Democratization," in Hewison, ed., *Political Change in Thailand*, pp. 58–76.

46 Myron Weiner, "Empirical Democratic Theory," in Myron Weiner and Ergun Ozbudun, eds., *Competitive Elections in Developing Countries* (Durham: Duke University Press, 1987), pp. 3–34.

47 Arend Lijphart, *Democracy in Plural Societies: A Comparative Exploration* (New Haven: Yale University Press, 1977).

48 Benedict R. O'G. Anderson, "Introduction," in *Southeast Asian Tribal Groups and Ethnic Minorities: Prospects for the Eighties and Beyond* (Cambridge MA: Cultural Survival Inc., and Department of Anthropology, Harvard University), p. 10.

49 Pasuk and Baker, *Thailand*, p. 315.

50 Peter A. Jackson, *Buddhism, Legitimation, and Conflict: The Political Functions of Urban Thai Buddhism* (Singapore: Institute of Southeast Asian Studies, 1989).

51 Pasuk and Baker, *Thailand*, p. 316.

52 Kittivuttho's notorious observations are quoted in Pasuk and Baker, *Thailand*, p. 310.

53 Peter A. Jackson, "Withering Center, Flourishing Margins: Buddhism's Changing Political Roles," in Hewison, ed., *Political Change in Thailand*, p. 89.

54 *National Identity Office, Thailand in the 1980s* (Bangkok: Muang Boran Publishing House, 1984), p. 69, quoted in Pasuk and Baker, *Thailand*, p. 319.

55 Andrew Brown, "Locating Working-class Power," in Hewison, ed., *Political Change in Thailand*, p. 171.

56 See Philip Hirsch, "The State in the Village: Interpreting Rural Development in Thailand," *Development and Change*, 20 (1989), pp. 35–56.

57 See Suchit Bungbongkarn, "Elections and Democratization in Thailand," in R.H. Taylor, ed., *The Politics of Elections in Southeast Asia* (Washington: Woodrow Wilson Center Press, 1996).

58 Pasuk Phongpaichit and Chris Baker, *Thailand's Crisis* (Chiang Mai: Silkworm Books, 2000), pp. 143–48).

59 Kevin Hewison, "Resisting Globalization: A Study of Localism in Thailand, *Pacific Review*, vol. 13, no. 2 (2000), pp. 279–96.

60 *The Sunday Nation* (Bangkok), December 31, 2000, pp. 1–2.

61 See Jackson, "Withering Center," pp. 80–85.

62 *The Sunday Nation* (Bangkok), December 31, 2000, p. 2.

63 Pasuk and Baker, *Thailand*, pp. 124–25.

64 Crouch, *Domestic Political Structures*, p. 67.

65 Pasuk and Baker, *Thailand*, p. 301.

66 Ibid., p. 306.

67 Ibid., p. 307.

68 Ibid., p. 310.

69 See William F. Case, "Can the Halfway House Stand? Elite Theory and Semidemocracy in Three Southeast Asian Countries," *Comparative Politics*, vol. 28, no. 4 (July 1996), pp. 437–64.

70 Anek Laothamatas, "Business and Politics in Thailand: New Patterns of Influence," *Asian Survey*, vol. 28, no. 4 (April 1988), pp. 451–70.

71 Chai-anan Sumadavanija, "Thailand: A Stable Semi-democracy," in Larry Diamond, Juan Linz, and Seymour Martin Lipset, eds., *Democracy in Developing Countries: Asia* (Boulder: Lynne Rienner, 1989), pp. 305–46.

72 See Pasuk Phongpaichit and Chris Baker, *Thailand's Boom* (St. Leonards: Allen and Unwin, 1996).

73 Samuel P. Huntington, *The Third Wave: Democratization in the Late Twentieth Century* (Norman: University of Oklahoma Press, 1991).

74 A concise account of this period is provided by Surin Maisrikrod, *Thailand's Two General Elections in 1992: Democracy Sustained* (Singapore: Institute of Southeast Asian Studies, 1992).

75 Daniel King and Jim LoGerfo, "Thailand: Toward Democratic Stability," *Journal of Democracy*, vol. 7, no. 1 (January 1996), p. 105.

76 Ibid., pp. 109–10.

77 Omar G. Encarnacion, "Beyond Transitions: The Politics of Democratic Consolidation," *Comparative Politics*, vol. 32, no. 4 (July 2000), pp. 479–98.

78 The best example is perhaps Michael Burton, Richard Gunther, and John Higley, "Introduction: Elite Transformations and Democratic Regimes," in Higley and Gunther, eds., *Elites and Democratic Consolidation*, pp. 1–37. See also Richard Gunther, P. Nikiforos Diamandourous, and Hans-Jurgen Puhle, eds., *The Politics of Democratic Consolidation: Southern Europe in Comparative Perspective* (Baltimore: Johns Hopkins University Press, 1995); and Huntington, *The Third Wave*, who evaluates consolidation in terms of the "two-turnover test."

79 See Juan Linz and Arturo Valenzuela, eds., *The Failure of Presidential Democracy* (Baltimore: Johns Hopkins University Press, 1994). Encarnacion (fn. 77) cites Scott Mainwaring and Timothy Scully eds., *Building Democratic Institutions: Party Systems in Latin America* (Stanford: Stanford University Press, 1995); Elizabeth Jelin and Eric Hershberg, eds., *Constructing Democracy: Human Rights, Citizenship and Society in Latin America* (Boulder: Westview Press, 1996); and Paul G. Buchanan, *State, Labor, Capital: Democratizing Class Relations in the Southern Cone* (Pittsburgh: University of Pittsburgh Press, 1995).

80 Juan J. Linz and Alfred Stepan, *Problems of Democratic Transition and Consolidation: Southern Europe, South America, and Post-Communist Europe* (Baltimore: Johns Hopkins University Press, 1996).

81 Encarnacion, "Beyond Transitions," pp. 487 and 491.

82 See Susan Pharr, Robert Putnam, and Russell Dalton, "A Quarter-Century of Declining Confidence," *Journal of Democracy*, vol. 11, no. 1 (April 2000), pp. 5–25; and Richard Rose, "The End of Consensus in Austria and Switzerland," *Journal of Democracy*, vol. 11, no. 1 (April 2000), pp. 26–40.

83 See Samuel Valenzuela, "Democratic Consolidation in Post-Transitional Settings: Notion, Process and Facilitating Conditions," in Scott Mainwaring, Guillermo O'Donnell, and Samuel Valenzuela, eds., *Issues in Democratic Consolidation* (Notre Dame: University of Notre Dame Press, 1992), p. 59.

84 Guillermo O'Donnell, "Illusions about Consolidation," in *Counterpoints: Selected Essays on Authoritarianism and Democratization* (Notre Dame: University of Notre Dame Press), pp. 175–94.

85 While the Democrat-led government was in power, the army chief, General Chetta Thanajaro, vowed to cooperate closely with Chuan. He pledged that "soldiers must stay completely away from politics – no involvement in the formation of governments, no criticism. . . . The coup d'etat is outdated. The more time passes, the more it's obsolete." *The Nation*, February 21, 1998, p. 1. He thus agreed first to accept deep budget cuts, then, in accordance with the constitution, even the loss of the army's television and radio stations, notwithstanding its impact on military revenues. *Bangkok Post*, March 11, 1998, p. 2. See also statements by Supreme Commander Sampao Chusri during the campaigning for the 2001 election, *Bangkok Post*, December 29, 2000, p. 3.

86 Huntington, *The Third Wave*, p. 276.

87 Peter Alford, Bangkok correspondent for *The Australian*, personal communication, December 28, 2000.

88 Phongpaichit and Baker, *Thailand's Crisis*, pp. 112–15 and 134–35.
89 Ibid., pp. 116–17.
90 For good accounts of the torturous passage of the "people's constitution," see Duncan McCargo, "Alternative Meanings of Political Reform in Contemporary Thailand," *Copenhagen Journal of Asian Studies*, vol. 13 (1998); and Pasuk and Baker, *Thailand's Crisis*, pp. 119–22.
91 See Pasuk Phongpaichit and Chris Baker, *Thailand's Boom and Bust* (Chiang Mai: Silkworm Books, 1998); Kevin Hewison, "Thailand's Capitalism Before and After the Economic Crisis," in Richard Robison, Mark Beeson, Kanishka Jayasuriya, and Hyuk-Rae Kim, eds., *Politics and Markets in the Wake of the Asian Crisis* (London: Routledge, 2000), pp. 192–21; Andrew MacIntyre, "Political Institutions and the Economic Crisis in Thailand and Indonesia," in T.J. Pempel, ed., *The Politics of the Asian Economic Crisis* (Ithaca: Cornell University Press, 1999), pp. 143–62; and Stephan Haggard, *The Political Economy of the Asian Financial Crisis* (Washington DC: Institute for International Economics, 2000), pp. 51–55 and 92–100. A prominent academic and constitution drafting assembly member, Suchit Bunbongkarn, observed, "we have never faced anything like this before." Interview, Chulalongkorn University, Bangkok, April 23, 1998.
92 Burton *et al*, "Introduction," pp. 20–22.
93 *Far Eastern Economic Review*, (hearafter *FEER*) November 6, 1997, p. 94.
94 Haggard, *Asian Financial Crisis*, pp. 11 and 14.
95 Laura Thornton, Senior Program Officer for Thailand, National Democratic Institute for International Affairs, personal communication, January 8, 2001.
96 Haggard, *Asian Financial Crisis*, p. 99.
97 See Haggard (with Nancy Birdsall), *Asian Financial Crisis*, pp. 195–96 and 206–8.
98 Anek Laothamatas, "A Tale of Two Democracies: Conflicting Perceptions of Elections and Democracy in Thailand," in Taylor, ed., *The Politics of Elections in Southeast Asia*, p. 201.
99 For a good analysis, see Surin Maisrikrod, "Political Reform and the New Thai Electoral System: Old Habits Die Hard?" in David Newman and John Fuhsheng Hsieh, eds., *How Asia Votes* (New York: Chatham House, forthcoming).
100 A permanent committee adviser and university academic stated in a discussion, "We knew when these things were written that they probably couldn't be paid for." Chulalongkorn University, Bangkok, April 10, 1998.
101 For a breakdown of the candidates' professional backgrounds and educational levels, see "Election Special," *Bangkok Post*, January 5, 2001, p. 5.
102 *Asian Wall Street Journal*, January 5–7, p. 1.
103 *FEER*, January 18, 2001, p. 18; and *The Nation*, January 8, 2001, pp. 1–2.
104 Discussions with academics and foreign journalists, Bangkok, January 2001.
105 Peter Alford, "Thailand: Magnate Sucks in Thai MPs," *The Australian*, April 28, 2000, p. 7.
106 See Ghita Ionescu and Ernest Gellner, eds., *Populism: Its Meanings and National Characteristics* (London: Weidenfeld and Nicholson, 1969); Ernesto Laclau, *Politics and Ideology in Marxist Theory: Capitalism, Fascism, Populism* (London: New Left Books, 1977); and Margaret Canovan, *Populism* (London: Harcourt, Brace, and Jovanovich, 1981).
107 Peter Alford, Bangkok correspondent for *The Australian*, personal communication, December 28, 2000.
108 *Bangkok Post, Business*, January 10, 2001, p. 2.
109 *Bangkok Post*, December 28, 2000, p. 3.

110 At a *Thai Rak Thai* election rally attended by the author in the country's impoverished northeast, Thaksin asked those who were farmers to raise their hands, to raise them again if they were indebted to banks and loan sharks, then raise them once more if they would benefit from three years of debt relief. Enthusiasm mounted among the 5–6000 in attendance with each raising of hands. Thaksin claimed that he had solved his own debt problems, and would now help farmers in solving theirs. What other party, he inquired, had ever approached them in this way? Nakhon Ratchasima, January 3, 2001.

111 *Bangkok Post*, December 28, 2000, p. 1.

112 *Bangkok Post*, January 4, 2001, p. 1.

113 *Bangkok Post*, December 28, 2000, p. 3.

114 At an election rally attended by the author in rural Buri Ram province, Newin Chidchob, deputy agriculture minister and one of several Chidchob family candidates contesting far parliament on the *Chart Thai* slate, displayed great charisma and folk humor while energizing his audiences. But in acknowledging the local appeal of *Thai Rak Thai*'s populism, he also highlighted in a savvy way the fiscal irresponsibility of debt relief and rural credit schemes. Buri Ram province, January 2, 2001.

115 *The Sunday Nation* thus characterized the rise of *Thai Rak Thai* in terms of "new money politics," January 7, 2001, p. 6. See also Ukrist Pathmanand, "The Thaksin Shinawatra Group: A Study of the Relationship between Money and Politics in Thailand," *Copenhagen Journal of Asian Studies*, vol. 13 (1998), pp. 60–81.

116 *Bangkok Post*, January 8, 2001, p. 6.

117 *Bangkok Post*, January 10, 2001, p. 2.

118 Samak Sundaravej, mayor of Bangkok and head of *Prachakorn Thai*, explained his party's having lost all its lower-house seats to the "money politics" of *Thai Rak Thai*. "With that kind of money, you can buy the country." Interview, Bangkok, January 17, 2001. See also Philip Bowring, "A Chance for the New Leader to Break with Thailand's Past," *International Herald Tribune* interactive, January 10, 2001.

119 As the results were released, Banharn exclaimed, "every time I watch TV I feel I'm going to faint." *The Nation*, January 9, 2000, p. 6.

120 *Bangkok Post*, January 9, 2001, p. 8.

121 *Bangkok Post*, January 6, 2001, p. 1.

122 A prominent academic at Chulalongkorn University observed that bureaucrats were involved in the disturbances, "but we are not sure how high up it goes." Discussion, Bangkok, January 12, 2001.

123 *The Nation*, December 30, 2000, p. 1.

124 For a breakdown of individual contests, see <http://www.bangkokpost.com/election2001/results.html>.

125 *Bangkok Post*, December 27, 2000. p. 1.

126 *The Nation*, January 13, 2001, p. 1.

127 Thomas Crampton and David Ignatius, "Thai Victor Says He would Obey Court Ruling," *International Herald Tribune* interactive, January 11, 2001.

128 Quoted in *FEER*, January 11, 2000, p. 22.

129 *The Nation*, January 9, 2001, p. 1.

130 *The Nation, Business and Finance*, January 8, 2001, p. B1.

131 Ibid., p. 1.

132 *The Nation, Business and Finance*, January 9, 2001, pp. B1-B4.

133 Ibid., p. B1.

134 *The Nation*, January 10, 2001.

135 *The Nation* interactive, January 25, 2001.
136 *Bangkok Post*, January 10, 2001, p. 3.
137 *The Nation*, January 4, 2001, pp. 1–2.
138 Ibid., p. 6.
139 Surichai Wun'gaeo, Institute of Asian Studies, Chulalongkorn Unversity, personal communication, January 13, 2001.
140 Shawn Crispin, Bangkok correspondent for the *Far Eastern Economic Review*, personal communication, January 11, 2001.
141 See *FEER*, November 2, 2000, pp. 30 and 34.
142 Suchit, "Thailand's Successful Reforms," p. 67.

6   The Philippines

1 Quoted in Mark R. Thompson, *The Anti-Marcos Struggle: Personalistic Rule and Democratic Transition in the Philippines* (New Haven: Yale University Press, 1995), p. 15.
2 James Putzel, "Survival of an Imperfect Democracy in the Philippines," in Peter Burnell and Peter Calvert, eds., *The Resilience of Democracy: Persistent Practice, Durable Idea* (Chippenham: Frank Cass, 1999), p. 214.
3 Ibid., p. 216.
4 Lucian Pye, *Asian Power and Politics: The Cultural Dimensions of Authority* (Cambridge: Harvard University Press, 1985), pp. 121–27.
5 Paul Hutchcroft, "Booty Capitalism: Business-Government Relations in the Philippines," in Andrew MacIntyre, ed., *Business and Government in Industrializing Asia* (St. Leonards: Allen and Unwin, 1994), p. 220.
6 John T. Sidel, "Philippine Politics in Town, District, and Province: Bossism in Cavite and Cebu, *Journal of Asian Studies*, vol. 56, no. 4 (November) 1997, pp. 947–66.
7 Thompson, *The Anti-Marcos Struggle*, pp. 3–4.
8 Andrew MacIntyre, "Business, Government and Development: Northeast and Southeast Asian Comparisons," in MacIntyre, ed., *Business and Government*, pp. 1–28.
9 See Hutchcroft, "Booty Capitalism," pp. 216–43.
10 Sidel, "Philippine Politics." See also John T. Sidel, *Capital, Coercion and Crime: Bossism in the Philippines* (Stanford: Stanford University Press, 1999).
11 Benedict Anderson, *The Spectre of Comparisons: Nationalism, Southeast Asia, and the World* (London: Verso, 1998), p. 196.
12 David Wurfel, *Filipino Politics: Development and Decay* (Ithaca: Cornell University Press, (1991), p. 9.
13 Thompson, *The Anti-Marcos Struggle*, p. 24.
14 Ibid., p. 19.
15 Wurfel, *Filipino Politics*, p. 79.
16 Sidel, "Philippine Politics," p. 954. The strategies of the Abines family in Santander, Cebu provide an illustration. "Those who did not vote for [Representative Crisologo] Abines's candidate would be reported to the congressman. After that, their water supply would be cut off and if they apply for a business permit they are given a hard time. The municipal waterworks system is owned by the Santander municipal government headed by Priscilla Abines. The Abineses also own the town's only bank and grocery store. There is no public market in Santander." *Philippine Daily Inquirer* (hereafter *PDI*), May 7, 1998, p. 16.
17 Wurfel, *Filipino Politics*, p. 37.

18 Thus, in 1998, as part of a nationalist celebration, the Philippine government proclaimed a centenary of independence, backdating its freedom from 1946 to Bonifacio's declaration in 1898.
19 Wurfel, *Filipino Politics*, p. 37. See also Thompson, *The Anti-Marcos Struggle*, pp. 29–32.
20 *PDI*, May 9, 1998, p. 20.
21 The day before the 1998 election, Catholic bishops pleaded before their flock, "Anybody but Erap." *PDI*, May 11, 1998, p. 1. Observers noted that when Estrada collected his endorsement in San Juan, it was the first time anyone could recollect his being seen at mass.
22 Benedict J. Tria Kerkvliet, "Contested Meanings of Elections in the Philippines," in Taylor, ed., *The Politics of Elections in Southeast Asia* (Cambridge: Cambridge University Press, 1996), pp. 149–50.
23 *PDI*, May 11, 1998, p. 1.
24 The columnist, Art A. Borjal, writes, "One major factor that could not destroy the *Lakas*'s demolition job [ie., moral appeals] against Erap – the rap that he was not a man of intellect – was the sad experience of the *masa* with leaders who were intellectuals. In the minds of many who belong to the lower classes, the country's experience with leaders who were brainy has been very bad. 'What did these so-called intelligent political leaders ever do [for] us who are poor?' many of the *masa* asked." *The Philippine Star*, May 13, 1998, p. 6.
25 Thompson, *The Anti-Marcos Struggle*, p. 32.
26 *PDI*, May 12, 1998, p. 1.
27 Benedict J. Tria Kerkvliet, *Everyday Politics in the Philippines: Class and Status Relations in a Central Luzon Village* (Berkeley: University of California Press, 1990).
28 Thompson, *The Anti-Marcos Struggle*, pp. 20–24.
29 Ibid., p. 15.
30 Kerkvliet, "Contested Meanings," p. 163.
31 Wurfel, *Filipino Politics*, p. 113.
32 Ibid., p. 169.
33 Ibid., pp. 130 and 138.
34 Ibid., p. 130.
35 Thompson, *The Anti-Marcos Struggle*, p. 52.
36 Wurfel, *Filipino Politics*, p. 124.
37 Thompson, *The Anti-Marcos Struggle*, p. 36. Thompson notes also Marcos's grievously violating elite understandings by proposing that his wife succeed him. "It was unprecedented for one clan to dominate the presidency indefinitely," p. 43.
38 Thompson, *The Anti-Marcos Struggle*, p. 40.
39 Ibid., p. 78.
40 Ibid., pp. 38–39.
41 Wurfel, *Filipino Politics*, p. 237.
42 For details on the coconut levy, see Nati Nuguid, "Cracking the Coconut," *Philippines Free Press*, May 2, 1998, pp. 14–15.
43 Thompson, *The Anti Marcos Struggle*, pp. 83–88.
44 Wurfel, *Filipino Politics*, pp. 137 and 239.
45 Thompson, *The Anti-Marcos Struggle*, p. 56.
46 Wurfel, *Filipino Politics*, p. 205.
47 For fuller accounts, see Karl D. Jackson, "The Philippines: The Search for a Suitable Democratic Solution, 1946–1986, in Larry Diamond, Juan J. Linz, and Seymour Martin Lipset, eds., *Democracy in Developing Countries: Asia* (Boulder: Lynne Rienner, 1989), pp. 231–66; David Wurfel, "Transition to Political

Democracy in the Philippines: 1978–1988," in Diane Ethier, ed., *Democratic Transition and Consolidation in Southern Europe, Latin America and Southeast Asia* (Houndmills: Macmillan Press, 1990), pp. 110–38; Anne Mackenzie, "People Power or Palace Coup: The Fall of Marcos," in Mark Turner, ed., *Regime Change in the Philippines: The Legitimation of the Aquino Government* (Canberra: Department of Political and Social Change, Australian National University, 1987); Gretchen Casper, *Fragile Democracies: The Legacies of Authoritarian Rule* (Pittsburgh: University of Pittsburgh Press, 1995). The authoritative account is offered by Mark Thompson, *The Anti-Marcos Struggle*.

48 Thompson, *The Anti-Marcos Struggle*, pp. 114–15.

49 Ibid., pp. 120.

50 Ibid., p. 181.

51 Samuel P. Huntington, *The Third Wave: Democratization in the Late Twentieth Century* (Norman: University of Oklahoma Press, 1991), pp. 142–49.

52 Thompson, *The Anti-Marcos Struggle*, p. 158.

53 Mark Thompson, "Off the Endangered List: Philippine Democratization in Comparative Perspective," *Comparative Politics*, vol. 28, no. 2 (January), 1996, p. 193.

54 Not all progressive forces were content with Aquino's performance, however. Maria Serena Diokno, director of the Third World Studies Center at the University of the Philippines and former member of Justice for Aquino, Justice for All (JAJA), assessed that "Cory" still had the people behind her during her presidency and could have effectively demanded from elites many more social reforms. Like many analysts, she rated Aquino's presidency as a missed opportunity. Discussion, University of the Philippines, Diliman, May 25, 1998.

55 This section borrows from William Case, "The Philippine Election in 1998: A Question of Quality," *Asian Survey*, vol. 34, no. 3 (May/June), 1999, pp. 468–85.

56 Philippe Schmitter, "Exploring the Problematic Triumph of Liberal Democracy and Concluding with a Modest Proposal for Improving its International Impact," in Axel Hadenius, ed., *Democracy's Victory and Crisis* (Cambridge: Cambridge University Press, 1997), p. 297.

57 Juan J. Linz, "Some Thoughts on the Victory and Future of Democracy," in Hadenius, ed., *Democracy's Victory*, p. 421.

58 Jon Elster, *Deliberative Democracy* (Cambridge: Cambridge University Press, 1998); and James Bohman, *Deliberative Democracy: Essays in Reason and Politics* (Cambridge: MIT Press, 1998).

59 Thompson, "Endangered List," pp. 197–98.

60 Discussions with Steven Rood, professor at University of the Philippines, Baguio, and member of board of directors, Social Weather Stations (SWS), Makati, May 18 and 20, 1998. SWS, on the Internet at http://www.sws.org.ph/, is an independent academic institute that conducts survey research on topics of public interest.

61 Gary Hawes, Manila-based Ford Foundation official, has suggested that much administrative decentralization had taken place in the Philippines and that it was now possible for city and municipal governments to be elected on the basis of good governance, rather than through clan connections and patronage machines. He cited Naga City under Mayor Jesse Robredo and Olongapo until recently under Mayor Richard Gordon as key examples. Gary Hawes, discussion, Makati, May 18, 1998. Mayor Robredo, who broke with his family clan in order to stand for office, estimated that perhaps a quarter of the 60-odd cities in the Philippines could now be classified as administered in professional ways. Interview, Naga City, May 29, 1998. For an assessment of Gordon's tenure as

head of the Subic Bay Metropolitan authority, as well as that of his successor, see Rigoberto Tiglao, "About Face," *Far Eastern Economic Review* (hereafter *FEER*), February 18, 1999, pp. 44–45.

62 Juan J. Linz and Alfred Stepan, *Problems of Democratic Transition and Consolidation: Southern Europe, South America and Post-Communist Europe* (Baltimore: Johns Hopkins University Press, 1996), pp. 200–204. They provide as examples President Alberto Fujimori in Peru and President Carlos Menem in Argentina, the first claiming to have suspended democracy in order to save it, the second having skirted statutory requirements while accumulating campaign funds and perhaps a personal fortune.

63 See Segundo E. Romero, "The Philippines in 1997: Weathering Political and Economic Turmoil," *Asian Survey*, vol. 38, no. 2 (February 1998), p. 197.

64 Giuseppe Di Palma, *To Craft Democracies: An Essay on Democratic Transitions* (Berkeley: University of California Press, 1999), pp. 48–49.

65 Neal H. Cruz, "Why Joe de V is Losing," *PDI*, May 15, 1998, p. 9.

66 Ibid., p. 9. See also *PDI*, May 24, 1998, p. 9.

67 *Philippine Star*, June 1, 1998, p. 15.

68 In a poll conducted by SWS in December 1996, respondents were asked which "personal qualities" they most wanted in presidential candidates. Only 34 per cent specified "never been involved in graft and corruption," placing it fifth in the list of qualities. *SWB* 97–17/18 (September 1997).

69 SWS conducted a series of four national surveys about attitudes toward possible presidential candidates during September 1996–June 1997. Respondents were asked whom they would vote for as president if the election were held that day. Joseph Estrada, Gloria Macapagal-Arroyo, and Miriam Defensor-Santiago consistently led the field, with Estrada the favorite in the last two surveys with 23 per cent. De Venecia gained 5 per cent in April 1997, then slumped to 3 per cent in June, tying with two others for sixth place. *SWB* 97–17/18 (September 1997), p. 6.

70 Gabriela R. Montinola, "Parties and Accountability in the Philippines," *Journal of Democracy*, vol. 10, no. 1 (January) 1999, p. 130.

71 *Philippine Star*, May 30, 1998, p. 21.

72 In a poll conducted by SWS in December 1996, before East Asia's economic crisis had set in, respondents were asked: "How closely should the next president follow Pres. Ramos's Policies?" A total of 45 per cent of the respondents thought that the next president should follow Ramos's policies "a little and change most things" or "not follow at all and change almost everything." *SWB* 97–17/18 (September 1997), p. 3. In the SWS exit poll conducted during the May 1998 elections, this question was asked again. The total of respondents wanting to "change most things" or to "change almost everything" rose to 54 per cent. Mahar Mangahas, *Manila Standard*, June 8, 1998, p. 17.

73 National Survey, *SWB* 97–17/18 (September 1997), p. 8. Approximately 64 per cent of respondents said that being "pro-poor" was the most important quality in presidential candidates. Being "approachable" was second at 40 per cent and "knowledge in running economic affairs" was third at 38 per cent.

74 The phrase "'helped' to do well" comes from O'Donnell and Schmitter, "Tentative Conclusions about Uncertain Democracies," in Guillermo O'Donnell, Philippe Schmitter, and Laurence Whitehead, eds., *Transitions from Authoritarian Rule: Prospects for Democracy*, (Baltimore: Johns Hopkins University Press, 1986), Part 4, p. 62. It refers to the importance of "artificially" bolstering parties that represent the "Right-Center and Right," perhaps by

"rigging the rules," in order to prevent an authoritarian backlash. Such "help" after a democracy has been consolidated, however, as in the Philippines, augurs poorly for that democracy's quality.

75 Discussion with David Wurfel, University of the Philippines, Diliman, April 31, 1998. Wurfel observed that Ramos had been behaving "rashly" for the previous year-and-a-half, sullying what up until then had been a largely favorable assessment of his presidency.
76 *PDI*, May 4, 1998, p. 8.
77 *Today*, April 29, 1998, pp. 1 and 12.
78 *PDI*, April 30, 1998, p. 1.
79 *Today*, April 29, 1998, p. 1.
80 *PDI*, May 5, 1998, p. 1.
81 Captain Carlos Magalang, YOU spokesman, quoted in *PDI*, May 8, 1998, p. 2.
82 Belinda Olivares-Cunanan, "Elusive Bro. Mike," *PDI*, March 5, 1998, p. 7.
83 *PDI*, May 5, 1998, p. 2.
84 See *Comparing SWS Exit Poll Results and Official Results: Presidential Votes, Philippines*, SWS 1998 National Exit Poll, posted June 22, 1998 at <http://www.sws.org.ph/exit-com.htm>
85 Joel Rocamora, "Who Won? Who Lost?," *Political Briefs* (Manila: Institute of Political Democracy, forthcoming).
86 Discussion with David Wurfel, University of the Philippines, Diliman, April 31, 1998.
87 *PDI*, May 5, 1998, p. 1.
88 *FEER*, March 5, 1998, p. 26.
89 Ibid., p. 26.
90 Ibid., p. 23.
91 *Today* (Makati), May 4, 1998, p. 12.
92 On the origins of the newly formed LaMMP, see Romero, "The Philippines in 1997," p. 197.
93 See, e.g., Estrada interview, *FEER*, January 15, 1998, p. 24. After his election, though, Estrada was more forthcoming, elaborating interest rate policies and commitments to "free-market institutions." *FEER*, May 14, 1998, p. 20.
94 Amando Doronila, *PDI*, May 15, 1998, pp. 1 and 9.
95 *PDI*, May 17, 1998, p. 17.
96 To sample the appeals that so resonated with mass audiences, consider the following journalistic account of one of Estrada's rallies in his home district of San Juan:
The portly actor-turned-politician eventually arrives. Current mayor (and Erap's son) Jose "Jinggoy" Estrada shouts: "It is my honor to introduce my own father, who is definitely better-looking than I am!" A whoop goes up among the 10,000-strong crowd. "He is definitely a better actor than I am!" continues Jinggoy. More cheers. "The next president of the Republic of the Philippines, Joseph 'Erap' Estrada!" As Estrada Sr. bounds onto the stage, his supporters break into a chant: "Erap, Erap, Erap, Erap!" Estrada throws a joke at his son: "Thank you for telling the truth. You can see the evidence – I am far better-looking than you." He introduces the local senatorial candidates for his LaMMP party and then turns to Luisa Ejercito, a doctor, whom he presents as "the only wife of Erap." The throngs understand this allusion to his reputed philandering (he has three children out of wedlock) and roar. "You don't seem to believe me," laughs Estrada. The people giggle and clap "Do you want me to sing?" A resounding yes. Erap warbles a line: "Of the many women I have loved, I married only one." That, he assures the crowd, "is Dr. Ejercito." The

people demand a more tangible proof of his fidelity. "Kiss, kiss, kiss," they shout. Ejercito stands up and kisses the vice-president, much to the crowd's delight.

Sangwon Sun and Antonio Lopez, "Is Estrada Unstoppable," *Asiaweek*, April 10, 1998, p. 16. Estrada ended all campaign appearances a week before the election, alleging that death threats had been made against him. *PDI*, May 9, 1998, p. 7.

97 See Amando Doronila, "Erap Cabinet Patchwork of Conflicting Interests," *PDI*, May 24, 1998, pp. 1 and 6.

98 Eduardo Cojuangco and Lucio Tan were both business people who rose to prominence under Marcos. Because of the Zamorra brothers' connections to Estrada, analysts advised a close monitoring of developments surrounding Cojuangco and the coco levy and the sequestered San Miguel shares, as well as several tax avoidance cases in which Tan was embroiled. Indeed, a month after Estrada's election, Cojuangco was elected president and chief executive of San Miguel, paving the way for his recapturing the sequestered shares. "Marcos's Beer Baron is Back," *The Australian*, July 8, 1998, p. 25.

99 Belinda Olivares-Cunanan alleged that Estrada, after winning the presidency, wished also to be secretary of the Department of Interior and Local Government in order that he could control the national police, then repay the underworld syndicates. "Can Estrada Abolish the Pork," *PDI*, May 24, 1998, p. 9.

100 *PDI*, May 5, 1998, p. B2.

101 Quoted in *PDI*, May 17, 1998, p. 2.

102 Ibid.

103 Montinola, "Parties and Accountability," p. 129.

104 *Sunday Inquirer Magazine* (Manila), May 10, 1998, p. 3.

105 See fn. 30.

106 Olivares-Cunanan, "Abolish the Pork," p. 9. Indeed, Jaworksi even assured supporters that his senatorial duties would not be allowed to compromise his game. Montinola, "Parties and Accountability," p. 126.

107 Joel Rocamora, "Revenge of the Masses? Or Snubbing the Snobs?," *Conjuncture* (forthcoming).

108 *PDI*, May 8, 1998, p. 18.

109 For an excellent analysis, see "Impeachment Trial or Resignation?" Kilosbayan, Bantay Katarungan, and Bantayog ng mga Bayani foundations, posted at http://www.livewire.com.ph/kilosbayan, November 2000.

110 See "The Elites vs. Estrada," *Asiaweek.com*, November 17, 2000.

111 *FEER*, February 1, 2000, p. 17. See also Peter Alford, "Philippines Asks: Was that a Coup We Just Had?" *The Australian*, January 22, 2001, pp. 1.

112 Peter Alford, "Estrada's Cronies Flee Manila," *The Australian*, January 23, 2001, p. 7.

113 Jinggoy Estrada attributed the non-violence to his father's moderation: "There is no blood on the hands of our family. It was very painful, but we made that sacrifice. And this is how they treat us?" Quoted in Cathy C. Yamsuan and Agnes E. Donato, "JV: Please Stop Persecuting My Family," in *PDI* interactive, January 23, 2001.

114 Quoted in *FEER*, February 1, 2000, p. 18.

115 Amando Doronila, *PDI*, May 10, 1998, p. 1. Doronila lamented also the "lack of commanding charismatic political personality that has captured the imagination of the nation."

7 Southeast Asia

1 Mark Thompson, *The Anti-Marcos Struggle: Personalistic Rule and Democratic Transition in the Philippines* (New Haven: Yale University Press), pp. ix–x.

2 Donald K. Emmerson, "A Tale of Three Countries," *Journal of Democracy*, vol. 10, no. 4 (October) 1999, pp. 35–53.

3 Roberto Tigalo and Michael Vatikiotis, "Estrada in Trouble," *Far Eastern Economic Review* (hereafter *FEER*), December 23, 1999, pp. 22–24.

4 See, e.g., Andrew MacIntyre, *Business and Politics in Indonesia* (North Sydney: Allen and Unwin, 1991); Ruth McVey, ed., *Southeast Asian Capitalists* (Ithaca: Cornell University Press, 1992); Anek Laothamatas, *Business Associations and the New Political Economy of Thailand* (Boulder: Westview Press, 1992); Edmund Terence Gomez and Jomo K.S., *Malaysia's Political Economy: Politics, Patronage and Profits* (Cambridge: Cambridge University Press, 1997); Peter Searle, *The Riddle of Malaysian Capitalism: Rent-seekers or Real Capitalists?* (St. Leonards: Allen and Unwin, 1999).

5 Eduardo Silva and Francisco Durand, "Organized Business and Politics in Latin America," in Francisco Durand and Eduardo Silva, eds., *Organized Business, Economic Change, Democracy in Latin America* (Miami: University of Miami, North-South Center Press, 1998), p. 5.

6 Silva and Durand, "Organized Business," p. 30.

7 Leigh A. Payne and Ernest Bartell, "Bringing Business Back In: Business-State Relations and Democratic Stability in Latin America," in Ernest Bartell and Leigh A. Payne, eds., *Business and Democracy in Latin America* (Pittsburgh: University of Pittsburgh Press, 1995), p. 272.

8 Silva and Durand, "Organized Business," p. 32.

9 Payne and Bartell, "Bringing Business Back In," p. 260.

10 Silva and Durand, "Organized Business," p. 30. Nigel Harris notes similarly that "[b]usinessmen are more sensitive to changes in profit expectation than the nature of the political order, and it is usually changes in the first which produce criticisms of the second." "New Bourgeoises?" *Journal of Development Studies*, vol. 24, no. 2, (January) 1988, p. 245.

11 Bertil Lintner, "Absolute Power: Burma's Army Controls Economy and Government," *FEER*, January 18, 1996, p. 25.

12 Guillermo O'Donnell and Philippe Schmitter, "Tentative Conclusions About Uncertain Democracies," in Guillermo O'Donnell, Philippe Schmitter, and Laurence Whitehead, eds., Transitions from Authoritarian Rule: Prospects for Democracy (Baltimore: Johns Hopkins University Press, 1986), Part 4, p. 27.

13 Michael Pinches, "The Philippines' New Rich," in Richard Robison and David Goodman, eds., *The New Rich in Asia* (London: Routledge), p. 119.

14 S.G. Redding, "The Distinct Nature of Chinese Capitalism," *Pacific Review*, vol. 9, no. 3, p. 431.

15 Eva Etzioni-Halevy writes, "The development of economic liberties, the free enjoyment of one's property, was . . . closely intertwined with the development of personal liberties. . . . These, in turn, were but the other side of the coin of political liberties that (by definition) are of the essence of democracy." *The Elite Connection: Problems and Potential of Western Democracy* (Cambridge: Polity Press, 1993), p. 131. See also John D. Sullivan, "Democratization and Business Interest," *Journal of Democracy*, vol. 5, no. 4, pp. 146–60.

16 Ruth McVey, "The Materialization of the Southeast Asian Entrepreneur," in McVey, ed., pp. 7–34.

17 For a contemporary account of the UMNO's business dealing during this period, see Edmund Terence Gomez, *Politics in Business: UMNO's Corporate Investments* (Kuala Lumpur: Forum, 1990).

18 The most thorough account of the UMNO assembly election made from a political economy perspective is Khoo Kay Jin, "The Grand Vision: Mahathir and Modernization," in Joel S. Kahn and Francis Loh Kok Wah, eds., *Fragmented Vision: Culture and Politics in Contemporary Malaysia* (North Sydney: Allen and Unwin, 1992), pp. 44–76.

19 A good example is Marina Yusof, managing director of Idris Hydraulic during the late 1980s.

20 In an interview, a Singapore journalist described UMNO behavior toward opposition supporters as more severe than in the past: "Now, they kill you. They kill your business. They go after relatives" (Kuala Lumpur, 16 February 1992).

21 Anek, *Business Associations*, p. 34.

22 Ibid., p. 35.

23 Ibid., p. 69–70.

24 Paul Handley, "More of the Same? Politics and Business, in Kevin Hewison, ed., *Political Change in Thailand: Democracy and Participation* (London: Routledge, 1997), pp. 98–99.

25 Ibid., p. 104.

26 Ibid., p. 108.

27 Thompson, *The Anti-Marcos Struggle*, p. 118.

28 Gary Hawes, *The Philippine State and the Marcos Regime: The Politics of Export* (Ithaca: Cornell University Press, 1987), p. 128.

29 Paul D. Hutchcroft, "Oligarchs and Cronies in the Philippine State: The Politics of Patrimonial Plunder," *World Politics*, vol. 43, no. 3 (1991), p. 445.

30 Thompson, *The Anti-Marcos Struggle*, p. 120.

31 Ibid., p. 160.

32 Ibid.

33 Handley, "More of the Same?" p. 108.

34 Ibid., p. 102.

35 Thompson, *The Anti-Marcos Struggle*, p. 174. Hutchcroft writes that while 'there were important efforts at liberalization and privatization . . . these efforts failed. . . . [A]s in pre-martial law years, a decentralized polity simply gives *more* oligarchs a chance to claw for the booty of the state." "Oligarchs and Cronies," p. 447.

36 Silva and Durand, "Organized Business," p. 2; and Payne and Bartell, "Bringing Business Back In," p. 259.

37 Barrington Moore Jr., *Social Origins of Dictatorship and Democracy: Lord and Peasant in the Making of the Modern World* (Boston: Beacon Press, 1966), p. 418.

Appendix

Basic Social, Adminstrative and Economic Data

Indonesia

population (July 2000 est.)	225 million
population density (people per sq. km.)	117
annual population growth	1.6
urban population (1999)	39.8%
major ethnic groups	Javanese (45%), Sudanese (14%), Madurese (7.5%)
official language	Bahasa Indonesia
other major languages	Javanese, Sundanese
major religions	Islam (88%), Christian (5%)
capital city and population	Jakarta, 12 million (est.)
other major cities	Surabaya, Medan, Bandung, Makassar
administrative division	23 provinces, 2 special regions, 1 capital city district
govt. budgetary expenditures (1999/2000 est.)	25.4 billion
land area (sq. km.)	1,919,440
forest area (sq. km., 1995	1,100.000
annual deforestation (1995)	1.0%
arable land	10%
life expectancy at birth (years)	68
fertility rate, total (births per woman)	2.6
infant mortality rate (per 1,000 births,1998)	43
population below poverty line	na
primary school enrolments (1995)	98.8%
secondary school enrolments (1995)	52.9%
literacy rates (adult male, 1999)	91.5%
personal computers (per 1,000 people, 1998)	8.2
internet hosts (per 1,000 people, 1998)	0.5

	1995	1998	1999
GNP (current US$)	194.4 billion	130.6 billion	119.5 billion
GNP per capita (current US$)	1,000	640	580
purchasing power parity (GDP per capita)	–	–	2,800 (est.)
GDP growth rate	–	–	0%
unemployment	–	15–20% (est.)	–
total labor force	–	88 million agriculture: 45% manufacturing: 11% services: 39%	–
trade (per cent of GDP)	15.9%	15.2%	
exports, value (current US$)	–	–	48 billion (est.)
imports, value	–	–	24 billion (est.)
foreign direct investment (current US$)	4.3 billion	–365 million	–
foreign debt (current US$)	–	144.7 billion	–

industries: petroleum and natural gas, textiles, apparel, footwear, mining, cement, chemical fertilizers, plywood, rubber, food, tourism
main exports: oil and gas, plywood, textiles, rubber
main imports: machinery and equipment, chemicals, fuels, foodstuffs
Freedom House ranking* (2000):   political rights: 4   civil liberties: 4   partly free

* Scores range from 1 to 7, with 1 representing the most free and 7 the least. "Free" countries have ratings averaging from 1–3; "partly free," from 3–5.5; and "non-free," from 5.5–7.

Singapore

population (July 2000 est.)	4.2 million
population density (people per sq. km.)	6 752
annual population growth	3.55%
urban population	100%
major ethnic groups	Chinese (77%), Malay (14%), Indian (7.6%)
official languages	Chinese, Malay, Tamil, English
major religions	Buddhism, Islam, Hinduism, Christian
administrative divisions	none
govt. budgetary expenditures (1998/1999 est.)	16.9 billion
land area (sq. km.)	622
forest area (sq. km.)	40
annual deforestation	0%
arable land	2%
life expectancy at birth (years)	80.5
fertility rate, total (births per woman)	1.16
infant mortality rate (per 1,000 births, 2000)	3.65
population below poverty line	na
primary school enrolments (1995)	93.6%
secondary school enrolments (1995)	73.9%
literacy rates (adult male, 1999)	91.1%
personal computers (per 1,000 people, 1998)	458.4
internet hosts (per 1,000 people, 1999)	208.1

	1995	1998	1999
GNP (current US$)	81.3 billion	96.7 billion	95.4 billion
GNP per capita (current US$)	27,230	30,560	29,610
purchasing power parity (GDP per capita)	–	–	27,800 (est.)
GDP growth rate	–	–	5.5%
unemployment	–	–	3.2%
total labor force		1.93 million	–
		agriculture: negl.	
		manufacturing: 21.6%	
		fin. services: 38%	
		commerce: 21.4%	
		construction: 7%	
trade (per cent of GDP)	354.7%	269.1%	–
exports, value (current US$)	–	–	114 billion
imports, value	–	–	111 billion
foreign direct investment (current US$)	7.2 billion	7.2 billion	–
foreign debt (current US$)	–	–	–

industries: electronics, financial services, petroleum refining, oil drilling equipment, ship repair, entrepot trade, biotechnology, rubber processing

main exports: electronics, machinery, mineral fuels, chemicals

main imports: machinery and equipment, mineral fuels, chemicals, foodstuffs

Freedom House ranking (2000):   political rights: 5   civil liberties: 5   partly free

Malaysia

population (July 2000 est.)	21.8 million		
population density (people per sq. km.)	66.1		
annual population growth (2000 est.)	2.01%		
urban population (1999)	56.7%		
major ethnic groups	Malay & other indigenous (58%), Chinese (26%), Indian (7%)		
official language	Bahasa Malaysia		
other major languages	Chinese dialects, Tamil, English		
major religions	Islam, Buddhism, Daoism, Hinduism, Christianity		
capital city and population	Kuala Lumpur, 2 million (est.)		
other major cities	Penang, Ipoh, Melaka, Johor Baru		
administrative division	13 states, 2 federal territories		
govt. budgetary expenditures (1999)	27.6 billion		
land area (sq. km.)	329,749		
forest area (sq. km., 1995)	154,700		
annual deforestation (1995)	2.4%		
arable land	3%		
life expectancy at birth (years)	71		
fertility rate, total (births per woman, 2000)	3.29		
infant mortality rate (per 1000 births, 2000)	20.1		
population below poverty line (1997 est.)	6.8%		
primary school enrolments (1995)	99.9%		
secondary school enrolments (1995)	58.7%		
literacy rates (adult male, 1999)	83.5%		
personal computers (per 1,000 people, 1998)	58.6		
internet hosts (per 1,000 people, 1999)	21.1		

	1995	1998	1999
GNP (current US$)	80.1 billion	81.5 billion	77.3 billion
GNP per capita (current US$)	3,890	3,680	3,400
purchasing power parity (GDP per capita)	–	–	10,700 (est.)
GDP growth rate	–	–	5%
unemployment	–	–	3% (est.)
total labor force	–	–	9.3 million (est.)
			agriculture: 16%
			manufacturing: 27%
			government: 10%
			services: 32%
			construction: 9%
trade (per cent of GDP)	85.6%	70.1%	–
exports, value (current US$)	–	–	83.5 billion (est.)
imports, value	–	–	61.5 billion (est.)
foreign direct investment (current US$)	4.1 billion	5.0 billion	–
foreign debt (current US$)	–	47.3 billion	–

industries: electronics, light manufacturing, rubber and palm oil, logging, tin, petroleum
main exports: electronics, petroleum and gas, chemicals, palm oil, rubber, textiles
main imports: machinery and equipment, chemicals, food, fuel, lubricants

Freedom House ranking (2000):	political rights: 5	civil liberties: 5	partly free

Thailand

population (July 2000 est.)	61.2 million		
population density (people per sq. km.)	119		
annual population growth (2000 est.)	0.93%		
urban population (1999)	21.3%		
major ethnic groups	Thai (75%), Chinese (14%), Lao		
official language	Thai		
other major languages	ethnic and regional dialects		
major religions	Buddhism (95%), Muslim (3.8%)		
capital city and population	Bangkok, 10 million (est.)		
other major cities	Chiang Mai		
administrative division	72 states		
govt. budgetary expenditures (1999 est.)	23 billion		
land area (sq. km.)	514,000		
forest area (sq. km., 1995)	116,300		
annual deforestation (1995)	2.6%		
arable land	34%		
life expectancy at birth (years)	68.5		
fertility rate, total (births per woman, 2000)	1.88		
infant mortality rate (per 1,000 births, 2000)	31.5		
population below poverty line (1998 est.)	12.5%		
primary school enrolments (1995)	84.7%		
secondary school enrolments (1995)	44.1%		
literacy rates (adult male, 1999)	93.8%		
personal computers (per 1,000 people, 1998)	21.6		
internet hosts (per 1,000 people, 1999)	3.3		

	1995	1998	1999
GNP (current US$)	161.9 billion	126.4 billion	121 billion
GNP per capita (current US$)	2,730	2,070	1,960
purchasing power parity (GDP per capita)	–	–	6,400 (est.)
GDP growth rate	–	–	4%
unemployment	–	4.5% (est.)	–
total labor force (1998)	–	32.6 million (est.)	–
		agriculture: 54%	
		manufacturing: 15%	
		services: 31%	
trade (per cent of GDP)	32.2%	26.7%	–
exports, value (current US$)	–	–	58.5 billion (est.)
imports, value	–	–	45 billion (est.)
foreign direct investment (current US$)	2.1 billion	6.9 billion	–
foreign debt (current US$)	–	–	80 billion (est.)

industries: tourism, textiles and apparel, agricultural processing, jewelry, electric appliances, electronics, automotive parts, tin, furniture

main exports: computers, parts, textiles, rice

main imports: capital goods, consumer goods, fuels

Freedom House ranking (2000):	political rights: 2	civil liberties: 3	free

The Philippines

population (July 2000 est.)	81.2 million
population density (people per sq. km.)	270
annual population growth (2,000 est.)	2.1%
urban population (1999)	57.7%
major ethnic groups	Indo-Malay (95.5%), Chinese (1.5%)
official language	Pkilipino (Tagalog), English
major religions	Roman Catholic (83%), Protestant (9%), Muslim (5%)
capital city and population	Manila (Quezon City), 10 million (est.)
other major cities	Cebu
administrative division	73 provinces
govt. budgetary expenditures (1998 est.)	12.6 billion
land area (sq. km.)	300,000
forest area (sq. km., 1995)	67,660
annual deforestation (1995)	3.5
arable land	19%
life expectancy at birth (years)	67.48
fertility rate, total (births per woman, 2000)	3.48
infant mortality rate (per 1000 births, 2000)	29.52
population below poverty line (1997 est.)	32%
primary school enrolments (1995)	99.9%
secondary school enrolments (1995)	77.4%
literacy rates (adult male, 1999)	94.6%
personal computers (per 1,000 people, 1998)	15.1
internet hosts (per 1,000 people, 1999)	1.2

	1995	1998	1999
GNP (current US$)	71.2 billion	78.9 billion	78.0 billion
GNP per capita (current US$)	1,010	1,050	1,020
purchasing power parity (GDP per capita)	–	–	3 600 (est.)
GDP growth rate	–	–	2.9%
unemployment	–	9.6%	–
total labor force	–	–	32 million (est.) agriculture: 39.8% manufacturing: 9.8% government: 19.4% services: 17.7% construction: 5.8%
trade (per cent of GDP)	17.7%	22.1%	–
exports, value (current US$)	–	–	34.8 billion (est.)
imports, value	–	–	30.7 billion (est.)
foreign direct investment (current US$)	1.5 billion	1.7 billion	–
foreign debt (current US$)	–	–	51.9 billion (est.)

industries: textiles, pharmaceuticals, chemicals, electronics, wood products, food processing, fishing
main exports: electronics, machinery and transport equipment, apparel, coconut products
main imports: capital goods, raw materials, consumer goods, fuels.

Freedom House ranking (2000):	political rights: 2 civil liberties: 3 free

Index

Notes
1 Most Indonesian, Malaysian, and Filipino names are inverted; Thai and ethnic Chinese names are not.
2 Endnote material is not indexed.